# RESEARCHING NATIONAL SECURITY INTELLIGENCE

Related Works from Georgetown University Press

*Analyzing Intelligence: National Security Practitioners' Perspectives, Second Edition*
Roger Z. George and James B. Bruce, Editors

*Intelligence Elsewhere: Spies and Espionage outside the Anglosphere*
Philip H. J. Davies and Kristian Gustafson, Editors

*Principled Spying: The Ethics of Secret Intelligence*
David Omand and Mark Phythian

*Spy Chiefs, Volume I: Intelligence Leaders in the United States and United Kingdom*
Christopher Moran, Mark Stout, Ioanna Iordanou, and Paul Maddrell, Editors

*Spy Chiefs, Volume II: Intelligence Leaders in Europe, the Middle East, and Asia*
Paul Maddrell, Christopher Moran, Ioanna Iordanou, and Mark Stout, Editors

*To Catch a Spy: The Art of Counterintelligence*
James M. Olson

# RESEARCHING NATIONAL SECURITY INTELLIGENCE

MULTIDISCIPLINARY APPROACHES

Stephen Coulthart
Michael Landon-Murray
Damien Van Puyvelde
EDITORS

Georgetown University Press
Washington, DC

© 2019 Georgetown University Press. All rights reserved. No part of this book may be reproduced or utilized in any form or by any means, electronic or mechanical, including photocopying and recording, or by any information storage and retrieval system, without permission in writing from the publisher.

The publisher is not responsible for third-party websites or their content. URL links were active at time of publication.

Library of Congress Cataloging-in-Publication Data

Names: Coulthart, Stephen, editor. | Landon-Murray, Michael, editor. | Van Puyvelde, Damien, editor.
Title: Researching National Security Intelligence : Multidisciplinary Approaches / Stephen Coulthart, Michael Landon-Murray, and Damien Van Puyvelde, editors.
Description: Washington, DC : Georgetown University Press, 2019. | The idea for Researching National Security Intelligence can be traced to a colloquium held at the University of Texas at El Paso (UTEP) in March 2017 and funded by the Intelligence Community Center for Academic Excellence program—Preface. | Includes bibliographical references and index. |
Identifiers: LCCN 2019003693 (print) | LCCN 2019016341 (ebook) | ISBN 9781626167056 (ebook) | ISBN 9781626167032 | ISBN (hardcover : alk. paper) | ISBN 9781626167049 (pbk.: alk. paper)
Subjects: LCSH: National security—Research—Congresses. | Military intelligence—Research—Congresses. | Intelligence service—Research—Congresses. | National security—Study and teaching—Congresses. | Military intelligence—Study and teaching—Congresses. | Intelligence service—Study and teaching—Congresses.
Classification: LCC UA10.5 (ebook) | LCC UA10.5 .R469 2019 (print) | DDC 327.12—dc23
LC record available at https://lccn.loc.gov/2019003693

20 19    9 8 7 6 5 4 3 2    First printing

Cover design by Martyn Schmoll.

*In memory of Sean Curtis (1992–2018)*

# Contents

*List of Illustrations* — ix

*Preface* — xi

*List of Abbreviations* — xiii

Introduction: A Pluralistic Approach to Intelligence Scholarship — 1
  *Stephen Coulthart, Michael Landon-Murray, and Damien Van Puyvelde*

## PART I. Framing Intelligence Research

1. Framing the Challenges and Opportunities of Intelligence Studies Research — 11
  *Mark Phythian*

2. Confessions of an Intelligence Historian — 29
  *John Ferris*

## PART II. Data Sources and the Study of National Security Intelligence

3. The Why, Who, and How of Using Qualitative Interviews to Research Intelligence Practices — 47
  *Damien Van Puyvelde*

4. The Use of Structured Behavioral Observation Systems to Address Research Questions in Intelligence — 63
  *Misty Duke*

5. A Sociological Approach to Intelligence Studies     79
   *Bridget Rose Nolan*

## PART III. Multidisciplinary Perspectives on National Security Intelligence Research

6. Enhancing Political Science Contributions to American Intelligence Studies     97
   *Stephen Marrin*

7. Can Decision Science Improve Intelligence Analysis?     117
   *David R. Mandel*

8. Charting a Research Agenda for Intelligence Studies Using Public Administration and Organization Theory Scholarship     141
   *Rick Caceres-Rodriguez and Michael Landon-Murray*

9. How the Field of Communication Can Contribute to the Understanding and Study of National Security Intelligence     163
   *Rubén Arcos*

## PART IV. Beyond the Ivory Tower: The Research and Practice of Intelligence

10. Bridging the Gap: The Scholar-Practitioner Divide in Intelligence     179
    *Brent Durbin*

11. The Ivory Tower and the Fourth Estate     193
    *Paul Lashmar*

12. The Ethics of Intelligence Research     211
    *Ross Bellaby*

    Conclusion: The Past, Present, and Future of Intelligence Research     225
    *Stephen Coulthart, Michael Landon-Murray, and Damien Van Puyvelde*

*List of Contributors*     237
*Index*     241

# Illustrations

| | | |
|---|---|---|
| 3.1. | Percentage of *Intelligence and National Security* articles using qualitative research interviews to gather data, 1986–2016 | 48 |
| 7.1. | Example of instructional material | 123 |
| 7.2. | Calibration curve plotted from data | 126 |
| 7.3. | Consistency rates of US, UK, and evidence-based lexicons | 130 |
| 9.1. | Map of communication processes and communication areas along the intelligence cycle | 164 |
| 9.2. | Intelligence cube | 166 |
| 11.1. | Examples of investigative journalists who have national security reporting experience | 196 |
| 11.2. | Intelligence cycle, academic research model (hourglass), and investigative journalism model | 200 |

# Preface

The idea for *Researching National Security Intelligence* can be traced to a colloquium held at the University of Texas at El Paso (UTEP) in March 2017 and funded by Intelligence Community Centers for Academic Excellence. At the event practitioners and scholars from five countries presented papers on navigating the realities of intelligence research. During the colloquium we realized the ideas were important enough to warrant a book-length treatment in an edited volume that would share insights with a wider audience and help advance the field.

Our motivation for this volume has been threefold. First, we wanted to create an interdisciplinary text that would provide guidance to fellow and emerging intelligence scholars. This volume also provided an outlet for us to explore some of the methodological and practical issues we have grappled with throughout our (relatively short) academic careers. Third—and perhaps most ambitiously—we wanted to create a volume that showcased the highly diverse perspectives of intelligence research. We sought out authors who had a wide array of disciplinary perspectives, ranging from journalism to sociology. We also wanted to capture a broad range of scholar-practitioner perspectives; our contributors have experience working in Canadian, UK, and US national security intelligence agencies. Bringing in diverse disciplinary and scholar-practitioner perspectives has not been without its challenges, requiring us to weave together a coherent narrative while leveraging the uniqueness of each contributor's perspective.

The purpose of this volume is thus to assist anyone interested in researching, and ultimately seeking to understand, intelligence and its many associated processes. We have designed it to provide an accessible introduction to the various theoretical perspectives and methods used in a field that has become increasingly dynamic in the last decade. Evolutions in the field—specifically the growing number of disciplines involved in intelligence research at universities and beyond and growing student interest—called for a new book on national security intelligence research. The task was made all the more important because writing about methodology is essential to anchoring this field in academia. Scholars and graduate students will find *Researching National Security Intelligence* useful for the light it sheds on a field that is in a state of flux. Throughout the volume contributors have identified emerging research themes and approaches to develop original and innovative intelligence research. A secondary, but important, audience is practitioners at intelligence agencies and in government generally. This book will provide them insights into the minds and multifaceted work of intelligence scholars.

This project was made possible thanks to the support of various colleagues, mentors, and friends. We are indebted to Larry Valero and to the staff and students of UTEP's National Security Studies Institute (NSSI). All three of us have worked or currently work in this unit and are deeply appreciative of Larry's tireless efforts to develop intelligence education and scholarship. This volume is a testament to his devotion to fostering interdisciplinary, rigorous intelligence research. We are also thankful to our editor, Don Jacobs, and two anonymous reviewers who helped us refine our ideas. Stephen would like to thank his doctoral advisers and good friends William N. Dunn and Michael Kenney at the University of Pittsburgh's Graduate School of Public and International Affairs. Over the years both have provided a sounding board for many ideas that came to fruition in this book. Michael would like to express his heartfelt thanks to Sydney Cresswell, whose support, guidance, and friendship over many years were essential and deeply rewarding (and continue to be!). Likewise, Michael would like to say how fortunate he has been to have the instrumental mentorship and motivation provided by Victor Asal and Jim Steiner. Damien thanks Peter Jackson, R. Gerald Hughes, Len Scott, and the late Chikara Hashimoto for challenging him to think about methodology and intelligence research. We will close by stating our thanks to the volume's contributors. When we began this project, colleagues warned us that coordinating among the various contributions and authors would be time-consuming. Ultimately, though, working with the authors has been one of the easiest—and most rewarding—parts of the job.

Stephen Coulthart, El Paso, TX<br>
Michael Landon-Murray, Colorado Springs, CO<br>
Damien Van Puyvelde, Glasgow, UK

# Abbreviations

| | |
|---|---|
| ACH | Analysis of Competing Hypotheses |
| APSA | American Political Science Association |
| BTG | bridging the gap |
| CBCA | Criteria-Based Content Analysis |
| CIA | Central Intelligence Agency (United States) |
| COMINT | communications intelligence |
| CSI | Center for the Study of Intelligence (United States) |
| DNI | director of national intelligence (United States) |
| EPA | Environmental Protection Agency (United States) |
| FBI | Federal Bureau of Investigation (United States) |
| GC and CS | Government Code and Cypher School (United Kingdom) |
| GCHQ | Government Communications Headquarters (United Kingdom) |
| HPSCI | House Permanent Select Committee on Intelligence (United States) |
| IC | intelligence community |
| *IJIC* | *International Journal of Intelligence and CounterIntelligence* |
| INR | Bureau of Intelligence and Research (United States) |
| IR | international relations |
| ISA | International Studies Association |
| ISS | Intelligence Studies Section |
| MEA | Middle East and Africa Division (Canada) |
| MI5 | Security Service (United Kingdom) |
| MI6 | Secret Intelligence Service (United Kingdom) |
| NCTC | National Counterterrorism Center (United States) |
| NIC | National Intelligence Council (United States) |
| NIE | national intelligence estimate |
| NSA | National Security Agency |
| OSS | Office of Strategic Services (United States) |

| | |
|---|---|
| PA | public administration |
| PEACE | planning and preparation, engage and explain, gaining an account, closure, and evaluation |
| RM | Reality Monitoring |
| SAT | structured analytic technique |
| SIGINT | signals intelligence |
| SSCI | Senate Select Committee on Intelligence (United States) |
| UN | United Nations |
| WEP | word of estimative probability |

# Introduction: A Pluralistic Approach to Intelligence Scholarship

*Stephen Coulthart, Michael Landon-Murray, and Damien Van Puyvelde*

Intelligence is often said to be the world's second oldest profession. Yet significant academic interest in the subject has only begun to blossom in recent decades, and new academic journals continue to be introduced. Dozens of universities around the world have also established intelligence degrees and funded new faculty positions on the subject.[1] In the United States, no fewer than sixteen intelligence studies degrees have been created since 2000, including seven in the past few years.[2] Many more minors and certificates pass curriculum and teaching review committees every year. Governments have also stimulated the growth of the field through teaching and research initiatives, such as the US government's Intelligence Community Centers for Academic Excellence program.[3] It is clear, then, that the study and teaching of intelligence have grown markedly.

Robust intelligence research has the potential to support better intelligence. One need only look at how evidence-based practice has assisted practitioners in a wide variety of fields, such as medicine and policing, to understand how scholarship can improve practice.[4] Still, expectations about the impact of intelligence research on performance should be tempered by humility, experience, and evidence.[5] This volume offers a perspective that aligns with that ethic but, at the same time, argues that diverse insights can make for more than marginal improvements to intelligence processes and outcomes. The chapters in this book demonstrate the problems that can follow from implementing practices that are not evidence based or up-to-date. More important, they highlight the opportunities that ongoing and prospective research agendas can offer intelligence scholars and practitioners.

Scholars can also bolster academia's educative and public accountability roles that stem from the new knowledge and reflections they develop. Just as intelligence services can enhance national security and liberty, they can also pose very real threats to those conditions and values. For some colleagues, such as intelligence scholar Ross

Bellaby, this means academics ought to pierce the "protective intelligence shield" to keep the public up-to-date with the general activities of intelligence services. This educative function is important because, in many countries, much of what the public thinks it knows about intelligence is "based more on fiction than fact."[6] Advancing intelligence scholarship can be one part of the larger framework of public engagement with intelligence that is so essential to contemporary democracies, attuned to performance as well as normative issues.

## Challenges of Researching National Security Intelligence

Studying intelligence poses significant challenges for scholars, largely because intelligence services are hard-to-access research subjects that seek to "guard their secrecy . . . [and] conceal their activities."[7] Researchers face high—but not insurmountable—barriers in the form of constrained access to information and sites and difficulty in meaningfully analyzing intelligence organizations and policies. Such challenges are not unique to intelligence studies but are more severe than in many other academic fields. Outside researchers do not have direct access to information on sensitive intelligence practices and therefore often rely on insiders to share relevant experiences and pieces of evidence.[8] Scholars previously employed in an intelligence agency and those who hold a security clearance (or once did) may have contacts that can provide special access to information or people of interest. However, their access is not unfettered, and they are limited in the information they can access and disclose. US intelligence agencies have set up prepublication boards to review the information current and former employees hope to publish. Whether it takes the form of a newspaper article, a conference presentation, or even a curriculum vitae, the information practitioners share about their past is limited by secrecy requirements.[9]

Other information sources exist in addition to insider accounts. Scholars can use declassified information, such as the "Family Jewels," documents released in 2007 detailing CIA abuses, and more recently, the millions of pages of formerly secret material the agency has made available online via its records search tool.[10] Though declassification provides an important window into the secret past, government officials necessarily select and limit what outsiders can learn through this lens.[11] In close to ninety countries, researchers can seek to obtain government documents through freedom of information requests.[12] The time required to get a response to these requests can be long; in recent years the median number of days for the CIA to respond to a Freedom of Information Act (FOIA) request was 153, and there was a backlog of 1,256 cases.[13] An FOIA request does not ensure that documents will be released or released in full.

Beyond planned releases of information on intelligence activities, data leaks provide another opportunity to learn about secret government practices. While this information can be helpful for research, using it can raise ethical issues. For example, an Associated Press review of the data repository of WikiLeaks, a nonprofit organization that publishes secret information including intelligence leaks, found the group posted data that "could put lives at risk or lead to people being jailed or harassed."[14]

Should a scholar should use leaked information—and therefore contribute to its wider dissemination—when its original release exposed and continues to endanger specific sources and methods, as well as helps adversaries, such as terrorists? These are not only academic questions but real considerations for many intelligence researchers.

Data limitations can slow the progress of intelligence research and scholarship. Without high-quality evidence it is difficult to conduct cutting-edge research and analysis that places intelligence scholarship in the pages of top disciplinary journals.[15] The difficulty of obtaining data and conducting comprehensive analysis also affects, to some extent, the career prospects of intelligence studies faculty because publishing in top-ranked disciplinary journals is key to attaining tenure and promotion at leading research universities, institutions that play an important role in generating new scholarship and legitimizing research fields. Perhaps one indicator of this dynamic is that, for a long time, there was a dearth of intelligence-focused academics at "powerhouse" institutions in the United States.[16] In recent years a number of these institutions has started to remedy this situation, which presages a new spring of intelligence studies, not only in the US but also in Europe and beyond.[17]

Another challenge is building and managing academic connections to the practitioner sphere to inform intelligence research and practice. For practice-minded scholars, robust engagement with intelligence agencies has the potential to facilitate evidence-based research and develop policy or practitioner-relevant projects. Government outreach on the study and teaching of intelligence has been on the rise in the United States as well as other parts of the world.[18] These relationships and programs stand to be strengthened, something that will require careful balancing on the part of government and academe because government sponsorship and consumption of intelligence research can be a double-edged sword and generate tensions between faculty intent on working directly with intelligence services and those who do not. Indeed, not all scholars seek to inform intelligence practice. Some prefer to keep more distance between the study and the practice of intelligence, to investigate overarching questions concerning theoretical matters, and to answer "big questions" related to the role of intelligence in policymaking and society. Recent research on this topic suggests that there is a growing schism in intelligence studies between two schools of thought. One argues that intelligence officials and scholars should work together to improve intelligence practices; the other would like to maintain learning and research opportunities that are free of government ties.[19] Our pluralist approach seeks to establish a field in which both schools can live together and learn from each other.

A further challenge—but also an opportunity—is disciplinary integration. Intelligence studies scholarship has traditionally suffered from a lack of engagement with related disciplines. Much of the most advanced knowledge pertinent to intelligence—whether on cognition, group and organizational dynamics, or communication, among others—exists in other domains and disciplines. Once called the "missing dimension" of international relations, intelligence studies has its own missing dimensions.[20] As a result, intelligence-relevant findings, theories, and frameworks can go unnoticed—sometimes for decades. For example, scholars have noted that some of the original findings on cognitive bias and intelligence analysis first explored in the 1970s and 1980s have not been updated in the intelligence studies literature in light of more recent advances in psychological research.[21] This problem is not intentional, but rather a by-product of academia's emphasis on specialization, complicated by intelligence scholarship's status as an multidisciplinary subject.

In recent years intelligence scholarship has shown promising signs of bridging disciplinary gaps, and more and more intelligence research is being published in some of the top disciplinary journals and university presses.[22] Intelligence studies journals also show encouraging signs: a recent special issue of *Intelligence and National Security* highlighted diverse disciplinary perspectives to improve and understand intelligence analysis, ranging from philosophy to computational social science.[23] Still, there is much work to be done, which is why this volume advances a resolutely multidisciplinary approach to the study of intelligence. Our hope is that identifying common opportunities within and between fields will sensitize researchers and contribute to a growing culture of disciplinary outreach.

## Addressing the Challenges of Intelligence Research: A Pluralistic Approach

Part 1 of this volume, "Framing Intelligence Research," defines and situates the field of intelligence studies. In the first chapter, "Framing the Challenges and Opportunities of Intelligence Studies Research," Mark Phythian argues that conceptualizing intelligence studies is difficult partly because "intelligence" is a contested term. Still, Phythian draws out common threads that weave together intelligence-related inquiry. He concludes that intelligence studies is a broad field rather than a solidified discipline with hard boundaries. In "Confessions of an Intelligence Historian," John Ferris discusses how historians have studied intelligence as a tool of statecraft—particularly in the twentieth century—and how broader interactions between history and political science have shaped the field and our understanding of international events. In particular, Ferris takes stock of how the study of intelligence has evolved and changed, with varying disciplines—history, political science, sociology, management—interacting and taking on prominent roles in different times and contexts.

With a firm conceptual and chronological framework in place, the volume then opens into three thematic sections on data collection, disciplinary perspectives, and research applications that offer a pluralistic approach to addressing intelligence research challenges.[24] An assumption of this pluralistic approach is that phenomena are "a huge fishnet of complex, mutually interacting relationships among constructs or variables" and that attempting to understand this tapestry of variables requires multiple ways of knowing.[25] In the foreign policy classic *Essence of Decision*, Graham Allison demonstrated this point by showing that the Cuban Missile Crisis is best explained using multiple theoretical perspectives rather than one.[26] A pluralistic approach then calls scholars to engage in an "exhaustive study of phenomena from as many different perspectives as possible."[27] Perspectives in this sense are defined broadly to include disciplinary lenses but also diverse data sources, methodologies, and national affiliation, among other factors. With each perspective the intelligence scholar receives a more nuanced understanding, increasing the relative completeness of what is known about the research subject. The result is not access to the "capital T truth" but a greater *confidence* that research results are valid.

Part 2, "Data Sources and the Study of National Security Intelligence," addresses key data and research challenges in intelligence studies. The contributors illustrate how applying a pluralistic approach is possible even in the most sensitive and secret intelligence activities. Damien Van Puyvelde, in chapter 3, "The Why, Who, and How of Using Qualitative Interviews to Research Intelligence Practices," illustrates the potential and procedures for conducting qualitative interviews, while highlighting the importance of combining interviews with other data-collection approaches. In chapter 4, "The Use of Structured Behavioral Observation Systems to Address Research Questions in Intelligence," Misty Duke examines how psychologists collect data through experiments to understand rapport building in interrogation. She also discusses the caveats and risks of generalizing findings from experimental studies outside the lab. Bridget Rose Nolan, a former analyst at the National Counterterrorism Center turned scholar, delves into ethnographic research and the way it can inform our understanding of analytic practices and organizational cultures in intelligence agencies in chapter 5, "A Sociological Approach to Intelligence Studies."

Part 3, "Multidisciplinary Perspectives on National Security Intelligence Research," highlights the importance of applying multiple disciplinary approaches to intelligence. Specifically, the chapters in this section provide researchers an opportunity to learn from other disciplines about how to study a difficult-to-access set of practices like intelligence.[28] Chapters in this section identify not only current research but also areas in which future scholarship is needed. Stephen Marrin's chapter 6, "Enhancing Political Science Contributions to American Intelligence Studies," surveys the various subfields of political science, highlighting many possible ways to integrate the study of intelligence as a function of government. David R. Mandel's chapter 7, "Can Decision Science Improve Intelligence Analysis?" is indicative of the prescriptive approach of part 3. Mandel relies on his experience at the intersection of national security research and practice to explain how decision science research helps practitioners and academics better understand analytic processes and performance. In chapter 8, "Charting a Research Agenda for Intelligence Studies Using Public Administration and Organization Theory Scholarship," Rick Caceres-Rodriguez and Michael Landon-Murray explore how theory and empirical studies in public administration can improve scholar and practitioner understandings of interorganizational and intraorganizational intelligence processes. Rubén Arcos, one of the leading Spanish scholars of intelligence, takes stock of the voluminous literature in communication sciences and identifies new avenues for research in areas such as semiotics in chapter 9, "How the Field of Communication Can Contribute to the Understanding and Study of National Security Intelligence."

Part 4, "Beyond the Ivory Tower: The Research and Practice of Intelligence," highlights the central difficulties and tensions that academic researchers face in conducting policy-relevant research. As in the previous sections, the contributors apply a pluralistic approach using diverse disciplinary perspectives. In chapter 10, "Bridging the Gap: The Scholar-Practitioner Divide in Intelligence," Brent Durbin, invoking Alex George's admonishment of academics to "bridge the gap," examines a number of initiatives to enhance collaboration between intelligence researchers and practitioners.[29] Former investigative journalist turned professor Paul Lashmar, in chapter 11, "The Ivory Tower and the Fourth Estate," describes how intelligence scholars can learn from and collaborate with journalists. In the process he describes some commonalities and differences between the two groups. In chapter 12, "The Ethics of Intelligence Research," Ross Bellaby makes a case for four ethical duties of intelligence scholars: to the people, to the nation's security, to intelligence and its practitioners, and to academia. The concluding chapter expands on some of the key ideas raised in this volume, such as the need to better integrate disciplines and the influence of intelligence scholarship on policy and practice.

Intelligence scholarship is advancing, but considerable challenges remain, namely, the continuing lack of data, disciplinary integration, and effective application of research to practice and policy. A pluralistic strategy offers a positive step in addressing these challenges. However, such an effort will be a long-term, incremental process. Our hope is that this volume provides a conceptual, empirical, and methodological tool kit informed by a variety of disciplines and approaches that can be used in intelligence studies. The contributions in this volume will offer a road map to researchers and students as they navigate the peculiarities of intelligence research and help propel intelligence studies forward.

## Notes

1. Jonathan Smith, "Common Thread? The Role of Professional Orientation in US and Non-US Intelligence Studies Programs," *Journal of Strategic Security* 10, no. 1 (2017): 118–42.
2. Stephen Coulthart and Matthew Crosston, "Terra Incognita: Mapping American Intelligence Education Curriculum," *Journal of Strategic Security* 8, no. 3 (2015): 46–68.
3. "Students at DIA," Defense Intelligence Agency, accessed November 16, 2018, http://www.dia.mil/Careers-and-Internships/Students/.
4. David L. Sackett, *Evidence-Based Medicine* (New York: John Wiley & Sons, 2000); Huw Davies, Sandra M. Nutley, and Peter C. Smith, *What Works? Evidence-Based Policy and Practice in Public Services* (Chicago: Policy Press, 2000); Lawrence Sherman, *Evidence-Based Policing* (Washington, DC: Police Foundation, 1998).
5. Richard K. Betts, "Is Strategy an Illusion?" *International Security* 25, no. 2 (2000): 5–50.

6. Amy Zegart, "Daggers and Ivory Towers: Why Political Science Professors Don't Study US Intelligence," in *Essentials of Strategic Intelligence*, ed. Loch Johnson (Santa Barbara, CA: Praeger Security International, 2015), 28; Patrick von Maravic, "Limits of Knowing or the Consequences of Difficult-Access Problems for Multi-method Research and Public Policy," *Policy Sciences* 45, no. 2 (2012): 153–68.
7. Von Maravic, 154.
8. Michael Warner, "Sources and Methods for the Study of Intelligence," in *Handbook of Intelligence Studies*, ed. Loch Johnson (New York: Routledge, 2007), 17–27.
9. See, for example, National Security Agency, "Prepublication Review," accessed August 10, 2018, https://www.nsa.gov/resources/everyone/prepub/.
10. "The Family Jewels," Central Intelligence Agency, accessed November 16, 2018, https://www.cia.gov/library/readingroom/collection/family-jewels. CREST was previously accessible only at the National Archives at College Park, Maryland. Central Intelligence Agency, "CIA Posts More than 12 Million Pages of CREST Records Online," press release, January 17, 2017, https://www.cia.gov/news-information/press-releases-statements/2017-press-releases-statements/cia-posts-more-than-12-million-pages-of-crest-records-online.html.
11. Richard Aldrich, "'Grow Your Own': Cold War Intelligence and History Supermarkets," *Intelligence and National Security* 17, no. 1 (2002): 148.
12. Greg Michener, "FOI Laws around the World," *Journal of Democracy* 22, no. 2 (2011): 145–59.
13. For more statistics on FOIA requests, see "What Is FOIA?" accessed August 10, 2018, https://www.foia.gov/index.html.
14. "Is Wikileaks Putting People at Risk?" BBC News, August 23, 2016, https://www.bbc.com/news/technology-37165230.
15. Amy Zegart, "Universities Must Not Ignore Intelligence Research," *Chronicle of Higher Education*, July 13, 2007, https://www.chronicle.com/article/Universities-Must-Not-Ignore/10353.
16. Peter Monaghan, "Intelligence Studies," *Chronicle of Higher Education*, March 20, 2009, https://www.chronicle.com/article/Intelligence-Studies/33353.
17. See, for example, Eric Denécé and Gérald Arboit, "Intelligence Studies in France," *International Journal of Intelligence and CounterIntelligence* 23, no. 4 (2010): 725–47; Eyal Pascovich, "Security and Intelligence Studies in Israel," *International Journal of Intelligence, Security, and Public Affairs* 19, no. 2 (2017): 134–48.
18. Stephen Marrin, "Improving Intelligence Studies as an Academic Discipline," *Intelligence and National Security* 31, no. 2 (2016): 269; Robert Pool, ed., *Field Evaluation in the Intelligence and Counterintelligence Context: Workshop Summary* (Washington, DC: National Academies Press, 2010); Cherie Chauvin and Baruch Fischhoff, eds., *Intelligence Analysis: Behavioral and Social Scientific Foundations* (Washington, DC: National Academies Press, 2011).
19. Loch K. Johnson, "Spies and Scholars in the United States: Wounds of Ambivalence in the Groves of Academe," *Intelligence and National Security* 34, no. 1 (2019): 1.

20. Richard J. Aldrich, "'A Profoundly Disruptive Force': The CIA, Historiography and the Perils of Globalization," *Intelligence and National Security* 26, no. 2-3 (2011): 139–58. Dilks initially called intelligence a "missing dimension" of international history. See Christopher Andrew and David Dilks, *The Missing Dimension: Governments and Intelligence Communities in the Twentieth Century* (London: Macmillan, 1984), 1.
21. Bess J. Puvathingal and Donald A. Hantula, "Revisiting the Psychology of Intelligence Analysis," *American Psychologist* 67, no. 3 (2011): 3.
22. There are too many to list here, but for recent examples from political science, see Brent Durbin, *The CIA and the Politics of US Intelligence Reform* (Cambridge: Cambridge University Press, 2017); Michael Poznansky, "Stasis or Decay? Reconciling Covert War and the Democratic Peace," *International Studies Quarterly* 59, no. 4 (2015): 815–26.
23. See "Understanding and Improving Intelligence Analysis by Learning from Other Disciplines," special issue, *Intelligence and National Security* 32, no. 5 (2017), http://www.tandfonline.com/toc/fint20/32/5/?nav=tocList.
24. Our use of "pluralism" is partially based on "critical multiplism." See T. D. Cook, "Postpositivist Critical Multiplism," in *Social Science and Social Policy*, ed. R. L. Shotland and M. M. Mark (Beverly Hills, CA: Sage, 1985), 21–62.
25. Nicole Letourneau and Marion Allen, "Post-Positivistic Critical Multiplism: A Beginning Dialogue," *Journal of Advanced Nursing* 30, no. 3 (1999): 624.
26. Graham T. Allison, *Essence of Decision* (Boston: Little, Brown, 1971).
27. Letourneau and Allen, "Critical Multiplism," 625.
28. Von Maravic, "Limits of Knowing."
29. Alexander George, *Bridging the Gap: Theory and Practice in Foreign Policy* (Washington, DC: US Institute for Peace, 1993).

PART I

Framing Intelligence Research

# 1.

# Framing the Challenges and Opportunities of Intelligence Studies Research

*Mark Phythian*

All indicators suggest that intelligence studies is in very good health. The number of degree courses in intelligence in the United States continues to grow; a recent Association of Former Intelligence Officers survey listed 156 "Institutions Teaching about Intelligence," largely in the United States.[1] Not only is the study of intelligence a growth industry, it is increasingly a global one. Moreover, an increasing number of online courses offered at universities draw together students with an interest in intelligence from a wider range of countries than usually brought together in campus-based courses. In addition, intelligence is increasingly taught as an element of more general political science, international relations, history, and other degree programs. As a consequence, there are now more people teaching intelligence; there are more people producing research on intelligence; there are more publishers looking to develop intelligence studies book lists; and there are more intelligence studies journals, providing more opportunities, publishing more intelligence articles, and being downloaded and read by more people.

## What Is Intelligence Studies?

The growth and spread of interest in studying and researching intelligence are to be welcomed. But before we discuss the challenges and opportunities of intelligence studies research, we need to address the nature of intelligence studies itself. There has been some, but only limited, reflection on what intelligence studies is.[2] In a sense, this is understandable because intelligence is relatively young as an established area of academic inquiry, and fundamental issues of its definition remain contested. We still debate the question, What is intelligence? so it is understandable that this question has taken precedence over the question, What is intelligence studies? Intelligence studies is not alone in this; there are parallels with, for example, the study of terrorism, or terrorism studies.[3] Terrorism is another subject rooted in the social sciences and history with its own literature, specialist journals, and key concepts and areas of focus. Terrorism has been described as an unruly field or a strange field. Here too the core definitional question—How is "terrorism" defined?—remains contested. Moreover, intelligence studies and terrorism studies share a relationship with the state that can cause tension within the fields and affect perceptions of their academic credibility. As Lisa Stampnitzky has observed, "Terrorism expertise has its origins as an adjunct to the developing counterterrorism apparatus of the state. . . . The state has been not just the primary *sponsor* of knowledge-production, but also the primary *consumer* of research."[4] The parallel with Stephen Marrin's view that "intelligence studies is an academic complement to the practice of national security intelligence" is clear.[5]

As the study of intelligence becomes more global, we can see several approaches emerging with differing emphases, each of which is informed by more general national political and intelligence cultures. For example, the bounds of the possible in the study of intelligence remain at least partly defined by differing levels of secrecy and openness that we can measure in terms of archival release policies, levels of interaction between professionals or former professionals and the academy, national approaches to the publication of intelligence memoirs (whether encouraged, tolerated, or discouraged in various ways), the nature of oversight mechanisms, and the depth of commentary generated by legislative oversight and postmortem investigations by various commissions of inquiry. Where the historical record relating to intelligence remains largely closed, historians can look for creative ways around this obstacle, but one likely consequence is an emphasis on research that is not dependent on archival openings. Moreover, the subject matter of intelligence studies is expanding as the practice of intelligence itself adapts to exploit the potential of technological advances. We can see this, for example, in the rapid rise of interest in cybersecurity issues and in the way in which surveillance studies has responded to the information released via the 2013 Edward Snowden leaks.

Increasingly, then, there is no single vision of "intelligence studies." However, in the United States the trend is toward intelligence education being understood as pre-professional training and the requirement of entry into the analytic profession. As Michael Landon-Murray has noted, in the United States "both the new and already established academic programs [in intelligence] are meant to prepare analytic professionals." The task confronting the US university system is "to ensure that what many consider the world's best higher education system is optimally serving the world's largest intelligence system."[6] This view could clearly result in a narrow understanding of the nature and purpose of intelligence studies, calling for a focus on the organization and nature of the US intelligence community and on perfecting analytic techniques for it.[7] One implication of these developments is that whereas academics usually reflect on the nature of a subject or discipline in relation to curriculum design and teaching preparation, it may be that "intelligence studies" as an idea can be better articulated through its research agenda than through the varied curricular forms it takes. But this requires some unpacking.

When in 2012 Loch Johnson asked *Intelligence and National Security* editorial board members, "What is the principal debate in intelligence studies?" he received a wide range of answers, with most rejecting the idea that a single central debate defined intelligence studies.[8] Is intelligence studies, then, rather like, for example, American studies, with no central defining questions driving its research program? Is it just the history, politics, and literature of intelligence, much like American studies is just the history, politics, and literature of America? However, if we think about this parallel, we will soon see that indeed overarching questions underpin American studies, such as the question posed by Jean de Crèvecoeur in his 1782 *Letters from an American Farmer*: "What is an American?" This question features as often in political culture discussions in American politics textbooks as it does in histories of American literature. Are there no corresponding foundational questions in intelligence studies? Just adapting de Crèvecoeur shows that there are. Indeed, doing so directs us to a core question without an agreed answer: What is intelligence? More specifically, we could ask, What is the role of intelligence? How does it fit and operate in different political systems or regime types? These are social science questions, but there are history variants: What was intelligence? How did it change, and with what consequences, in times of war or times otherwise held to be exceptional? What role does intelligence play in the broader culture? Other questions are rooted in the humanities: What is the nature of cultural representations of intelligence? How do these cultural representations influence thinking about questions relating to intelligence? And across all contributing disciplines, there are questions such as, What has been the impact of intelligence, and at what cost? What difference has it made? There are, then, foundational questions out there, but intelligence studies could be more systematic about identifying, refining, and presenting them. Doing so would provide clearer definition of the subject.

Intelligence studies, as an academic project, is based on an idea, one that links both historical and social science approaches to its study. The idea is encapsulated in the term used by Christopher Andrew and David Dilks as the title of their 1984 edited volume, *The Missing Dimension*.[9] It is the idea that something important to a full understanding of the past, to how the contemporary state works and acts internationally, and to the relationship between citizen and state either had been ignored by historians and social scientists or had evaded them because of the high levels of secrecy attached to it. It is the idea that *full* understanding required the incorporation of this missing dimension. To illustrate the point, Andrew has reflected on how, when he was conducting PhD research into the 1904 entente cordiale and French foreign minister Théophile Delcassé in the mid-1960s,

> I began to realise that the French must have had access to some German diplomatic telegrams. I remember being in the University Library here and having open on my library desk *Die Grosse Politik*, the German diplomatic documents, and the *Documents Diplomatiques Français* and concluding that one could only understand Delcassé's policy if he had read some of the documents in *Die Grosse Politik*—but he couldn't have read them, could he?

Oh, perhaps he could! When I got to see his papers I realised that he did, and this is still a period when in the published diplomatic documents all [signals intelligence] was edited out.[10]

## The Four Projects of Intelligence Studies

Wesley Wark made an early and thoughtful attempt to address the question, What is intelligence studies? in research terms in his introduction to a special issue of *Intelligence and National Security*, based on papers delivered at a 1991 conference in Toronto. Wark identified eight overlapping intelligence "projects": the research project (by which he meant making available archival collections); the historical project; the definitional project; the methodological project (applying social science concepts to intelligence); memoirs; the civil liberties project; investigative journalism; and the popular culture project.[11] Nearly thirty years later, Wark's 1991 prospectus can be considered to have consolidated around four overlapping projects: the research/historical; the definitional/methodological; the organizational/functional; and the governance/societal/policy.[12] The popular culture project identified by Wark continues to have considerable potential but remains underdeveloped. In addition to these ongoing projects, we have reached a point in the evolution of intelligence studies at which we should begin to think about an additional project: the technological.

Greater openness around archival releases has facilitated much new historical research in recent years, although international intelligence history remains problematic. In the United Kingdom this project has been described as the "British school" of intelligence studies, reflecting both the strength of the British community of historians and the centrality of the two twentieth-century world wars to much historical research on intelligence.[13] This body of work includes, for example, Richard Aldrich on UK-US cooperation in the Cold War, Government Communications Headquarters (GCHQ), and the relationship between British prime ministers and intelligence (this latter with Rory Cormac).[14] The work of Rory Cormac has shown that it is possible to produce detailed historical accounts of the sensitive ("deniable") area of covert action.[15] It also includes several official or authorized histories of the Security Service (MI5), the Secret Intelligence Service (MI6), GCHQ, the Joint Intelligence Committee (the first volume), and cabinet secretaries (which has an intelligence dimension).[16] There have also been historical works facilitated by government, which constitute a kind of quasi-authorized project, such as Christopher Andrew's two-volume collaboration with Vasili Mitrokhin.[17] While welcoming the publication of official or authorized histories of intelligence organizations, we should also remain alert to any limits imposed on their authors. For example, it was no accident, and was not the author's wish, that Keith Jeffery's official history of MI6 goes no further than 1949. Some areas of national security and intelligence history remain contentious. For example, Northern Ireland is treated quite sparingly in Christopher Andrew's authorized history of MI5, suggesting an official reticence. It is not just in transitional states that we find contests over secrecy and openness in file releases or that we see evidence of file destruction.[18]

In parts of Europe the intelligence literature has been dominated by historical approaches. This is the case, for example, in Germany, where the International Intelligence History Association had its origins and has produced the *Journal of Intelligence History* since 2001 (now published by Taylor and Francis). The opening of state security archives in the former Communist bloc states of Central and Eastern Europe since 1991 has transformed the possibilities for research on the intelligence organizations, practices, and relations of these states.[19] In particular, the availability of the Stasi archives (in relation to which this process has been fullest) has made possible several detailed studies of Stasi activity and effectiveness and has added to our understanding of Western governments' activities during the Cold War.[20] Acts of resistance in relation to file releases and their part in reconciliation processes have also been the subject of academic scrutiny.[21]

The canvas of intelligence history is a busy one, but the key point here is that there are still many important big spaces. Some of these reflect major obstacles to writing international intelligence history. Perhaps most significant, Soviet archives remain closed. Use of these archives must await the passage of time, although it is worth noting that the Mitrokhin archive at Churchill College, Cambridge, has proved very useful to historians; it is the third most-visited archive at Churchill College after the Winston Churchill and Margaret Thatcher archives. We are still learning important things about the role of intelligence in the First World War, the Second World War, and even more so, the Cold War.[22] Calder Walton has demonstrated the potential for research into the role of MI5 in the decolonization process.[23] File releases can transform and deepen understandings of key events and be of enormous value to biographical projects.[24] Nevertheless, it would be wrong to imply that progressive archival openings and the commissioning of official histories have eliminated the core challenge of secrecy that confronts the intelligence researcher. We would do well to remember Richard Aldrich's warning that official file releases are "pre-selected, cleaned and processed by officials who are the institutional successors to those who we wish to study" and that those working in archives "have no external guarantee that what is preserved there is necessarily an analogue of reality."[25] Triangulation is clearly important. For example, the subjects of MI5 surveillance were objects of suspicion, and surveillance on them proceeded on the basis that the institutional suspicion was well founded. All their reported actions—travel, speaking engagements, and meetings—are interpreted through this prism of suspicion. However, this suspicion can prove to have been misplaced. When contrasted with other accounts of the life—personal diaries, memoirs, the recollections of others—the account offered in the MI5 personal file can appear distorted.

Even progress in file releases can coexist with ongoing classification resulting in the creation of a fuller, rather than the fullest possible picture. For example, in 1989 the US State Department published the volume in its *Foreign Relations of the United States* series that dealt with US-Iranian relations from 1951 to 1954, but this essentially ignored the 1953 coup that removed Prime Minister Mohammad Mossadegh from power and the CIA's role in this coup. In 2017 a volume was released that dealt with the 1953 coup. This new volume demonstrated how partial the initial 1989 release had been but itself fell some way short of providing a comprehensive account given the number of document sections that remain classified.[26]

While *Intelligence and National Security* was founded as a multidisciplinary journal, in its early years intelligence history provided the core focus. In the years since the terrorist attacks of September 11, 2001 (9/11), however, a higher proportion of articles have been rooted in social science than were previously. There have also been a greater number of articles addressing the question, What is intelligence? and dealing with intelligence futures.[27] This reflects the continued relevance of a second research project, one that Wesley Wark termed the definitional/methodological project.[28] The importance of this was set out by Harry Howe Ransom in 1980, in the early days of academic intelligence studies, when he identified an "impediment to understanding" rooted in "the conceptual confusion, indeed, terminological chaos, surrounding this topic. The term 'intelligence' is commonly used interchangeably to refer to a variety of disparate functions, including evaluated information, espionage, counterintelligence, and covert political action."[29] While some despair that intelligence studies has not transcended definitional debates, these debates remain important to clarifying what is to be studied and why and should be seen as a necessary feature of intelligence studies, given that the subject is so affected by rapid technological advance. One central question is whether "intelligence" should be defined purely as an information or knowledge process or whether it is also a power process involving policy and action. Peter Gill and I, in framing our approach to studying intelligence, have taken the latter view and defined intelligence in terms of surveillance, understood as both the gathering and storing of information and the supervision of people's behavior—that is, both knowledge and power. Our definition of intelligence is as follows: "The mainly secret activities—targeting, collection, analysis, dissemination and action—intended to enhance security and/or maintain power relative to competitors by forewarning of threats and opportunities."[30] As this definition suggests, the definitional/methodological project is also about developing frameworks for understanding—for example, debating the utility of and alternatives to the intelligence cycle model and considering organizing principles and ideas around which thinking about intelligence may proceed, such as surveillance and the role of intelligence in relation to concepts of risk and uncertainty.[31]

The research/historical project discussed earlier provides the foundation for the third project: the organizational/functional. This project focuses on intelligence organizations and their functions (and not just at the state level). There has been important and distinctive theoretical work here by, for example, Michael Herman, Philip Davies, and Amy Zegart, deploying ideas of organizational process.[32] Recent years have seen important contributions from behavioral science perspectives and an increasing number of contributions to debates on analytical techniques and the way, and to what extent, these can be improved. Within these contributions, there have been thoughtful efforts to draw parallels with and lessons from other professions and from academic disciplines. The work done to date provides a clear indication of the future potential of this line of inquiry.[33]

Surveillance is also a key theme here, one of the key legacies of the Snowden leaks for intelligence studies. The information revealed about organizational practices via the Snowden leaks has led to a renewed focus on surveillance and a questioning of previous understandings and conceptualizations. As Zygmunt Bauman, Didier Bigo, and colleagues put it in a 2014 root and branch reevaluation of approaches to surveillance in light of Snowden,

> Much of this information, especially about the scale, reach, and technical sophistication of these practices, came as a surprise even to seasoned observers, and its significance remains unclear. This is partly because the extensive details about the complex systems that have been exposed are difficult to track, although many of them seem to have serious and immediate consequences. It is also because these details seem to imply significant transgressions of established understandings of the character and legitimacy of those institutions concerned with security and intelligence operations, thus stimulating intense political controversy. And it is partly, and even more disconcertingly, because some revelations seem to confirm long-term transformations in the politics of states; in relations between states; and in the institutions and norms established in relation to democratic procedures, the rule of law, relations between state and civil society, relations between public policy and corporate or private economic interests, the acceptability of cultural norms and even concepts of subjectivity.[34]

This seems to me to be the basis of a coherent post-Snowden research project around surveillance that intelligence studies should be taking up. It contains within it several key themes that have been explored separately, such as public-private partnerships, the role of the private sector in intelligence, and the question of the ethics of intelligence. As David Lyon has written, "Surveillance is a site of struggle, of controversy. Its currency is terms such as privacy, civil liberties, and human rights. Each of these is profoundly ethical and thus confronts us with questions that are unavoidably philosophical and even spiritual as well as political."[35]

This agenda takes us into the territory of the fourth project—governance/societal/policy—which addresses the impact that intelligence has on government and society and the impact that government and society have on intelligence. Harry Howe Ransom touched on this in his agenda-setting 1980 article when he highlighted "the perhaps unresolvable normative problem of balancing the requirements of American democracy with the presumed need for intelligence agency secrecy."[36] Hence, we can see consideration of this problem as being core to the intelligence studies research agenda. It gave rise to early works by Loch Johnson on intelligence oversight and accountability and by Greg Treverton on covert action and democracy, establishing accountability as a key dimension of the academic study of intelligence.[37] It reminds us how, from its earliest days, intelligence studies has been concerned with the relationship between intelligence, the state, and the broader society—or, if you like, between power, knowledge, and secrecy—and not simply with intelligence as a process per se.

This agenda is also concerned with the societal impact of intelligence technologies; the extent to which societies have consented to the forms, range, and depth of surveillance facilitated by technological advance; the ways this consent can be taken to have been given; and the ways it can be regularly renewed.[38] It is concerned with the oversight and accountability challenges that arise from technological advance (exposed by the Snowden leaks) and also with the post-9/11 rise in international intelligence cooperation.[39] Indeed, the very possibility of national oversight is challenged by developments in these areas. A normative dimension is brought to this project through the ethics of cooperating with states that use methods amounting to torture to extract information and the responsibilities of intelligence at the level of the organization and individual in these contexts.

Here too I would locate the study of intelligence failure. Stephen Marrin made the astute point some years ago that the study of failure provides a theoretical focus, or "big question," for intelligence studies equivalent to that of the causes of war in international relations.[40] Linked to this, one central aspect of the literature, especially in the United States, is the extent to which intelligence does or does not affect government policy.[41] Postmortem inquiries into the Iraqi weapons of mass destruction intelligence issue have also highlighted a contrasting problem: when policy determines what is defined as "intelligence." All of these approaches reflect the point that intelligence is a preeminently social and political phenomenon, not simply a technical discipline. Consequently, the intelligence studies research agenda must go beyond a focus on issues of process.

## Issues Cutting across the Intelligence Studies Projects

The intelligence studies research agenda overlaps clearly at points with that of strategic studies. This should come as no great surprise, and a number of key figures in intelligence studies are also key figures in strategic studies. The important point here is that as a subject area, strategic studies has attracted criticism for being too narrowly focused on military power and on the state as the referent object and for being Western-centric.[42] Critical security studies developed in response to this narrow focus, extending the range—empirically and conceptually—of strategic studies. In essence there are currents within the three social science projects outlined previously that perform the same role in intelligence studies that critical security studies performs within the broad field of strategic studies. Efforts toward theorization of intelligence have developed forms of critical intelligence studies that draw on insights and approaches deployed in the area of critical security studies, of the kind also evident in the development of critical terrorism studies.[43] This is an area rich with potential for further development.[44] There are no clear lines separating critical security studies and critical terrorism studies from some approaches evident in the research projects that make up intelligence studies, nor should there be. This lack of delineation is evident, for example, in approaches to the framing of and normative issues raised by the post-9/11 "war on terror."[45]

Technology has long been part of the intelligence studies research agenda, reflecting its central role in the protection, transmission, and theft o10f important secrets, going back to the use of invisible ink in the ancient world.[46] The rise of the armed drone has meant that issues of violent technologies remain relevant to intelligence studies, just as they are to strategic studies and international relations more broadly. Research concerning normative issues raised by armed drone use have drawn on just war theory, and a debate concerning just war theory's utility in relation to intelligence is set to develop in the future.[47]

Technology is central to surveillance, and surveillance is in turn central to social science approaches to understanding intelligence. "Technology" was used by Michel Foucault in his work on social control "to describe exertions of power that are based less on overt violence than on the subtle manipulation of human behavior—in which bodies are prodded in certain directions, molded according to particular forms, and forced to act in coordination with one another."[48] In focusing on technology in this way, Foucault's interest lay in how the manipulation of society by technology could be resisted. There is clearly something of this approach in post-Snowden social science interventions around surveillance. Hence, technology has been part of the three social science–based research projects discussed earlier. However, we have now reached a point at which contemporary intelligence practice is so dependent on technological innovation that "technology" needs to be seen as a project in its own right. The focus on cybersecurity is changing the shape of the intelligence studies research agenda. Social scientists clearly have a role to play in this change, but the center of gravity is shifting toward academics in the fields of mathematics and computer science. We can see this shift in the recent expansion of journals in this area. Some of these are interdisciplinary and have a social sciences dimension (for example, the *Journal of Cyber Security* and the *Journal of Cyber Policy*), but others have a more exclusively technical focus (for example, the *Journal of Cyber Security Technology* and *Computers and Security*). Universities that deliver intelligence programs are looking to bolster their expertise in all matters cyber, and when they do, they are usually looking for people with mathematics and computer science backgrounds rather than backgrounds in the social sciences. The shift in the nature of intelligence studies is set to become more pronounced in the future.

As the geographical range of research on intelligence gradually expands and our understanding of intelligence beyond the Anglosphere develops, so the potential for comparative analysis increases.[49] Comparative analysis is relevant to each of the projects identified earlier. In general, progress in developing an information base from which comparative analysis can proceed has been frustratingly slow, and some areas remain apparently immune to analysis. Without comparative analysis our capacity to conduct social science research at the level of *national systems* of intelligence is severely limited. The production of detailed national case studies must precede comparative analysis. These case studies are the raw material of it. Given that comparative analysis has not developed far, neither have we gotten very far in developing comparative frameworks—of identifying precisely what we study when we do comparative analysis of intelligence systems. Should we focus on intelligence organizations, or more broadly to include, for example, oversight and accountability mechanisms and facilitate reflection on wider questions of how the form of the state affects the nature of intelligence and how intelligence affects the nature of the state?

There is no escaping the fact that most of the intelligence studies literature still focuses on a relatively small number of countries. A 2016 survey, by Damien Van Puyvelde and Sean Curtis, of the content of *Intelligence and National Security* and the *International Journal of Intelligence and Counterintelligence* to 2015 found that over 70 percent of the published articles had a geographical focus on the United States or United Kingdom.[50] The leading countries of focus were the United States (the subject of 996 articles), the United Kingdom (519), Russia (215), Germany (140), Israel (82), France (67), and Canada (60). China was the focus of a relatively small number of articles (31), while work on intelligence in countries in Africa was largely absent. Hence, the increasingly globalized picture of the study of intelligence is not being matched by a geographical spread of research focus. This raises the question, Why is this the case? There are models that show what can be achieved in the face of very limited information; the work by Hal Klepak on security intelligence in Cuba and by Carl Thayer on Vietnam are very good illustrations, as is the edited collection *Intelligence Elsewhere*.[51] In addition, the work of Paul Maddrell, Christopher Moran, and colleagues has shown how a biographical approach to intelligence leaders can illuminate national contexts.[52] There are also examples in which models of change are used to compare the causes of shifts in intelligence systems in different parts of the world.[53] Nevertheless, comparative analysis remains one of the key challenges for intelligence studies research, and the dearth of this analysis holds back the development of intelligence studies as an academic subject area.

## Opportunities of Intelligence Studies

Intelligence studies is fortunate in having a good range of well-regarded and widely read specialist international journals. A number of these are published by Taylor & Francis—*Intelligence and National Security*, the *International Journal of Intelligence and Counterintelligence*, the *International Journal of Intelligence, Security, and Public Affairs* (formerly *Inteligencia y Seguridad: Revista de Análisis y Prospectiva*), the *Journal of Intelligence History*, and based in Australia, the *Journal of Policing, Intelligence and Counter Terrorism*. The existence of these journals provides great opportunities for publication and dissemination but also points toward a research challenge. It is important that these journals continue to develop, but it is also important that intelligence studies academics continue to engage in outreach and cooperate with academics working in mainstream security studies, strategic studies, sociology, politics, international relations, and so forth. Together these academics can construct conference panels, produce special themed issues of journals and edited book collections, and also build a presence in the more generalist disciplinary journals to raise the profile of intelligence studies within the disciplines from which it draws and to dispel any suspicions that it is a narrow technical subject primarily designed to service the state. This will mitigate the risk of "ghettoization" of intelligence research. Then again, success here brings the challenge of keeping track of the intelligence literature, of knowing where to find it. Research that falls within the expanding boundaries of intelligence studies can appear in a wide range of journals across several disciplines. The Snowden leaks, for example, have resulted in important responses in a range of disciplinary and interdisciplinary journals, such as the *Journal of Information, Communication and Ethics in Society*, the *International Journal of Human Rights*, and *Digital Journalism*, to name just three.[54]

Intelligence remains largely absent from international relations theory. The exception may be the cyber realm, where there has been significant work aimed at situating the cyber revolution and its implications within broader international relations theory.[55] Elsewhere in mainstream international relations theory, though, intelligence may have an implicit presence, but it is not considered explicitly. This is particularly true of foundational approaches, such as structural realist theoretical contributions, both offensive and defensive realist variants. For example, in his classic statement of offensive realism, *The Tragedy of Great Power Politics*, John Mearsheimer identifies three factors that determine how great powers behave, the third of which is "the fact that states can never be certain about other states' intentions."[56] Elsewhere, he elaborates on the implications of this:

> States ultimately want to know whether other states are determined to use force to alter the balance of power, or whether they are satisfied enough with it that they have no interest in using force to change it. The problem, however, is that it is almost impossible to discern another state's intentions with a high degree of certainty. Unlike military capabilities, intentions cannot be empirically verified. Intentions are in the minds of decision-makers and they are especially difficult to discern. One might respond that policy-makers disclose their intentions in speeches and policy documents, which can be assessed. The problem with that argument is policy-makers sometimes lie about or conceal their true intentions. But even if one could determine another state's intentions today, there is no way to determine its future intentions. It is impossible to know who will be running foreign policy in any state five or ten years from now, much less whether they will have aggressive intentions. This is not to say that states can be certain that their neighbours have or will have revisionist goals. Instead, the argument is that policy-makers can never be certain whether they are dealing with a revisionist or status quo state.[57]

This serves as a great summary of *why* intelligence is required. Indeed, the assumption that intelligence is a necessity rests on essentially neorealist assumptions about the nature of the international system. Yet you will look in vain to find an entry for "intelligence" in Mearsheimer's *The Tragedy of Great Power Politics*, let alone explicit discussion in the text. This remains true of the updated edition published in 2014. Intelligence remains a "missing dimension" in core international relations theory. And this is of considerable significance; Mearsheimer does not factor in a dimension that has the capacity to affect the utility of his analysis. Through investments in intelligence, states seek the capacity to break down this uncertainty, to mitigate it. This means that there are intermediate possibilities for states in dealing with the structural problems arising from the nature of the international system and that Mearsheimer's prescription is not the only possibility. Moreover, the growth of intelligence capabilities and communities in the great powers since the nineteenth century means that drawing conclusions largely based on patterns of state behavior in that century might well be problematic; the growth of organized national intelligence has generated a greater range of state options. Hence, if incorporated, intelligence studies can inform thinking about international relations theory at least as much as international relations theory can inform thinking about intelligence.

Earlier I referred to the canvas of historical research into intelligence. In social science terms, intelligence was, until thirty years or so ago, a relatively blank canvas, featuring just a small number of colorful and bold interventions from figures such as Loch Johnson, Richard Betts, Michael Herman, and Greg Treverton. This canvas has seen a good number of important additions during the last decade. But there are still big spaces where social science theories could be adapted to illuminate aspects of intelligence. Moreover, the canvas has expanded during this time. Intelligence studies is a broad intellectual project that incorporates a variety of perspectives from several disciplines—for example, history, politics, international relations, sociology, psychology, criminology, media and communication studies, and increasingly, computer science and mathematics. It is a dynamic subject area featuring not just a wide range of conceptual possibilities but also the emergence of new areas on which to apply them—the developing literatures about the cyber realm, the implications of drone development and use, the post-Snowden surveillance debate, for example. The emergence of these new areas also requires us to revisit and reassess established understandings and concepts—for example, the intelligence cycle, the meaning of surveillance, and the relationship between ethics and intelligence. These spaces constitute an opportunity-rich environment for the intelligence researcher. Overall, as an academic project intelligence studies is still defined as much by gaps as it is by coverage. If it could be better at articulating these as a research agenda, it would also acquire clearer definition as an academic subject area.

## Notes

1. For a list of programs, see "Academic Exchange," Association of Former Intelligence Officers, accessed August 8, 2018, https://www.afio.com/12_academic.htm.

2. See, for example, Stephen Marrin, "Improving Intelligence Studies as an Academic Discipline," *Intelligence and National Security* 31, no. 2 (2016): 266–79; Peter Gill and Mark Phythian, "What Is Intelligence Studies?" *International Journal of Intelligence, Security, and Public Affairs* 18, no. 1 (2016): 5–19.
3. I first discussed this parallel in Mark Phythian, "Intelligence Theory and Theories of International Relations; Shared World or Separate Worlds?" in *Intelligence Theory: Key Questions and Debates*, ed. Peter Gill, Stephen Marrin, and Mark Phythian (London: Routledge, 2009), 54–72.
4. Lisa Stampnitzky, "Disciplining an Unruly Field: Terrorism Experts and Theories of Scientific/Intellectual Production," *Qualitative Sociology* 34, no. 1 (2011): 7. Emphasis in original.
5. Marrin, "Improving Intelligence Studies," 266.
6. Michael Landon-Murray, "Moving US Academic Intelligence Education Forward: A Literature Inventory and Agenda," *International Journal of Intelligence and Counterintelligence* 26, no. 4 (2013): 744, 746.
7. For a textbook example, see Carl J. Jensen III, David H. McElreath, and Melissa Graves, *Introduction to Intelligence Studies*, 2nd ed. (New York: Routledge, 2018).
8. Loch K. Johnson and Allison M. Shelton, "Thoughts on the State of Intelligence Studies: A Survey Report," *Intelligence and National Security* 28, no. 1 (2013): 109–20.
9. Christopher Andrew and David Dilks, eds., *The Missing Dimension: Governments and Intelligence Communities in the Twentieth Century* (London: Macmillan, 1984).
10. Mark Phythian, "Profiles in Intelligence: An Interview with Professor Christopher Andrew," *Intelligence and National Security* 32, no. 4 (2017): 397.
11. Wesley K. Wark, "Introduction: The Study of Espionage: Past Present, Future?" *Intelligence and National Security* 8, no. 3 (1993): 1–13.
12. These categories are identified in Gill and Phythian, "What Is Intelligence Studies?"
13. See Donald Cameron Watt, "Intelligence Studies: The Emergence of the British School," *Intelligence and National Security* 3, no. 2 (1988): 338–42.
14. Richard J. Aldrich, *The Hidden Hand: Britain, America and Cold War Secret Intelligence* (London: John Murray, 2001); Richard J. Aldrich, *GCHQ: The Uncensored Story of Britain's Most Secret Intelligence Agency* (London: HarperPress, 2010); Richard J. Aldrich and Rory Cormac, *The Black Door: Spies, Secret Intelligence and British Prime Ministers* (London: William Collins, 2016).
15. Rory Cormac, *Disrupt and Deny: Spies, Special Forces, and the Secret Pursuit of British Foreign Policy* (Oxford: Oxford University Press, 2018).
16. Christopher Andrew, *The Defence of the Realm: The Authorized History of MI5* (London: Allen Lane, 2009); Keith Jeffery, *MI6: The History of the Secret Intelligence Service, 1909–1949* (London: Bloomsbury, 2010); Michael Goodman, *The Official History of the Joint Intelligence Committee*, vol. 1, *From the Approach of the Second World War to the Suez Crisis* (London: Routledge, 2014); Ian Beesley, *The Official History of the Cabinet Secretaries* (London: Routledge, 2016).

17. Christopher Andrew and Vasili Mitrokhin, *The Mitrokhin Archive: The KGB in Europe and the West* (London: Allen Lane, 1999); Christopher Andrew and Vasili Mitrokhin, *The Mitrokhin Archive II: The KGB and the World* (London: Allen Lane, 2005).
18. For example, see Phil Miller, "Foreign Office Destroyed 200 Files on UK Role in Sri Lanka Insurgency," *The Guardian*, May 24, 2018. More generally, see Ian Cobain, *The History Thieves: Secrets, Lies and the Shaping of a Modern Nation* (London: Portobello Books, 2016).
19. Paul Maddrell, "The Opening of the State Security Archives of Central and Eastern Europe," *International Journal of Intelligence and Counterintelligence* 27, no. 1 (2014): 1–26.
20. The literature using the Stasi archives is large. Three good examples from the intelligence literature that cover the areas I mention here are Jens Gieseke, "East German Espionage in the Era of Détente," *Journal of Strategic Studies* 31, no. 3 (2008): 395–424; Kristie Macrakis, *Seduced by Secrets: Inside the Stasi's Spy-Tech World* (New York: Cambridge University Press, 2008); Paul Maddrell, "What We Have Discovered about the Cold War Is What We Already Knew: Julius Mader and the Western Secret Services during the Cold War," *Cold War History* 5, no. 2 (2005): 235–58.
21. For example, the Romanian Orthodox Church's efforts to prevent the release of the names of priests identified as collaborators with the Securitate, the Nicolae Ceaușescu–era internal security/political police organization. See Lavinia Stan and Lucian Turescu, "The Devil's Confessors: Priests, Communists, Spies, and Informers," *East European Politics and Societies* 19, no. 4 (2005): 655–85.
22. The subject of a series of articles that appeared in John Ferris and Mark Stout, eds., "Military Intelligence during the First World War," special issue, *Intelligence and National Security* 32, no. 3 (2017).
23. Calder Walton, *Empire of Secrets: British Intelligence, the Cold War, and the Twilight of Empire* (London: HarperCollins, 2013). Mention should also be made of the important earlier work of Philip Murphy, e.g., "Creating a Commonwealth Intelligence Culture: The View from Central Africa, 1945–1965," *Intelligence and National Security* 17, no. 3 (2002): 131–62.
24. As, for example, with recent biographies of Guy Burgess and Donald Maclean that draw on National Archives file releases. Stewart Purvis and Jeff Hulbert, *Guy Burgess: The Spy Who Knew Everyone* (London: Biteback, 2016); Roland Philipps, *A Spy Named Orphan: The Enigma of Donald Maclean* (London: Bodley Head, 2018).
25. Richard J. Aldrich, "Grow Your Own: Cold War Intelligence and History Supermarkets," *Intelligence and National Security* 17, no. 1 (2002): 148.
26. The two volumes share the same title: *Foreign Relations of the United States, 1952–1954, Iran, 1951–1954*. The 1989 volume is available at https://history.state.gov/historicaldocuments/frus1952-54v10; the 2017 volume is available at https://history.state.gov/historicaldocuments/frus1951-54Iran.
27. For example, Alan Breakspear, "A New Definition of Intelligence," *Intelligence and National Security* 28, no. 5 (2013): 678–93; Kira Vrist Rønn and Simon Høffding, "The Epistemic Status of Intelligence: An Epistemological Contribution to the

Understanding of Intelligence," *Intelligence and National Security* 28, no. 5 (2013): 694–716. On intelligence futures, see, for example, the articles that appeared in *Intelligence and National Security* 18, no. 4 (2003), particularly the introduction by Wesley Wark, "Learning to Live with Intelligence," 1–14.

28. Main examples include Michael Warner, "Wanted: A Definition of Intelligence," *Studies in Intelligence* 46, no. 3 (2002), https://www.cia.gov/library/center-for-the-study-of-intelligence/csi-publications/csi-studies/studies/vol46no3/article02.html; Kristan Wheaton and Michael Beerbower, "Towards a New Definition of Intelligence," *Stanford Law and Policy Review* 17, no. 2 (2006): 319–30; Peter Gill, "Theories of Intelligence: Where Are We, Where Should We Go and How Might We Proceed," in Gill, Marrin, and Phythian *Intelligence Theory*, 208–26.

29. Harry Howe Ransom, "Being Intelligent about Secret Intelligence Agencies," *American Political Science Review* 74, no. 1 (1980): 141.

30. Peter Gill and Mark Phythian, *Intelligence in an Insecure World*, 3rd ed. (Cambridge: Polity Press, 2018), see 5 and the discussion at 33–36.

31. See the various perspectives on the intelligence cycle presented in Mark Phythian, ed., *Understanding the Intelligence Cycle* (London: Routledge, 2013).

32. Michael Herman, *Intelligence Power in Peace and War: Intelligence Services in the Information Age* (Cambridge: Cambridge University Press, 1996), chs. 16–18; Philip H. J. Davies, *MI6 and the Machinery of Spying* (London: Frank Cass, 2004); Amy B. Zegart, *Spying Blind: The CIA, the FBI and the Origins of 9/11* (Princeton, NJ: Princeton University Press, 2007).

33. Stephen Marrin is a key figure in these efforts. For a range of perspectives, see Stephen Marrin, ed., "Understanding and Improving Intelligence Analysis by Learning from Other Disciplines," special issue, *Intelligence and National Security* 32, no. 5 (2017).

34. Zygmunt Bauman, Didier Bigo, Paulo Esteves, Elsepth Guild, Vivienne Jabri, David Lyon, and R. B. J. Walker, "After Snowden: Rethinking the Impact of Surveillance," *International Political Sociology* 8 (2014): 122.

35. David Lyon, *Surveillance after Snowden* (Cambridge: Polity Press, 2015), viii.

36. Ransom, "Being Intelligent," 141.

37. Loch K. Johnson, *A Season of Inquiry: The Senate Intelligence Investigation* (Lexington: University Press of Kentucky, 1985); Gregory F. Treverton, *Covert Acton: The Limits of Intervention in the Post-War World* (New York: Basic Books, 1987).

38. On this see the discussion in David Omand and Mark Phythian, *Principled Spying: The Ethics of Secret Intelligence* (Washington, DC: Georgetown University Press, 2018).

39. Hans Born, Ian Leigh, and Aidan Wills, eds., *International Intelligence Cooperation and Accountability* (London: Routledge, 2011).

40. Stephen Marrin, "Intelligence Analysis Theory: Explaining and Predicting Analytic Responsibilities," *Intelligence and National Security* 22, no. 6 (2007): 821–46.

41. See, for example, Stephen Marrin, "Why Strategic Intelligence Analysis Has Limited Influence on American Foreign Policy," *Intelligence and National Security* 32, no. 6 (2017): 725–42.

42. See, for example, Ole Waever, "The History and Social Structure of Security Studies as a Practico-Academic Field," in *Security Expertise: Practice, Power, Responsibility*, ed. Trine Villumsen Berling and Christian Bueger (London: Routledge, 2015), 76–106; Pascal Vennesson, "Is Strategic Studies Narrow? Critical Security and the Misunderstood Scope of Strategy," *Journal of Strategic Studies* 40, no. 3 (2017): 358–91.
43. For example, Gill and Phythian, *Intelligence in an Insecure World*; Gill, Marrin, and Phythian, eds., *Intelligence Theory*; and Peter Gill, Stephen Marrin, and Mark Phythian, eds., "Developing Intelligence Theory," special issue, *Intelligence and National Security* 33, no. 4 (2018), particularly the articles by Hamilton Bean, Gunilla Ericksson, and Peter Gill.
44. See also the discussion in Didier Bigo, "Rethinking Security at the Crossroads of International Relations and Criminology," *British Journal of Criminology* 56, no. 6 (2016): 1068–86.
45. See, for example, Amy Zalman and Jonathan Clarke, "The Global War on Terror: A Narrative in Need of a Rewrite," *Ethics and International Affairs* 23, no. 2 (2009): 101–13.
46. See Kristie Macrakis, *Prisoners, Lovers, and Spies: The Story of Invisible Ink from Herodotus to al-Qaeda* (New Haven, CT: Yale University Press, 2014).
47. On violent technologies, ethics, and intelligence, see Grégoire Chambayou, *Drone Theory* (London: Penguin, 2015); Elke Schwarz, *Death Machines: The Ethics of Violent Technologies* (Manchester: Manchester University Press, 2018). On just war's utility when extended to intelligence, see, for example, Omand and Phythian, *Principled Spying*; Adam Diderichsen and Kira Vrist Rønn, "Intelligence by Consent: On the Inadequacy of Just War Theory as a Framework for Intelligence Ethics," *Intelligence and National Security* 32, no. 4 (2017): 479–93.
48. Michael C. Behrent, "Foucault and Technology," *History and Technology* 29, no. 1 (2013): 84.
49. See, for example, Philip H. J. Davies and Kristian C. Gustafson, eds., *Intelligence Elsewhere: Spies and Espionage outside the Anglosphere* (Washington, DC: Georgetown University Press, 2013).
50. Damien Van Puyvelde and Sean Curtis, "'Standing on the Shoulders of Giants': Diversity and Scholarship in Intelligence Studies," *Intelligence and National Security* 31, no. 7 (2016): 1040–54.
51. The chapters by Klepak and Thayer are in Stuart Farson, Peter Gill, Mark Phythian, and Shlomo Shpiro, eds., *PSI Handbook of Global Security and Intelligence: National Approaches*, vol. 1, *The Americas and Asia* (Westport, CT: Praeger, 2008); Davies and Gustafson, *Intelligence Elsewhere*.
52. Paul Maddrell, Christopher Moran, Ioanna Iordanou, and Mark Stout, eds., *Spy Chiefs*, Volume 2: *Intelligence Leaders in Europe, the Middle East, and Asia* (Washington, DC: Georgetown University Press, 2018).
53. For example, Marina Caparini, "Comparing the Democratization of Intelligence Governance in East Central Europe and the Balkans," *Intelligence and National Security* 29, no. 4 (2014): 498–522; Marco Cepik and Cristiano Ambros, "Intelligence,

Crisis and Democracy: Institutional Punctuations in Brazil, Colombia, South Africa, and India," *Intelligence and National Security* 29, no. 4 (2014): 523–51; Eduardo Estévez, "Comparing Intelligence Democratization in Latin America: Argentina, Peru and Ecuador Cases," *Intelligence and National Security* 29, no. 4 (2014): 552–80.

54. Christian Fuchs and Daniel Trottier, "Internet Surveillance after Snowden: A Critical Empirical Study of Computer Experts' Attitudes on Commercial and State Surveillance of the Internet and Social Media Post-Edward Snowden," *Journal of Information, Communication and Ethics in Society* 15, no. 4 (2017): 412–44; Nick Taylor, "To Find the Needle Do You Need the Whole Haystack? Global Surveillance and Principled Regulation," *International Journal of Human Rights* 18, no. 1 (2014): 45–67; Heikki Heikkilä and Risto Kunelius, "Surveillance and the Structural Transformation of Privacy: Mapping the Conceptual Landscape of Journalism in the Post-Snowden Era," *Digital Journalism* 5, no. 3 (2017): 262–76.
55. See, for example, Lucas Kello, *The Virtual Weapon and International Order* (New Haven, CT: Yale University Press, 2017).
56. John J. Mearsheimer, *The Tragedy of Great Power Politics* (New York: W. W. Norton, 2001), 3.
57. John J. Mearsheimer, "Structural Realism," in *International Relations Theories: Discipline and Diversity*, ed. Tim Dunne, Milja Kurki, and Steve Smith (Oxford: Oxford University Press, 2007), 73.

# 2.

# Confessions of an Intelligence Historian

*John Ferris*

This chapter reflects on my experience as a historian of intelligence, beginning as a PhD student in 1979, to my present status as the authorized historian for the British communications intelligence agency, the Government Communications Headquarters (GCHQ). It examines the evolution of the study of intelligence, particularly of its history, over that period and considers how the study of its history has shaped academic understanding of intelligence.

## *Apologia Pro Vita Sua* (A Defense of One's Life)

As a boy scout, during the international geophysical calendar for 1968, I listened for electromagnetic transmissions on a ham radio, gaining the only practical experience I ever have had in signals intelligence (SIGINT). As an undergraduate in the mid-1970s, I was interested in intelligence and struck by the announcement of Ultra.[1] I read some key books in the area that later proved helpful to me, especially David Kahn's *The Codebreakers* and Roberta Wohlstetter's *Pearl Harbor*, alongside works by political scientists on related themes, such as the politics of decision-making, and perception and action, like Graham Allison's *Essence of Decision*.[2] However, when I began my PhD in 1979, I did not intend to work on intelligence. I stumbled into that field by accident. My dissertation addressed British strategic policy between the end of the Great War and 1926, seeking to reconstruct how decision-makers made foreign policy, financial, and military decisions and formulated strategy.[3] Where most of my elders and peers focused on files from just one department, alongside the Cabinet Office and private papers, I attacked files from many departments and scanned their indexes, which were available only on paper. Without realizing it, I had chosen a topic for which I had to address the perceptions of decision-makers, and thus the way information and intelligence were interpreted and shaped thought and action. Some of those records on intelligence, moreover, survived. In my period, material on intelligence had not been so thoroughly "weeded" from the files as was true of those a decade later. For that reason, and given the scope of my research, I frequently came across intelligence records. In particular I found a few files about the British crypt-analytical organization of the interwar years, the Government Code and Cypher School (GC and CS), and some of its solutions of foreign diplomatic traffic. I was not the first to find all these solutions; Adam Ulam and Christopher Andrew had used some of them well.[4] However, I found increasing amounts of material that no one else had used. When I discussed this issue with other historians, many believed that I could not have found what I had, or else, even if I had, the history of GC and CS and its influence still could not be reconstructed.

By 1982 I had completed the research for my thesis and was writing it up and thinking about my next project. Potential topics for research were plentiful. In the mid-1980s there were few students in strategic history and many topics that I knew had promise. I decided to work on British signals intelligence because it was the most interesting, original, and difficult topic I could find and because I seemed to be the only person able to find new material on it. Instead of doing so by accident, I hunted systematically for evidence. I also chose not to focus on the areas where other people had done or were doing work, like Ultra or Room 40, but on those where I knew SIGINT had been practiced but not yet studied, like the interwar years or the British army in the First World War.[5] I haunted the paper-finding aids at the British Public Record Office (PRO) because I knew that only a wide swathe through the records could produce enough grist for my mill.[6] I doubt that any other scholar went through as many of those indexes as I or that anyone can do so again, as those aids often have vanished. I discovered that files on signals were a fruitful source of material on signals security and, in turn, cryptography, which transformed my understanding of how signals intelligence shaped operations and command as well. Though the British army attempted to destroy its records on SIGINT from the First World War, six months of working through all the files on signals, operations, and intelligence from the corps level up yielded enough fragments to reconstruct how the system worked and affected the war. Moreover, when I examined Admiralty files on the Great War, I found that without any public notice, GCHQ had released much of the Room 40 material—and hundreds of records on army SIGINT from 1914 to 1918. Six months of research through military, diplomatic, naval, and private papers between 1793 and 1914 and a year in the India Office Records and Library enabled me to understand the nature and role of intelligence in other times and places. I learned things in which I had no background, like wireless communication and cryptography; until I understood them, ignorance damaged my ability to understand documents that I read. When I mastered them, however, they enabled me to make my bones among SIGINTers. I finished my dissertation in 1986 and spent the next year completing my study of primary documents, which allowed me to publish works in signals intelligence. For the next twenty years, I thought of myself as a strategic historian with a specialization in intelligence. Over the past decade, as the field has evolved, I have come to see myself as being a historian of signals intelligence who uses knowledge of strategic issues as context for communications intelligence (COMINT).

In the process I met other scholars working in intelligence. I was self-taught in that area, unlike military, diplomatic, or naval matters, in which I was well schooled by military historians. I was what I would call a first-generation historian of intelligence, though; when I began work, a few other historians, like Wesley Wark, were supervised by an intelligence specialist, Chris Andrew. Being a first-generation scholar had disadvantages, particularly the need to learn from experience things that I might have been taught, but it also meant that I learned matters my own way. When Michael Handel first met me, he said (kindly) that I had reinvented the wheel, though he did not understand how much I (like he) had imbibed from Roberta Wohlstetter. I was fortunate in friends, like David French and Keith Neilson, who had worked on intelligence and provided advice, encouragement, and source references.[7] I was blessed with the opportunity to work for a few years in the archives alongside Brad Smith, the best of all the intelligence historians of the 1980s and 1990s and the only one besides myself to focus on signals intelligence at the time.[8] After I had begun to publish, David Kahn, the doyen of students of signals intelligence, immediately offered encouragement and advice, as he characteristically did to young people working in the area. The same was true with Michael Handel, great as theorist of intelligence and friend, who taught me strategy through osmosis and whom I miss every day.

By the time I began to publish, intelligence was becoming a recognized topic for study, marked by the founding of a specialized academic journal in 1986, *Intelligence and National Security*, and the rise of regular conferences and seminars. I would not call intelligence a field at this time, but there was a sense that one might be created, that scholars could work meaningfully in the area, learn from practitioners in other disciplines, and create a critical mass of scholarship. What first emerged was largely an encounter between British-trained historians, many of them Canadian, and American-trained political scientists, many of them Israelis. In the 1970s several political scientists—Michael Handel, Bob Jervis, and Dick Betts, to name but a few—produced pioneering theoretical works on issues fundamental to intelligence, like perception, deception, and intelligence failure.[9] Their works were based on analysis of a small number of well-documented case studies, like the Yom Kippur War, Pearl Harbor, and the scandals surrounding the Central Intelligence Agency during the 1970s, in which liberal Western governments were forced to disgorge their secrets to the public. Many of these writers also had experience as advisers to intelligence agencies or congressional committees. In the 1980s they were the dominant group of academics working on intelligence. These men had created the largest corpus of connected work on the topic, while we historians handled difficult evidence, hidden by secrecy, on matters that were hard to connect. However, with the exception of Loch Johnson, these political scientists also increasingly disengaged from the field because they saw no more major issues of theory to tackle in intelligence and became interested elsewhere.[10] Ironically, they withdrew precisely as the historical base started to become solid, providing an excellent opportunity (which no one really pursued) to test and refine their theories.

Whereas I, a historian, luxuriated in the opportunity to find a new dimension to historical events—every bloody one of them after another—Michael Handel thought they simply proved theories he already knew and sometimes regarded historical knowledge as mere anecdote. He also, however, believed that every historian at least knew something, which was more than he thought true of political scientists, and regarded teaching intelligence at the Naval War College as a calling. Meanwhile, a few historians tackled intelligence and published some important monographs and articles, but the gaps in knowledge were great, and even basic facts were hard to establish. For me simply to demonstrate the number of solutions of foreign diplomatic traffic that the GC and CS published between 1919 and 1941 took great effort. As Brad Smith said at this time, to take one step from established fact was to risk sinking in quicksand, yet facts were hard to find or connect. The knowledge that the intelligence agencies retained much key evidence from 1917 onward made scholars cautious about moving beyond what one could prove. The absence of evidence, and the cult of secrecy that marked the agencies, also provided room for conspiracy theorists and theories to flourish, made works of speculation hard to refute, and led many commentators to overestimate the importance of intelligence on decision-making.

From the mid-1980s the number of students and scholars working in intelligence history steadily grew, while students of public administration, policy, and management became prominent in the study.[11] So increasingly did retired intelligence officers, whether by writing or merely talking to students of intelligence. Though initially this process involved veterans of the Second World War, like Patrick Beesly, by the late 1980s it included practitioners from the iciest days of the Cold War, such as Michael Herman, and it continues today with Michael Warner, among others.[12] Initially, historians could participate in this process only if they were accepted in old boys' networks, but with the establishment of permanent seminars and regular conferences in the field, these contacts became constant. Then, more cautiously, serving intelligence personnel began to interact with scholars. By the late 1990s young researchers could attend venues and expect to meet established scholars, old hands, and serving intelligence officers. In the process many discoveries were made, including the similarities in personality between intelligence analysts and academics and the fact that the agencies did not know their own history, which in some cases historians knew better, and expected—wanted—us to answer their "So what?" questions. Simply by knowing intelligence officers as people, we better understood their agencies.

Meanwhile, the agencies shaped the field, in a different way than they had before, which essentially had been to block our ability to understand them. During the early and middle parts of the Cold War, many scholars (mostly old hands) aided the agencies, as, during its last decade, did some political scientists who had developed theories of intelligence. The agencies enabled demi-official histories by giving old hands privileged access to records but generally maintained as much secrecy as they could. The end of the Cold War changed the political environment of their work. The agencies began to question their cult of secrecy, though their personnel were divided as to how open they could or should become. Under pressure from their political masters, they began massive releases of documents into the public domain. By 2001 the American and British archives held virtually all the intelligence records from between

1917 and 1945, outside internal security and personnel records. For the first time, there was a broad and reliable database on intelligence in that period; basic facts became easier to establish and connect, and quicksand to avoid. A continuous historical narrative emerged, though much of it has not yet been written up, and probably is known only to the historians working with the documents.

In the past few years, the agencies have decided to be as open as possible without really compromising operational security—as some officers say, to be translucent, though transparency is impossible. A surprising amount of material from the Cold War already has reached the archives in the United Kingdom and the United States, and soon far more records on the matter will be released. The single biggest change for historians of intelligence was the sudden availability of documents. In 1990 we worked despite a lack of records—that was the charm of the field. To study twentieth-century intelligence was like examining classical or medieval history; deserts of lacunae separated some tolerably documented areas. From 2001 modern intelligence increasingly was no harder to study than the military or diplomatic issues that it shaped, so long as you knew what intelligence was.

This interaction between academics and agencies also produced a new market for students of intelligence, particularly a focus on managerial approaches to analysis. The existence of academic intelligence centers, intended to teach programs in the study of intelligence, partly to prepare students for a professional career, bear witness to the influence of that relationship. Moreover, historians within the intelligence agencies have developed personal and professional relationships with academics, through which much was learned by both sides. Under the enlightened leadership of Col. Bill Williams, the Cryptologic History branch of the National Security Agency regularly assisted historians, including Larry Valero and myself, to write works on SIGINT history as scholars in residence and established a biennial conference (the Center for Cryptologic History Symposium) that has shaped public knowledge of the field. Several agencies commissioned official or authorized histories in which respected academics were free to examine documents on specific topics and to write about them.[13] That development has shaped my career as one of the few academic students of the history of signals intelligence. For a decade some of my closest professional relationships have been with historians within the intelligence community, especially those working on the coalface of COMINT. As an authorized historian, I have learned what it is like to participate in discussions in which I must not hint at classified knowledge I happen to possess. A framed copy of the Official Secrets Act sits over my work desk. In this process both academics and the agencies must beware a devil's bargain, but so far the practice has aided both sides—though, one might cavil, "'e would say that, wouldn't 'e?"

## The Continuous Narrative of Intelligence History

What has study of its history contributed to our knowledge of intelligence, and what more have historians to offer? The influence of intelligence history on intelligence knowledge is tied to theorists. Theorists tried to illuminate an unknown and hidden topic by refining usable generalizations from well-documented case studies; historians do so by mining the evidence and broadening the base of what is known. In the process they have created the largest connected body of works in the literature on intelligence.

This statement must be put in perspective. The archives always held more evidence about intelligence than generally was realized, the problem being that finding it took much time and effort. The new releases make intelligence much easier to discover, but at a price. Once, when found, such records were embedded in their decision-making context, easing judgment as to what they affected and how. Now, intelligence is more accessible but stands alone; the problem is to find its context. Much good work about intelligence history emerged between 1914 and 1980. The modern school of intelligence history essentially emerged after 1960 and centers on the twentieth century, but in 1959 the strongest area of scholarship on the topic, high in quality, addressed Renaissance and early modern Europe.[14] Our present knowledge of intelligence history, though greater than ever before, has chronological and thematic limitations. A continuous narrative, with long and thick connections, has emerged about the role of intelligence in war and power politics from 1914 to 1945 and increasingly between 1945 and the 1980s. This narrative is strongest regarding Anglophone states and great powers and weakest about small states, especially non-Western peoples. If forgotten, this focus can produce an unconscious and unfortunate bias. Thus, the intelligence services of liberal Anglophone states are bad models for understanding the *mukhabarat* (intelligence services) of Arab countries.[15] In different ways, however, the services of fascist and communist states offer better comparisons, and all those instances, added together, produce a model of a security-intelligence service different from Anglophone institutions and assumptions.[16] So too, intelligence before 1914 worked differently than it did afterward, as illustrated by the works in a thinner narrative, which links intelligence between 1400 and 1914; study of the past of intelligence helps one to see how it may change again.

Nonetheless, the rise of a continuous narrative has produced great gains. Good literatures exist on the intelligence services of most great powers between 1914 and 1945 and a surprising amount is available on those of European neutrals.[17] The missing dimension of many issues has been uncovered. In some cases the evidence about intelligence has been integrated with that of the events it shaped, or that from every country in a competition has been synthesized. Some works have compared the quality or effect of intelligence services at any time or the way the struggle of intelligence affected competitions of power politics or war.[18] Myths about intelligence, and founding myths about intelligence services, have been eliminated. The share of speculation, and also of conspiracy theory, in the writing about intelligence has declined, though they never will vanish, and conspiracies sometimes happen. This is my gloss of the continuous narrative, which focuses on instrumental intelligence in power politics and war. Other versions could address political warfare or internal security or surveillance.

Intelligence has offered advantages to states for millennia, though not consistently—here essential to events, there irrelevant. Most states have received some intelligence sometimes, but not always from permanent and specialized agencies for collection, nor through assessment by bureaucracies. They conducted intelligence through systems and traditions—means by which people gather and assess data for specific purposes, as against loose combinations of ideas and practices about how to do so if one must. In response to changes in supply and demand, intelligence might switch from systems to traditions and back again. Advances could be abandoned by any practitioner and overlooked by its neighbors. Until 1860 staffs were a secretariat. Kings and commanders handled even minor functions of command. They organized the collection of their own intelligence, working through ad hoc means and a few aides. Intelligence was personalized, the service of so and so, rather than a state. This approach had advantages. Decision-makers could direct their intelligence and receive exactly the information they wanted; on many matters the best personalized systems matched any bureaucratized ones of modern times, their effect redoubled because their enemies tended to be poor in the field. When intelligence was least common, it offered a greater return to its practitioners by making one-sided relationships more common. Most premodern systems, however, were worse than mediocre modern ones since intelligence was not thoroughly handled, while major gaps existed in key areas.

The modern age of intelligence began in 1914 through the sudden synthesis of developments in sources, organization, and communication. Intelligence aided military forces, especially in operations, to unprecedented degrees during the First World War. Collection and assessment agencies exploded in size. Bureaucracy and technology enabled a transformation simultaneously in intelligence, power, and war. The parts of intelligence changed, but more the whole and its interaction with knowledge and strategy. A tight cycle of command, control, communications, and intelligence (C3I) emerged for operations, as it had done for strategy by the 1860s, enabling the deployment of Union forces against Confederates, Prussians against Austrians and French, and British power across the globe. Knowledgeable states turned practices of information processing to intelligence. Secrecy and secret sources became more important to decisions than ever before, and so remained until the end of the Cold War. Once, only unusual ability by an actor created quality in intelligence, which almost automatically yielded superiority over enemies. Now, quality became systematic, open to all, making superiority harder to create. Superiority could emerge only through constant efforts in an open-ended competition. The average level of military intelligence matched the best known before. The best were better.

Intelligence proved more powerful for strategy than ever before, drawing from subjects and citizens, neutrals and enemies. Intelligence for operations on land—doubly so at sea—and communications in war were revolutionized. Imagery and signals intelligence, joined to the general staff system, telegraph, and radio, produced more powerful means to collect, assess, and use data. By 1918 intelligence services used virtually every technique deployed between 1939 and 1945, including operational deception, controlled agents, and data-processing systems able to synthesize material from thousands of sources in real time and to guide immediate actions by forces or fire, as Britain did with blockade intelligence and defense against German strategic bombers. World War II rested on a long and evenly matched struggle between great armies. Intelligence affected it everywhere, varying with operational circumstances. In Russia, Palestine, and Iraq, intelligence shaped victories on an epic scale.[19] Force-to-space ratios were low, breakthrough and exploitation possible, and the weight of intelligence lay heavily with one side, Austria and Germany on the eastern front and Britain in the Middle East.[20] The western front between 1915 and 1917, conversely, was characterized by dense force-to-space ratios, elaborate defensive systems, and firepower that could kill but not move. Breakthrough was difficult to achieve—exploitation impossible. The armies of Britain, France, and Germany also possessed able intelligence. Each side penetrated the other's intentions and capabilities, making surprise rare. The aggregate quality of intelligence in the First World War matched that of the Second, but in strategic terms each side's successes cancelled each other out, while at the operational plane, intelligence was harder to use for dramatic results. Forces were too slow and clumsy to maximize the opportunities that intelligence enabled. Nonetheless, in a war in which power was measured by the ability to produce hundreds of thousands of soldiers and millions of tons of steel, intelligence mattered. It multiplied force more than in any previous conflict, as much as in any later one.

After the war, intelligence services shrank in size but still remained far larger than before it. They became permanent bureaucracies. Human intelligence agencies collected more material on military and diplomatic topics than they had before 1914. Since the techniques of cryptographic and physical security remained primitive, any systematic attack found easy meat. Never before in peacetime had acquisition been so powerful. Diplomatic intelligence was high in quality, widely distributed, and competitive. The great powers possessed decent to excellent intelligence services, which often aided policy. Yet in the 1930s intelligence mattered less than incomprehension, stemming from ideological differences. Statesmen of every country misunderstood each other's aims and character. Everywhere, assessment was confused and politicized. Neville Chamberlain, Adolf Hitler, Benito Mussolini, and Joseph Stalin did not wish to hear contrary analyses from subordinates, merely echoes of their opinions. Intelligence should provide only facts, which they filtered through ideology and the belief that their will created reality. The politicization of intelligence had an ironic systematic effect. Hitler, Stalin, and Mussolini mistook military power more than other statesmen. They got their own forces wrong because their subordinates deceived them, as well as foreigners. Between 1933 and 1941, far more than in 1905–14, decision-makers misunderstood the fundamentals of power and policy. German (and to a lesser degree, Italian) strength was exaggerated and that of everyone else underrated, especially Japanese, Soviet, and American. The greatest victim of the overstatement of German power was the Axis. Mussolini and Japanese decision-makers made the decisions that ruined their countries because they believed Germany too powerful to lose. So too, Hitler.

Despite the quality of collection, the policy of every great power failed. Their code breakers did not stop Britain and Germany from stumbling into a war neither planned in 1939. The Russian interior ministry, the Narodnyy Komissariat Vnutrennikh Del (NKVD), did not shield Russia from disaster in 1941, nor was the United States saved by Magic. Reason, raison d'état, and intelligence were bad guides for these statesmen because they viewed events and played the game so differently, in a reciprocal, multilateral, and atomized system, with so many actors affecting each other through such unpredictable ways, in which ideas, knowledge, policy, and cause and effect were linked in an ironic fashion. Intentions were not affected, nor effects intended, amid low systemic certainty. Statesmen thought the state system was a machine in which all one needed to create an effect was to pull a lever. In fact, the machine was baroque and broken. There were more levers to be pulled than in 1914, but with less certain outcome and more people pulling to opposite effect. People thought they knew how to get what they wanted but failed to do so because they did not understand the system and the way it worked. These statesmen thought they all were playing a game with one set of rules, but each played a different game with the same pieces. They all lost.

In 1939 another total war broke out among the industrialized states. Again, economic and demographic power shaped victory as much as skill in operations. Until 1942 the two coalitions were comparable in economic terms, but the Axis powers were superior at operations, except against British air and naval forces in Europe. From that point the Allies became stronger and better. In this match, intelligence routinely served as force multiplier and sometimes as tiebreaker. It shaped the Second World War more than the First because intelligence supported firepower that could kill and move, enabling more decisive actions, while the effect was one-sided for a long run. The story of intelligence in the Second World War is told uncritically, from the perspective of Allied sword against Axis shield, at the peak of the success of Ultra.[21] Actually, the intelligence war was a real competition, involving Axis successes and Allied failures. At sea Axis intelligence matched Ultra until the German and Italian navies sank and achieved a success comparable to Ultra (in effect, though not technique) against the Red Army in 1941–43. Axis intelligence services ranged from incompetent to good, mostly mediocre. Allied ones were poor to great, mostly good. Initially, however, the states superior in intelligence and material misused these advantages. American, British, and Soviet forces often were too poor to exploit the advantages provided by intelligence, while failures of assessment exposed them to devastation from surprise attack. Before 1942 intelligence worked marginally in the Axis favor by multiplying the value of their large and good forces. From 1942 the balance of intelligence and power turned simultaneously and systematically toward the Allies. Intelligence did little to cause Axis defeat but much to shape how the Allies achieved victory. It was the greatest force multiplier that the Western allies had. Ultra gave the Western allies a powerful grip on enemy forces, allowing an effective use of resources, and supported a campaign of deception that enabled regular success in the most difficult form of the military art: amphibious assault. In the Pacific, superiority in intelligence was fundamental to American successes against a large and powerful foe.

Nor did superiority with intelligence end at collection. For every belligerent, strategic assessments and decisions were made by rational bureaucracy joined to charismatic leadership. British and American leaders made errors in such areas, especially regarding Japanese intentions in 1941. At worst they were as bad as anyone but better on average and unmatched at their best. Their decision-making system in Europe combined the best of British and American approaches, with Britain handling the collection and analysis of intelligence and its use in planning, and both states driving strategy and action. Anglo-American leaders treated intelligence as essential to action. They emphasized the source best suited to provide these gains—signals intelligence—and accepted the need for specialized assessment and a rational process of decision-making. Good consumers even of mediocre material, their fare often was excellent. The Western Allies multiplied each other's strengths. German and Axis agencies divided them. They competed not against the enemy but against each other. They could not transfer best lessons, nor pool their power, nor acquire the resources their rivals did, nor understand the need to do so. Cooperation between the Western Allies in intelligence was not perfect, merely better than anything ever known before. It was honed by cooperative competition in the pursuit of common tasks. British services worked better with American ones than German agencies (or for that matter, the US Army and Navy) did with each other. The payoff was most particular in signals intelligence. The Germans failed to attack high-grade American or British cryptographic machines because the task was hard, resources were scarce, and only massive and centralized cryptanalysis could break them. This the divided German system could not provide. One German cryptanalyst called a unified system "a monster organization."[22] Britons named it Bletchley Park.

Between 1914 and 1945, several trends emerged in intelligence. A process once dominated by personality became systematized. Bureaucracies, with their characteristic strengths and weaknesses, became the chief producers and consumers of intelligence. Intelligence became a profession rather than a subdivision of police or military services—bureaucratized, industrialized, and militarized. Though agencies were larger in war than in peace, during both periods their size and sophistication grew exponentially. They systematically built on advances, which were common, combining the leading edges of technology, especially in communications, information processing, and aerial platforms. Far more material was collected than ever before, straining analytical capabilities. Economies of scale aided acquisition, in which technical sources could deploy mass-production techniques and switch them between targets, more than analysis, which is labor-intensive craftwork. Instrumental intelligence affected power politics in peace as much as ever before; both the average and upper levels raised in quality, but in part for that very reason, by ratcheting up the level of competitors and competitions, it was hard to use effectively. Compared to previous conflicts, especially at the operational level but also the strategic one, the heightened power of intelligence reduced the density of the fog of war for all belligerents, often to the benefit of one side. This development reduced some—not all—of the impact of uncertainty, friction, and chance; so did other improvements in technology and organization, like communications and rational bureaucracies. Each of these factors reinforced the rest reciprocally.

During the Cold War an integrated and multilateral system of power politics spurred the development of the largest, most sophisticated, and most technologically advanced intelligence services ever seen. Many of them were linked in two great international alliances of states and intelligence services. Supply and demand grew in unprecedented ways. Intelligence on the broadest forms of technology, the narrowest characteristics of weapons and the most secret of programs, expanded exponentially in value. Signals intelligence became industrialized, mechanized, and mathematized, as cryptology and computers drove each other to revolutions. Every year brute force became stronger and chisels sharper. Imagery expanded in an even more stratospheric fashion. Intelligence focused on supporting millions of soldiers and thousands of nuclear warheads in a worldwide competition of power politics against a peer, which never went hot but might have done so at any time. In the Cold War's early years, each side occasionally gained through intelligence—most notably the Soviets by acquiring technological data on nuclear weapons—but neither could be sure of the other's capabilities. This problem was exacerbated by Soviet deception; the Soviets intended to counter American nuclear superiority by indicating that they had more strategic bombers and missiles than was true. US authorities accepted this disinformation, which fit their ideas of what the Soviets would do if they could, but with counterproductive effects—it triggered greater expansion programs that reinforced American superiority. These problems of ignorance were mitigated, however, because neither side wanted an all-out war; the consequences were too obvious.

In any case, between 1955 and 1961, the United States, later followed by the Soviets, developed technical means to determine the current nuclear strength of its rival, although expansion programs and qualitative developments always remained uncertain. The U-2s eliminated American fears of a bomber gap, as the Keyhole satellites did of a missile gap.[23] The years 1939–45 had witnessed a communications intelligence war; traffic analysis and imagery dominated the Cold War. Each day intelligence agencies, East and West, monitored each other's capabilities and intentions, their main task being to say, "World War III will not start today." This news was good to know. Intelligence agencies eliminated ignorance, uncertainty, and alarm about nuclear forces and stabilized the balance of terror. US national intelligence estimates (NIEs) often are taken to represent everything that mattered about Cold War intelligence; in fact, most of them were tertiary in value. The central intelligence products of the Cold War were those linked to strategic monitoring and target acquisition, including NIEs on Soviet strategic units and the target folders for nuclear forces, an all-source product with direct application.[24]

These strengths came at a cost. More is not always better. Intelligence and strategic bureaucracies could not handle the host of material they received—photographic analysts routinely were six to eighteen months behind in their examination of imagery. Intelligence services faced a new problem, which continued after the Cold War. Once most pieces of intelligence were false; now they were true but trivial in quality and overwhelming in quantity, producing bewilderment and information overload. Heightened security crippled distribution of material—far more intelligence was collected than ever before, with a higher proportion of it never circulated to those who needed it. Security restrictions limited the value of Western signals intelligence almost as much as the enemy's defenses did. While excellent for strategic purposes, security was less useful for operations than it had been during 1918 or 1943.

For strategic intelligence during the Cold War, the triumph lay in military spheres. Despite all the effort on espionage and analysis, otherwise it failed, but without fatal consequences. The USSR is the classic case of wasted intelligence: no state ever was better in collection; few gained less from the practice.[25] The greatest effect was defensive, to limit hostile collection, rather than to give its own leaders actionable evidence. Both sides misunderstood fundamental points of power and policy in an unbalanced system. These problems, however, were overcome because nuclear weapons and their effect were hard to mistake, and intelligence on them was good enough. These facts linked the net estimates of both sides in the Cold War. This situation forced everyone to minimize risky strategies and to play much of the game the same way. Nuclear weapons crippled the value of conventional power and left the struggle to center on economic growth and political stability—the trump suits of the West. Intelligence was secondary in the emergence and the end of this struggle. The USSR lost the Cold War because it did not know itself. The West knew itself, and something of the enemy, but won without quite knowing it had done so, or how.[26]

Clearly, at some point, adding yet another mite to a continuous narrative becomes one damn thing after another. To stave off this fate, historians of intelligence must find topics relevant to their audiences. One obvious area is to test the classic works of theory against new evidence, which has the added benefit of combining the two greatest areas of continuous work in the field and using each to hone the other. Works on the history of intelligence constantly confirm the predictions of theorists about the politics of intelligence, though they force modifications in detail to arguments derived predominantly from recent American experiences. These works make the literature on perceptual bias, surprise, the use of intelligence, and the determination of intelligence success and failure even more problematic than they were. Against this, the theoretical writings on deception rested on a limited base of evidence, combined with brilliant analyses of one case of deception: Fortitude. Handel and the British analyst he analyzed, Roger Hesketh, overgeneralized their case.[27] In wars of the past century, deception was a standard operating procedure, applied by everyone against all. It centered on security, aiming to cause confusion and uncertainty (rather than to control an enemy's sources) and leading the enemy to act in a specific way. Deception, that is, is an adjunct to security, which sometimes can become far more.

## The Impact of the Continuous Narrative

The continuous narrative on intelligence and international history has affected many audiences in different ways. Perhaps more than students of intelligence realize, nonspecialists find the matter intriguing and mysterious. Merely to discuss anecdote or icon attracts attention, as does telling a true, or new, story in an interesting fashion. The greatest influence of the continuous narrative has been among the academic historians who address power, power politics, and war. Twenty years ago diplomatic, military, strategic, and international historians knew that intelligence was important to their concerns, were not sure that it really could be studied, and were dismayed by the large proportion of sensationalist accounts in the small literature. Today, conventional military or diplomatic historians read specialist accounts of intelligence agencies or techniques, often do some primary research in intelligence for their own projects, and sometimes write specialist works on the topic. Some intelligence scholars seek to integrate intelligence with the matters it affects, though not enough of us; that is our chief failure as a group. Equally, there are limits to this effect. I remain staggered by the failure of students of British diplomacy between 1915 and 1945 to examine the diplomatic SIGINT record, which then shaped decisions and now is easily available. If Winston Churchill, George Curzon, and Neville Chamberlain had read such material, perhaps students of their policies might do so. Nonetheless, members of these fields accept the power and value of intelligence history and the works of intelligence historians, which, over the next generation, will affect their representation of power politics and war over the past century, including the Cold War.

The story is different with academic historians who address the relationship between security services and internal politics. Many of these historians identify with radical or popular groups that have been monitored by the state and view that surveillance with abhorrence. People of such persuasions also have written many of the studies on the relationship between security services and internal politics, and those on surveillance, from many disciplines. Their position has much power. It fits a mainstream opinion in Anglo-American views of political liberty. As a historian and citizen, I have different views about the use of intelligence against external rivals and fellow citizens. The latter topic is messier, and judgments very often must be complex. Thus, from 1930 to 1960, members of the Communist Party USA were simultaneously agents of Moscow and among the few white Americans who fought the terrorist lynching of black men. The Federal Bureau of Investigation's actions on political policing often were awful. Much of the evidence on political policing remains closed, which raises further suspicion, some of which, I think, would be justified were it all released. Yet historians of intelligence accept documented proof of unpleasant or illegal behavior by security services. My authorized history of GCHQ will address how far the state monitored its many peoples. The reluctance of Americans of leftist views, including historians, to accept that Venona proved many American communists were agents of Moscow demonstrates that problems with historical truth occur in many places.[28] Political policing and surveillance should be important topics in any country's political and social history, which cannot be handled well unless all sides of the story are studied and specialists cooperate. In this area the continuous narrative of intelligence history has had limited effect, which is unlikely to improve through anything short of generational change.

How far this historical work has affected students of intelligence from other disciplines is another question. Over the past decade, the academic study of intelligence has been dominated by three groups: historians, students focused on training and management, and practitioners of public policy. We all use the theories generated long ago by political scientists. For intelligence historians this has been an exciting period; our understanding has been transformed. Have any of you cared? And if so, how? This point has broad consequences. I have a multidisciplinary approach and see myself almost as much a student of strategy as of history. Yet I always have doubted the idea of a field called "intelligence studies"; those of us from different disciplines attacking similar issues have much in common now but may not necessarily in the future. Military historians and strategists have been associated for centuries; we share canonical texts, tackle parallel issues, often read each other's work—yet do not belong to one and the same field. So I ask members of other disciplines looking at intelligence: How would you rate the importance of this revolution in the history of intelligence to your knowledge of the topic? Your answers to these questions will say something about whether there is a field of intelligence studies, or, say, a situation in which strategists, economists, historians, and sociologists look at similar phenomena, like armed forces or intelligence services, but remain part of different disciplines.

The effect of the continuous narrative on serving intelligence officers is strong, and growing, though still less than that of the theorists. Intelligence officers are professionally, and often personally, interested in history. They realize that academic historians know things about their past that their agencies do not. I believe that intelligence history soon will have the influence on intelligence officers that military history does on military officers. One of the ties that may bind a field of intelligence studies together is the pedagogical needs of the intelligence community, which must combine different disciplinary approaches to the topic, just as a military academy and staff college does with their professional concerns.

The impact of academic work on any public is hard, or perhaps impossible, to disentangle from any kind of knowledge at all, and also varies by country. Any person who can get a platform shapes public attitudes; here intelligence scholars compete with Hollywood and social media. Public attention is driven by anecdote, sensation, and scandal. The greatest conduits for public influence by academic intelligence history are forms of education. To some degree, and a growing one, the continuous narrative of intelligence history affects courses in diplomatic, strategic, military, intelligence, and international history. I see few examples of its influence on the most common textbooks for intelligence studies, which spend little time on history before the Cold War. Again, institutions like the National Cryptologic Museum, the International Spy Museum, or the Bletchley Park Trust often are run by people with a good grasp of the academic literature on intelligence, who make valuable research contributions of their own and, to varying degrees, cooperate with the intelligence agencies. Naturally, they filter academic research through a museum focus on artifacts, displays, labels, and personalities, but still they bring it to public attention. Generally, however, public opinion in all Western countries remains naive about all aspects of intelligence. Ignorance and conspiracy theory remain powerful in public views, as do simplistic accounts of success. Scholars of all persuasions have a long way to go in changing that fact.

## Notes

1. Frederick Winterbotham, *The Ultra Secret* (New York: HarperCollins, 1974). See also Harold C. Deutsch, "The Historical Impact of Revealing the Ultra Secret," *Parameters* 7, no. 3 (1977): 16–32.
2. David Kahn, *The Codebreakers: The Story of Secret Writing* (New York: Macmillan, 1967); Roberta Wohlstetter, *Pearl Harbor: Warning and Decision* (Boston: Little, Brown, 1971); Graham Allison, *Essence of Decision: Explaining the Cuban Missile Crisis, 1962* (Stanford, CA: Stanford University Press, 1971).
3. John Ferris, "The Evolution of British Strategic Policy, 1916–1926" (PhD diss., University of London, 1986).
4. Adam B. Ulam, *Expansion and Coexistence: Soviet Foreign Policy, 1917–1973* (New York: Praeger, 1974); Christopher Andrew, "The British Secret Service and Anglo-Soviet Relations in the 1920s. Part I: From the Trade Negotiations to the Zinoviev Letter," *Historical Journal* 20, no. 3 (1977): 673–706.
5. See, for example, Patrick Beesly, *Room 40: British Naval Intelligence, 1914–1918* (London: Hamish Hamilton, 1982).
6. The Public Record Office was the guardian of the national archives of the United Kingdom from 1838 to 2003, when it became the National Archives.
7. See, for example, David French, "Spy Fever in Britain, 1900–1915," *Historical Journal* 21, no. 2 (1978): 355–70; and Keith Neilson, "'Joy Rides': British Intelligence and Propaganda in Russia, 1914–1917," *Historical Journal* 24, no. 4 (1981): 885–906.
8. Brad Smith, *The Shadow Warriors: O.S.S. and the Origins of the C.I.A.* (New York: Basic Books, 1983).
9. Robert Jervis, *Perception and Misperception in International Politics* (Princeton: Princeton University Press, 1976); Michael I. Handel, "The Yom Kippur War and the Inevitability of Surprise," *International Studies Quarterly* 21, no. 3 (1977): 461–502; Richard Betts, "Analysis, War and Decision: Why Intelligence Failures Are Inevitable," *World Politics* 31, no. 1 (1978): 35–54.
10. Loch K. Johnson, *A Season of Inquiry: The Senate Intelligence Investigation* (Lexington: University Press of Kentucky, 1985).
11. See, for example, Glenn P. Hastedt, "The Constitutional Control of Intelligence," *Intelligence and National Security* 1, no. 2 (1986): 255–71; Philip H. J. Davies, "Organizational Politics and the Development of Britain's Intelligence Producer/Consumer Interface," *Intelligence and National Security* 10, no. 4 (1995): 113–32.
12. See Michael Herman, *Intelligence in Peace and War* (Cambridge: Cambridge University Press, 1996).
13. On British intelligence, see Christopher Andrew, *The Defence of the Realm: The Authorized History of MI5* (London: Allen Lane, 2009); Keith Jeffery, *MI6: The History of the Secret Intelligence Service, 1909–1949* (London: Bloomsbury, 2010); Michael Goodman, *The Official History of the Joint Intelligence Committee*, vol. 1, *From the Approach of the Second World War to the Suez Crisis* (Abingdon: Routledge, 2014).

14. See Mildred Gladys Richings, *Espionage: The Story of the Secret Service of the English Crown* (London: Hutchinson, 1935).
15. See, for example, Owen L. Sirrs, *A History of the Egyptian Intelligence Service: A History of the Mukhabarat, 1910–2009* (Abingdon: Routledge, 2010).
16. See Christopher Andrew and Oleg Gordievsky, *KGB: The Inside Story of Its Foreign Operations from Lenin to Gorbachev* (London: HarperCollins, 1990); Robert Gellately, *The Gestapo and German Society* (Oxford: Oxford University Press, 1991); and David Childs and Richard Popplewell, *The Stasi: The East German Intelligence and Security Service* (New York: New York University Press, 1996).
17. See, for example, C. G. McKay and Bengt Beckman, *Swedish Signal Intelligence, 1900–1945* (London: Frank Cass, 2003); Neville Wylie, "'The Importance of Being Honest': Switzerland, Neutrality and the Problems of Intelligence Collection and Liaison," *Intelligence and National Security* 21, no. 5 (2006): 782–808.
18. Herman, *Intelligence in Peace*.
19. Francis Harry Hinsley et al., eds., *British Intelligence in the Second World War*, vols. 1–4 (London: HMSO, 1979, 1981, 1984, 1988).
20. David Kahn, *Hitler's Spies: German Military Intelligence in World War II* (New York: Macmillan, 1978).
21. See, for example, Edward J. Drea, *MacArthur's ULTRA: Codebreaking and the War against Japan, 1942–1945* (Lawrence: University Press of Kansas, 1992).
22. John Ferris, *Intelligence and Strategy: Selected Essays* (London: Routledge, 2005), 165.
23. Jonathan Renshon, "Assessing Capabilities in International Politics: Biased Overestimation and the Case of the Imaginary 'Missile Gap,'" *Journal of Strategic Studies* 32, no. 1 (2009): 115–47.
24. Donald P. Steury, ed., *Intentions and Capabilities: Estimates on Soviet Strategic Forces, 1950–1983* (Washington, DC: Center for the Study of Intelligence, 1996).
25. For a recent history of Soviet intelligence, see Jonathan Haslam, *Near and Distant Neighbors: A New History of Soviet Intelligence* (Oxford: Oxford University Press, 2015).
26. Bruce D. Berkowitz, "U.S. Intelligence Estimates of the Soviet Collapse: Reality and Perception," *International Journal of Intelligence and CounterIntelligence* 21, no. 2 (2008): 237–50.
27. Michael I. Handel, *War, Strategy and Intelligence* (London: Frank Cass, 1989), 361–451.
28. Venona was a US counterintelligence effort to decrypt messages transmitted by Soviet intelligence, which led to the detection of spies in the West. On Venona, see John Early Haynes and Harvey Klehr, *Venona: Decoding Soviet Espionage in America* (New Haven, CT: Yale University Press, 1999).

# PART II

# Data Sources and the Study of National Security Intelligence

# 3.

# The Why, Who, and How of Using Qualitative Interviews to Research Intelligence Practices

*Damien Van Puyvelde*

Since the origins of the field of intelligence studies in the 1950s, scholars have researched empirical evidence on the conduct of national security and intelligence in various settings, focusing mostly on government practices.[1] The paucity of sources to study secret government practices has long shaped the study of national and international security. To learn about intelligence practices, researchers working outside the government developed explorative projects based on fragments of evidence discovered in publicly available government documents, memoirs, private papers, and interviews.[2]

Research in the field of intelligence studies has been significantly affected by the secrecy that characterizes national security.[3] Government intelligence archives are available only in select democratic countries, and even then many documents remain unavailable. Government intelligence activities themselves often rely on fragile sources and methods to acquire and understand information about perceived threats. Michael Warner, an intelligence historian working for the US government, notes that disclosing these sources and methods can provide an informational, analytical, or operational advantage to a rival.[4] Thus, governments prefer to keep a significant part of their intelligence practices secret and severely punish unauthorized disclosures of information. The case of former Central Intelligence Agency (CIA) officer John Kiriakou, who recently served prison time after pleading guilty to one count of passing classified information to the media, offers a stark reminder of the risks insiders take when they decide to disclose sensitive government information without authorization. Current and former national security professionals need to be extremely careful regarding what they can and cannot disclose to outsiders and might prefer not to discuss their work with researchers. The secrecy that characterizes national security restricts research and necessarily shapes the field of intelligence studies. Exploring this condition can help researchers understand the limits of their knowledge and identify strategies to mitigate these limits and communicate their findings effectively.

This chapter focuses on a specific data-collection method—qualitative research interviews—in the field of intelligence studies. The chapter addresses methodological questions relating to the engagement with interviewees as primary sources and related epistemological concerns with notions of bias and objectivity. A frequently cited estimate suggests that around "90 percent of all social science investigations use interview" data.[5] Interviewing has long been a prominent data-collection strategy in intelligence studies, though not as frequent as this estimate suggests. A systematic review of all the research articles published in *Intelligence and National Security*, the flagship journal in intelligence studies, from the inception of the journal in 1986 to 2016, shows that researchers conducted and referred to their interviews in 15 percent of all articles published during this period.[6] The trend plot in figure 3.1 shows that interviews have become an increasingly common data-gathering technique in intelligence studies over the last three decades. Despite the widespread use and importance of this method, very little has been written about the challenges of interviewing in national security research.[7]

This chapter discusses the rationales and limitations of qualitative interviews as a research method in intelligence studies and identifies best practices to inform researchers' decisions regarding who to interview and how to conduct interviews effectively. The sensitivity of the objects and subjects of intelligence studies requires careful preparation and follow-up. Intelligence researchers must solve several methodological and logistical puzzles, not only before but also during and after their data-collection effort. Most of these puzzles are not unique to the study of intelligence and national security, but the sensitivity of the issues being researched reinforces their

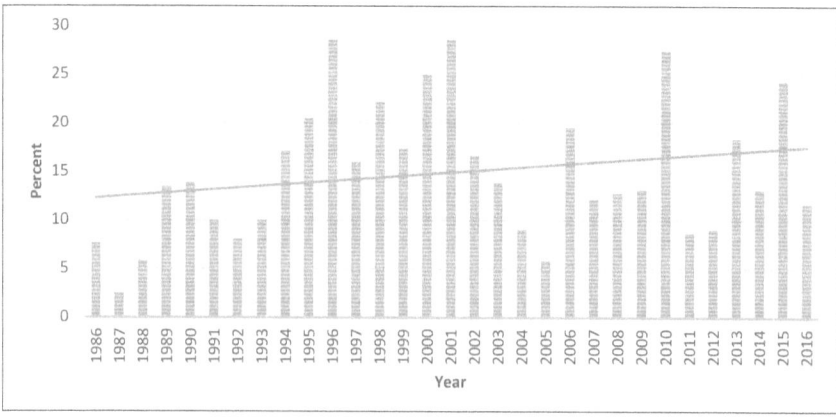

Figure 3.1. Percentage of *Intelligence and National Security* articles using qualitative research interviews to gather data, 1986–2016

importance. The secrecy of intelligence limits research opportunities and influences key methodological choices. Developing an awareness of this condition and its implications and developing strategies to mitigate its effects are essential to maximize the potential of qualitative research interviews in this difficult field of research.

## Why Qualitative Research Interviews Are Essential to the Study of Intelligence

Researchers across multiple disciplines seek to obtain primary sources because they can provide a firsthand account from actors who have a direct connection with a topic. What constitutes a primary source varies depending on the discipline and the research question that is asked. Students of government often rely on documents and interviews to collect primary data, to reveal and analyze processes and practices that have not received enough attention in the literature. Both types of data sources—documents and interviews—present substantial challenges of accessibility and reliability in the field of intelligence studies.

Despite Western governments' efforts toward greater transparency regarding their intelligence practices, severe data constraints continue to limit national security research.[8] Nevertheless, information about government intelligence programs and activities often becomes public when agencies meet certain hurdles. For instance, the US intelligence community's failure to prevent the terrorist attacks of September 11, 2001, led to the publication of a government report disclosing information on national intelligence practices.[9] The unauthorized disclosure of classified information orchestrated by former National Security Agency contractor Edward Snowden is another case in point, this time of forced transparency. While investigations of intelligence failures and leaks of sensitive government information have provided much material to intelligence researchers and the public, they do not tell the whole story. Governments tailor their reports for public dissemination, and unauthorized disclosures, even when they are extensive, do not provide a complete account of the practices of intelligence agencies. Rigorous scholarship on intelligence exhausts all documentary sources—including government archives, memoirs, media reports, and secondary literature—to contextualize processes and practices. Interviews can add to the information gleaned through these sources and help reconstruct a comprehensive account of complex issues.

When limited information is publicly available through documentary research, interviews can help fill the gaps left by missing documentary sources. Information about intelligence services is notoriously sparse. Official documents available online and at national archives are limited in scope and availability because government officials sanitize public records to protect intelligence sources and methods. Researchers can use interviews in combination with memoirs and public records, for instance, to provide more exhaustive accounts of a phenomenon. Here qualitative research interviews complement a strategy of triangulation through which the researcher cross-references different data sources and data types.[10] However, the declassification of sensitive government documents, when it occurs at all, often takes place decades after those documents were written. For example, the United Kingdom follows a thirty-year rule, but the Security and Intelligence Services are exempt from this provision. The British National Archives note that in many cases, security-classified material is released to the public after a period of fifty years or more.[11] In the United States an executive agency must declassify its documents after twenty-five years, but there are nine exemptions to this rule, including intelligence sources and methods.[12] When sensitive information is declassified, many of the officials with firsthand knowledge of these documents might not be alive anymore or remember specific documents and the events surrounding them.[13]

For outside researchers seeking to understand national security, interviews are a useful tool to clarify the practices and inner workings of the national security state beyond the information available on paper.[14] Qualitative interviews can reveal human interactions, insiders' interpretations of key facts, and assorted beliefs and preferences. From a constructivist perspective, conducting interviews can assist researchers who want to reveal how insiders create and sustain government security practices.[15]

Interviews are not a perfect data-collection method. Conducting interviews is costly and time-consuming. Plus, interviews are only as reliable as their narrator, whose reminiscences and memories can be deceitful. Interviewees might not remember events or practices accurately, either because of memory lapses or because of personal attitudes and political preferences. For instance, David Murphy, a former CIA station chief in Berlin and chief of the agency's Soviet Russia Division, has criticized publications about the US ability to verify arms limitation agreements. According to Murphy, "the information contained in these books is derived from interviews from retired CIA and Federal Bureau of Investigation officials so that much of it is hearsay covering events which occurred decades ago. Thus, it reflects the inevitable distortion caused by memory lapses, often colored by personal attitudes. In many cases, the statements on individuals and events contained in these books are simply not true."[16] Insiders can be driven by self-serving motives and can seek to present themselves in a good light or selectively disclose negative information about a rival unit or organization. Allison Shelton notes that national security professionals who participated or have knowledge of political assassinations "might feel compelled to prevaricate on their true responsibility."[17] Intelligence historian Rhodri Jeffreys-Jones compares oral interviews with governmental figures to official memoirs. In both cases the subject "can be expected to put the best possible spin on his period of office, and to withhold information that might embarrass him, or discredit his motives."[18] Following the publication of former National Security Agency and CIA director Michael Hayden's memoir, the vice chair of the Senate Select Committee on Intelligence, Senator Dianne Feinstein (D-CA), released a summary pointing out dozens of "factual errors and other problems."[19] Feinstein's rebuttal reminds us that researchers should maintain a healthy dose of skepticism when analyzing the accounts of serving and former officials as well as their critics.

## Whom to Interview

The objectives and research questions driving a project are the best reference points to determine whom to interview. Intelligence scholar Philip Davies notes that elite interviewing is particularly relevant in the study of intelligence because intelligence is created for the consumption of senior decision-makers.[20] Senior officials have firsthand experience of important events and high-level policy processes and can be expected to be familiar with key pieces of information. These officials are often interviewed after they have left government, when they have more time to engage with researchers and more latitude to share select pieces of information and opinions with outsiders. Occasionally, scholars are able to interview serving senior officials. Political scientist Loch Johnson, for instance, interviewed then–director of national intelligence James Clapper.[21] Such interviews provide current and topical material, but serving officials might not be able to discuss issues as freely as retired officials. Serving officials' answers are often prepared in advance and reviewed by a public affairs office.

Elites should be construed not only as senior officials but more broadly as persons who are able to "exert influence" thanks to their intellectual and social capital.[22] Various midlevel and entry-level professionals also contribute to national security processes and policies and constitute valuable sources to understand government security practices beyond the institutionalized view from the top. From this perspective the prominence of interviews with senior officials limits our understanding of national security practices. Researchers have much to gain from interviewing a variety of practitioners and stakeholders to learn about their different perspectives. Depending on the specific subject of study, interviewing outsiders (for example, actors from civil society who research or publicly write about national security intelligence) can also provide relevant information. For example, interviews with congressional staffers, journalists, and members of public interest groups can shed light on the role of intelligence in democracies.[23]

Once categories of potential interviewees have been identified, further methodological questions arise to decide whom to interview. Scientific approaches to research often rely on sampling to select cases and subjects that are representative of a wider universe. In intelligence studies systematic sampling has thus far remained very rare, not to say inexistent. Few intelligence researchers have sought to generalize their inferences beyond the limited number of cases they looked at.[24] Outside researchers do not have enough access to information to identify all the employees of an agency or a specific unit at a certain point in time. Random sampling risks excluding important respondents, whom researchers cannot afford to overlook in a field marked by limited access to information.[25] One notable exception is Stephen Coulthart's survey of the use of structured analytic techniques at the Bureau of Intelligence and Research (INR) at the US State Department.[26] By and large intelligence scholars have relied on purposive sampling to select their sources, interviewing specific individuals they were particularly keen to hear from because of their participation in specific events and processes. In general the population of interviewees that is identified and willing to be interviewed is so small (a few dozen) that intelligence scholars are forced to rely on convenience sampling, interviewing whomever they manage to obtain an interview with. Government secrecy often prevents the use of refined methodological frameworks and limits the external validity of the findings made in the field of intelligence studies.

Identifying potential interviewees can prove particularly challenging for outside researchers. Unlike other public organizations, intelligence and security agencies protect their employees' identity, except for the most senior officials. Consequently, finding officials with firsthand knowledge of a specific issue or event can be particularly difficult. Yet various techniques exist to identify potential interviewees. The name of senior intelligence officials, especially those of agency directors and their assistants, are often publicly available. In many Western democracies, these officials appear in the media to explain their agencies' policies and to testify at parliamentary hearings to justify their actions. A simple internet search for the name of former directors and deputy directors of the CIA will reveal that some of them are now teaching at top-tier US universities and have publicly available university email addresses. Others have worked in the private sector since they retired from government, and their company email addresses are also publicly available. The home address of former senior officials can sometimes be found in phonebooks and specialized publications like *The International Who's Who*. Professional networking websites offer another venue to identify and contact serving and former intelligence officers at all levels. A LinkedIn search for "Central Intelligence Agency" reveals 778 results, though searches for other agencies, like the French Direction Générale de la Sécurité Extérieure or the British Secret Intelligence Service, return no result. Identifying potential interviewees is one thing; getting them to reply to requests for interviews is quite another, especially if they are contacted out of the blue.

To obtain interviews with national security professionals, scholars often must rely on networking. In the United States, various serving and retired officers attend academic and professional conferences that are open to the public, including the International Studies Association annual convention and conferences organized by the International Association for Intelligence Education and the Strategic and Competitive Intelligence Professionals Association. Associations of retirees, like the Association of Former Intelligence Officers, can also help identify and find potential interviewees. Seminar series, like those organized by the METIS research group on intelligence in democratic societies at SciencesPo Paris in France and the Cambridge Intelligence Seminar in the United Kingdom, provide similar opportunities to get a foot in the door. Using a strategy of snowballing—asking each interviewee to recommend and introduce the researcher to one or more other sources—can help identify additional interviewees and open doors. Snowballing is particularly well suited to the study of intelligence because the population of interest is often invisible to outside researchers.[27] However, this strategy increases the likelihood that all the interviewees will belong to the same social network and be like-minded. One way to reduce this type of sampling bias is to enlist individuals who are not introduced by other interviewees and ask them to provide contact information for other participants.[28]

Researchers can then adopt different strategies, based on the positions of the respondents, to decide on the order of their interviews. One strategy starts with individuals on the periphery of the agencies—retirees, journalists, and outside experts—then moves to low-level and midlevel employees, and finishes with senior officials involved in specific governmental processes. Starting from the periphery can help build a solid knowledge base to develop important questions for later interviews with senior officials. Alternatively, interviewing senior officials first can indicate to other serving and former employees that a research project is serious and worthy of engagement. Often, availability and convenience, more than a specific research strategy, affect the interview order.

## How to Prepare an Interview

Once the researcher has identified a pool of interviewees and decided on a strategy, a host of methodological and logistical issues still need to be addressed before field research can start. Simply chatting with insiders is unlikely to elicit valid information from them. Conducting exhaustive research on the interviewees' biography will help scholars understand their subjects' background and ensure that they have firsthand knowledge of the issues being studied. This initial research on the interviewee will subsequently help to eliminate irrelevant questions and to interpret the significance of what the interviewee says.

The researcher also needs to decide whether to conduct structured, semistructured, or unstructured interviews. Structured interviews rely on a standardized set of questions to frame interactions with interviewees. This type of interview can, for instance, take the form of a questionnaire survey, like the one used by Coulthart to investigate the use of analytic techniques at the INR. The context and process of structured interviews is repeated exactly with all the interviewees to ensure that results can be aggregated reliably. Questions need to be clear and specific enough for the sources to respond to them effectively. Structured interviews standardize the data-collection process and make it easier to compare answers from one interviewee to another. When interviews are structured enough, quantitative analysis can be applied to the collected data. This type of approach has become relatively common in political sciences and public administration but has never been used in intelligence studies.[29] The predetermined character of structured interviews limits the discovery of new and potentially relevant information that was initially overlooked by the researcher. This risk is particularly important in the field of intelligence studies, where information is often shrouded in secrecy. The relatively small pools of interviewees accessible in intelligence studies also limit the potential for quantitative research.

Unstructured and semistructured interviews are more common in intelligence studies. Their prominence can be explained by the exploratory approach adopted by most researchers in a field that is severely constrained by government secrecy.

Unstructured interviews take the form of open conversations with one or more respondents. The researcher prepares a list of issues to discuss ahead of time and gives the interviewee(s) plenty of latitude to drive the discussion. In semistructured interviews the researcher prepares a list of questions that he or she will ask the respondent. The interviewer might ask further questions and probe the respondent as the interview unfolds to gather more information on replies that seem particularly significant. Rob Johnston, who used semistructured interviews in his ethnographic study *Analytic Culture in the U.S. Intelligence Community*, notes that this format "helps put respondents at ease and makes the entire process seem somewhat less contrived."[30] This type of interview imposes some standardization but leaves the door open for the conversation to digress and possibly reveal new issues and angles. Unstructured and semistructured interviews require more attention from the interviewer to keep the conversation in line with the research objectives and more work to transcribe and make sense of the interview data.

Aberbach and Rockman identify three considerations in deciding on the type of interview: the degree of prior research, the need for validity, and the receptivity of respondents. First, when significant prior research exists on a subject, the researcher is more likely to have sufficient knowledge to design refined, closed-ended questions to be used in a more structured interview. Second, open-ended questions—most frequently used in semistructured interviews—give more leeway to the respondents, who can share their knowledge based on their own cognitive frameworks, and are ideal for exploratory projects. Third, some respondents might prefer to articulate their views rather than being limited by close-ended questions. The two political scientists conclude that concerns with reliability should drive the choice of method and not the pressures to produce "an analytically rigorous treatment of less reliable and informative data."[31]

Once the type of interview has been decided and questions have been identified, the time has come for the researcher to contact potential interviewees. Drafting an effective message, leading to a positive reply, requires preparation. This initial message should provide an honest and brief overview of the research project and situate the role of the respondent in this context. Given the sensitivity of intelligence practices, explaining that one is not looking for any sensitive information and offering confidentiality can help increase response rates. Aberbach and Rockman advise researchers "to be persistent and to insist firmly, but politely (and with a convincing explanation) that no one but the person sampled, i.e., the principal, will do for the interview."[32] Once this initial message is ready, the researcher needs to consider how to contact the source. While sending an interview request by email is common, some interviewees might prefer to be contacted by written letter or even by phone. Understanding the source's status and his or her cultural setting will inform this decision. Lilleker contacted British members of parliament by letter, but a letter would be unlikely to yield results when approaching a Mexican law enforcement officer, an American activist, or a Danish journalist.[33]

When a respondent agrees to an interview, several practical parameters still need to be agreed on. Will the interview take place in person, by telephone, or by email? A face-to-face interview, in person or via video chat, provides opportunities to directly observe the respondent's body language, which might grant additional clues. Interviewing a source within his or her work environment can provide further information regarding his or her professional status, for instance. Sometimes interviewing sources in their office is simply impossible. Foreign researchers will struggle to get permission to enter the headquarters of an intelligence agency where they will be perceived as a security risk. Public spaces, preferably quiet ones, are the typical fallback option. Researchers and interviewees sometimes agree to interact over the phone. In such cases the researcher will still be able to hear intonations and direct reactions from the interviewee, but observing body language and the surroundings will not be possible. Establishing rapport without eye contact is also harder. Finally, more structured interviews can be conducted via email or letter. This method provides more flexibility for the interviewee to prepare his or her responses, which might then lack in spontaneity. Visual and auditory sources of information are lost, as well as some opportunities to digress and uncover unexpected but relevant memories and opinions. In sum, whenever possible, face-to-face interviews are the best option.

The next step is to determine a list of topics or questions so that the respondent is not questioned aimlessly. Interview questions generally seek to fill knowledge gaps in the literature and to corroborate information. Depending on the preferred approach, the interviewer can seek to establish, confirm, or deny facts and beliefs about specific events, processes, and policies that are relevant to the project. A typical set of interview questions might start with a biographical question to establish the interviewee's expertise and shed light on past experiences. Open-ended questions on the concepts examined by the research project should be asked early on, to leave enough time to satisfyingly answer them. More pointed questions, probing the memory of the interviewee to verify facts and beliefs, can follow. Sensitive and difficult questions can be kept for the end of the interview to minimize their impact on the discussion in case they irritate the interviewee. The interviewer might also want to keep some time at the end of the interview for the informant to answer questions off the record. This is particularly important in intelligence research because respondents tend to be concerned about what they can and should not say. Answers to questions off the record cannot be mentioned as such in the research, but they help frame and contextualize the research.

Positionality, the relationship between the interviewer and the interviewee, is another factor that affects the effectiveness of interviews as a research method. Throughout the interview researchers should refrain from exposing their views, even when prompted. Maintaining a degree of neutrality or distance with the respondent limits the interviewer's influence on the responses. However, questions inevitably steer the interview and reveal the researcher's agenda, which constrains the informant's responses. Respondents are likely to engage differently with different types of interviewers. Cunningham-Sabot finds that local elites tend to trust foreign researchers more than their fellow citizens because they are not perceived as a threat to their status.[34] The situation is quite different in the field of intelligence studies, in which the nationality of an interviewer can cause concerns about his or her intentions. In other cases the background of the interviewer can facilitate interactions with the interviewee. A respondent who served in the military is likely to perceive an interviewer who served in the same branch to be more trustworthy than, for example, a foreigner. Whatever the circumstances, researchers should develop in-depth knowledge of the research topic and effectively communicate their academic credentials and expertise to the respondent. This knowledge will help the researcher maintain critical distance, demonstrate commitment, and facilitate rapport with the interviewee before, during, and after the interview.[35]

Conducting interviews raises several ethical concerns related to the respondents and the researcher.[36] Institutional requirements, through institutional review boards in the United States, are often designed to protect respondents.[37] This is particularly important in intelligence studies, a field in which respondents can risk their career, if not more, when they engage with outsiders. Scholars are asked to provide information to assess the degree to which their research could harm their respondents and develop mitigation strategies to minimize any potential harm. Several best practices exist to do so, including the preparation of an information sheet summarizing the key objectives of their project and a consent form to be shared with the respondents ahead of the interview. These formalities will provide the respondents with an opportunity to assess whether they are at ease with the proposed interview process and, if not, to request changes. For example, respondents could agree to be recorded but ask to review each paragraph in which the researcher will refer to their interview. From the researcher's perspective, recording an interview can reduce data distance—the amount of information lost in the interview process—and provide more room for the researcher to concentrate on what the interviewee is saying. However, using a recorder or even taking notes might make the respondent feel uncomfortable. Some respondents might prefer not to be recorded at all.

One additional concern that arises more prominently in the field of intelligence studies is information security. National security professionals can be expected to know and respect their professional obligations and refrain from disclosing sensitive information. However, interviewees may occasionally discuss sensitive issues. In this case the main issue, from the researchers' point of view, is to protect their sources so that they do not incur any harm. A national security professional who discloses sensitive information to a researcher might breach government policies or even the law and damage his or her career as a result. General David Petraeus, a former director of the CIA and commander of the International Security Assistance Force in Afghanistan, was sentenced to two years of probation and $100,000 fine for sharing classified information with his biographer.[38] In this case the scandal also significantly affected the career of Petraeus's interviewer and biographer.[39] Given the sensitivity and riskiness of research involving human subjects, research ethics issues should not only orient methodological choices before and during interviews but also after their conduct.

## Using Interview Material

After the interview the researcher needs to conduct several additional tasks in order to use the interview material as effectively and ethically as possible. These steps are important because the use of data is one of the main factors determining the quality of a research output. Directly after the interview, the researcher should take some time to write down impressions and review his or her notes, if any, to add details and transcribe the interaction while memories are still fresh. Transcribing audio records, if they are available, is preferable and provides an opportunity for the researcher to ponder the interview data. When recording is not possible, the researcher should be aware that personal bias can affect his or her memory of the interview, subsequent field notes, and data analysis efforts.[40] Respondents can also be a source of bias. The information they share raises questions of validity and meaningfulness. In the best cases, interviewees tell the truth as they see it; in the worst cases, they deceive or lie to the researcher.[41] Interviewees might prefer to discuss specific events and memories over others, or they might simply not know the truth. After all, intelligence itself tends to be based on fallible sources that might have been manipulated by adversary services.[42]

To address these limitations, researchers should seek to understand their interviewees' point of view and consider how different perspectives might affect their responses. Thorough preparation and in-depth knowledge of documentary evidence can help researchers recognize pieces of information that differ from established facts. To systematically evaluate the plausibility of the responses they obtain, researchers should, whenever possible, corroborate information with other data sources, including other interviews and primary documents.[43] Taking a step back and considering broader questions, such as who is speaking to whom, for what purpose, and under what circumstances, will help the researcher maintain a critical distance from the respondents.[44] Researchers should also make sure not to "privilege the views of the people who talked to them" over other equally reliable sources of evidence.[45] If an interviewee's account of an event differs from other sources, it might still be worth including it in the research to highlight discrepancies and alternative perspectives. However, not all the evidence gathered through an interview will serve the project, and some data will need to be discarded.[46] In turn, while a researcher can hardly escape his or her own bias when selecting interview extracts, maintaining an awareness of his or her own position can minimize the impact of bias on the research output. Some researchers prefer to accept—perhaps even embrace—this subjectivity and argue that the interaction between the interviewer and interviewee coproduces the interview material and the research narrative in which data will be used.[47]

Researchers use a variety of techniques to incorporate interview material in their writing. Block quotes put a strong emphasis on the interviewee's experience and are more frequent in ethnographic projects exploring organizational cultures, for instance.[48] Frequent and lengthy quotations can overpower the researcher's voice and limit the amount of analysis. Most researchers prefer to use short quotations or to paraphrase key information in order to prevent interviews from dominating their study. Multiple conventions exist to refer to interview material. Respondents sometimes give their consent for the researcher to refer to them by name and to specify the date and location of the interview. In intelligence studies this is most common with retired intelligence officers who served at senior levels. These interviewees are used to dealing with media and researchers' requests and are better placed to share information and personal opinions without damaging their careers. Even when an interviewee does not disclose sensitive information, they might be reticent to publicly express their opinions about their work and organization. Respondents might request to see the specific paragraph in which their interview will be mentioned and ask for the citation not to refer to them by name. Such requests can be helpful to the extent that they provide further opportunities to clarify the meaning of what interviewees said. If the researcher did not obtain consent, then the interviews cannot be cited and the information discussed in the interview should not be directly used in the research output—but it can inform the research.

Given the sensitivity of national security practices, serving and former practitioners often prefer to speak anonymously. As a result intelligence researchers have developed various practices to quote anonymous sources. Whenever possible the researcher should try to describe the occupation of the interviewee and give a sense of his or her expertise. References can, for example, mention "a national security expert with experience in Congress," "a former operation officer," or "an intelligence analyst working on Middle Eastern issues in the 1990s." Further anonymity can be provided using nicknames or codes, such as Mrs. White, Mr. Blue, informant 1, informant 2. Referring to the specific day, month, and year and the city where the interview took place is preferable. These details will help readers assess the validity of the sources that were consulted and the broader context. Sometimes anonymity can be difficult to maintain if dates and locations are mentioned. There are not so many intelligence officers from a specific unit or agency with knowledge of issue x that met with researcher y on day z. Scholars can then refer to "private information," "interview data," "confidential interview," or "unattributable" information, and sometimes they avoid attributing sources altogether.[49] While these practices protect respondents, they prevent other researchers from independently verifying information, especially when confidential interviews are the only sources the author refers to.[50]

Researchers might need to take additional measures to protect their respondents, especially when interview sources are based in nondemocratic countries or have discussed particularly sensitive matters.[51] To protect the identity of their interviewees, researchers can decide not to make note of their names at all and not to record the interview in any way. Several technical means, including encryption, can be used to secure the storage and transmission of interview data on computers.[52] However, information stored on computer is always at risk of being disclosed, particularly by well-resourced nation-state actors.

## Conclusion

Qualitative research interviews, just like archival research, provide a limited window into intelligence practices. As Michael Warner suggests, a researcher "has to appraise his or her sources in the knowledge that they are surely fragmentary."[53] Triangulating between and within each data type is key to overcoming some of the limits of interviews and, when possible, to improving the validity of the findings. Documentary sources such as government reports are important because they can provide the necessary epistemological and empirical foundations to conduct and corroborate interviews. In turn, interviews can help cut through the surplus of documents available in government archives and online to identify the most significant sources and make sense of them.[54] Yet altogether interviews and documents cannot tell the full story. As historian Peter Jackson points out, "It is, in any case, a dubious proposition to assume that we can ever know the 'full story' of any historical event. Our understanding of complex historical phenomena is too contingent on the temporal and ideological context in which we operate."[55] Interviews can help a researcher uncover memories, beliefs, and sometimes facts, but objectivity is necessarily constructed. This limitation is not unique to the study of intelligence but is felt more strongly in this field characterized by a limited number of sources.

## Notes

The author would like to thank Mark Phythian for his comments at the National Security Studies Institute's annual colloquium held March 23–24, 2017, at the University of Texas at El Paso. An earlier version of this chapter was published as an article in *International Studies Perspectives*, a journal published by Oxford University Press.

1. Loch K. Johnson, "The Development of Intelligence Studies," in *The Routledge Companion to Intelligence Studies*, ed. Robert Dover, Michael S. Goodman, and Claudia Hillebrand (London: Routledge, 2013), 4–9.
2. R. Gerald Hughes, "Of Revelatory Histories and Hatchet Jobs: Propaganda and Method in Intelligence History," *Intelligence and National Security* 23, no. 6 (2008): 842–54; R. Gerald Hughes, Peter Jackson, and Len Scott, *Exploring Intelligence Archives: Enquiries into the Secret State* (London: Routledge, 2008).
3. Peter Jackson, "Introduction," in Hughes, Jackson, and Scott, *Exploring Intelligence Archives*, 3.
4. Michael Warner, "Wanted: A Definition of 'Intelligence,'" *Studies in Intelligence* 46, no. 3 (2002): 17.
5. James A. Holstein and Jaber F. Gubrium, *The Active Interview* (Thousand Oaks, CA: Sage, 1995), 1. This claim can be traced to Michael Brenner, *Social Method and Social Life* (London: Academic Press, 1981), 115.
6. A database of all the articles published in *Intelligence and National Security*, including those that use interview as a data-collection method, is on file with the author and available on request. The other flagship journal in the field, the *International Journal*

*of Intelligence and CounterIntelligence*, was not included in this database because articles published in this venue do not systematically follow academic conventions regarding citation. Given its centrality to the field, *Intelligence and National Security* can be considered representative of broader trends in the field of intelligence studies.

7. Philip H. J. Davies, "Doing Politics: Spies as Informants: Triangulation and the Interpretation of Elite Interview Data in the Study of the Intelligence and Security Services," *Politics* 21, no. 1 (2001): 73–80; Brenda L. Moore, "In-Depth Interviewing," in *Routledge Handbook of Research Methods in Military Studies*, ed. Joseph Soeters, Patricia M. Shields, and Sebstiaan Rietjens (London: Routledge, 2014), 116–28.
8. Office of the Director of National Intelligence, "Statistical Transparency Report Regarding Use of National Security Authorities," Washington, DC, April 30, 2016.
9. National Commission on Terrorist Attacks upon the United States, *The 9/11 Commission Report: Final Report of the National Commission on Terrorist Attacks upon the United States* (Washington, DC: National Commission on Terrorist Attacks upon the United States, 2004).
10. Davies, "Doing Politics," 77–78.
11. "The 30-Year Rule—A Briefing Note," National Archives, last modified May 6, 2009, http://webarchive.nationalarchives.gov.uk/20090516124223/http://www.30yearrulereview.org.uk/background.htm.
12. White House, Executive Order 13526, December 29, 2009, section 3.3.
13. Richard J. Aldrich, "'Grow Your Own': Cold War Intelligence and History Supermarket," *Intelligence and National Security* 17, no. 1 (2002): 147.
14. Davies, "Doing Politics," 74; Darren G. Lilleker, "Interviewing the Political Elite: Navigating a Potential Minefield," *Politics* 23, no. 3 (2003): 208.
15. Dvora Yanow and Peregrine Schwartz-Shea, *Interpretation and Method: Empirical Research Methods and the Interpretive Turn* (New York: M. E. Sharp, 2006).
16. David E. Murphy, "Sasha Who?" *Intelligence and National Security* 8, no. 1 (1993): 102.
17. Allison M. Shelton, "Framing the Oxymoron: A New Paradigm for Intelligence Ethics," *Intelligence and National Security* 26, no. 1 (2011): 37.
18. Rhodri Jeffreys-Jones, "Commentary: Loch Johnson's Oral History Interview with William Colby, and Johnson's Introduction to That Interview," in Hughes, Jackson, and Scott, *Exploring Intelligence Archives*, 270–72.
19. Michael V. Hayden, *Playing to the Edge: American Intelligence in the Age of Terror* (New York: Penguin Books, 2017). For the rebuttal, see Dianne Feinstein, "Factual Errors and Other Problems in 'Playing to the Edge: American Intelligence in the Age of Terror,' by Michael V. Hayden," Staff Summary, March 2016, https://www.feinstein.senate.gov/public/_cache/files/e/7/e7fde6e8-4053-454a-a15c-47234daf175e/1FB727F237C5E0C97F075462081B6DAC.hayden-book-response-march-2016.pdf.
20. Davies, "Doing Politics," 76; Warner, "Wanted: A Definition," 17–18.
21. Loch K. Johnson, "A Conversation with James R. Clapper, Jr., the Director of National Intelligence in the United States," *Intelligence and National Security* 30, no. 1 (2015): 1–25.

22. William S. Harvey, "Strategies for Conducting Elite Interviews," *Qualitative Research* 11, no. 4 (2011): 433.
23. Damien Van Puyvelde, "Intelligence Accountability and the Role of Public Interest Groups in the United States," *Intelligence and National Security* 28, no. 2 (2013): 139–58.
24. See, for example, Joshua Rovner, *Fixing the Facts: National Security and the Politics of Intelligence* (Ithaca, NY: Cornell University Press, 2011), 13–14.
25. Oisín Tansey, "Process Tracing and Elite Interviewing: A Case for Non-probability Sampling," *PS: Political Sciences and Politics* 40, no. 4 (2007): 765.
26. Stephen Coulthart, "Why Do Analysts Use Structured Analytic Techniques? An In-Depth Study of an American Intelligence Agency," *Intelligence and National Security* 31, no. 7 (2016): 933–48.
27. Tansey, "Process Tracing," 770–71.
28. Rob Johnston, *Analytic Culture in the US Intelligence Community: An Ethnographic Study* (Washington, DC: Central Intelligence Agency, 2005), 122.
29. Joel D. Aberbach and Bert A. Rockman, "Conducting and Coding Elite Interviews," *PS: Political Science and Politics* 35, no. 4 (2002): 675; Sandra Groeneveld, Lars Tummers, Babette Bronkhorst, Tanachia Ashikali, and Sandra van Thiel, "Quantitative Methods in Public Administration: Their Use and Development through Time," *International Public Management Journal* 18, no. 1 (2015): 61–86.
30. Johnston, *Analytic Culture*, 121.
31. Aberbach and Rockman, "Conducting and Coding," 674.
32. Aberbach and Rockman, 674.
33. Lilleker, "Interviewing the Political Elite," 209.
34. Emanuelle Cunningham-Sabot, "Dr. Jekyl, Mr. H(i)de: The Contrasting Face of Elites at Interview," *Geoforum* 30, no. 4 (1999): 329–35.
35. Robert Mikecz, "Interviewing Elites: Addressing Methodological Issues," *Qualitative Inquiry* 18, no. 6 (2012): 485; Zoë Slote Morris, "The Truth about Interviewing Elites," *Politics* 29, no. 3 (2009): 212–14.
36. Stephane J. Baele, David Lewis, Anke Hoeffler, Olivier C. Sterck, and Thibaut Slingeneyer, "The Ethics of Security Research: An Ethics Framework for Contemporary Security Studies," *International Studies Perspectives* 19, no. 2 (2018): 105–27.
37. Dvora Yanow, "Reforming Institutional Review Board Policy: Issues in Implementation and Field Research," *PS: Political Science and Politics* 41, no. 3 (2008): 483–94.
38. United States v. David Howell Petraeus, Judgment in a Criminal Case, Case number: DNCW315CR000047-001, US District Court, Western District of North Carolina (2015).
39. Jessica Bennett, "Paula Broadwell, David Petraeus and the Afterlife of a Scandal," *New York Times*, May 28, 2016.
40. Cameron G. Thies, "A Pragmatic Guide to Qualitative Historical Analysis in the Study of International Relations," *International Studies Perspectives* 3, no. 4 (2002): 351–72.

41. John Ferris, "Coming in from the Cold War: The Historiography of American Intelligence, 1945–1990," *Diplomatic History* 19, no. 1 (1995): 92.
42. Isaac Ben-Israel, "Philosophy and Methodology of Intelligence: The Logic of Estimate Process," *Intelligence and National Security* 4, no. 4 (1989): 672.
43. Janet Buttolph, Johnson H. T. Reynolds, and Jason D. Mycoff, *Political Science Research Methods* (Washington, DC: CQ Press, 2008), 343.
44. Alexander L. George and Andrew Bennett, *Case Studies and Theory Development in the Social Sciences* (Cambridge, MA: MIT Press, 2004), 100.
45. Michael Warner, "Sources and Methods for the Study of Intelligence," in *Handbook of Intelligence Studies*, ed. Loch K. Johnson (London: Routledge, 2006), 26.
46. Hughes, "Of Revelatory Histories," 848.
47. Mary Manjikian, "Reading Lolita in Langley: The Unreliable Narrator as a Device to Evaluate Intelligence Credibility," *Intelligence and National Security* 30, no. 5 (2015): 709–10.
48. Johnston, *Analytic Culture*, 13–16; Bridget Rose Nolan, "Information Sharing and Collaboration in the United States Intelligence Community: An Ethnographic Study of the National Counterterrorism Center" (PhD diss., University of Pennsylvania, 2013), 28–30.
49. Bob Woodward, *Veil: The Secret Wars of the CIA, 1981–1987* (New York: Simon & Schuster, 1987); Philip H. J. Davies, "Organizational Politics and the Development of Britain's Intelligence Producer/Consumer Interface," *Intelligence and National Security* 10, no. 4 (1995): 130; Jeffrey T. Richelson, *A Century of Spies: Intelligence in the Twentieth Century* (Oxford: Oxford University Press, 1995), 498; Stuart Farson, "Parliament and Its Servants: Their Role in Scrutinizing Canadian Intelligence," *Intelligence and National Security* 15, no. 2 (2000): 255.
50. Graham Brown, "The Perils of Terrorism: Chinese Whispers, Kevin Bacon and Al Qaeda in Southeast Asia—A Review Essay," *Intelligence and National Security* 21, no. 1 (2006): 151.
51. Baele et al., "Ethics of Security Research."
52. Leonie Maria Tanczer, Ryan McConville, and Peter Maynard, "Censorship and Surveillance in the Digital Age: The Technological Challenges for Academics," *Journal of Global Security Studies* 1, no. 4 (2016): 350–51.
53. Warner, "Sources and Methods," 21.
54. Tansey, "Process Tracing and Elite Interviewing," 767.
55. Jackson, "Introduction," 9.

# 4.

# The Use of Structured Behavioral Observation Systems to Address Research Questions in Intelligence

*Misty Duke*

The study of human behavior and cognition can reveal valuable information pertaining to the field of intelligence and national security. For example, Rose McDermott advocated for the use of experimental research design to examine factors relevant to supporting quality intelligence analysis, such as analyst personality, cognitive bias, and training.[1] Understanding human behavior is also important when investigating such issues as propaganda, human-machine interactions, human intelligence collection, and the way consumers interpret, and act on, intelligence products.

Researchers who study behavior must develop a plan for its measurement, referred to as *operationalization*. Operationalization of behavior is done using one of three general methods. The first is physiological. Researchers can observe brain activity using functional magnetic resonance imaging or electroencephalographs, for example, or they can observe other physiological processes, such as heart rate, galvanized skin response, and respiration, in response to some stimulus. The second method is self-report, asking individuals to describe their own mental states, cognitive processes, intended behavior, or actual behavior. Since these behavioral exchanges occur so quickly, individuals may not be consciously aware of their own behaviors, and their reports may not capture the richness of their actual behavior. Self-reports of behavior can be inaccurate because they can be influenced by respondents' memory and self-perceptions. The third way to measure behavior is through direct observation. Observation may provide a more valid measure of behavior than self-report, such as when measuring complex social interactions.[2]

The study of behavior through direct observation can be used to address research questions in at least three areas of intelligence and national security studies. The first area is human intelligence collection, in which the goal is to obtain useful, accurate information through questioning an asset, detainee, witness, or informant. What strategies do questioners use during debriefs, interviews, or interrogations? How do those being questioned—hereafter referred to as *sources*—respond to such strategies? The answers to these questions may prove crucial to supporting effective collection efforts, which may, in turn, inform tactical and strategic decisions. The second area of intelligence and national security that may be addressed through behavioral observation is counterintelligence and security. How do people in secure environments respond to *social engineering*, psychologically manipulative efforts to access sensitive information? How can people be trained to recognize social engineering and respond appropriately? Studies exploring these issues may enable businesses, intelligence agencies, and other organizations to reduce information loss and protect the integrity of information systems. The third area in which the direct observation of behavior may be relevant is ideological and behavioral radicalization. What factors (demographic, attitudinal, personality, situational, cultural) contribute to the development of radical beliefs and violent behavior in support of those beliefs? What types of messages are effective in countering radical beliefs and, thereby, reducing violent behavior? The answers to these questions may be useful for identifying and targeting individuals who are at risk for engaging in extremist behavior.

## Overview of Behavioral Observation Methodology

Researchers have developed two main approaches to behavioral observation. In experimental studies they manipulate variables and determine their impact on behavior. For example, studies have examined the effect of certain persuasion methods on individuals' willingness to agree to do things they would not normally do.[3] While experimental studies allow researchers to isolate the effect of variables on behavior, these effects may not transfer to settings in which the behavior naturally occurs. Alternatively, behavior can be observed in settings in which it naturally occurs. For example, Rob Johnston conducted an ethnographic study of analysts from across the intelligence community in which he directly observed the conduct of analysis in agency settings.[4] However, the substantial number of factors, both known and unknown to the researcher, that determine behaviors occurring in natural settings can reduce the *validity of causal inferences*. In other words, researchers' conclusions about causal effects are constrained because they are unclear about which variables in particular have affected behavior.

The level of structure inherent in any observation system is related to the nature of the data required. Researchers who want to obtain quantitative data will prefer a more structured system of observation, whereas researchers who require qualitative data will use less structured observation methods. On the one hand, unstructured systems are more flexible and allow for interpretation of observations. Structured systems, on the other hand, are amenable to quantitative measures of behavior, such as frequency, timing, and intensity, which allow for generalizing from a sample of observations to the population of observations from which the sample was derived. Because researchers in intelligence studies may be interested in such generalization, this chapter will focus on structured observational systems. It is important to note that these systems require consideration of several factors that are pertinent to valid, objective measurement of behavior, such as reliability, validity, context-dependent versus generalized behavior, level of specificity, and timing of behavior. These factors will be discussed later in the chapter.[5]

Researchers conducting structured observation must demonstrate two psychometric properties of behavior measurements: reliability and validity. *Reliability* is concerned with the consistency of the measure. If a measure of a person's behavior is taken more than once under the same conditions, will both measurements be similar? If more than one person takes the measure under the same conditions, will both measurements be similar? The type of reliability addressed in the latter question is called *inter-rater reliability*, which is especially relevant for quantitative observational measures that are a function of both the observation target and the observer.[6] As the level of interpretation required by the observer increases, the consistency of observations made by different observers decreases. Researchers who use observational measures must demonstrate cross-observer consistency. They typically do so by having more than one observer code some or all cases so that indicators of inter-rater reliability, such as Kappa or the intra-class correlation coefficient, can be calculated.

*Validity* is concerned with the accuracy of the measure. Measures of behavior are not the same as the construct that the behavior represents. Constructs cannot be directly observed, because they represent classifications of ideas and knowledge. Researchers depend on behavioral observations to make inferences about these constructs.[7] For example, the number of times the target smiles at another person can be used as a measure of pro-social behavior. The validity of this depends on whether the behavior *smiling* captures any or all of the meaning of the construct *pro-social behavior*. Sometimes behaviors are measured not to understand something about a construct but to understand behaviors in specific contexts.[8] For instance, juror behavior during deliberation is unique to the *juror* role and to the *verdict* task. Observing such behavior can help one understand how people communicate under these constraints rather than measure a more general construct. In such cases validity of measurement is not as relevant an issue as reliability.

Observations can be used to make inferences about constructs that are context dependent, such as social behavior in the presence of peers versus professional colleagues, or constructs that are stable across contexts, such as aggressive behavior.[9] Most of the observational measures discussed in this chapter are used to make inferences about context-dependent constructs, which vary across settings and stimuli and are easily reversible. For example, when a person is being interrogated about information they wish to keep secret, they would likely refuse to provide many details and try to avoid developing rapport with their interrogator. However, this same person may be quite verbose and share great affinity for a close friend. Communicativeness and rapport are context-dependent behaviors.

Observations of both verbal and nonverbal behavior are often captured through video recording, which allows for detailed coding. Verbal behavior may also be captured through written accounts. Nonverbal behavior can be coded on several levels, moving from global, or large scale, to specific.[10] The frequency of large-scale movements, such as gestures, may be recorded or categorized according to the meaning or function of the behavior. For example, a gesture may be categorized as a display of affect. Further along the continuum are coding systems that identify more specific aspects of behaviors, such as the relation of body parts with one another. At the furthest point of specificity, coding systems identify microbehaviors, such as the blink of an eye. These systems can become very complex, nesting microbehaviors in large-scale behaviors and periods and examining the meaning of behaviors and correlates with verbal behaviors. Verbal behaviors can also be measured according to various levels of specificity, ranging from turns in a conversation to phrases, words, and syllables.[11] The level of specificity that is appropriate for coding behaviors depends on the research question.

Structured observations may be either static or dynamic in nature.[12] On the one hand, *static* observations are made at one point in time, such as observations made of people who pass by a specific location. There is only one opportunity to observe each target. On the other hand, *dynamic* observations, which are made across time, allow for evaluation of behavioral patterns. One example of dynamic observation would be observing how well a border security agent implements practices learned in training over time. Dynamic observations are recorded using *interval coding*, in which measures are taken during discrete periods. For example, the observer would note the number of times the agent applies the learned behavior during each eight-hour job shift. The researcher may be interested in evaluating whether the agent applies the behavior less frequently across time.

Researchers record structured observations using either a count system or a rating scale.[13] Observers using the *count system* identify the frequency of a specific behavior during a specified period, such as the number of times one person smiles at another person during a conversation. Observers using *rating scales* choose one of several rank-ordered categories that reflects the extent to which a behavior or construct is present. An observer may rate the attentiveness of an interviewer toward an interviewee on a four-point Likert-type scale with the following categories: very attentive, somewhat attentive, minimally attentive, and completely inattentive. Because count systems of measurement involve less interpretation than rating scales, they are more reliable.

The remainder of this chapter reviews the application of behavioral observation to three areas of intelligence and national security research: intelligence interviewing and interrogation, individual behavior in secure environments, and religious and political radicalization. Examples of research studies in which behavioral observation has been used as a source of data will be provided in each area.

## Behavioral Observation of Intelligence Interviewing and Interrogation

In the last decades, the US intelligence community has relied heavily on human intelligence collection methods—specifically on the interrogation of individuals suspected of facilitating terrorist activities—to learn more about terrorism.[14] To support these efforts, a large body of research has been conducted to develop evidence-based interrogation methods that maximize the likelihood of obtaining accurate information from sources. The following sections distinguish between observations of actual interviews or interrogations, observations of simulated interviews or interrogations, and efforts to classify deceptive behavior in these contexts.

### Observation of Actual Interviews or Interrogations

In some studies researchers decide to code verbal and nonverbal interrogator and source behaviors displayed during video- or audio-recorded interrogations. This method has been used to examine a model of interviewing used by police officers in the United Kingdom and comprising five stages: planning and preparation, engage and explain, gaining an account, closure, and evaluation (PEACE).[15] In one study of the model, researchers reviewed 142 tapes and transcripts of PEACE interviews conducted with individuals suspected of social security benefit fraud.[16] They measured the skillful implementation of interviewer behaviors specified for each stage on a five-point Likert-type scale, ranging from "need further training" to "highly skilled performance." They also provided an evaluation of the overall quality of each phase of the interview and the quality of the entire interview on five-point Likert-type scales. These measures were intended to capture the construct *interviewer skill*. However, one could argue that the reliance on rating-scale measures of behavior introduced a level of subjectivity that might not be present if the researchers had used a measure of the frequency of behavior.

This research has also sought to measure the construct *interview outcome*. This is challenging because "ground truth" regarding culpability is unknown. Arguably, a successful interview is one that obtains a full account of information, regardless of whether it results in a confession or denial. Interview outcomes were coded according to five categories: (1) "no comment," in which suspects refused to provide any information; (2) "denial," in which suspect denials were accepted by the interviewer without being tested; (3) "partial admission," in which suspects provided some information about the crime but not enough to proceed with a legal case; (4) "comprehensive account," in which admissions were fully explored or denials were fully tested; and (5) "confession," in which a confession was given and accepted by the interviewer without much detail being provided. According to the researchers, the most desirable outcomes were either "comprehensive account" or "confession."

The study then divided interviewers into either a high-skill or a low-skill group for each stage, according to their overall performance at that stage. These two groups were compared to determine the relationship between ratings of the quality of interviewer skill at each stage of the interview and overall ratings of the quality of interviewer skill. Furthermore, interviews with outcomes coded as "comprehensive account" or "confession" (the best outcomes) were compared to interviews with outcomes coded as "denials" or "partial admissions" (the worst outcomes) regarding ratings of the quality of interviewer skill. The results of the study indicated that interviewers classified as high skill within each stage conducted interviews rated higher in overall quality. This suggests that behaviors at each stage of the interview are important to overall interview quality. Additionally, interviews that were rated highest in overall quality were those most likely to have the best outcomes, indicating that interviewers who were more skilled in PEACE interviewing techniques conducted more successful interviews.

Some observational studies of actual interviews focus on source behavior rather than interviewer behavior. In a study of counterinterrogation strategies, researchers examined audio and video recordings of 181 police interviews of international, right-wing, and terrorist suspects conducted in the United Kingdom and Ireland.[17] The researchers developed a coding manual based on a review of the scientific literature and instruction manuals written by terrorist groups, consultation with police interview trainers, and experience observing police interrogations. The interviews were coded using an initial list of thirty-one strategies. After coding had been completed, only nine strategies occurred in more than 10 percent of the interviews; these nine strategies were included in subsequent analyses.

The researchers coded for the presence or absence of a strategy during each forty-five-minute section of an interview, a form of interval coding. These strategies were coded at a macro level rather than at the level of conversational turns. In other words, for the presence of a strategy to be coded, an entire section of the interview had to be characterized by the use of that strategy rather than only a few answers to interview questions. The mean number of times each strategy was used per interview was entered into a principal components analysis, which identified five statistically independent counterinterrogation factors meant to reflect constructs: *verbal* (discussing an unrelated topic, providing well-known information, or providing an unscripted response), *passive verbal* (providing monosyllabic responses or claiming to have no memory), *passive* (refusal to make eye contact or complete silence), *no comment*, and *retraction*. Comparison of the three categories of terrorists with use of each type of counterinterrogation strategy revealed that all strategies except *retraction* were most commonly used by paramilitary groups.

In another study, Christopher Kelly and his colleagues used a dynamic measure of interview and source behavior to examine how behaviors change over time during an interrogation.[18] They used interval coding to code twenty-nine video- and audio-recorded police interrogations of twenty-one individuals suspected of committing various crimes. Behaviors were coded in five-minute intervals, resulting in a total of 519 intervals across all interviews. Interviewer behaviors were coded according to sixty-five specific techniques identified in a previous study to make up six domains or constructs of interrogation methods: rapport and relationship building, presentation of evidence, emotion provocation, confrontation/competition, context manipulation, and collaboration. Two of these domains were removed from the analysis because of coding difficulties and low frequency of usage. Coding of each behavior was conducted on a three-point rating scale intended to measure the degree to which each behavior was exhibited during the interview: "none," "moderate," or "major/exclusive." This rating scale is similar to a count system of coding; the scale is measuring frequency and intensity. The coding system was pilot tested and then a new domain was added; the new domain was called "direct questioning" because it was intended to capture questioning that could not be categorized as consistent with a specific domain. Source behavior was initially coded according to whether information provided was cooperative (i.e., nonincriminating or self-incriminating information) or resistant (i.e., denials, claims of poor memory, retractions) on a three-point scale: "not present," "somewhat present," and "strongly present." The cooperative and resistant scales were combined to create one scale with five points: "strong resistance," "weak resistance," "neutral," "weak cooperation," and "strong cooperation." This coding system was pilot tested before it was used to code all interviews.

To control for interviews of different lengths, all interviews were divided into three sections, with each section having an equal number of five-minute intervals. Analyses were done to examine how the intensity of each interrogation domain used during each section of the interview was related to (1) the intensity of domains used during other parts of the interview and (2) suspect cooperation in each part of the interview. Separate analyses were conducted for interviews that resulted in confessions versus those that resulted in denials. Additional analyses were conducted to examine relationships between the intensity of interview domains used during each five-minute interval and suspect cooperation in subsequent intervals. These analyses evaluated the dynamic effect of interrogation methods over time. The results of the study indicate that the nature of the relationship between interviewer behaviors and source behaviors changes during the interview in complex ways.

In summary, researchers have developed several coding systems to examine interviewer and source behavior during real investigative interviews and interrogations. These observations of behavior have provided insight into naturally occurring interviewer-source behaviors. The following section provides an overview of experimental research studies that evaluate how specific situational and individual difference factors affect interviewer-source behaviors.

### Observation of Simulated Interviews or Interrogations

In experimental studies on interviews and interrogations, researchers use simulations to test various interrogation methods and settings and their effect on source behavior. In some experimental studies, participants willingly act out the role of "suspect" or "witness" in a simulated interrogation. Psychology professor Par Anders Granhag and his colleagues conducted an experiment to evaluate the effectiveness of a method of elicitation called the Scharff technique on information gain.[19] The goal of the Scharff technique is to obtain information from sources without them knowing the interviewer's collection requirements or how much information they revealed. In this study, participants were given information about an impending terrorist attack and told that they would participate in an interview about the attack. They were then questioned using either the Scharff technique or a direct-questioning technique that asked for a narrative of the event and then followed up with specific questions. Interviews were video recorded and coded to measure the amount of information provided by sources. Since "ground truth" is known in experimental studies, it is easier to apply count systems of coding. In this study, if sources either provided a detail related to the terrorist attack or agreed to a detail suggested by the interviewer, that detail was coded "yes." Details were coded "yes" only if they had not been mentioned during an earlier part of the interview. The ratio of details provided by sources to the total number of details about the terrorist attack was calculated. This provided a measure of the construct *information gain*, which was greater for sources who participated in Scharff technique interviews than for sources who participated in direct-questioning interviews.

Other studies involve deception to convince participants that they are taking part in a real interview or interrogation. In one such study, college students were falsely informed that they were participating in a study to assess general knowledge and induced to cheat on a test by an experimenter posing as another participant.[20] Other similarly deceived participants were induced to violate rules but not to cheat. Later, all participants were "interrogated" about the alleged cheating event using one of two combinations of interrogation methods from the *Army Field Manual*.[21] This study had better ecological validity than role-playing studies on interrogation because participants believed that they were really being interrogated about an issue that could have real consequences.

Researchers coded audio recordings of interrogations to determine the amount of information obtained during each interview. Two types of information were coded: information about the cheating behavior (admission details) and information about other noncheating aspects of the testing session (nonadmission details). Innocent participants could accurately report only on nonadmission details since they did not cheat during the testing session. Like Granhag et al., the researchers coded details according to whether they were mentioned, or agreed to, by the source. Each participant was interrogated using several different methods, and the number of details mentioned by sources was calculated after each part of the interview, a form of interval coding. This approach allowed the researchers to assess how information gain increased as each new interrogation method was introduced within each group. The researchers found that participants questioned using the *Army Field Manual's* We Know All approach had provided twice as much nonadmission information and three times as much admission information after it had been implemented, compared to after only the direct-questioning method had been implemented. In the We Know All approach, the interrogator convinces a source that interrogation is merely required to confirm information already known to the interrogator. In summary, the studies reviewed in this section demonstrate how behavioral observations of simulated interrogations can be useful to examine the effectiveness of interrogation methods.

### Observation and Classification of Deceptive Behavior in Interviews and Interrogations

Human detection of deception is one of the most robust areas of research on interrogation. Most research in this area has been conducted using analogue, experimental studies in which participants are asked to lie or tell the truth about a past event or behavior or about future intentions. A different group of participants then judges the veracity of statements made by liars and truth tellers. In some studies observers make simple "truth" or "lie" classifications, and calculations derived from signal detection theory are used to evaluate the accuracy of deception judgments. For example, Stephen Porter and his colleagues examined the impact of two factors on deception judgments: (1) the judge's motivation to correctly classify truth tellers and liars and (2) accurate feedback about deception judgments.[22] High- or low-motivated participants made deception judgments about video-recorded interviewees after receiving accurate, inaccurate, or no feedback about previous judgments. The postfeedback judgments were classified, according to signal detection theory, as "hits" (proportion of correct "lie" judgments out of all judgments made of liars) or "false alarms" (proportion of incorrect "lie" judgments out of all judgments made of truth tellers).[23] Hit and false alarm rates were used to calculate *discrimination accuracy*, which is the ability to correctly discriminate between instances of deception and instances of truth telling. This study found that people who had low motivation and no feedback had the highest discrimination accuracy scores. The researchers also examined another important measure in signal detection theory: *response bias*, or an indication of the threshold of evidence required for an observer to make a "lie" judgment. Observers who have a more liberal response bias will be less inclined to make "lie" judgments, resulting in fewer hits and fewer false alarms, whereas observers who have a more conservative response bias will be more inclined to make "lie" judgments, resulting in more hits and more false alarms. The researchers found that low-motivated observers who were provided with feedback were more conservative in their judgments than low-motivated observers who received no feedback, whereas high-motivated observers provided with feedback were more liberal in their judgments than high-motivated observers who received no feedback.

Other studies on deception detection have applied verbal and nonverbal behavioral coding systems intended to aid observers in making accurate judgments of lying and truth telling. One system, the Criteria-Based Content Analysis (CBCA), is based on nineteen verbal criteria for judging deception, such as whether statements have a logical structure or include information about subjective mental states.[24] These criteria are more prevalent in truthful statements. Another system, Reality Monitoring (RM), is derived from the source-monitoring framework, which postulates that real memories of events contain sensory (e.g., "I heard music in the background") and contextual (e.g., "I was wearing a blue sweater that day") information.[25] Alternatively, false memories include information about cognitive operations (e.g., "I know I walked down Elm Street because that is near my house") because confabulating details about an event that was not experienced requires significant thought and reasoning. Thus, deceptive verbal statements include more information about cognitive operations, and true statements include more sensory and contextual details.

Aldert Vrij and his colleagues conducted a study to determine the most effective type of interview for yielding statements that observers could accurately classify as true or deceptive.[26] Both CBCA and RM were used to classify statements made during three types of interviews: information-gathering (participants provided a statement and answered follow-up questions), accusatory (participants were asked accusatory questions), and behavior-analysis (participants provided a statement and were then asked questions intended to elicit cues to deception). Coding on CBCA criteria differentiated between liars and truth tellers in information-gathering interviews but not in accusatory or behavior-analysis interviews. Coding statements using the RM system differentiated between truth tellers and liars in the information-gathering and behavior-analysis interviews but not in the accusatory interviews. These results indicate that information-gathering interviews may be most useful when an interviewer is using CBCA or RM to determine whether a source is deceptive or honest. The research studies presented here are only a few examples of the large body of research that has applied behavioral observation to answer research questions related to human intelligence collection through interviews and interrogations. Given the importance of these questions to tactical and strategic security planning, it is likely that this area of research will continue to thrive.

## Behavioral Observation in Behavior in Secure Environments

In the last decade a growing body of research has explored the human factor in cybersecurity.[27] Users of technology can be susceptible to phishing, malware downloads, and other cybercrimes. These behaviors increase the employers' vulnerability when users engage in careless behavior using work computers. Intelligence agencies, businesses, and other organizations must address employee behavior to decrease susceptibility to cybercrime. Most studies of cybersecurity evaluate secure user behavior through self-report measures.[28] A few studies have directly observed behavior as users respond to socially engineered attempts to obtain sensitive information. For example, Jemal Abawajy tested the effectiveness of three cybersecurity training delivery methods (instructor-led, online, and game-based) on users' ability to distinguish between phishing emails and websites and legitimate emails and websites.[29] Both before and after training, participants were asked to classify ten emails or websites as legitimate or illegitimate. This study examined only a small number of participants, and therefore the author was unable to generalize results to the population of trained users. Nonetheless, the results indicated that the game-based delivery method was most effective in helping users correctly identify illegitimate websites, while the online delivery method was most effective in helping users correctly identify illegitimate emails.

One could argue that users who know that they are being tested on their information security awareness will perform better than users who are unaware that their online behavior is being observed. To obtain a more valid measure of user behavior, several studies have made observations of unaware users. Researchers in one study tested the effectiveness of a cybersecurity exercise called Social Engineering Resistant User Model (SERUM).[30] Users in an unspecified "institution," who were not aware that they were participating in an experiment, were sent mock phishing emails. If they responded to those emails, they were sent to a screen warning them that there may have been a breach of security, and then they were sent an email that provided the same warning. The email included a link to a training program in which users could choose to participate. After training, users were offered the option to answer questions to evaluate how much new knowledge they gained during the training. The following week users were sent a second mock phishing email. The same procedure was followed for users who responded to the email. Most users ignored both emails. A very small percentage of those who responded to the phishing emails took part in the training. However, 75 percent of the people who responded to a phishing email during the first week did not respond to the phishing email sent during the second week, indicating that they may have learned to ignore such emails.

Social engineering efforts may also take place in person. Christian Happ and colleagues conducted a study to evaluate how elicitors who use the norm of reciprocity, in which people feel compelled to respond pro-socially to pro-social behaviors, may be successful in convincing targets to reveal secure information.[31] Researchers posing as interviewers asked passersby in a public location to participate in a survey about their online behavior. After asking several questions about internet security at work, interviewers asked participants to provide their computer password. To trigger the norm of reciprocity, all participants were offered a chocolate. However, the timing of the offer varied in three ways. Participants were offered the chocolate before the interview began, immediately before the interviewer asked for the password, or after the interview had concluded. Participants were more likely to provide their password if they were given a chocolate immediately before the interviewer asked for the password than if the chocolate was given at the beginning or the end of the interview. This indicated that those who provided their password were acting consistently with behavior predicted by the norm of reciprocity.

In these studies, participant behavior (classify an email or website as legitimate or not, click on an email link or ignore the email, provide a password or not) was measured as an indicator of the construct *security awareness*. The behavior was coded in a binary fashion, either *secure* or *insecure*. However, one could argue that secure behaviors vary along a continuum from secure to insecure.[32] Research on user behavior should apply more flexible coding strategies to accommodate the measurement of a variety of insecure behaviors. For example, the type of information that is disclosed may range from "minimally sensitive" to "highly sensitive." A variety of behaviors could be coded, such as using social media sites on workplace devices, accessing illegitimate websites through web searches, being careless with workplace devices and computers, and installing untrusted applications on work computers.[33]

Another area for future research is the effectiveness of in-person social engineering methods. The Federal Bureau of Investigation has identified several methods of elicitation of information that primarily rely on social contact between the elicitor and the target.[34] For example, when using a *provocative statement*, the elicitor says something intended to provoke the target to ask a question of the elicitor. If the elicitor says, "This has been the worst day ever," the target asks, "What happened?" In this way, it seems as if the target has initiated the conversation, making him or her less suspicious of the elicitor, who engages the target in subsequent conversation directed toward accessing sensitive information. There is limited research on the effectiveness of elicitation methods in obtaining sensitive information from targets. Such studies would be amenable to direct observation of targets' responses to various elicitation methods.

Few research studies have directly observed user responses to socially engineered efforts to access sensitive information. Yet behavioral observation is uniquely amenable to answering questions about naive user behavior and the effectiveness of training efforts to improve secure behavior. The application of these methods can be expanded to measure a broad range of behaviors in response to both online and in-person contact.

## Behavioral Observation of Political and Religious Radicalization

Researchers have recently become interested in personality, demographic, and situational factors that define pathways toward ideological radicalization and extremism.[35] Many of these studies have collected data through content analysis of official records relating to terrorist incidents or foiled terrorist plots or interviews with terrorists.[36] Fewer studies have used experimental methods, which rely on self-report data.[37] However, none of these experimental studies have directly observed behavior in response to radicalizing stimuli.

Experimental studies can use observation to measure the constructs *radicalization* and *extremism* under varying individual difference and situational factors. One measure of these constructs is an individual's response to encountering stimuli on social media sites, which may radicalize behavior by providing a forum for radical discourse.[38] An experiment could expose participants to various forms of extreme messages via mock social media sites and provide opportunities to respond via liking the post, sharing the post, responding to the post, or ignoring the post. Demographic, attitudinal, and personality factors would also be measured to predict the extent to which participants are willing to engage in radicalized responding. Messages with varying characteristics can be examined to determine which lead to more radicalized responding. Studies such as these would provide a more valid assessment of the factors contributing to radicalization than self-report measures alone.

## Conclusion

Direct observation of behavior can be a rich source of data for research in areas relevant to intelligence and national security. This method of data collection can be applied to a variety of research designs that may be used to answer diverse research questions. Behavioral observations can be valid indicators of underlying constructs, such as cooperation in interrogation, and they can help researchers understand how people behave under various circumstances, such as responding to social engineering efforts. While these methods are widely used in psychological research, they have not been regularly applied in intelligence studies research. Intelligence studies scholars should consider incorporating this method of data collection to produce interesting and groundbreaking findings in future research.

## Notes

1. Rose McDermott, "Experimental Intelligence," *Intelligence and National Security* 26, no. 1 (2011): 82–98.
2. Paul Yoder and Frank Symons, *Observational Measurement of Behavior* (New York: Springer, 2010).
3. Thomas Hugh Feeley, Ashley E. Anker, and Ariel M. Aloe, "The Door-in-the-Face Persuasive Message Strategy: A Meta-analysis of the First 35 Years," *Communication Monographs* 79, no. 3 (2012): 316–43.
4. Rob Johnston, *Analytic Culture in the US Intelligence Community* (Washington, DC: Center for the Study of Intelligence, Central Intelligence Agency, 2005).
5. For more information on qualitative coding of behavior, see Johnny Saldaña, *The Coding Manual for Qualitative Researchers* (London: Sage, 2016).
6. Kevin A. Hallgren, "Computing Inter-rater Reliability for Observational Data: An Overview and Tutorial," *Tutorials in Quantitative Methods for Psychology* 8, no. 1 (2012): 23–34.
7. William R. Shaddish, Thomas D. Cook, and Donald Thomas Campbell, *Experimental and Quasi-experimental Designs for Generalized Causal Influence*, 2nd ed. (Boston: Houghton Mifflin, 2002).
8. Yoder and Symons, *Observational Measurement of Behavior*.
9. Yoder and Symons.
10. Ronald H. Rozensky and Laurie Felman Honor, "Notation Systems for Coding Nonverbal Behavior: A Review," *Journal of Behavioral Assessment* 4, no. 2 (1982): 119–32.
11. Louis A. Gottschalk, *Content Analysis of Verbal Behavior: New Findings and Clinical Applications* (London: Routledge, 2013).
12. Yoder and Symons, *Observational Measurement of Behavior*.
13. Yoder and Symons.
14. Mark W. Pearce, *The Evolution of Defense HUMINT through Post-conflict Iraq* (Carlisle Barracks, PA: US Army War College, 2009).
15. Colin Clarke, Rebecca Milne, and Ray Bull, "Interviewing Suspects of Crime: The Impact of PEACE Training, Supervision, and the Presence of a Legal Advisor," *Journal of Investigative Psychology and Offender Profiling* 8, no. 2 (2011): 149–62; David W. Walsh and Rebecca Milne, "Keeping the PEACE? A Study of Investigative Interviewing Practices in the Public Sector," *Legal and Criminological Psychology* 13, no. 1 (2008): 39–57.
16. David W. Walsh and Ray Bull, "What Really Is Effective in Interviews with Suspects? A Study Comparing Interviewing Skills against Interviewing Outcomes," *Legal and Criminological Psychology* 15, no. 2 (2010): 305–21.

17. Laurence Alison, Emily Alison, Geraldine Noone, Stamatis Elntib, Sara Waring, and Paul Christiansen, "Whatever You Say, Say Nothing: Individual Differences in Counter Interrogation Tactics amongst a Field Sample of Right Wing, AQ Inspired and Paramilitary Terrorists," *Personality and Individual Differences* 68 (2014): 170–75.
18. Christopher E. Kelly, Jeaneé C. Miller, and Allison D. Redlich, "The Dynamic Nature of Interrogation," *Law and Human Behavior* 40, no. 3 (2016): 295–309.
19. Par Anders Granhag, Simon Oleszkiewicz, Leif A. Strömwall, and Steven M. Kleinman, "Eliciting Intelligence with the Scharff Technique: Interviewing More and Less Cooperative and Capable Sources," *Psychology, Public Policy, and the Law* 21, no. 1 (2015): 100–110.
20. Misty C. Duke, James M. Wood, Justin Magee, and Hector Escobar, "Effectiveness of Army Field Manual Interrogation Approaches for Educing Information and Building Rapport," *Law and Human Behavior* 42 (2018): 442–57.
21. Department of the Army, *Army Field Manual FM2-22.3: Human Collector Operations* (Washington, DC: Department of the Army, 2006).
22. Stephen Porter, Sean McCabe, Michael Woodworth, and Kristine A. Peace, "'Genius Is 1% Inspiration and 99% Perspiration' . . . or Is It? An Investigation of the Impact of Motivation and Feedback on Deception Detection," *Legal and Criminological Psychology* 12 (2007): 297–309.
23. Thomas D. Wickens, *Elementary Signal Detection Theory* (New York: Oxford University Press, 2002).
24. Max Stellar and Guenter Köhnken, "Criteria-Based Content Analysis," in *Psychological Methods in Criminal Investigation and Evidence*, ed. David C. Raskin (New York: Springer-Verlag, 1989), 217–45.
25. Marcia K. Johnson, "Memory and Reality," *American Psychologist* 61, no. 8 (2006): 760–71.
26. Aldert Vrij, Samantha Mann, Susanne Kristen, and Ronald P. Fisher, "Cues to Deception and Ability to Detect Lies as a Function of Police Interview Styles," *Law and Human Behavior* 31, no. 5 (2007): 499–518.
27. Jemal Abawajy, "User Preference of Cyber Security Awareness Delivery Methods," *Behavior and Information Technology* 33, no. 3 (2014): 237–48; Brenda Wiederhold, "The Role of Psychology in Enhancing Cybersecurity," *Cyberpsychology, Behavior, and Social Networking* 17, no. 3 (2014): 131–32.
28. For example, see Sarah Burns and Lynne Roberts, "Applying the Theory of Planned Behaviour to Predicting Online Safety Behavior," *Crime Prevention and Community Safety* 15, no. 1 (2013): 48–64.
29. Abawajy, "User Preference."
30. Kenny Jansson and R. von Solms, "Phishing for Phishing Awareness," *Behavior and Information Technology* 32, no. 6 (2013): 584–93.
31. Christian Happ, André Melzer, and Georges Steffgen, "Trick with Treat—Reciprocity Increases the Willingness to Communicate Personal Data," *Computers in Human Behavior* 61 (2016): 372–77; Robert Cialdini, *Influence*, 5th ed. (Boston: Pearson, 2009).

32. Sharul Tajuddin, Wendy Olphert, and Neil Doherty, "Relationship between Stakeholders' Information Value Perception and Information Security Behavior," *Proceedings of the 4th International Conference on Integrated Information (IC-ININFO 2014)* (Madrid: AIP Conference Proceedings, 2015), 69–77.
33. Amanda M. Y. Chu and Patrick Y. K. Chau, "Development and Validation of Instruments of Information Security Deviant Behavior," *Decision Support Systems* 66 (2014): 93–101.
34. Federal Bureau of Investigation, *Elicitation Techniques*, accessed August 10, 2018, https://www.fbi.gov/file-repository/elicitation-brochure.pdf/view.
35. Angela McGilloway, Priyo Ghosh, and Kamaldeep Bhui, "A Systematic Review of Pathways to and Processes Associated with Radicalization and Extremism amongst Muslims in Western Societies," *International Review of Psychiatry* 27, no. 1 (2015): 39–50.
36. For example, see Jytte Klausen, Selene Campion, Nathan Needle, Giang Nguyen, and Rosanne Libretti, "Toward a Behavioral Model of 'Homegrown' Radicalization Trajectories," *Studies in Conflict and Terrorism* 39 (2015): 67–83; Tahir Abbas and Assma Siddique, "Perceptions of the Processes of Radicalization and De-radicalisation among British South Asian Muslims in a Post-industrial City," *Social Identities: Journal for the Study of Race, Nation and Culture* 18, no. 1 (2012): 119–34.
37. Michael A. Hogg, Christie Meehan, and Jayne Farquharson, "The Solace of Radicalism: Self-Uncertainty and Group Identification in the Face of Threat," *Journal of Experimental Social Psychology* 46, no. 6 (2010): 1061–66.
38. Maura Conway, "Determining the Role of the Internet in Violent Extremism and Terrorism: Six Suggestions for Progressing Research," *Studies in Conflict and Terrorism* 40, no. 1 (2017): 77–98; Martin Rudner, "'Electronic Jihad': The Internet as Al Qaeda's Catalyst for Global Terror," *Studies in Conflict and Terrorism* 40, no. 1 (2017): 10–23.

# 5.

# A Sociological Approach to Intelligence Studies

*Bridget Rose Nolan*

Sociology is the systematic study of society, social structures, institutions, and relationships. Within the discipline, sociologists specialize in a wide variety of subfields, including race, class, gender, organizations, religion, politics, education, culture, inequality, and social interaction. Though sociology is related to and overlaps with other social sciences, its value lies in its focus mostly on contemporary domestic populations (as opposed to anthropology), informal as well as formal structures of power (as opposed to political science), and a group-level orientation (as opposed to psychology). Levels of analysis can range from the macro (large-scale social processes, such as stability and change among big groups or structures) to the micro (small-scale interactions among individuals or small groups, such as the dynamics of conversation). Depending on the type of research question sociologists are asking, they may use a variety of methods to collect data. These include interviews, surveys, participant observation or ethnography, experiments, and the use of existing data sources such as the US Census. The types of data these methods generate can be qualitative, quantitative, or a mixture, and sociologists use statistics and other analytical tools to demonstrate patterns among their observations and make generalizable claims.

The study of intelligence is missing a sociological perspective. Understanding international cooperation among friendly intelligence agencies—and lack of cooperation among unfriendly agencies—requires knowledge of the principles of group dynamics, inequality, and power. Because intelligence work in industrialized countries is inextricably intertwined with sociological notions of complex formal organizations and bureaucracies, an approach at the meso level of individual intelligence agencies requires the theory and empirical findings of Max Weber and Lewis Coser.[1] Their work can help us understand why the group dynamics that make individual agencies strong also complicate cooperation across those agencies. At the micro level of everyday interaction, intelligence work relies heavily on the contributions of

Erving Goffman's and Arlie Hochschild's notions of impression management, presentation of self, conversation analysis, emotion work, and the social construction of reality.[2] Their work can help us understand how the role of the intelligence analyst is constructed and how the organization and the individual are mutually constitutive. Rob Johnston's work in anthropology, sponsored by the Center for the Study of Intelligence (CSI) at the Central Intelligence Agency (CIA), provides an important inside look at intelligence work in the era immediately following the terrorist attacks of September 11, 2001.[3] Yet there is no extant literature on the sociology of intelligence work or counterterrorism. I explore some of these gaps in this chapter, which is organized in three parts. The first section offers a summary of my own background as a practitioner-turned-scholar and discusses the methodological opportunities and limitations of conducting fieldwork research inside the US intelligence community (IC). The second section shows how sociology's theories and methods can generally contribute to our understanding of intelligence work. The third section identifies future research questions in intelligence studies that sociology can help us answer.

## Practical Considerations: Opportunities and Challenges

I worked as a counterterrorism analyst for the CIA between 2007 and 2011. During my time there, I sought and received permission to conduct an ethnography of the National Counterterrorism Center (NCTC), which is the organization that was created after 9/11 to address the 9/11 Commission Report's finding that intelligence agencies were not sharing information the way they could or should.[4] NCTC houses officers from all around the intelligence community under one roof with the hopes that working alongside representatives from other agencies would encourage analysts to share information. During the course of my participant observation, I wanted to explore whether and how that information sharing occurs. As a sociologist, I was interested in learning about the small, day-to-day interactions that make up the life of the analyst and about the larger organizational dynamics that accomplish intelligence work.

Access to the IC is imperative to the process of conducting systematic data collection and analysis. Certainly for ethnography—the descriptive documentation of a living culture—there is no other way; the researcher must have access to a culture in order to study it. An interview study could conceivably be done without such access, but this approach would likely introduce significant bias; without insider status, current IC personnel would likely respond with reticence to an interview request, even if the researcher were a friend of a friend or had some other tangential connection. This would leave a population of former employees of two main types: retired IC employees, who may have spent too much time removed from the IC to know its current goings on, and employees who have left the IC before retirement and, depending on their reasons for leaving, could bring a negative overall bias to the sample.

Even if a representative interview sample were achievable from the outside, though, there can be stark differences between what people say and what they actually do—not because people are necessarily purposefully trying to mislead but because people are sometimes unaware that their words and actions do not match. Focusing solely on interviews can therefore be valuable but may not give us the overall picture we are seeking as intelligence researchers. Furthermore, access to the IC allows researchers to explore the micro-level, day-to-day workings of the organization, whereas outsiders are more likely to have to focus on more macro-level realities, such as organizational structure changes, legislative or budgetary issues, and the public rhetoric from IC leaders. Thus, the security clearance provides the researcher with entrée—it gets the researcher in the door both literally and figuratively—and the opportunity to build rapport with the people who do this work daily. I worried that my fellow analysts would be reluctant to participate in my study and that they would respond with the very reticence they are taught to show to reporters and other outsiders, but I was pleasantly surprised to find the opposite: my coworkers were enthusiastic about being interviewed because they felt that someone who understood their plight—which I did, as I also lived it daily—was finally giving them a voice.

Despite the opportunities it affords, access to what has been called "Top Secret America" also presents challenges.[5] The two main limitations of the security clearance are time and space. First, the security clearance itself takes time to process. A background check can take more or less time depending on the subject's background, personal circumstances, and foreign national contacts. The minimum seems to be around six months, but I worked with people whose clearances took two or more years to come through. The process is not fun or easy either. Applicants must open their lives up to the federal government with no guarantees, and for the highest clearances, they must undergo what can be harrowing procedures, like the polygraph and psychiatric evaluation. Once the clearance is granted, it takes significant additional time to adjust to the culture shock that frequently accompanies a journey inside the bubble. People cannot truly know what life inside the IC is like before they join, and some may have adopted Hollywood's imaginings, which can create a sense of overwhelm when they are faced with the reality. Many of my former colleagues echoed this feeling when they described their sense of "sand shifting beneath the feet" or said the reality of the IC hit them with the force of "water from a fire hose." Once a person has acculturated, a significant time investment goes into getting to know colleagues and building a social network. This is true not only because these relationships are necessary to do the job well, but also because there is no known organizational mechanism through which one can conduct research in the first place. If it is possible to do research, it is all done on an ad hoc basis, organically developed and pursued through personal relationships. In other words, the organization has no office or other formal structure through which researchers can officially request permission to conduct a study; researchers must build up and rely on their own relationships, which are largely personality driven and therefore vary widely such that a well-connected or charismatic person would probably be more likely to get permission from their management chain. The exceptions to this rule are researchers conducting studies officially on behalf of the CIA, as Rob Johnston did for the CSI.[6] CIA-sponsored research comes with its own set of challenges, though; while the backing of the CSI provides organizational legitimacy and access, this research may also run the risk of pro-CIA bias that research backed by non-CIA-affiliated organizations does not face.

Second, space limitations affect insiders' research. When conducting research inside a highly secured government facility, there will inevitably be interactions and conversations that are sociologically rich but that cannot be separated from the sensitive environment in which they occurred. These data must be sacrificed to protect the work and the employees, and there is no way to make up for those losses.

## Theoretical Considerations

Despite these limitations, sociology can still teach us a great deal about intelligence work. Intelligence scholars tend to present intelligence as both a process and an organization.[7] Classical sociology can contribute to our understanding of both perspectives.

### Symbolic Interactionism

If we think about intelligence work as a process, there are various kinds of processes we could choose to focus on: the process of collecting, handling, and exploiting intelligence; the processes of social interaction among representatives of the various agencies; or even the processes of recruiting assets to conduct espionage. Erving Goffman's work in sociology speaks directly to all of these.[8] Goffman was a symbolic interactionist, meaning he focused primarily on "thin" slices of behavior at the micro level—the seemingly insignificant moments in daily life that when taken together construct and reflect our social reality. He focused on the exchange of symbols through language and suggested that we can infer things about the larger invisible structures that shape our lives from very small interactions, such as a conversation between two people. If we look at the transcript of that conversation, we may notice, for instance, that John is able to successfully interrupt Sally and take the floor back, whereas Sally is not able to successfully interrupt John. Usually patterns of interruption are indicators of status—and in this case, we may infer that John is of a higher status than Sally. Symbolic interactionists argue that larger social structures are aggregates of these millions of tiny interactions and that these dynamic social processes both inform and are informed by the larger structure, which is performed and reproduced in social interaction.

Goffman's 1959 book, *The Presentation of Self in Everyday Life*, details his concept of dramaturgy: borrowing terminology from the theater, he suggested that social life is really no different from what actors are doing on the stage.[9] We all have roles to play—parent, colleague, citizen, friend—and those roles come with socially constructed and widely understood notions of how they should ideally be performed. We go about social life according to scripts, or shared expectations of how situations should unfold. We use costumes and props, like a doctor's white coat or stethoscope, and we are engaging nearly all the time in what Goffman calls "impression management"—efforts to maintain positive impressions in the minds of others that we are competent social actors. Impression management also features what Goffman calls "face work," which is a social actor's efforts to maintain a certain public self-image. If we err in our performance, we may "lose face" and employ strategies to rescue the performance, or "save face." We may also engage in "misrepresentation," when actors sometimes engage in strategies that fall short of outright lying but involve innuendo, omission, or purposeful ambiguity to maintain a credible performance. This dramaturgical approach to social life is socially constructed, and all these performances together constitute what we experience as reality.

Because we experience thousands of moments of interest to Goffman in a day, I offer just a few examples of how we can use Goffman's dramaturgical approach to understand intelligence work. The work of recruiting spies is a salient example of how intelligence work processes depend heavily on the maintenance and subversion of Goffmanian principles. The method of recruiting spies or assets is called the agent recruitment cycle.[10] The first step in the process is called "spotting": recruiters find people that they perceive may have access to information the US government might want to know. Recruiters then "assess" and "develop" the targets, essentially building a relationship with them that appears to be a normal friendship or business partnership. Recruiters must rely heavily on impression management through these stages because they must keep their affiliation with the US government a secret until they are as sure as they can be that the target will agree to be a spy. Indeed, living undercover is perhaps the clearest example of Goffmanian principles in action; to maintain one's cover, one must engage in strategies of impression management, face work, and presentation of self to make the performance come off as effortless and therefore go unquestioned. Underneath the surface the "true" self still lives, and as a social actor the recruiter must suppress this self and perform the role of another, less-authentic self. This performance requires a tremendous amount of emotional energy to appear effortless. It is similar to a duck swimming across a pond: the duck appears to glide smoothly along the water's surface, but its feet and legs are paddling furiously beneath the water to make the gliding possible. This is the work of impression management. Goffman would likely classify undercover work as a "cynical" performance, meaning that the social actor may not be taken in by their own performance and does not believe it reflects a "real" self; the performer tries to convince the audience of their authenticity only as a means to some other end—in this case, the successful recruitment and handling of a spy.

Once recruiters have successfully recruited—or "pitched"—the asset, the case officers can drop the performance a bit since the target now knows their true affiliation. But the handling of the spy requires an alternative set of Goffmanian performances. The relationship between the spy and the handler and each party's true affiliations obviously have to remain secret to outsiders, but the relationship must still be maintained in order to communicate information between them. Here, both parties rely on others to maintain the fabric of society and the perception that nothing is amiss, and then the spy and the handler can subvert these shared understandings for their own ends. This is the concept behind a dead drop—a seemingly ordinary location hiding in plain sight where information between the spy and the case officer can be exchanged without risking the danger of a face-to-face meeting. Spies capitalize on widely understood notions of how social life is constructed and performed, and they manipulate these scripts in order to keep their work from being discovered.

While presentation of self and impression management are easily observable in the agent recruitment cycle, one of Goffman's central points is that we are all doing this every day—not just in special circumstances like the delicate balancing act of recruiting a spy. Unlike "cynical" performances, which the actors themselves do not believe, what Goffman terms "sincere" performances are given by actors who believe that the reality they are trying to convey is their true, authentic self. We can therefore apply Goffman's ideas to more ordinary, everyday circumstances as well, such as daily interactions among colleagues in the intelligence community, to understand how the work of intelligence is done day to day. Additionally, we can see how ordinary processes of interaction that we may take for granted are highlighted and made explicit in this unexpected social space.

## Greedy Institutions

Sociology provides useful perspectives for approaching intelligence as an organization. Goffman and sociologist Lewis Coser coined terms that can help us understand how the various agencies within the intelligence community relate to each other—or perhaps how they do not relate to each other quite so well—and how these organizational dynamics create and reproduce status inequality among the agencies.

In his book *Asylums*, about psychiatric hospitals, Goffman introduced the concept of the total institution—an organization that has 24-7 physical control over its members.[11] In addition to hospitals, we might think of institutions like prison or the military as total institutions; each member is beholden to all the organization's rules and regulations, and upon entering, the institution makes many demands of each member, which has the effect of radically altering that person's behavior. Coser built on Goffman's notion of the total institution to coin the term "greedy institution"—an organization that does not have 24-7 physical control over its members but nonetheless makes many demands, exerts emotional and psychological control, and engenders great loyalty among its participants.[12]

The CIA certainly embodies the greedy institution. Coser states that greedy institutions "seek exclusive and undivided loyalty . . . they attempt to reduce the claims of competing roles . . . and erect strong boundaries between insiders and outsiders so as to hold the insider in close bonds to the community to which he owes total loyalty."[13] The CIA draws that boundary with the very first communication it has with prospective employees and reinforces the line each step of the way before an applicant ever walks through the front door of the headquarters building. Before the agency even makes an offer of employment, the processing paperwork states, "Be discreet about your employment processing. Do not discuss information about your processing or prospects for employment with individuals beyond immediate family." All the onboarding processes happen without ever really getting any information from the agency itself: the nature of the job is unclear, contact people only ever give their first names, and caller ID does not reveal agency phone numbers, so the applicant must remain passive and beholden to the agency's schedule, ready to jump when the agency says to jump. The prospective employee simply must take everything on faith. This is an excellent way for the CIA to engender loyalty. The agency features a self-selecting group of patriotic volunteers, and everything is freely given up front with no guarantees, both of which create a bond with the organization before the first day. In the language of the greedy institution, Coser puts it this way: "Nor are greedy institutions typically marked by external coercion. On the contrary, they tend to rely on voluntary compliance and to evolve means of activating loyalty and commitment. . . . Greedy institutions aim at maximizing assent to their styles of life by appearing highly desirable to the participants."[14]

The ways in which the agency appears "highly desirable to the participants" hardly need elucidation; for most people there is some combination of a sense of patriotism or civic duty mixed with Hollywood's imagery, which, though inaccurate, is essentially the only imagery available to the applicant before the agency makes an offer. At this point the CIA has created great loyalty, and many perceive this clearance process to be head and shoulders above those of the rest of the intelligence community's agencies. Each agency is different in terms of the rigor of the clearance process. Some agencies do not require a polygraph, for instance, or require a less severe form of it. Certainly a sense of pride or camaraderie—some call it smugness—comes with having survived what is understood to be the most difficult onboarding process in the intelligence community.

The acculturation process for new CIA employees quickly socializes them into the CIA identity. By psychologically shadowing employees, effectively limiting relationships with "outsiders," and overwhelming other spheres of life, the CIA creates a strong in-group. The CIA teaches its employees that they are the best and the brightest and that they sit atop the intelligence community hierarchy. It is no surprise, then, that the CIA resisted the post-9/11 organizational restructuring of this hierarchy and the mandate that requires *the* agency to collaborate with other agencies. In fact, all the intelligence agencies, with their own onboarding and socialization processes, may be considered their own in-groups. Creating a strong in-group usually requires the designation of clear out-groups as well, often with accompanying negative sentiments and stereotypes, and these well-institutionalized notions cannot be overcome overnight.

The organizational mechanisms of the greedy institution coupled with the agencies' preexisting status inequality suggest the following: as long as the home agencies remain the primary focus of loyalty, and as long as the CIA sits atop the intelligence hierarchy, the current structure and acculturation processes in the intelligence community may be considered barriers to information sharing and collaboration, even—perhaps especially—when the agencies work together under the same roof. In other words, the very qualities that make the CIA so strong make collaboration with other agencies difficult. These patterns are the opposite of what the 9/11 Commission Report was hoping for when it recommended the creation of NCTC—a place where representatives from the various agencies would work together. The thinking was that the lack of information sharing among agencies was caused by interagency isolation and hostility, so to reverse these trends, putting representatives from these agencies together seemed the logical choice. But the lessons from Goffman and Coser help us see why the organizational dynamics at work make the adoption of this restructuring so difficult.

## Emotion Work

In addition to considering how we can think of intelligence work separately as organizational and procedural, an examination of Arlie Hochschild's notion of emotion work provides a way to weave these two perspectives together. In *The Managed Heart*, Hochschild defines "emotion work" or "emotional labor" as "the management of feeling to create a publicly observable facial and bodily display." Hochschild's work mainly examines service sector jobs in which "the emotional style of offering the service is part of the service itself." She studied flight attendants specifically, but it is easy to see how retail workers, nurses, wait staff, and bank tellers are all expected to "induce or suppress feeling in order to sustain the outward countenance that produces the proper state of mind in others."[15] For example, retail workers cannot let on that they are annoyed or angry when customers are rude to them. Instead, they must continue to smile and be pleasant while serving the customer because the way the service is rendered is part of the service itself. For these types of jobs, emotional labor is a two-step process. First, workers must suppress any "real" feelings of anger they may feel toward the belligerent or rude customer; second, they must conjure the demeanor expected of their job despite the customer's rude behavior in an effort to produce the experience of "good service"—however that is defined in a particular context—in the mind of the customer.

I suggest that emotion work is present in the intelligence community, even though the secretive, hidden-from-view analyst in some ways could not be more different from the bubbly flight attendant or the caring nurse. In service jobs, workers interact directly with the consumers of that service: flight attendants smile directly at the passengers as they deliver beverages. In the intelligence community, however, the analysts interact with the consumers of their intelligence products far less frequently. In fact, it is not uncommon for an analyst to labor over a paper, only to have no knowledge of whether it was impactful or was even read by any consumers. One analyst described it to me this way: "There's a distance between us and the policymakers and even the NCS [National Clandestine Service, now the Directorate of Operations]; am I making an impact? If it is, you kind of have a right to know, it would be nice to know. Otherwise it's a black hole of intelligence. It's like, I spent six months on this paper—what happened to it?"[16] At the same time, analysts may be called on to give briefings on a particular topic on which they are considered "subject matter experts."

It is in these interactions, as well as in the day-to-day interactions with colleagues, that the emotion work of an analyst takes place.

I suggest, however, that emotion work in the intelligence community involves only the first step of the two-step process described previously. Intelligence analysis is highly stressful and chaotic; it also requires analysts to deal with countless types of upsetting knowledge and disturbing images. This is where the first step of emotion work occurs: analysts are expected to suppress their emotive reactions to stress, anxiety, fear, and uncertainty. But instead of inducing an opposing emotive state, analysts' emotion work seems to rest solely with the suppression. Rather than replacing their "real" emotions with the "proper" emotions, they are expected to develop unemotional and almost mechanical personas, essentially turning off their emotions altogether. They must take upsetting experiences in stride, they must hear about terrible events without batting an eye, and they must develop the ability to let the chaotic and unusually stressful quality of daily life slide off their backs. These notions are illustrated by the two highest compliments an analyst can be paid: being called a "machine" or "made of Teflon" by a fellow analyst. We can see echoes of this language in the ways in which other intelligence services describe their work. For instance, practitioners and scholars in the UK talk about "central intelligence machinery" and "machinery of government," though these references seem more to describe the organizational structure of intelligence bureaucracies rather than individual approaches to work.[17] My colleagues also frequently used machine imagery to communicate the idea that their work was urgent or important; I heard analysts say they were "crashing" or "cranking" on a paper, for example. Analysts must therefore develop what might be called a clinical detachment to the work of counterterrorism.

Part of this type of emotion work is managed by the institution, in this case the CIA and NCTC. Hochschild addresses the role of the institution when she writes that "as a farmer puts blinders on his workhorse to guide its vision forward, institutions manage how we feel." In medical schools, for example, the institution can "prearrange what is available to the worker's view" in order to manage the emotions of medical students. When a class is viewing an autopsy, the instructor covers the face, genitals, and hands to depersonalize the body; the instructor uses deft maneuvers to complete the procedures quickly and cleanly; and the body itself is removed as quickly as possible so that only organs remain to be examined. This keeps the students from feeling and showing extreme reactions that might otherwise occur when seeing a human body cut and disassembled, and it teaches them instead to display the clinical interest of a doctor.[18]

In the intelligence community, the institutional process for bringing new members aboard is a useful tool for weeding out applicants who may be unable to handle the stresses of the job and perform the necessary emotion work. If applicants cannot endure the harrowing polygraph exam in a levelheaded manner, they are not likely to fare well in the job itself. Even getting suited up for the polygraph is a thoroughly nerve-wracking experience. Lindsay Moran, a former Directorate of Operations officer, describes the process in her book *Blowing My Cover: My Life as a CIA Spy*:

Like the other polygraphers, Kathy seemed incapable of managing so much as a smile. Wordlessly, she led me to a small windowless room and seated me in a Barcalounger, stationed in front of a desk. Behind the desk was a swivel chair, and a computer whose screen I couldn't see. She handed me a waiver stating that if, during my polygraph, I revealed having committed any serious crimes (such as murder, rape, or any federal offenses), the CIA was required by law to turn that information over to the Department of Justice or the FBI. . . . Kathy had strapped coils around my chest and waist, a blood-pressure gauge around my arm, and nodes around two fingers on each hand. . . . One thing I would come to realize for the first time that morning, and on several occasions later in my career: The prospect of taking a lie-detector test is a surefire cure for constipation.[19]

The CIA builds observation periods into the polygraph to see how the applicant is coping. In my case, for example, the examiner left me alone in the room several times to "consult with supervisors" about my answers. These periods of isolation were sometimes twenty to thirty minutes apiece, and while I never saw a camera, I am certain that I was being watched to see how I reacted to the upsetting line of questioning. Moran had this sense during her polygraph as well: "Meanwhile, I glanced around the room, wondering where the hidden camera must be; we had heard that all of the rooms were equipped with a discreet video-surveillance apparatus so that the testers could observe your behavior while they were out of the room."[20]

Psychological testing is also an effective tool to ensure that only the most even-keeled people are hired. The applicant must answer hundreds of bizarrely worded true-or-false questions, such as "I would rather be a florist than a firefighter" and "I rarely like to torture small animals."[21] These facets of the onboarding process are important for several reasons. Both the polygraph and the psychological testing serve to get the skeletons out of the closet for prospective employees so that they cannot be blackmailed by a foreign government. But from an emotion work perspective, they are also part of the institution's role in ensuring that only the coolest, most sensible people make it to the inside, and these organizational practices go on to inform the processes of social interaction.

The institution also has ways of channeling its employees' focus after they have been hired so that they are constantly on high alert and in crisis mode. Not surprisingly, the most significant event in most counterterrorism analysts' lives was the terrorist attacks of September 11, 2001; both NCTC and CIA place visual reminders of that awful day around the premises so that it always feels recent. As an analyst told me, "Every day is a reminder of those crazy times."[22] At the CIA's Counterterrorism Center, for example, there is supposedly a sign over the entrance that says, "Today is September 12, 2001." When employees walk into NCTC's lobby, they must look at a glass case containing pieces of rubble and grotesquely twisted steel from the World Trade Center. The CIA's hallways contain similar items, such as Osama bin Laden's guns and other artifacts. The idea is to keep the mission at the front of the mind, but from an emotion work perspective, the prevalence of these artifacts also serves to encourage employees to be in "machine" mode all the time.

The institution therefore plays a role in managing the emotions of its workers, but the analysts themselves also reinforce this emotion work through their interactions with each other. Turning off the emotions and remaining stoic, logic, and machine-like are encouraged. Sometimes the analysts jokingly refer to themselves and each other disparagingly as "drones" or "androids," but these jokes actually underscore the point that these qualities are prized. I was always surprised by the nonchalance with which my colleagues could wave off threatening situations, as this excerpt from my field notes illustrates:

> Yesterday I went to Africa Day at Bolling Air Force Base.... Around 10:30am there was an announcement that there was a suspected CBRN [chemical, biological, radioactive, or nuclear] device on the base and we were on lockdown. Later they were like, "It's a HAZMAT [hazardous materials] situation and no one is permitted to enter or leave." I was kind of freaked out. But [my colleague] Sophie said, "Don't worry, the last thing the military wants on its hands is 250 dead bodies. They will protect us!" I was like, that's just great. It turned out to be an anthrax scare. When stuff like that happens, I realize all over again how weird this world is. This stuff doesn't happen at home. When I got back to the office today, everyone was like, "I heard you had a good time at Bolling yesterday!" They just made a big joke out of it like it was no big deal, I think to convince me that it was no big deal....
>
> Today I went out to lunch with some of the REM [Radicalization and Extremist Messages Group, my group at NCTC] girls. On the way back we were stopped at the light where you turn into NCTC, and Rose had left about two car lengths between us and the car in front. I asked her why she didn't pull up, and she looked at me like I was crazy and said, "In case someone starts shooting." Of course. Who *doesn't* think about getting shot at 24/7?[23]

Leaving significant space between one's car and the car ahead is a rather routine precaution people take in response to the 1993 shooting in which Aimal Qazi killed two employees and wounded three others who were waiting at the traffic light to turn into CIA Headquarters. The thinking is that if someone starts shooting, the extra space between cars will allow drivers to escape more quickly. This normalization of risk is part of an analyst's emotion work. Most people would not flourish in such circumstances, but the analysts take it in stride. More than that, they help *each other* take it in stride.

Analysts also use language to perform emotion work. Specifically, I found that my colleagues frequently used language to create emotional distance both from terrorist targets and from fellow analysts—in Hasler's terms, to turn off the "squishier" parts of the brain.[24] In the case of terrorist targets, analysts used language to take away the adversary's power and to dehumanize the target. I heard several examples of language that used rhyme to euphemize certain jobs: "You track 'em, we whack 'em." "Give that guy a warhead to the forehead." "We're gonna work until he's got flies on the eyes." The word "kill" is seldom used to describe terrorist targeting; instead, euphemisms—such as "neutralize," "take out," "counter," "silence," and "smoke"—abound.[25]

The contention that counterterrorism analysts are particularly logical and level-headed is not surprising. Analysis is a product of logical thinking, and so it is not unusual that this profession would attract people who already have a relatively logical disposition. The CIA and its counterparts must be "objective," defined as "expressing or dealing with facts or conditions as perceived *without distortion by personal feelings*, prejudices, or interpretations."[26] The job is to report the facts as the analyst sees them to the policymakers; the job is not to influence or suggest policy, and it is not supposed to change depending on which political party occupies the White House. Indeed, intelligence community employees are not even permitted to display their own political leanings in the workplace; through legislation known as the Hatch Act, employees are forbidden from donating to a partisan political campaign, running for office, or even wearing political buttons. An employee theoretically cannot even drive a car onto the compound if it bears a partisan political bumper sticker. From all angles, analysts must be impartial, logical, and unemotional to the point that their very personalities seem to be suppressed. What is interesting here are the ways in which the institution encourages the suppression of emotion as well as the ways in which that suppression is reinforced through processes of social interaction.

## Future Considerations

Looking ahead, some of the most important sociological questions in intelligence studies concern organizational failure. We need to know more about what makes organizations fail generally, but we also need to know more specifically about how intelligence agencies fail. Diane Vaughan's study on the *Challenger* disaster and Charles Perrow's work on what he calls "normal accidents" provide a solid sociological basis for understanding organizational failure in general.[27] Amy Zegart's work specifically on the organization and effectiveness of American security agencies also makes crucial theoretical and empirical contributions, but as it is situated within political science, the nexus of sociology and national security organizations is still lacking.[28] If secretive organizations are to be understood as a different kind of formal organization, and I think they should be, then they must be studied and understood separately and, in my view, within the discipline of sociology. Sociology is singularly suited to improve our understanding of how these organizations are constructed and reproduced through social interaction every day because it uniquely addresses those kinds of relationships among the social sciences. Sociology can also help us interrogate what is sometimes perceived as the government's knee-jerk reaction to failure: throwing more money, personnel, and bureaucracy at the problem. More may not always be better.

Intelligence research would also benefit from looking more closely at organizational successes. Admittedly this is a more difficult task in intelligence agencies because many of their successes must remain secret, but there are plenty of public successes or partial successes with which to start. It may also be possible to separate content from process: while the specific details of a plot disruption may need to remain secret, the mechanisms may not. We need to know more about the onboarding and acculturation processes of American intelligence agencies other than the CIA as well. As a CIA person working at a CIA-dominated organization, most of what I have been able to show comes from that organization's perspective. We need to know more about how the Federal Bureau of Investigation, the National Security Agency, the Defense Intelligence Agency, and others create strong in-groups (if indeed they do) so that we can learn how successful and unsuccessful dynamics affect information sharing and collaboration down the road. It is important to find out, for instance, how lower-status organizations frame narratives about their place in the status hierarchy, particularly in relation to higher-status organizations. Officers who have worked in more than one agency would be especially important in helping to understand how American agencies do things differently or similarly. We could expand this approach to the international level, too, to explore international mechanisms of information sharing among the US and our allies or even other countries' organizational approaches to their own domestic intelligence.

There are also opportunities to discover whether and how the IC addresses organizational identity and other impediments to effective sharing. My research shows that these impediments are not adequately addressed, especially with regard to organizational incentives, and these findings have both practical and scholarly implications. While the official rhetoric of the IC touts sharing and collaboration as being of primary importance, the officers are still individual people who want to succeed in those individual careers. Like academics, analysts are under pressure to publish their reports via classified outlets such as the President's Daily Brief, and these publications are of paramount importance for getting promoted. Yet the organization does not properly incentivize people to collaborate with each other to produce those publications. In almost all cases it is faster to publish solo. Like journalists, analysts feel a significant amount of time pressure to get the best scoop on a current topic of interest to policymakers. Although the analysts are theoretically all on the same team, they are competing against each other to get the hottest topics published in the most elite classified publications. Unless and until the performance appraisal system is retooled to incentivize group interest as well as individual interest, it is unrealistic to expect employees to do things for which they know they will not be individually rewarded. But we need to know more.

From a sociology perspective, some of the most pressing research programs and questions for intelligence studies center on the ways in which presentation of self, impression management, and misrepresentation may interfere with effective information sharing and collaboration among domestic intelligence agencies as well as among the US intelligence community and foreign intelligence services. Much of the official rhetoric from government leaders since 9/11 has focused on moving from a "need to know" model to a "need to share" approach. But this official rhetoric often clashes with the everyday experiences of the people who do this work, and Goffman's approach can help us see how micro-level interactions can be understood to enhance or inhibit legitimate information sharing. More visibly, we can use dramaturgy to analyze the failed performances of national leaders and their ripple effects across the world. What starts out as losing face owing to a poor execution of a script and a role can lead to uncertainty, volatility, and a lack of confidence in the White House from other world leaders.

This research may be difficult to do, however. Although I obtained written permission from the appropriate offices to conduct my study and my colleagues and interview subjects were on board with my project, I did encounter resistance from other entities at the CIA when I began to write, which delayed my progress significantly and ultimately resulted in my resignation (although I also had other reasons for leaving). I do not know if any other officers have attempted to carry out research there, but my sense is that the agency would be even more resistant to the idea now than they were in 2009, when I got permission. They may be more open to research conducted under the auspices of the CIA's Center for the Study of Intelligence. Some of this depends on political realties—who occupies the White House, our relationships with our allies, whether American interests are attacked in the foreseeable future, the public perception of the intelligence community, and whether the public is generally sympathetic to or suspicious of the CIA. These political realities are variable. For instance, people had an unfavorable view of the agency in the lead-up to and aftermath of the Iraq weapons of mass destruction (WMD) debacle, but public opinion soared immediately after the 2011 killing of Osama bin Laden. Perhaps even less surprisingly, public opinion tends to fracture along political lines. Historically, Democrats have had a less favorable view of the CIA than Republicans have, but as of 2016, that pattern has flipped.[29] I have argued elsewhere that on paper the CIA should prefer having an insider conduct this kind of research as opposed to, say, Congress, but since timing is critical, there is no blanket answer to whether the agency would allow it again.[30] Despite the many challenges, these kinds of empirical findings—and putting them in conversation with theory and other research—demonstrate not only what we can learn from a sociological approach to data collection in intelligence studies but also how sociology can help intelligence agencies better achieve their missions to protect the country.

## Notes

Disclaimer: All statements of fact, opinion, or analysis expressed are those of the author and do not reflect the official positions or views of the CIA or any other US government agency. Nothing in the contents should be construed as asserting or implying US government authentication of information or agency endorsement of the author's views. This material has been reviewed by the CIA to prevent the disclosure of classified information.

1. Max Weber, *Economy and Society* (Berkeley: University of California Press, 1922); Lewis Coser, *Greedy Institutions: Patterns of Undivided Commitment* (New York: Free Press, 1974).
2. Arlie Hochschild, *The Managed Heart: Commercialization of Human Feeling* (Berkeley: University of California Press, 1983); Erving Goffman, *The Presentation of Self in Everyday Life* (New York: Anchor Books, 1959).
3. Rob Johnston, *Analytic Culture in the U.S. Intelligence Community: An Ethnographic Study* (Washington, DC: Central Intelligence Agency Center for the Study of Intelligence, 2005), xiii.
4. National Commission on Terrorist Attacks, *The 9/11 Commission Report: Final Report of the National Commission on Terrorist Attacks upon the United States* (New York: W. W. Norton, 2004), xvi.
5. Dana Priest and William Arkin, "Top Secret America: A Hidden World, Growing beyond Control," *Washington Post*, July 19, 2010, http://projects.washingtonpost.com/top-secret-america/.
6. Johnston, *Analytic Culture*, xiii.
7. Mark Lowenthal, *Intelligence: From Secrets to Policy* (Washington, DC: CQ Press, 2015), 11.
8. Goffman, *Presentation of Self*, 30–34; Erving Goffman, *Strategic Interaction* (Philadelphia: University of Pennsylvania Press, 1967), 1–82.
9. Goffman, *Presentation of Self*, 30–34.
10. Randy Burkett, "An Alternative Framework for Agent Recruitment: From MICE to RASCALS," *Studies in Intelligence* 58, no. 1 (March 2013): 7–17, https://www.cia.gov/library/center-for-the-study-of-intelligence/csi-publications/csi-studies/studies/vol.-57-no.-1-a/vol.-57-no.-1-a-pdfs/Burkett-MICE%20to%20RASCALS.pdf.
11. Erving Goffman, *Asylums: Essays on the Social Situation of Mental Patients and Other Inmates* (New York: Anchor Books, 1961), 4.
12. Coser, *Greedy Institutions*, 4–5.
13. Coser, 4–5.
14. Coser, 6.
15. Hochschild, *Managed Heart*, 5, 7.
16. Bridget Rose Nolan, "Information Sharing and Collaboration in the United States Intelligence Community: An Ethnographic Study of the National Counterterrorism Center" (PhD diss., University of Pennsylvania, 2013), 48.
17. "National Intelligence Machinery," UK government, last modified November 2010, https://www.gov.uk/government/publications/national-intelligence-machinery; Philip Davies, "Intelligence and the Machinery of Government: Conceptualizing the Intelligence Community," *Public Policy and Administration* 25, no. 1 (2010): 29–46, http://journals.sagepub.com/doi/abs/10.1177/0952076709347073.
18. Hochschild, *Managed Heart*, 49–50.
19. Lindsay Moran, *Blowing My Cover: My Life as a CIA Spy* (New York: Berkeley Books, 2005), 15–16.
20. Moran, 9.

21. Moran, 12.
22. Nolan, "Information Sharing," 25.
23. Nolan, 51–52.
24. Susan Hasler, *Intelligence: A Novel of the CIA* (New York: Thomas Dunne Books, 2010), 25.
25. Nolan, "Information Sharing," 52, 53.
26. *Merriam-Webster Online*, s.v. "objective," accessed July 8, 2018, http://www.merriam-webster.com/dictionary/objective (my emphasis).
27. Diane Vaughan, *The Challenger Launch Decision: Risky Technology, Culture, and Deviance at NASA* (Chicago: University of Chicago Press, 1996), 40; Charles Perrow, *Normal Accidents: Living with High-Risk Technologies* (Princeton: Princeton University Press, 1984), 4.
28. Amy Zegart, *Spying Blind: The CIA, the FBI, and the Origins of 9/11* (Princeton, NJ: Princeton University Press, 2007), 1–14.
29. Carrie Dann, "Democrats Now Give the CIA Higher Marks than Republicans Do. That's a Really Big Shift," *NBC News*, January 4, 2017, https://www.nbcnews.com/politics/first-read/democrats-now-give-cia-higher-marks-republicans-do-s-really-n703206.
30. Nolan, "Information Sharing," 6.

# PART III

# Multidisciplinary Perspectives on National Security Intelligence Research

# 6.

# Enhancing Political Science Contributions to American Intelligence Studies

*Stephen Marrin*

Political science—as the study of power, government, and governance—has already contributed much to American intelligence studies through the theories and concepts developed in its respective subfields, but it could contribute much more. Political scientists such as Harry Howe Ransom, Robert Jervis, Richard Betts, Loch Johnson, Amy Zegart, Glenn Hastedt, Joshua Rovner, and many others have made significant contributions to American intelligence studies, or the general understandings of the function of intelligence in the United States. But given the breadth and depth of political science as an academic discipline, there is not a lot of scholarship being produced by political scientists about intelligence, to the point that Amy Zegart has suggested that political scientists are not studying intelligence much at all.[1]

In part, political scientists' limited emphasis on intelligence studies is because most American research universities treat intelligence studies as if it were an experiential field rather than a scholarly one. For the most part, they do not hire intelligence studies scholars as full-time faculty, instead hiring adjuncts (current or former practitioners) to teach intelligence studies courses based more on experience than on theory and scholarship. As an illustration of this dynamic, the American Political Science Association's annual conference has only one or two panels on intelligence studies–related topics, and they struggle for both purchase and attendance. Some research universities even discourage PhD students from focusing on intelligence studies–related topics for their dissertations.

Because political scientists have not yet devoted much time or attention to intelligence studies, there are plenty of opportunities to apply political science concepts to intelligence studies issues in ways that make contributions to the body of knowledge. Concepts from many of the subfields of political science—to include political theory, international relations (IR), and American politics—provide scholars with the opportunity to frame many different kinds of intelligence studies questions and topics in order to develop deeper understandings about intelligence as a function of government. To that end, this chapter provides a conceptual framework that links political science to intelligence studies based on their common focus on power and then addresses the potential contributions that political science can make to intelligence studies in the areas of political theory, IR, and American politics.

## Using Power to Link Political Science to Intelligence Studies

The relationship between political science and intelligence studies can be established based on the correspondence of the key construct in both domains: power. The field of political science defines itself as the study of power, not only the study of politics. In all subfields of political science, the emphasis is on how power is organized and used.

Intelligence primarily enables the application of governmental power of all forms to include military, economic, political, and social. According to one explanation for the purpose of intelligence,

> information or intelligence can enable the application of power with greater efficiency or effectiveness. Properly understood, the role of intelligence is to collect information and analyze it as a way to produce knowledge about a competitor or adversary. The primary benefit of intelligence is that it enables power to be applied with greater precision and with less collateral damage. . . . Despite its simplicity, this explanation provides the rationale for the creation of every intelligence organization and collection operation.[2]

With the purpose of intelligence defined as the knowledge that enables the effective and efficient application of governmental power, putting the intelligence function into a governmental context then requires explaining what the purpose of government is, and that leads directly to political science and specifically to the subfield of political theory.

## Political Theory

One area of political science that can significantly improve our understanding of intelligence as a function of government is political theory. Intelligence is frequently framed along the lines of protecting the security of the state and advancing state interests, but to explain that effectively requires addressing the purposes of the state (to include in terms of power), conceptualizations of state interests and security, and the linkage between intelligence and state purposes.

For example, political scientists could approach the study of intelligence using an approach similar to the political "state of nature." The "state of nature" was an ahistorical construct used by political theorists, such as Thomas Hobbes, John Locke, Jean-Jacques Rousseau, and Immanuel Kant, in the sixteenth to eighteenth centuries to conceptualize different kinds of societies and purposes of government. As

John Owen points out, each of these social contractarians has a different view on the power of the state over society, as developed out of a hypothesized state of nature.[3] Specifically, these political theories allow political scientists to develop a typology that identifies different kinds of governments and the relationships they have with their people, to include monarchies and dictatorships on one end and representative and popular democracies on the other end.

These ideas provide the framework for exploring the implications of different kinds of political theories for the development of intelligence as a function of government. They also introduce the fact that how those in power define "interests," "security," and "threats" establishes the parameters of the roles and responsibilities of the intelligence services.[4] For example, national security can be defined in narrow terms, such as winning wars and military conflicts, or more broadly to include a range of social, political, and economic factors, and this can affect perceptions of the role and function of intelligence organizations. Regardless of how broadly the function of intelligence is operationalized, in this "state of nature," the purpose of intelligence remains the same across space and time: to collect, analyze, and relay to decision-makers the kind of information that would enable them to use their power with greater effectiveness and efficiency.

For example, in terms of intelligence collection, first there were spies. Spies acquired intelligence for the person in charge. Spies existed because there was no other easy way to get the information. Spies could be pure observers—essentially, reconnaissance—who looked out over battlefields to count the number of troops and the weapons possessed. Or they could be more espionage-oriented, to get close to where the information was by infiltrating the adversary's decision-making process and then relaying the information acquired back to whomever they reported to. Closely related to spies was the interception of communications. One side would intercept the letter carriers or messengers of the other side to try to get at the message that was being communicated. As codes were developed in writing, that then led to code breaking. And as communications technology evolved (via the telegraph, telephone, radio, and so on), intelligence collection systems developed in order to find ways to break into those systems, acquire the message, break the code, and read the message. Additional forms of technology also led to additional forms of intelligence collection based on airplanes and dirigibles or blimps. The intelligence collected from these platforms had the potential to provide decision-makers with information or knowledge that allowed them to use their power more effectively and efficiently.

Regarding the relationship between intelligence analysis and policymaking, intelligence services support policymaking by supplementing openly acquired information with secret information collected secretly, analyzing that intelligence with all the other information that is available, and disseminating that analysis to policymakers who—in theory—can use that information to make or implement policy more effectively.[5] In practice, while intelligence analysis can influence policy, because it is a delegated, duplicative, and frequently redundant function, it often has less impact on the most important national security decisions than many would expect.[6]

Much of this kind of content—the understanding of the intelligence function outside historical or national context—has been developed as "intelligence theory."[7] While some efforts have been made to develop intelligence theories that explore and exploit "state of nature"–like approaches to intelligence studies, few bridges have been developed between the political science subfield of political theory, on the one hand, and intelligence studies, on the other. The development of more bridges between political theory and intelligence studies would provide a more solid foundation for understanding the purposes of intelligence in light of existing explanations for government and governance.

## International Relations

A second area of political science that can contribute to intelligence studies is IR. The levels of analysis approach in IR provides a useful frame of reference for emphasizing different roles and functions for intelligence. The basic idea underlying levels of analysis is that events are caused by multiple factors with overlapping influences, and isolating causal forces at different levels of generality will simplify the analysis and provide greater understanding of the forces at play. Kenneth Waltz's *Man, the State, and War* introduced levels of analysis to IR theory by locating the causes of war at the level of the individual, the state, and the system.[8] The level chosen for analysis creates a specific kind of cognitive filter that determines which facts and implications are deemed relevant to study. As Waltz observes, "Our estimates of the causes of war are determined by our presuppositions as much as by the events of the world about us."[9] In a 1961 article, David Singer took Waltz's level of analysis framework and applied it more generally to state behavior and IR.[10]

However, while these categories are useful in thinking through questions of causation, they are not complete in and of themselves. The use of the three levels of analysis construct is not intended to accurately reflect the complexity of causation in IR. The reality is that more than three levels of analysis exist. Other causal factors between the level of the individual and the state and between the level of the state and the system demonstrate that the ordinal ranking system of individual, state, and system is incomplete. Different theories have focused on levels between the individual and the state, including group decision-making and the role of bureaucratic politics and organizational culture, areas that will be returned to in the next chapter.[11] Other theories have located causal importance between the level of the state and that of the system, including transnational actors and global forces, such as ideological and religious belief systems. Although the existence of these additional causal factors demonstrates that the ordinal ranking system is incomplete, this does not affect the utility of the levels of analysis framework for understanding both IR and the role of intelligence at the different levels.

The different levels of analysis are intentionally distinct for analytical purposes, but as Waltz acknowledges—using the term "images" to mean "levels"—real causal forces are interrelated: "The third image describes the framework of world politics, but without the first and second images there can be no knowledge of the forces that determine policy; the first and second images describe the forces in world politics, but without the third image it is impossible to assess their importance or predict their results."[12] Or put more succinctly, Waltz notes that "some combination of our three images, rather than any one of them, may be required for an accurate understanding of IR."[13]

The outcome of interactions between two or more states can be understood, explained, and predicted by addressing—in order—the structural constraints imposed by the distribution of power or prevailing normative views; the domestic issues that have relevance in the interaction, such as ideology or wealth; and finally, the decision-making process within each state, including the preferences and proclivities of individual leaders. Structural theories are best at illuminating the broad strokes of history by focusing on the structural constraints that shape state behavior. State-level theories are best at explaining how states pursue their general interests within these constraints, while individual-level theories are best at explaining why specific policies were chosen over others. The integration of the theories is necessary to provide proper explanation of any particular outcome. In the end each kind of theory illuminates the causal impact of different kinds of variables that affect IR but does so by layering its insights on top of those provided by the others. The value of each theory in explaining international outcomes depends entirely on the question asked and the level of specificity desired in the answer. Rather than pursue a zero-sum competition between theories, a different approach would entail admission of the value of each theoretical school but also—perhaps more important—its limits.

In the intelligence studies context, there have been few efforts to link IR theories at any particular level or all together to the role and function of intelligence. There have been some efforts to address the contributions that intelligence makes to state behavior and its impact on international politics, including Jennifer Sims's theory of intelligence and international politics and Richard Aldrich's review essay on intelligence and international security.[14] For the most part, the limited work in this space provides an opportunity for IR and foreign policy scholars to contribute to intelligence studies.

## Systemic-Level IR Theories

IR theories at the systemic or structural level—realism and constructivism, specifically—will have least to contribute to intelligence studies. Realist theories emphasize power and explain conflict and war, with earlier authors referencing the writings of Thucydides, Machiavelli, and Hobbes to emphasize the persistence of conflict and importance of power, with state "interests defined as power."[15] In that sense realist theories may provide a rationale for the existence of intelligence as a function of government. Later realist theories were more abstract, explaining conflict and war based on rational states with unequal distribution of power operating in an anarchic system and attempting to achieve security to the degree they are able to acquire it.[16]

While the policy implications of realism have been hotly debated, the role of intelligence in this framework has been underdeveloped. There have been few efforts to use systemic-level IR theories to contribute to intelligence studies, with the primary exception being Mark Phythian's exploration of intelligence and structural realism. Phythian suggests a tight connection between intelligence and structural realism in that the latter provides theoretical insights to important intelligence studies questions, such as why intelligence functions are needed and why, "particularly in the case of the US, intelligence agencies did not wither away with the passing of the Cold War." Specifically, Phythian suggests that the need to reduce uncertainty about other states' current and future intentions provides an explanation of the need for intelligence and that "a structural realist perspective also provides an explanation for the centrality of secrecy to intelligence."[17]

By way of contrast, the other kind of structural theory is constructivism, which emphasizes the autonomous impact of ideas, identity, and norms on the behavior of states. Constructivism is structural because it views international society—both practices and interaction—as the independent variable, considering how the norms and identities prevalent within international society constrain and shape the behavior of states. Alexander Wendt specifically argues that a relaxation of the sovereignty norm—which in his view is a social construct—and the resulting evolution of cooperation will provide the means for states to redefine their interests and identities.[18] Constructivism could be used in intelligence studies as a way of explaining how intelligence services help reinforce the sovereignty norm through the concept of "national intelligence" and the self-fulfilling expectation of conflict in the way that intelligence services define their role as the identification of threats to security. As Hamilton Bean observes, when combined with other kinds of critical theories, including critical-cultural theory, feminist theory, and postmodern theory, constructivism can also provide "improved understanding of the interrelationships among discourse, power, structure, and identity" by addressing "(a) how intelligence is used to insulate public officials from accountability and security institutions from democratic control; (b) how national security decision-making becomes centralized in the hands of elites at the expense of congressional and public debate; (c) how intelligence activities interfere with legitimate democratic processes; and (d) how the economic imperatives of intelligence contractors distort public policy and shape understandings of security threats."[19]

For the most part, however, structural theories have relatively limited utility for intelligence studies because of their general and abstract nature. As Kenneth Waltz suggests, "Structures shape and shove; they do not determine the actions of states." Instead, per Waltz, how states respond to structural pressures "is a task for theories about how national governments respond to pressures on them and take advantage of opportunities that may be present."[20] In other words, structural theories have limited explanatory power on their own, and the incorporation of domestic-level variables provides the specificity necessary to determine whether states will abide by structural constraints. Since the intelligence function is part of the "actions of states," state-level theories will have more to contribute to intelligence studies than systemic or structural theories.

## State-Level IR Theories

IR theories at the state level—attributing the behavior of states internationally to forces or characteristics at or within the unit levels—have more to contribute to intelligence studies. There are a variety of different ways to focus on the internal factors that affect state behavior, including but not limited to regime type.[21] Democratic peace theory, for example, is a strand of liberal theory that focuses on the internal political dimensions that affect state behavior. Extrapolating from Immanuel Kant's observation that a world of republics would lead to "perpetual peace," Michael Doyle observes that democracies have not gone to war with each other and then speculates that this is due to the greater difficulty that democracies have in conducting warfare because of open debate, electoral constraints on action, and implicit checks and balances inhibiting aggressive behavior.[22] Yet even with these restrictions, Doyle says that democracies wage war against nondemocracies. The reasons he provides are internal to the state and relate to ideological affinity. Michael Poznansky's recent research observes that democracies will conduct covert war and forcible regime change against other democracies when the latter are not expected to remain well-functioning democracies.[23]

Similar explanations oriented to domestic-level factors, such as regime type, have been developed in the intelligence studies literature, specifically in the Cold War context addressing the intelligence services of communist versus democratic states or in the post–Cold War context focusing on the intelligence services of democracies versus nondemocratic states.[24] For example, regime type could explain why some nondemocracies combine foreign and domestic intelligence services in the same organizations, while democracies tend to separate foreign from domestic intelligence services as a way to protect the privacy and civil liberties of citizens. More research on whether regime type affects the role, responsibility, and actions of intelligence services and other related issues would provide the opportunity for political science to more effectively contribute to intelligence studies.

Another kind of state-level theory addresses the way governments focus on both internal and external policies simultaneously. For example, Stephen David argues that third-world states do not just balance against external power capabilities but instead "omni-balance," or balance against both internal and external threats.[25] In addition, Robert Putnam explores how sequencing can be used to improve positions in both domestic and international interactions simultaneously, by using a staggered negotiation process to acquire greater domestic support at home and then using that heightened support to achieve more at the negotiating table.[26] These theories can help inform intelligence studies by explaining the broad requirements for both internal and external intelligence services to provide information and assessments to help governments achieve their goals against both internal and external threats simultaneously, especially in the context of transnational forces with domestic ramifications such as communism during the Cold War or violent Islamic extremism in a post-9/11 context.

## Individual-Level IR Theories

IR theories at the individual level—which posit that individual decision-makers affect state behavior and that study of individual characteristics and thinking processes can help explain and predict state behavior—have the most to contribute to intelligence studies. This level assumes that the starting point for an assessment of any country is its leaders, for policy does not emerge whole cloth out of a country or its foreign policy process. People occupy positions of power and decide which interests to pursue internationally and which policies might best achieve them. Individual-level theories also focus on psychological processes that confound the rational actor or perfect information assumptions that abound in rational choice and strategic interaction theories. These individual-level theories clash directly with theories that assume states are unitary rational actors operating with perfect information.[27]

Robert Jervis is the most prolific author in this space, spanning both individual-level IR theories and intelligence studies. Jervis focuses on individual cognition and emphasizes ways that "misperceptions" arise through development of concepts shaped by beliefs about one's own domestic system, previous experiences, and international history.[28] Jervis also focuses on the use of analogies and argues that past events influence a leader's current perceptions and lead to biases that shape the interpretation of incoming information in ways inconsistent with a "perfect information" assumption.[29] Misperceptions can arise from overusing historical analogies or from overemphasizing lessons arising from events that were personally salient, were experienced firsthand, occurred early in life, or had important consequences, such as revolutions or wars. These misperceptions can lead to flawed or suboptimal decisions even when information to make better decisions may have existed. Other theorists extend this approach by, for example, explaining poor decision-making by referencing how motivational or emotional distortions and cognitive dissonance can manifest in suboptimal decision-making processes.[30] Again, the focus of these theories is on individual decision-makers and the way their thinking processes can lead to decisions inconsistent with rational actor and perfect information assumptions. In terms of contributions to intelligence studies, Jervis has used this approach quite successfully to explain the causes of intelligence failure, and Keren Yarhi-Milo has extended the discussion of intelligence as shaping policymaker perceptions and misperceptions.[31]

There are both challenges and opportunities at the intersection of intelligence studies and individual-level IR theories. While individual-level theories have the most to contribute to intelligence studies, they are also a challenge to apply because of the requirement for substantial amounts of precise and sometimes intimate information regarding policymaker thinking and decision-making processes. In addition, they are much better at explaining suboptimal decisions with the benefit of hindsight than they are at predicting when distortions—such as those arising from the use of inappropriate analogies—will occur. Yet significant insight can arise when national security decision-making incorporating intelligence is evaluated at the level of the individual decision-maker. For example, Uri Bar-Joseph and Rose McDermott have evaluated the relative success of surprise attacks and the degree to which states recover from such attacks by examining the psychological factors associated with the learning processes of different kinds of national security leaders—to include the effects of personality style, temporal urgency, and emotional priming—in addition to their relative receptivity to intelligence.[32] More research along these lines, focusing on the characteristics of leaders that contribute to the relative success or failure of the integration of intelligence into their decision-making processes, would make a significant contribution to intelligence studies.

At the same time, there is an opportunity for intelligence studies scholars to contribute to the development and testing of individual-level theories. Individual-level data regarding decision-makers and their decision-making processes is utilized frequently in national security policymaking. Intelligence agencies have an advantage in providing this kind of analysis since they have access to more precise information providing greater insight into cognitive and decision-making processes than most other institutions. Intelligence agencies also have leadership analysts who use concepts derived from political psychology—including personal history, biography, personality, and other factors—to assess the effect that the leaders could have on their respective state's behavior. The personal factors are assessed in the context of constraints, including amount of political support or limitations in economic or military capabilities, but in the end the analysis rests on a determination of human agency in driving state behavior. Evaluating declassified intelligence reports that include information about foreign leaders may provide IR scholars with a variety of empirical tests of theoretical presumptions about the degree to which the individual shapes state behavior. It is not a coincidence that some of the more recent contributions made to the IR literature on individual-level theories were developed by former Central Intelligence Agency analysts.[33]

## American Politics

A third area of political science that is applicable to intelligence studies is the subfield of American politics, including national political institutions and processes, the separation of powers between the branches of government and the "invitation to struggle" through checks and balances, the role of Congress in authorizing and overseeing intelligence, and the judicial role in interpreting the constitutionality of intelligence practice. This is the fit of intelligence structures and processes into the frameworks of the American machinery of government. Doing that requires understanding the Constitution as well as how the machinery and operations of the US government have changed since its creation in the late 1700s. It also requires exploring the relationship between secrecy and society in a democracy and the role and function of intelligence services in that context.[34]

In a democracy the intelligence services—as a part of the government—are supposed to serve the interests of "we the people," whereas in nondemocracies they serve the interests of those in power. For the US the purposes of the government can be found in the preamble to the Constitution, which lays out different goals and objectives. Providing for the common defense is one of a number of purposes, but sometimes trying to achieve common defense (or national security) conflicts with other important goals that the government is trying to achieve, including general welfare and the blessings of liberty. People can and do disagree over which goal is more important for particular issues and policies, and that is what leads to political fights over domestic intelligence in general (which comes up against Fourth Amendment provisions against unreasonable searches), exploitation of National Security Agency acquisition of metadata from various communications, enhanced interrogation practices, extraordinary rendition, and others. These controversies open the door to a broader discussion of the various ways in which political science describes and explains oversight and accountability, either through a "check and balance" or through internal executive branch platforms and mechanisms.

Political scientists who use concepts from American politics to explain intelligence as a function of government include Roger Hilsman and Harry Howe Ransom, and later Loch Johnson, Glenn Hastedt, and Amy Zegart.[35] There has also been an effort to use Plato's concept of the ship of state as an extended metaphor to explore the role, responsibility, and function of intelligence services in an American governmental context.[36] But these contributions are on the margins of political science, and there remains ample opportunity for "Americanists" to do more to contribute to intelligence studies.

## Congressional Oversight

One area of intelligence studies in which the American politics subfield of political science could make additional contributions is explaining congressional oversight of intelligence. Congress's role overseeing the intelligence community has increased markedly since the creation of the Senate Select Committee on Intelligence (SSCI) in 1976 and the House Permanent Select Committee on Intelligence (HPSCI) in 1977, following revelations a few years earlier of extensive intelligence abuses. Congress created these committees to provide needed legislation, such as to authorize funding and to strengthen and institutionalize intelligence oversight by "conduct(ing) investigations, audits, and inquiries regarding intelligence activities."[37] SSCI and HPSCI have maintained an active role in oversight and over time have also become so entwined in the operations of the intelligence community that they have become substantial consumers of finished intelligence and originators of reform proposals.[38]

One important question not yet definitively answered is the degree to which congressional oversight of intelligence is shaped by partisan or ideological considerations.

The political science literature on congressional oversight indicates that members will act based on electoral considerations, or in the case of intelligence oversight, the "electoral disconnection."[39] Michael Madigan, counsel to former SSCI member Senator Howard Baker, noted that service on SSCI "has no political benefit. In fact, it is a vast political detriment. The time it takes up. You get no benefits from serving on the intelligence committee. There are no pork-barrel benefits to be obtained and no state issues involved."[40] The HPSCI staff also notes, "Service on HPSCI has more overt drawbacks than attractions: it likely offers no help vis-à-vis the interests of the Members' districts; it detracts time and attention from issues of direct interest to constituents; and there is little Members can say about what they do on HPSCI."[41] This may help explain why congressional overseers have historically been comparatively less active when it comes to intelligence, with conventional political science models of oversight—reactive "fire alarm" and proactive "police patrol"—having less explanatory value.[42]

Controversies periodically erupt providing opportunities for congressional intelligence committee members opposed to intelligence activities to publicly criticize the intelligence community while others defend it. Recent research suggests that intelligence agencies could better and more proactively manage their relations with Congress to help address such circumstances.[43] To explain the performance and decisions of those who serve on the intelligence oversight committees, Frank Smist developed the "institutional oversight" and "investigative oversight" models to differentiate cooperative and adversarial relationships between the committees and their overseen institutions.[44] In addition, HPSCI's 1996 staff study characterized member approaches to oversight by using the terms "adversary" and "advocate."[45] To examine the degree of congressional support or opposition to the intelligence community, Loch Johnson evaluated the extent to which a variety of factors shaped the kinds of questions (hardball versus softball) posed in open hearings from 1975 to 1990 and concluded that ideology and partisanship appear to have the strongest predictive value for hardball questioning.[46]

In the years since, much has changed in terms of partisan engagement with the intelligence community. Therefore, Johnson's assessment of the degree to which ideology or partisanship affects attitudes toward intelligence may no longer apply in the same way.[47] He has updated his analysis by creating a typology of different kinds of intelligence overseers, to include ostriches ("content to bury their heads in the sand and continue the earlier era of trust"), cheerleaders ("supporting intelligence missions with robust funding and encouragement"), lemon suckers (finding "fault with America's attempts to spy on adversaries or overthrow regimes that fail to accommodate US interests"), and guardians ("striking a balance between serving as partners of the intelligence agencies . . . and demanding competence and law-abiding behavior from these agencies").[48] Additional study and examination of congressional oversight of intelligence is where political science research could make both a methodological and substantive contribution to our understanding of the congressional intelligence committees' functioning.

## American Foreign and National Security Policy

It is also possible for the study of American foreign and national security policymaking to contribute more to intelligence studies. In terms of broad understandings of American foreign policy, many theoretical approaches explain what the US government does and why it does it.[49] The role of intelligence collection and analysis in the foreign policy process is to highlight knowledge about adversaries and competitors (both real and potential), their capabilities and intentions, and the operating environment in general.

In political science there is an extended discussion about how groups of individuals—and then organizations—fail to operate in ways consistent with the rational actor model, in the context of perfect information. These approaches could easily be adapted to the study of the use of intelligence in a foreign policy and national security decision-making context.

For example, political scientists could contribute to intelligence studies by further developing explanations for strategic surprises and their impact. For decades they have studied suboptimal decision-making in the context of a particular set of foreign policy outcomes (strategic surprise, specifically, entailing failures of policy omission rather than commission), and this effort then morphed into the "intelligence failure" subfield of intelligence studies. These studies emphasize a variety of historical cases, including Pearl Harbor, the Korean War, the Vietnam War, the Iranian Revolution, the end of the Cold War, the 2001 terrorist attacks, and the Iraq War, extensively relying on counterfactual analysis to evaluate how the negative outcome could have been prevented.[50] This is now one of the more developed areas of the intelligence studies literature, which is full of a wide variety of explanations, interpretations, and perspectives. However, while intelligence studies scholars have explored this issue extensively, it is not well integrated with concepts from political science. More could be done to bring aspects of foreign policy analysis and processes into the study of these kinds of failures.

But it is also possible to evaluate the way in which intelligence intersects with decision-making in organizations more generally. One example here is the classic Graham Allison approach to developing three models of decision-making (rational actor, bureaucratic politics, and organizational process) and using those different models to explain foreign policymaking and, ultimately, state behavior.[51] Using this approach to evaluate the creation of foreign policy also provides an opening to address the role and function of intelligence in this decision-making process, in different ways and at different levels of analysis, to include organizational, behavioral, institutional, small group, and individual. Here the question is: How much does intelligence or intelligence analysis matter in the making and implementation of foreign policy?

Answering this question entails an evaluation of the degree to which intelligence actually affects foreign policy, national security, and the behavior of states. This is a fascinating question in terms of both theory and practice because it is where knowledge meets power, with historical case studies providing the opportunity to explore how and in what ways intelligence matters. Several scholars have approached this question from the perspective of intelligence studies, but political scientists are also exploring this space now too.[52] More judicious exploitation of theories from political science would provide significant added value on these questions related to the intersection of knowledge and power and help us better understand the use—as well as the nonuse—of intelligence in a broader foreign policy and national security decision-making context.

Another area of intelligence studies that political scientists could contribute to is the study of covert action. Covert action is a kind of secret foreign policy intended to retain plausible deniability in terms of US sponsorship and implementation. The intelligence studies literature on covert action is generally well developed but does not incorporate key concepts from political science and IR.[53] This is currently changing, as several researchers are exploring different aspects of covert action from a foreign and national security policy perspective. Examples include research on the impact of covert action on conflict escalation management, the use of covert action as a means of communicating intent and credibility through indirect signals, and examinations of covert action in a critical context.[54] Another important new study found that overt electoral interventions are more effective than covert ones as a foreign policy tool, but that such covert actions do still increase the likelihood of the favored party winning.[55]

## Improving the Role of Political Science in American Intelligence Studies

The disciplinary prism of political science provides valuable concepts and theories for those who desire to understand, explain, and evaluate intelligence as a function of government and will continue to be important for the further development of intelligence studies. Both fields are oriented to power, and there is significant overlap in terms of the kinds of questions asked and the kinds of answers developed.

In addition to the potential value of the political science subfields addressed in this chapter, other subfields also have utility for understanding and explaining intelligence as a function of government. For example, comparative politics could help conceptualize and frame intelligence as a function of government across different kinds of societies, cultures, political systems, and governments.[56] In addition, public administration could address the actual functioning of intelligence as a product, process, organization, and community and the way it intersects with politics and governance. Additionally, policy analysis could be used to put the product of intelligence services into broader policy context, specifically by addressing the challenges—and perhaps impossibility—of fully separating intelligence from politics.

But bringing more political science into intelligence studies will require that research universities in the US treat intelligence studies as both a scholarly discipline and an experiential one. In the US, intelligence studies is not yet integrated into most university political science and public policy programs. Many large universities offer popular and well-attended courses on intelligence at both the undergraduate and graduate levels, and some have developed intelligence programs. But the faculty members who teach these courses are frequently not scholars relying on the accumulated body of knowledge in the intelligence studies field. Instead, they tend to be current or former practitioners teaching about their experiences. As a result, research universities are treating intelligence studies as if the primary value is experience rather than concepts or theories. In addition, PhD students—rather than being encouraged to contribute to intelligence studies as an academic discipline integrated with the theories and concepts of the broader discipline—are in some cases actively discouraged from doing so. Discouraging PhD students from specializing in intelligence topics is a dysfunctional approach that limits the potential scholarship rather than developing it further.

As a result, in the US, intelligence studies remains at the margins of academia, relegated to applied intelligence programs, which are like "intelligence schools" preparing students for jobs as intelligence analysts rather than producing knowledge about intelligence as a function of government. In most of these programs, knowledge about intelligence provides a kind of professional context about intelligence before the students devote more of their attention to mastering practitioner-oriented skills. The result is frequently more like professional preparation than education. Because there are so few academic institutions with intelligence studies scholars on their respective faculties, PhD students who want to study intelligence topics in the US generally choose a committee of advisers who have expertise on subjects that are congruent but not directly overlapping with intelligence studies. This is having the effect of functionally degrading intelligence studies development in the US.

To further develop intelligence studies and integrate it more effectively into political science in the US, American universities should hire more intelligence studies scholars to teach in security-oriented public policy programs, create intelligence studies centers, and provide more opportunities for PhD students to specialize on intelligence topics.[57] Doing this will enable political science to more effectively contribute to our understandings of intelligence as a function of government, improve intelligence policy, and build societal understanding of intelligence more generally.

## Notes

1. Amy Zegart, "Cloaks, Daggers, and Ivory Towers: Why Academics Don't Study US Intelligence," in *Strategic Intelligence*, ed. Loch Johnson (Westport, CT: Praeger, 2007), 21–34; Amy B. Zegart, "Opinion: Universities Must Not Ignore Intelligence Research," *Chronicle of Higher Education* 3 (July 2007), https://www.chronicle.com/article/Opinion-Universities-Must-Not/123365.
2. Stephen Marrin, "Intelligence Analysis Theory: Explaining and Predicting Analytic Responsibilities," *Intelligence and National Security* 22, no. 6 (December 2007): 821–46.
3. John Owen, "Liberalism and Security," in *The International Studies Encyclopedia*, vol. 8, ed. Robert A. Denemark (New York: Wiley-Blackwell, 2010), 4920–39.

4. Marrin, "Intelligence Analysis Theory."
5. Marrin.
6. Stephen Marrin, "Why Strategic Intelligence Analysis Has Limited Influence on American Foreign Policy," *Intelligence and National Security* 32, no. 6 (2017): 725–42.
7. See the following chapters in Peter Gill, Stephen Marrin, and Mark Phythian, eds., *Intelligence Theory: Key Questions and Debates* (London: Routledge, 2009): David Kahn, "An Historical Theory of Intelligence," 4–15; Michael Warner, "Intelligence as Risk Shifting," 16–32; Loch Johnson, "Sketches for a Theory of Strategic Intelligence," 33–53; Jennifer Sims, "Defending Adaptive Realism: Intelligence Theory Comes of Age," 151–65; Peter Gill, "Theories of Intelligence: Where Are We, Where Should We Go, and How Might We Proceed?" 208–26. Also see Michael Warner, "Building a Theory of Intelligence Systems," in *National Intelligence Systems: Current Research and Future Prospects*, ed. Gregory F. Treverton and Wilhelm Agrell (Cambridge: Cambridge University Press, 2009), 11–37.
8. Kenneth Waltz, *Man, the State, and War: A Theoretical Analysis* (New York: Columbia University Press, 1959).
9. Waltz, 224–25.
10. J. David Singer, "The Level-of-Analysis Problem in International Relations," *World Politics* (1961): 77–92.
11. Graham T. Allison, "Conceptual Models and the Cuban Missile Crisis," *American Political Science Review* 63, no. 3 (1969): 689–718; Irving Janis, *Victims of Groupthink* (Boston: Houghton Mifflin, 1972); Irving Janis, *Groupthink: Psychological Studies of Policy Decisions and Fiascoes* (Boston: Houghton Mifflin, 1982); Irving Janis, *Crucial Decisions: Leadership in Policymaking and Crisis Management* (New York: Free Press, 1989).
12. Waltz, *Man, the State, and War*, 238. The first image is the individual level, the second image is the state level, and the third image is the system level.
13. Waltz, 14.
14. Jennifer Sims, "A Theory of Intelligence and International Politics," in Treverton and Agrell, *National Intelligence Systems*, 58–92; Richard Aldrich, "Intelligence and International Security," in *International Studies Encyclopedia*, ed. Robert A. Denemark (Malden, MA: Wiley-Blackwell, 2010), 3824–42.
15. Hans J. Morgenthau, *Politics among Nations*, 5th ed. rev. (New York: Knopf, 1978); E. H. Carr, *The Twenty Years Crisis* (London: Macmillan, 1946).
16. Kenneth Waltz, *Theory of International Politics* (Reading, PA: Addison-Wesley, 1979).
17. Mark Phythian, "Intelligence Theory and Theories of International Relations," in Gill, Marrin, and Phythian, *Intelligence Theory*, 54–72.
18. Alexander Wendt, "Anarchy Is What States Make of It," *International Organization* 46, no. 2 (Spring 1992): 391–425.
19. Hamilton Bean, "Intelligence Theory from the Margins: Questions Ignored and Debates Not Had," *Intelligence and National Security* 33, no. 4 (2018): 527–40. See also James Der Derian, *Antidiplomacy: Spies, Terror, Speed and War* (Cambridge,

MA: Blackwell, 1992); Hamilton Bean, "Rhetorical and Critical/Cultural Intelligence Studies," *Intelligence and National Security* 28, no. 4 (2013): 495–519.
20. Kenneth Waltz, "Structural Realism after the Cold War," *International Security* 25, no. 1 (Summer 2000): 24, 27.
21. Examples of theorists who have attempted to locate the critical causal variable at the level of the state and its internal processes include Andrew Moravcsik, "Taking Preferences Seriously: A Liberal Theory of International Politics," *International Organization* 51, no. 4 (Autumn 1997): 513–55; Matthew Evangelista, "Domestic Structure and International Change," in *New Thinking in International Relations Theory*, ed. Michael Doyle and G. John Ikenberry (Boulder, CO: Westview, 1997); James Fearon, "Domestic Political Audiences and the Escalation of International Disputes," *American Political Science Review* 88, no. 3 (September 1994): 577–92; James Fearon, "Domestic Politics, Foreign Policy, and Theories of International Relations," *Annual Review of Political Science* 1, no. 1 (1998): 289–313; and Stephen David, "Explaining Third World Alignment," *World Politics* 43, no. 2 (1991): 233–56.
22. Michael W. Doyle, "Reflections on the Liberal Peace and Its Critics," *International Security* 19, no. 4 (1995): 180–84.
23. Michael Poznansky, "Stasis or Decay? Reconciling Covert War and the Democratic Peace," *International Studies Quarterly* 59, no. 4 (December 2015): 815–26.
24. Roy Godson, ed., *Comparing Foreign Intelligence: The U.S., the USSR, the U.K. and the Third World* (Washington, DC: Pergamon-Brassey's, 1988); Adda B. Bozeman, *Strategic Intelligence and Statecraft: Selected Essays* (Washington, DC: Brassey's, 1992).
25. David, "Explaining Third World."
26. Robert D. Putnam, "Diplomacy and Domestic Politics: The Logic of Two-Level Games," *International Organization* 42, no. 3 (1988): 427–60.
27. Singer, "Level-of-Analysis Problem," 88–89.
28. Robert Jervis, "A Hypotheses on Misperception," *World Politics* 20, no. 3 (April 1968): 454–79.
29. Robert Jervis, *Perception and Misperception in International Politics* (Princeton, NJ: Princeton University Press, 1976).
30. Richard Ned Lebow, *Between Peace and War* (Baltimore: Johns Hopkins University Press, 1981); Deborah W. Larson, *Origins of Containment: A Psychological Explanation* (Princeton, NJ: Princeton University Press, 1985).
31. Robert Jervis, *Why Intelligence Fails: Lessons from the Iranian Revolution and the Iraq War* (Ithaca, NY: Cornell University Press, 2010); Keren Yarhi-Milo, *Knowing the Adversary: Leaders, Intelligence, and Assessment of Intentions in International Relations* (Princeton, NJ: Princeton University Press, 2014).
32. Uri Bar-Joseph and Rose McDermott, *Intelligence Success and Failure: The Human Factor* (New York: Oxford University Press, 2017).
33. Daniel L. Byman and Kenneth M. Pollack, "Let Us Now Praise Great Men: Bringing the Statesman Back In," *International Security* 25, no. 4 (2001): 107–46.
34. Rhodri Jeffreys-Jones, *The CIA and American Democracy* (New Haven, CT: Yale University Press, 1989); Loch K. Johnson, *America's Secret Power: The CIA in a Democratic*

*Society* (New York: Oxford University Press, 1989); Daniel Patrick Moynihan, *Secrecy: The American Experience* (New Haven, CT: Yale University Press, 1998); Stansfield Turner, *Secrecy and Democracy: The CIA in Transition* (Boston: Houghton Mifflin, 1985); Stansfield Turner, *Burn before Reading: Presidents, CIA Directors, and Secret Intelligence* (New York: Hyperion, 2005).

35. Roger Hilsman, "Intelligence and Policy-Making in Foreign Affairs," *World Politics* 5, no. 2 (1952): 1–45; Loch Johnson, "Harry Howe Ransom and American Intelligence Studies," *Intelligence and National Security* 2, no. 3 (2007): 402–28; Loch Johnson, "Intelligence Shocks, Media Coverage, and Congressional Accountability, 1947–2012," *Journal of Intelligence History* 13, no. 1 (2014): 1–21; Glenn Hastedt, "Public Intelligence: Leaks as Policy Instruments—The Case of the Iraq War," *Intelligence and National Security* 20, no. 3 (September 2005): 419–39; Amy B. Zegart, *Flawed by Design: The Evolution of the CIA, JCS, and NSC* (Stanford, CA: Stanford University Press, 1999).

36. Stephen Marrin, "The United States," in *Routledge Companion to Intelligence Studies*, ed. Robert Dover, Michael Goodman, and Claudia Hillebrand (New York: Routledge, 2014), 145–53.

37. Select Comm. on Intelligence, "Legislative Oversight of Intelligence Activities: The U.S. Experience," S. Rep. No. 103-88 at 14–19 (1994).

38. L. Britt Snider, *Sharing Secrets with Lawmakers: Congress as a User of Intelligence* (Washington, DC: Central Intelligence Agency Center for the Study of Intelligence, February 1997); and Permanent Select Comm. on Intelligence, "IC21: The Intelligence Community in the 21st Century," staff study (1996) (hereafter cited as IC21).

39. David R. Mayhew, *Congress: The Electoral Connection* (New Haven, CT: Yale University Press, 1974); Amy Zegart and Julie Quinn, "Congressional Intelligence Oversight: The Electoral Disconnection," *Intelligence and National Security* 25, no. 6 (December 2010): 744–66.

40. Frank Smist, *Congress Oversees the United States Intelligence Community, 1947–1989* (Knoxville: University of Tennessee Press, 1990), 33.

41. IC21, chap. 15.

42. Matthew McCubbins and Thomas Schwartz, "Congressional Oversight Overlooked: Police Patrols and Fire Alarms," *American Journal of Political Science* 28 (February 1984): 165–79; Joel Aberbach, *Keeping a Watchful Eye: The Politics of Congressional Oversight* (Washington, DC: Brookings Institution, 1990); Joel Aberbach, "Improving Oversight: The Endless Task of Congress," *Society* 40, no. 1 (November/December 2002): 60–63; Zegart and Quinn, "Congressional Intelligence Oversight."

43. Glenn Hastedt, "The CIA and Congressional Oversight: Learning and Forgetting Lessons," *Intelligence and National Security* 32, no. 6 (2017): 710–24.

44. Smist, *Congress Oversees*.

45. IC21.

46. Loch Johnson, "Playing Hardball with the CIA," in *The President, the Congress, and the Making of Foreign Policy*, ed. Paul Peterson (Norman: University of Oklahoma Press, 1994), 49–73.

47. Zegart and Quinn, "Congressional Intelligence Oversight"; Amy Zegart, *Eyes on Spies: Congress and the United States Intelligence Community* (Stanford, CA: Hoover Institution Press, 2011).
48. Loch Johnson, "Ostriches, Cheerleaders, Skeptics, and Guardians: Role Selection by Congressional Intelligence Overseers," *SAIS Review* 28, no. 1 (Winter-Spring 2008): 93–108. Also see Loch Johnson, "The Church Committee Investigation of 1975 and the Evolution of Modern Intelligence Accountability," *Intelligence and National Security* 23, no. 2 (2008): 198–225.
49. G. John Ikenberry, ed., *American Foreign Policy: Theoretical Essays*, 2nd ed. (New York: HarperCollins, 1996).
50. Jervis, *Why Intelligence Fails*; Erik J. Dahl, *Intelligence and Surprise Attack: Failure and Success from Pearl Harbor to 9/11 and Beyond* (Washington, DC: Georgetown University Press, 2013); James J. Wirtz, *Understanding Intelligence Failure: Warning, Response and Deterrence* (New York: Routledge, 2016).
51. Allison, "Conceptual Models." See also Graham Allison and Philip Zelikow, *Essence of Decision: Explaining the Cuban Missile Crisis*, 2nd ed. (New York: Longman, 1999).
52. Robert Jervis, "Why Intelligence and Policymakers Clash," *Political Science Quarterly* 125, no. 2 (2010): 185–204; Stephen Marrin, "The 9/11 Terrorist Attacks: A Failure of Policy Not Strategic Intelligence Analysis," *Intelligence and National Security* 26, no. 2–3 (2011): 182–202; Paul R. Pillar, *Intelligence and U.S. Foreign Policy: Iraq, 9/11, and Misguided Reform* (New York: Columbia University Press, 2011); Joshua Rovner, *Fixing the Facts* (Ithaca, NY: Cornell University Press, 2011); Stephen Marrin, "Why Strategic Intelligence Analysis Has Limited Influence on American Foreign Policy," *Intelligence and National Security* 32, no. 6 (2017): 725–42; Patrick Roberts and Robert Saldin, "Why Presidents Sometimes Do Not Use Intelligence Information," *Political Science Quarterly* 131, no. 4 (2016): 779–802.
53. Gregory F. Treverton, *Covert Action: The Limits of Intervention in the Postwar World* (New York: Basic Books, 1987); Twentieth Century Fund, *The Need to Know: The Report of the Twentieth Century Fund Task Force on Covert Action and American Democracy* (New York: Twentieth Century Fund, 1992); Roy Godson, *Dirty Tricks or Trump Cards: U.S. Covert Action and Counterintelligence* (Washington, DC: Brassey's, 1995); William J. Daugherty, *Executive Secrets: Covert Action and the Presidency* (Lexington: University Press of Kentucky, 2004).
54. Austin Carson and Keren Yarhi-Milo, "Covert Communication: The Intelligibility and Credibility of Signaling in Secret," *Security Studies* 26, no. 1 (2017): 124–56; Oliver Kearns, "State Secrecy, Public Assent, and Representational Practices of U.S. Covert Action," *Critical Studies on Security* 4, no. 3 (2016): 276–90; Austin Carson, "Facing Off and Saving Face: Covert Intervention and Escalation Management in the Korean War," *International Organization* 70, no. 1 (Winter 2016): 103–31.
55. Dov H. Levin, "When the Great Power Gets a Vote: The Effects of Great Power Electoral Interventions on Election Results," *International Studies Quarterly* 60, no. 2 (June 2016): 189–202.

56. Adda Bozeman, "Political Intelligence in Non-Western Societies: Suggestions for Comparative Research," in *Comparing Foreign Intelligence: The U.S., the USSR, the U.K. and the Third World*, ed. Roy Godson (Washington, DC: Pergamon-Brassey's, 1988), 115–55; Adda Bozeman, *Politics and Culture in International History* (Princeton, NJ: Princeton University Press, 1960); Philip H. J. Davies, "Ideas of Intelligence: Divergent National Concepts and Institutions," *Harvard International Review* 14, no. 3 (Fall 2002): 62–66.
57. For more on these recommendations, see Stephen Marrin, "Intelligence Studies Centers: Making Scholarship on Intelligence Analysis Useful," *Intelligence and National Security* 27, no. 3 (2012): 398–422.

# 7.

# Can Decision Science Improve Intelligence Analysis?

*David R. Mandel*

Sherman Kent, the father of modern intelligence analysis, noted that the majority of the most important passages of substantive intelligence are instances of human judgment made under conditions of uncertainty.[1] Few of such passages are based on "cold, hard facts." Not that the facts are absent, but as Kent put it, they lie at the base of a pyramid whose apex is judgment. This disproportion between the two kinds of statements is no accident. It may even be an inevitable feature of intelligence.

Kent hinted as much, noting that judgments in intelligence are necessary because useful information is collected in competitive environments in which capable opponents are sufficiently competent to hide critical information or to deceive others about its true nature. In such cases inferences must typically go beyond the facts. In other cases, when intentions are at issue, the truth may not only be unknown; it may very well be unknowable. Perhaps an adversary's intentions have not even been well formed at the time an analyst is called on to make an assessment. Then, it is vital that the uncertainty of the analyst's judgments be well calibrated, being neither boldly overconfident nor timidly underconfident. Likewise, such cases demand that intelligence assessments be communicated to the decision-maker with clarity and precision and without policy prescription.

Intelligence analysis is thus best viewed as an exercise in expert judgment under uncertainty in which the judgments serve decision-makers who are responsible for acting on high-stakes national security and foreign policy issues. Intelligence analysis is therefore an ideal beneficiary of decision science, if we understand the latter as signifying no more than the intersection of sciences devoted to understanding (a) how people actually judge and decide (i.e., descriptive models or theories), (b) how they ought to judge and decide if they were to fully respect a set of logical constraints or axioms (i.e., normative models or theories), and (c) how their judgments and decisions can be improved, either in general or in specific contexts (i.e., prescriptive models or theories).[2]

Decision science forms a nexus among the social, behavioral, cognitive, and computational sciences. As with other sciences, it is replete with theories, empirical findings, and methods. These facets, like the legs of a tripod, give stability to the scientific enterprise. They work in concert to advance the field and increase the likelihood that its advances are productive. Theories guide experiments and shape research methods. Research findings strengthen theories or prompt revisions or refutations of theories. And advances in research methods open new pathways for important scientific discoveries.[3]

The aims of this chapter are primarily illustrative. The next section contrasts two examples of decision science exploitation from within the intelligence community. I use the examples to illustrate two main points. First, prospects for *hypothesis generation* about effective intelligence methods are better when they are closely tied to relevant scientific findings than when they are less carefully tethered. Second, intelligence professionals leverage decision science for hypothesis generation, but they seldom apply it to the critical step of *hypothesis testing*. The subsequent section forms the chapter's core and illustrates three applications of decision science to problems in intelligence analysis that focus on testing either process or product quality. The examples illustrate a diversity of research methods and areas of practical application. The first example focuses on training of analysts to improve their skill at probabilistic belief revision. The second focuses on the verification and improvement of forecasting accuracy in strategic intelligence. The third example illustrates research efforts to improve the communication of uncertainty to intelligence consumers. I conclude the chapter with reflections on why scientific hypothesis testing is rare in the intelligence community and sketch some avenues for future work.

## Examples of Decision Science Exploitation in Intelligence

There has been some leveraging of decision science in the world of intelligence, and this section will provide two such examples. The first is quite well-known and involves the seminal contributions of Richards Heuer Jr. to elucidating the psychology of intelligence analysis (also the title of his influential book).[4] Heuer drew heavily from psychological research of the 1970s and 1980s on perceptual limitations and cognitive biases. His attention to research on confirmation bias in particular led him to formulate structured analytic techniques (SATs) such as Analysis of Competing Hypotheses (ACH).[5] For our purposes, only a few critical elements of ACH must be mentioned. In particular, the technique requires analysts to externalize their hypotheses and evidence in the form of a matrix in which mutually exclusive hypotheses are listed in columns and pieces of evidence are listed in rows. The analyst is required to consider each piece of evidence separately in relation to each hypothesis, moving across rows. For each cell in a row, the analyst is to decide on the degree to which the evidence is consistent with the hypothesis on a five-level ordinal scale effectively ranging from "highly inconsistent (−2)" to "highly consistent (+2)," with a neutral midpoint. The final key feature is that the plausibility of the alternative hypotheses is gauged by adding up the number of inconsistent scores only (i.e., −1 and −2).

Positive scores indicating consistency are recoded to a value of 0. Thus, the hypothesis that is "least negative" is deemed to be the most plausible, and so forth. The last information-integration feature of ACH reflects the influence of Karl Popper's theory of falsification on Heuer.[6] Popper argued that an idea can be considered "scientific" only if it can be proven false. However, Heuer took this to mean that *only* disconfirmatory evidence should be given weight in hypothesis testing. ACH has become a mainstay of analytic training programs and tradecraft primers, although some evidence suggests that analysts are resistant to using the method.[7]

The second example of leveraging decision science I will mention is one that, by comparison, is barely known. In developing a lexical standard for communicating uncertainty in intelligence assessments, my colleague Alan Barnes first undertook a systematic review of the decision science literature on the interpretation of verbal probabilities, or words of estimative probability (WEPs), as they are often called in the intelligence community. He examined the research findings bearing on how people's interpretations of WEPs such as "unlikely" or "almost certain" map onto numerical probability ranges.[8] A qualitative meta-analysis of those studies (and unpublished studies in the intelligence community) guided his selection of WEPs and their stipulated numerical meanings in the lexical standard he devised and subsequently implemented while serving as a director of a strategic intelligence division in the Canadian government.

These two examples have important similarities. Both involve intelligence practitioners who were not decision scientists but who went outside their areas of expertise to leverage decision research in order to improve intelligence practice. In both cases the *findings* of decision research were central to the leveraging process—more so than decision theories or scientific methods. And critically, in neither case was the method developed subsequently subjected to scientific validation attempts by its originator. In other words, decision science was leveraged in the constructive process of method development (i.e., hypothesis generation) but not in the evaluation of method quality (i.e., hypothesis testing).

The consequence of not scientifically evaluating the effectiveness of a given method, however, differs in severity in the two examples because of their differential reliance on evidence-based methods in the hypothesis-generation process. In the case of Barnes's uncertainty lexicon, the findings of many experiments were used as an evidence base for selecting WEPs and their stipulated meanings expressed as numerical probability equivalents. It is perhaps unsurprising, then, that an experiment I conducted a few years ago revealed that intelligence analysts and university students alike provided numerical best estimates for the WEPs in Barnes's lexicon that, on average, were very close to their stipulated numerical meaning.[9] In only a few cases out of the twenty WEPs in the lexicon were the stipulated numerical equivalents outside the 95 percent confidence interval around the median best estimates provided by participants. Moreover, in those few cases, the WEPs were ones that were infrequently used by analysts in their written intelligence products.

Heuer's development of ACH was undoubtedly inspired by scientific evidence, but ACH did not follow as an almost inevitable result of such evidence, as did

Barnes's lexicon from the body of findings he reviewed. Rather, ACH was more or less Heuer's own innovation. It is perhaps also unsurprising, then, that the effectiveness of ACH remains very much in doubt. Few studies of its effectiveness have been conducted, and those that have offer little support for the technique. Paul Lehner and colleagues found that ACH reduced confirmation bias in a nonexpert sample but that ACH did not mitigate confirmation bias among intelligence analysts.[10] A recent experiment by Mandeep Dhami, Ian Belton, and myself compared the quality of hypothesis testing of intelligence analysts who were trained in ACH and asked to use it in a hypothesis-testing task with that of analysts not trained in ACH (but drawn from the same cohort) and not asked to use any specific SAT. We found that base-rate neglect—the tendency to ignore statistically relevant information about the relative frequency of a hypothesis, such as a 0.1 percent prevalence of a disease in a given population—was more prevalent among analysts who were taught ACH and required to use it than among analysts who were not taught ACH and who were not required to use any SAT.[11]

Aside from such studies, there are also several theoretical reasons to be skeptical of ACH. Rather than a full exposition of these problems, I will briefly focus on one issue—namely, that there is no normative basis for ignoring the confirmatory evidence for alternative hypotheses that ACH advises for analysts, not even within Popper's own writings.[12] Popper was primarily focused on the problem of demarcation between what is and is not science. His focus on falsifiability was directed mainly at tests of universal hypotheses, such as "all swans are white," for which the observation of a single nonwhite swan is sufficient to reject the hypothesis, even if a million white swans had already been observed. Intelligence problems, in contrast, seldom give rise to tests of universal hypotheses. Rather, they usually focus on hypotheses about particular cases. Moreover, they seldom deal with perfectly definitive test data, such as whether a swan is white or not. Thus, slam-dunk instances of disconfirmation that might otherwise warrant an uncontestable basis for hypothesis rejection are few and far between in intelligence analysis. The analysts' subjective assessment of how consistent or inconsistent a piece of evidence is with a given hypothesis is not the kind of disconfirmation the realist Popper had in mind. However, even if intelligence problems were just the sort Popper had in mind, counting up the number of disconfirmatory pieces of evidence (and doubling their value when they are judged to be "highly inconsistent" as opposed to just "inconsistent"), as ACH advises analysts to do, is neither Popperian nor sound. Simply put, no normative theory of hypothesis testing or belief revision supports the kind of evidential bean counting that ACH attempts to formalize.

From the aforementioned examples of knowledge exploitation, some preliminary observations could be made. First, the intelligence community could improve the effectiveness and efficiency of process development by using evidence-based methods that draw on decision science. The commendable example of this approach taken by Barnes remains very much the exception rather than the rule in intelligence. Second, and more important, intelligence organizations could improve both their processes and their products by adopting a self-skeptical, scientific mind-set in which the quality of processes and products are routinely verified using scientific research methods and principles.[13] The aim of this mind-set would be to routinely test which *good* ideas in intelligence work and which *good* ideas in intelligence do not work so that the former could be retained and refined and the latter rejected or revised.[14]

It strikes me as plausible that the urgency of achieving this aim hinges on one's beliefs about the relative likelihood of good ideas succeeding versus failing. If one believes that most good ideas are effective, then routine verification may seem unnecessary. Alternatively, if one believes that most good ideas fail to deliver on their promises, verification becomes central to resource efficiency and effectiveness. A skeptical prior thus guides the skeptic, for whom the opinion that a particular process is good for intelligence practice serves merely as evidence in support of the claim that the process is worth testing scientifically in order to verify its actual effectiveness. For the nonskeptic, however, the same opinion serves a preemptive function, effectively nullifying the requirement for verification by hypothesis testing.

I have encountered this defense many times in discussions of the effectiveness of processes to support intelligence analysis, such as standards designed to promote analytic rigor and SATs like ACH. Proponents will preemptively self-criticize their position by admitting that such techniques are not perfect, yet they are quick to point out that the techniques are still better than unstructured "intuition"—as if the latter claim were uncontroversial.[15] Yet the claim clearly is controversial given that analysts report that they doubt the efficacy of SATs.[16] The frequency with which one encounters this dogmatic belief inside the practitioner sphere suggests that the view of scientific testing as a necessary requirement for sound process and outcome accountability is not firmly entrenched.

Greater contact between intelligence and decision-science communities could help change the belief that a good idea is tantamount to an effective method—provided that intelligence practitioners keep an open mind. This does not mean that experimental methods and conclusions drawn from research findings should not be carefully scrutinized—indeed they should—but the scrutiny should be intellectually sincere and not due to motivated reasoning aimed at derailing the application of scientific methods to the practice of intelligence, just as a policymaker should not reject the veracity of an estimate because it does not agree with a preferred policy stance.[17] In neither case do we benefit from advisers who are cajoled or incentivized to operate in an ideational echo chamber.[18]

## Applications of Decision Science to Intelligence Analysis

### Example 1: Instruction to Improve Analysts' Probabilistic Reasoning

It is widely recognized that intelligence analysts must handle evidence, test hypotheses, and revise their beliefs under conditions of uncertainty.[19] There are alternative ways to represent uncertainty and to reason under uncertainty, but most training programs for intelligence analysts devote little or no serious attention to the matter. Bayesian reasoning represents one normative perspective. In this approach an individual's prior subjective probability that a hypothesis is true is revised using Bayes's rule in light of new probabilistic evidence.[20] Bayes's rule does not ensure that one's beliefs are accurate but rather that they are internally consistent or coherent. Several studies show that individuals can be taught to improve their Bayesian reasoning through instruction, especially when they are taught how to structure evidence in the form of a natural sampling tree or other visualization method in which nested sets of features are made visually explicit.[21]

To examine whether instruction in Bayesian reasoning using natural sampling trees might also be useful for improving intelligence analysts' ability to reason coherently with probabilistic information, I first gave military intelligence analysts enrolled in intelligence training courses a probabilistic reasoning task similar to ones tested in previous studies.[22] In the task, analysts received probabilistic information about the possible group membership of an individual. There were two possible groups, each of which made up half the population (i.e., the groups had equal base rates). Analysts were required to judge the probability of the individual's membership in each group.

After this task I provided in-class instruction to the analysts on how to represent probabilistic information in natural sampling trees and how to extract information from the tree in order to answer questions of the general form, How likely is this hypothesis to be true given the evidence provided?[23] The following problem was used in one variant of the training:

> Imagine that you are an analyst and you suspect that one of your targets (Nargis) might be an insurgent (INS). Nargis has been tested for explosive residue and the test result was positive. Now, you would like to know the probability of his actually being INS given that he tested positive. Assume the following statistics are accurate: 10% of the population in this area is involved with insurgent activity, and 90% of people who are INS test positive on the same test you gave to Nargis. As well, 40% of people who are not INS also test positive for explosive residue. Thus the test is not a 100% accurate diagnostic for INS. It makes an incorrect diagnosis 10% of time for people who are INS and 40% of time for people who are not INS. Now, if you wanted to assess the probability that Nargis is an INS given that he tested positive, how would you go about doing that?

Analysts were first asked to solve the problem on their own, and then they were shown step-by-step how to arrive at a coherent estimate. For example, figure 7.1 shows the final step of the solution to the aforementioned problem. That is, analysts are shown how to represent the statistical information in the original problem description in a nested-set format that makes the application of Bayes's rule fairly intuitive. The equation presented at the bottom of the slide shows analysts how to combine the relevant subsets and captures the short form of Bayes's rule, which reduces the number of mental

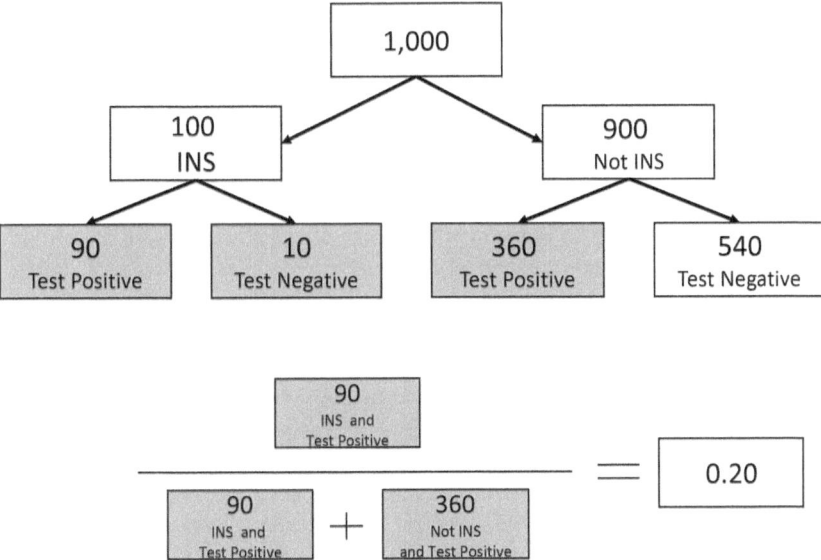

Figure 7.1. Example of instructional material from David Mandel, "Accuracy of Intelligence Forecasts from the Intelligence Consumer's Perspective," *Policy Insights from the Behavioral and Brain Sciences* 2 (2015): 111–20.

steps required to calculate an estimate.[24] The short form equates the probability of the hypothesis ($H$) given the data ($D$) to the conjunctive frequency of the hypothesis and data normalized by the frequency of the data: $P(H|D) = f(H \cap D)/f(D)$.

The instructional phase lasted between twenty and thirty minutes, and then analysts were given a second task that was equal in form and difficulty to the first. The findings showed that on average analysts substantially improved their ability to coherently assess the likelihood of mutually exclusive and exhaustive alternative hypotheses on the basis of probabilistic evidence. Specifically, after training, analysts were more likely to respect an axiom of probability calculus called unitarity (or sometimes called additivity), which requires that the probability of an event and the probability of the complement of the event equal 1. Several studies have shown that people do not respect this axiom in their judgments.[25] For instance, the probability assigned to a terrorist attack occurring in a given location and time frame tends to be much less than the probability assigned to a terrorist attack *not* occurring in the same location and time frame when that value is subtracted from 1.[26]

The same logical error was evident in intelligence analysts' probability judgments. Before instruction, analysts' mean probability estimates of the two mutually exclusive and exhaustive hypotheses summed to 0.91 (i.e., 91 percent). However, after instruction the magnitude of the error was significantly attenuated, and the mean probabilities summed to 0.99 (i.e., 99 percent). The level of consistency between analysts' probability judgments and their binary decisions regarding which category was more likely to represent the target person was also significantly improved after training.

Although it remains to be verified how long these salutary effects persist among analysts given such training, the initial positive results indicate that additional research on the topic is warranted. Moreover, the literature on such training effects offers cause for encouragement given that significant improvements in the coherence of probability judgments following similar brief training in Bayesian reasoning have been reported to persist for as many as five weeks after training (i.e., in the research cited, the longest post-training interval that was examined was five weeks).[27] As well, training that focuses on practical statistical advice for making probabilistic judgments has been linked to improvements in forecasting skill in a recent geopolitical forecasting tournament funded by the Intelligence Advanced Research Projects Activity under the Office of the Director of National Intelligence.[28]

More generally, the aforementioned experiment offers a useful transactional model for developing evidence-based training for analysts. In this model, analysts in training take an active role as participants in testing the effectiveness of the training and can usually be fully debriefed about the research aims, if not the research findings, after they have participated. Thus, they come to learn that their involvement in evidence-based verification of training methods will shape decisions about future training programs. In many instances, a subset of analysts will want to maintain contact with scientists, increasing the likelihood of future partnerships between the intelligence and scientific communities. This model seems to fulfill at least two key tenets of Kent's vision of professionalism in intelligence: promoting intellectual rigor and fostering the systematic use of outside experts.[29]

### Example 2: Verifying and Improving Forecasting Skill in Intelligence

Providing timely, relevant, and accurate forecasts to decision-makers is among the most vital of intelligence assessment functions. Terms like "estimative intelligence" or "anticipatory intelligence" hint at that fact, and intelligence doctrine often makes it explicit.[30] For instance, the North Atlantic Treaty Organization's intelligence doctrine states, "Analysis does more than look at the current situation, it should be predictive and therefore should address what might happen next, based upon alternative assumptions regarding the actions and reactions of different actors (including the impact of any intervention)."[31] Yet the quality of intelligence forecasts is seldom examined in any proactive manner.[32]

Decision science can be of considerable benefit in enabling forecast verification because it is well equipped with quantitative methods for scoring aspects of forecasting skill, theoretical approaches for interpreting the findings, and practical methods for improving forecasts once a forecaster's characteristics are known. These advantages can provide intelligence organizations with sorely lacking outcome-based metrics of quality control. Such metrics may also help buttress the intelligence community from the effects of "accountability ping pong"—reactive measures that overcorrect the last politicized and sensationalized intelligence failure, thus paving the way for flipside errors.[33]

In 2007 Alan Barnes and I began collaborating on a long-term study of the quality of strategic intelligence forecasts made in the Middle East and Africa (MEA) Division of the Intelligence Assessment Secretariat, which provides the Privy Council Office and other senior Government of Canada clients with original, policy-neutral assessments of foreign developments and trends that may affect Canadian interests.[34] At the time Alan directed the MEA Division, and he wanted to keep track of the forecast accuracy of its products. Toward that end—and the ultimate goal of improving analytic processes and products—he implemented procedures that enabled such evaluation. For instance, analysts in his division routinely identified which of their assessments were forecasts and which were not, and they assigned numerical probabilities to forecasts based on the lexicon discussed earlier.[35] For the study we enlisted subject matter experts to code the outcomes of the forecasted events after a suitable period had elapsed. We assessed the interrater reliability of the coders on a subset of forecasts to ensure that there was sufficient agreement in interpreting what actually happened. While the 90 percent rate of agreement observed was not perfect, it was acceptable.

We examined roughly six years of intelligence assessments produced by the MEA Division.[36] We extracted from intelligence products 1,514 forecasts for which numerical probabilities were assigned and the forecasted outcomes either occurred or did not occur. That is, these forecasts excluded the subset composed of murkier cases in which the analyst did not assign a probability term from the lexicon or the forecasted event was described with too much imprecision to be coded with confidence. The excluded cases were about one-third of the sample of forecasts. The exclusion rate is itself informative. Ideally, forecasts should be devoid of vague or ambiguous language so as to be evaluable by a "clairvoyance test," meaning that a clairvoyant able to look into the future would need no additional clarification or details about a forecast to say if something predicted actually came to pass (e.g., "What do you mean by X term?").[37] Whether a particular candidate would be elected in a specific upcoming election would pass the test, whereas whether tensions would rise in the Middle East in the next six months would not.

The two-thirds of the forecast sample that was amenable to quantitative evaluation showed impressive skill characteristics. The accuracy rate—namely, the proportion of cases comprising true positives and true negatives—was 94 percent.[38] A more sensitive measure, the normalized discrimination index, expresses the proportion of variance in the outcome that is explained by the forecasts.[39] This measure showed that roughly 76 percent of the variance in outcomes was explained by the forecasts. The forecasts also exhibited good calibration, although forecasts in general were underconfident. Calibration refers to the degree to which forecasted probabilities are directly proportional to the relative frequency of event occurrence. Thus, forecasts are perfectly calibrated when 0 percent of 0 percent–chance forecasts occur, 10 percent of 10 percent–chance forecasts occur, 90 percent of 90 percent–chance forecasts

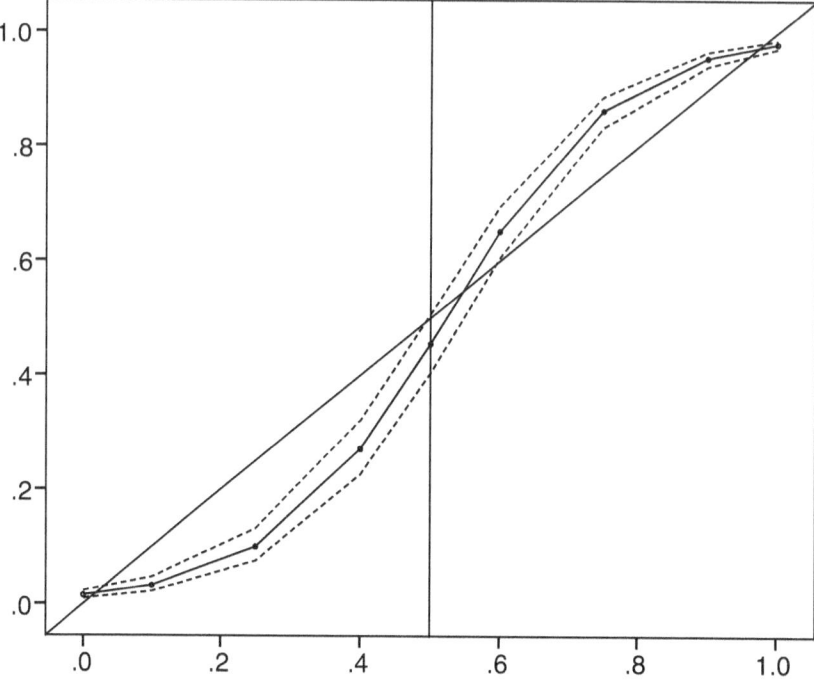

Figure 7.2. Calibration curve plotted from data in David Mandel and Alan Barnes, "Accuracy of Forecasts in Strategic Intelligence," *Proceedings of the National Academy of Sciences* 111, no. 30 (2014): 10984–89.

*Note:* Dotted lines show 95 percent confidence intervals. Triangular regions show zones of underconfidence and quadrilateral regions show zones of overconfidence. The 45° line shows the slope of perfect calibration.

occur, and 100 percent of 100 percent–chance forecasts occur. The calibration curve plotted in figure 7.2 shows that most points along the sigmoid curve fall in the triangular zones of underconfidence (i.e., below the 45° slope for probabilities less than 0.5 and above the 45° slope for probabilities more than 0.5).

It is hopefully clear from the preceding summary of results that the analytic methods of decision science can help intelligence organizations verify many aspects of their judgmental skill. For instance, from the preceding research we know that strategic forecasts are expressed with greater uncertainty than is required given their high degree of accuracy. This was true of forecasts produced by junior and senior analysts in the MEA Division. Moreover, an extension of this research to a larger, more diverse sample, including forecasts that were made using WEPs rather than numerical probabilities, shows that the key findings—good accuracy coupled with underconfidence—replicate.[40]

Such knowledge is important because by knowing the direction and magnitude of bias in intelligence forecasting, steps can be taken to effectively mitigate it. One option is to intervene early. Analysts undergoing training on mind-sets and biases tend to be warned of the perils of confirmation bias, unrealistic optimism, and overconfidence—all biases that seem overtly self-serving—but they are unlikely to be educated about the flipside of these biases and their potential costs.[41] For instance, the CIA's tradecraft primer warns analysts that overconfidence is a common bias in estimating probabilities, but it does not say anything about underconfidence.[42] However, the flipside of overconfidence is underconfidence, and training or tradecraft guidance that focuses on the risk of overconfidence without also educating analysts about the risk of underconfidence might be inadvertently making underconfident analysts even more underconfident.[43] Analysts could be informed that underconfidence has the deleterious effect of making their assessments less informative for intelligence consumers by shrouding them in more uncertainty than is justified.

In conjunction with such training, analysts could be given on-the-job calibration feedback so that they can learn about their skill characteristics and where they may need to make improvements.[44] Calibration feedback involves informing analysts about whether their predictions were correct or incorrect and about the magnitude and direction of the discrepancy between their confidence levels and accuracy rates. Analysts whose confidence levels surpassed their accuracy rates learn that they were overconfident, whereas analysts whose accuracy rates surpassed their confidence levels would learn that they were underconfident. Even more important, analysts might learn about the conditions that make them prone to underconfidence or overconfidence. For example, a well-documented research finding called the hard-easy effect refers to the tendency for people to be overconfident when assessing their performance on difficult problems and underconfident when assessing their performance on easier problems.[45] Calibration feedback could provide analysts with direct insight into the degree to which their confidence levels are insensitive to task difficulty, consistent with the hard-easy effect. Such feedback could provide intelligence organizations with credible estimates of the effect of endemic factors such as time pressure on calibration and accuracy.

The previous recommendations for early intervention target intelligence analysts for improvement. However, intelligence organizations could also target intelligence products directly through late interventions. For example, an organization that observes that its assessments are underconfident could recalibrate the assessments before their release to intelligence consumers. Alan Barnes and I adopted this approach in the forecasting study described earlier. We showed that we could substantially attenuate underconfidence in intelligence forecasts by shifting all probability values to their more extreme adjacent value on the nine-point probability scale used in the MEA Division (leaving only the endpoint and midpoint values of 0, 0.5, and 1 unaltered). Thus, values of 0.1, 0.25, 0.4, 0.6, 0.75, and 0.9 were remapped onto values of 0, 0.1, 0.25, 0.75, 0.9, and 1, respectively.[46] An organization that has credible evidence on its skill profile could invoke similar recalibration procedures to correct known biases before the dissemination of intelligence products to consumers. Recalibration could also be tested at the individual analyst level, with forecasts from underconfident analysts being made more extreme and forecasts from overconfident analysts being made less extreme.

The organizational implementation of recalibration methods such as those just described must be handled with care. Analysts should be notified if their assessments are going to be transformed. They need to know not only why but also how the transformation process works so that they can understand their transformed assessments. Still, some analysts would likely object to any statistical alteration of their assessments, and managers would have to effectively address their concerns. Monitoring to ensure that analysts are not making their assessments even less extreme to compensate for the recalibration process would also need to be conducted. Consumers might also need to be informed, at least partly because they may already intuitively adjust forecasts they receive to correct for what they believe are inherent organizational biases. For instance, if policymakers view an intelligence organization's forecasts as timid, they might already subjectively recalibrate assessments, making them more extreme. For example, if they read "likely" in an assessment, they might interpret it as "very likely," whereas if they read "unlikely," they might interpret it as "very unlikely," and so on.[47]

### *Example 3: Communication of Uncertainty in Intelligence*

The value of intelligence depends not only on the accuracy, coherence, relevance, and timeliness of assessments but also on the fidelity with which those assessments are communicated to intelligence consumers. As Kent surmised long ago, it does little good for the decision-maker if accurate assessments are expressed in fuzzy or misleading language that causes the decision-maker to interpret the assessments in a way that substantially differs from that intended by the analyst.[48] Given that uncertainty in most intelligence is communicated using WEPs, there is ample opportunity for miscommunication, not to mention weaseling out of estimative commitments.

It is unsurprising that analysts prefer to use words rather than numbers. Studies have shown that communicators like to express uncertainties with words even though people receiving communications prefer to have uncertainties expressed numerically.[49] What strikes the receiver as imprecision, vagueness, or ambiguity tends to be regarded as precious wiggle room by the communicator. Interestingly, recent research suggests that the latter perception may be erroneous. In two experiments Sarah Jenkins and colleagues presented probabilistic estimates to participants in one of four formats—numerical (e.g., "20% likelihood"), numerical-verbal (e.g., "20% likelihood [unlikely]"), verbal-numerical (e.g., "unlikely [20% likelihood]"), or verbal (e.g., "unlikely").[50] Participants were then informed that the prediction was erroneous (e.g., for a low probability estimate, the event occurred). On average, participants viewed the numerical estimate as the least incorrect and the verbal estimate as the most incorrect, and the forecaster was viewed as least credible in the verbal probability condition.

Studies also show that people tend to interpret WEPs as corresponding to numerical probability ranges, and those ranges can vary substantially across individuals, especially those who are demographically heterogeneous.[51] Nor does the evidence suggest that expertise working with uncertain estimates immunizes individuals from interpretational disagreements. In one remarkable study, members of the Executive Committee of the Environmental Protection Agency's (EPA) Science Advisory Board provided numerical range estimates of the terms "likely" and "not likely."[52] These were WEPs that the EPA was considering adopting for communicating uncertainty, and hence they had been given some forethought. Nevertheless, the minimum numerical probability associated with "likely" spanned four orders of magnitude, whereas the maximum numerical probability associated with "not likely" spanned five orders of magnitude. The ranges that committee members assigned to these overtly contradictory terms were even found to overlap.

Within the intelligence community, there remains much opposition to quantifying uncertainties with numerical probabilities.[53] Institutional responses to the challenge of communicating uncertainty have instead focused on promulgating WEP lexicons that are intended to standardize the language of uncertainty. Sometimes the WEPs are accompanied by stipulated numerical ranges, which are intended to standardize the meaning of the accepted terms. However, these lexicons are seldom developed using an evidence-based (i.e., scientific) approach.[54]

In a recent study, Emily Ho, David Budescu, Mandeep Dhami, and I applied an evidence-based approach to this topic.[55] We drew on research methods commonly used in decision science to study interpretations of verbal probability phrases.[56] We compared the WEPs used in the US (promulgated by the Office of the Director of National Intelligence through Intelligence Community Directive 203) and in the UK (promulgated by the Ministry of Defence).[57] We collected data from two samples of intelligence analysts. We used one sample to optimize the numerical ranges associated with the terms, and we tested two quantitative procedures for doing so. Then we tested the communication fidelity of the original standards and our evidence-based standards on a second, independent sample of analysts. Communication fidelity was defined as the consistency rate—that is, the proportion of analysts' best numerical probability equivalents for the WEPs that fell within the terms' stipulated ranges.

Figure 7.3 shows the consistency rates for the US and UK lexicons alongside the more favorable of the two evidence-based lexicons we tested.[58] It is evident that both the UK and evidence-based lexicons outperform the US lexicon for extreme probability terms "remote chance" and "almost certainly." For the less-extreme phrases, the US and evidence-based lexicons outperformed the UK lexicon. The average consistency rate across the terms is 53 percent for the US lexicon, 56 percent for the UK lexicon, and 79 percent for the evidence-based method. The evidence-based lexicon therefore substantially increased communication fidelity by optimizing the numerical probability ranges assigned to the WEPs used in the existing lexicons.

Of course, these findings do not imply that evidence-based improvements to current institutional approaches are necessarily optimal. While such approaches are

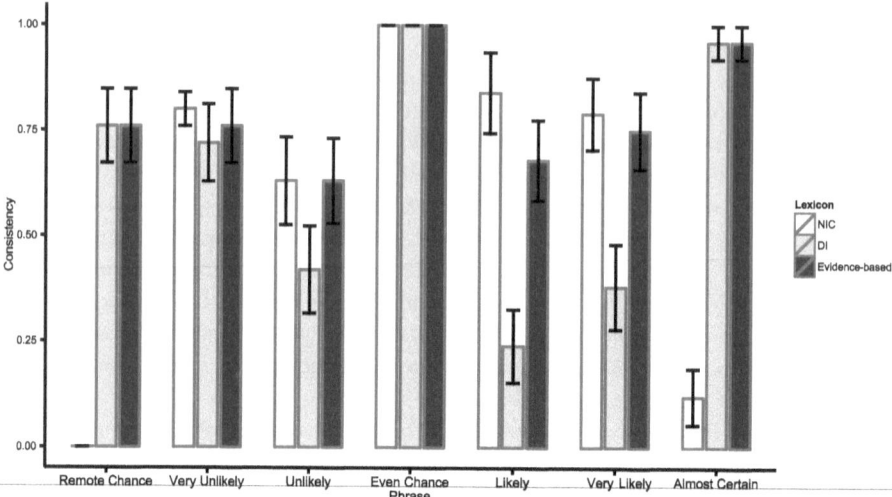

Figure 7.3. Consistency rates of US (NIC = National Intelligence Council), UK (DI = Defence Intelligence), and evidence-based lexicons

*Source:* Adapted from Emily Ho, David Budescu, Mandeep Dhami, and David Mandel, "Improving the Communication of Uncertainty in Climate Science and Intelligence Analysis," *Behavioral Science and Policy* 1, no. 2 (2015): 43–55.

*Note:* Error bars show 95 percent confidence intervals.

surely the best way to make practice better, important limits remain. For instance, even well-crafted lexicons are likely to be out of sight and out of mind when consumers read intelligence products. Some products, such as US National Intelligence Estimates, include an explanatory note that describes the lexicon, but is it likely that consumers keep the stipulated meanings in mind?[59] Research by David Budescu and colleagues suggests that consumers of reports expressing uncertainties using lexicons of WEPs with stipulated numerical ranges lose track of those precise meanings and default to their personal interpretations of the WEPs.[60]

Other research shows that communicators are more apt to use verbal probabilities (i.e., WEPs) than numerical probabilities when their aim is to spin a message to bolster their preferred views rather than to be accurate.[61] WEPs are also susceptible to context effects that alter their meaning. For instance, a range of factors including event base rates, the severity of the events, and event valence influence people's interpretations of verbal probabilities.[62] WEPs, as noted earlier, exhibit substantial variation in interpretation across individuals, especially those who are demographically heterogeneous. Moreover, the interpretation of WEPs is culturally specific; for instance, British and Chinese individuals predictably differ in their interpretations of terms such as "likely" or "unlikely."[63] In short, for several good reasons, intelligence professionals should consider whether their continued dependence on WEPs and their correspondent aversion to numerical probabilities is serving well their community and the decision-makers they support.

## Concluding Remarks: Moving beyond the Goodness Heuristic

The research examples showcased in this chapter illustrate some of the ways in which decision science could be used to verify and improve the quality of intelligence processes and products. I selected these examples in the hope that they suffice to show that decision science offers a variety of empirical and analytical methods for addressing specific challenges in intelligence analysis, and that the application of such methods to practical problems in intelligence analysis can yield new insights into how good current practices are and how they might be improved.[64] It should be equally evident from the preceding discussion that a careful analysis of current practices intended to support expert judgment under conditions of uncertainty—namely, what intelligence analysis is virtually all about—can benefit greatly from knowledge of pertinent theories and findings in decision science. Such knowledge is vital for properly calibrating practitioner beliefs about the efficacy of alternative methods for intelligence.

As I intimated early on in this chapter, the absence of verification of the quality of analytic processes, such as SATs and standards for communicating uncertainties in assessments to decision-makers, through scientific hypothesis testing indicates that support for these practices might itself be poorly calibrated and, more specifically, overconfident. Antiskeptical beliefs in the soundness of methods that have never been scientifically tested reflect what I will call the goodness heuristic, which can be expressed in the following manner: *if, upon mental inspection, an idea seems good, then act on it as if it were good because it probably is good.*

The goodness heuristic is related to Daniel Kahneman's WYSIATI principle, but it is not exactly the same.[65] WYSIATI stands for "what you see is all there is." In other words, when thinking about something, people tend to focus on what they perceive, what they are told about, or what they are consciously aware of, and they give little thought to what is not "seen" in these ways. When we believe that we have thought up a good idea, both the idea and our positive evaluation of it serve as constituent parts of "what we see." The WYSIATI principle implies that at that initial *aha* moment, we will be unduly influenced by these items of "knowledge" and we will not automatically search for unobservable items that might temper our enthusiasm, such as the multitude of reasons why our ostensibly good ideas might nevertheless fail. Following the WYSIATI principle, and regarding some event $x$ (e.g., a method to help analysts reason better), *if what I see about $x$ is good, then I will judge that $x$ probably is good.* The goodness heuristic thus draws from WYSIATI its performative conclusion: *if $x$ probably is good, then I will use $x$ or advocate for its use.*

The goodness heuristic is too frequently allowed to take charge of process-selection decision-making in intelligence. If the intelligence community were to develop a culture of skepticism that insisted on evidence-based verification for proposed methods, it would likely serve as a useful antidote. Given what intelligence is—expert judgment designed to support decision-making in a highly uncertain world—decision science (and more generally, the disciplines it draws from) has an important future role to play in shaping the practice and organization of intelligence.[66] Such a cultural shift in intelligence and its fuller exploitation of decision science could be mutually reinforcing, reflecting a coevolutionary process that accelerates over time. This would most certainly have a professionalizing effect on intelligence analysis, along the lines Kent envisioned.[67] Yet the realization of such a scenario is far from certain. The opportunity exists, but only time will tell how fully it will be realized.

Should it be taken, there are many areas in which important contributions could be made. I have already touched on some, but let me note a few others. One is the *selection* of analysts, which could be improved through research that identifies individual difference predictors of analytic skill. We know, for example, that actively open-minded thinking, a measure of cognitive style, predicts better forecasting skill.[68] A research program could test a wide range of individual difference measures to verify which ones predict important facets of analytic performance—and how strongly the predictive effects are in order to determine which measures are worth considering for inclusion in future selection screening processes.

Decision science could also yield significant benefits for intelligence in *training and education*. This is perhaps the area where an infusion of outside expertise into the intelligence community could be most beneficial. Not only would topics such as "mind-sets and biases" and "confidence and uncertainty" be best taught by genuine experts (namely, by those who research those topics for a living), but decision scientists could introduce relevant topics that are unlikely to even be on the radar as far as curriculum goes. To give one example, twenty-first-century intelligence training should prepare analysts and managers to harness the so-called wisdom of the crowd. Early work on this topic has shown that the average of individual estimates from members of a crowd was often more accurate than the majority of individual estimates.[69] However, research on methods for aggregating human judgments has progressed rapidly in recent years. We know more about the conditions under which aggregation across individuals benefits judgment.[70] We have developed and continue to develop more effective methods for aggregating estimates from multiple individuals.[71] And we have generalized the wisdom-of-the-crowd effect from basic numerical estimation tasks to complex problem-solving tasks that resemble the puzzles if not the mysteries of intelligence.[72]

There are many examples such as this that intelligence organizations should know about and be able to capitalize on in selection, training, and analytic practice. Those organizations that fail to do so will be at a disadvantage in a highly competitive race for actionable knowledge on wide-ranging topics. For these reasons alone, the intelligence community should leverage decision science to its fullest capacity. The community should ensure that decision scientists are enlisted in that effort, and its policymakers should, above all else, keep an open, yet skeptical, mind.

## Notes

Send correspondence to david.mandel@drdc-rddc.gc.ca. I wish to thank Alan Barnes, Stephen Coulthart, and Michael Landon-Murray for their feedback on earlier drafts of this chapter.

1. See, e.g., Sherman Kent, "Estimates and Influence" and "Words of Estimative Probability," both in *Sherman Kent and the Board of National Estimates: Collected Essays*, ed. D. P. Steury (Washington, DC: Center for the Study of Intelligence, 1994), 51–59, 133–46.
2. On these three theoretical perspectives, see David E. Bell, Howard Raiffa, and Amos Tversky, "Descriptive, Normative, and Prescriptive Interactions in Decision Making," in *Decision Making: Descriptive, Normative, and Prescriptive Interactions*, ed. David E. Bell, Howard Raiffa, and Amos Tversky (Cambridge: Cambridge University Press, 1988), 9–32; David Mandel, "On the Meaning and Function of Normative Analysis: Conceptual Blur in the Rationality Debate?" *Behavioral and Brain Sciences* 23, no. 5 (2000): 686–87; Jonathon Baron, "The Point of Normative Models in Judgment and Decision Making," *Frontiers in Psychology*, December 24, 2012, doi:10.3389/fpsyg.2012.00577.
3. Anthony G. Greenwald, "There Is Nothing So Theoretical as a Good Method," *Perspectives on Psychological Science* 7, no. 2 (2012): 99–108.
4. Richards Heuer Jr., *Psychology of Intelligence Analysis* (Washington, DC: Center for the Study of Intelligence, 1999).
5. In addition to *Psychology of Intelligence Analysis*, see Richards Heuer Jr., "Computer-Aided Analysis of Competing Hypotheses," in *Analyzing Intelligence: Origins, Obstacles, and Innovations*, ed. Roger Z. George and James B. Bruce (Washington, DC: Georgetown University Press, 2008), 251–65.
6. See Karl Popper, *The Logic of Scientific Discovery* (New York: Routledge, 2002). Originally published 1935 as *Logik der Forschung* (Vienna: Verlag von Julius Springer).
7. For example, US Government, *A Tradecraft Primer: Structured Analytic Techniques for Improving Intelligence Analysis*, March 2009, https://www.cia.gov/library/center-for-the-study-of-intelligence/csi-publications/books-and-monographs/Tradecraft%20Primer-apr09.pdf. For an example of resistance to SATs, see Stephen Coulthart, "Why Do Analysts Use Structured Analytic Techniques? An In-Depth Study of an American Intelligence Agency," *Intelligence and National Security* 31, no. 7 (2016): 933–48.
8. Alan Barnes, "Making Intelligence Analysis More Intelligent: Using Numeric Probabilities," *Intelligence and National Security* 31, no. 3 (2016): 327–44.
9. David Mandel, "Accuracy of Intelligence Forecasts from the Intelligence Consumer's Perspective," *Policy Insights from the Behavioral and Brain Sciences* 2 (2015): 111–20.
10. Paul Lehner, Leonard Adelman, Brant Cheikes, and M. J. Brown, "Confirmation Bias in Complex Analyses," *IEEE Transactions on Systems, Man, and Cybernetics-Part A: Systems and Humans* 38, no. 3 (2008): 584–92.

11. Preliminary results are reported in Mandeep Dhami, Ian Belton, and David Mandel, "Annex G: Report on SAS-114 Experiment on Analysis of Competing Hypotheses," in *Proceedings of SAS-114 Workshop on Communicating Uncertainty, Assessing Information Quality and Risk, and Using Structured Techniques in Intelligence Analysis*, ed. David Mandel (Brussels: NATO STO, 2018), doi: 10.14339/STO-MP-SAS-114.
12. See Popper, *Logic of Scientific Discovery*.
13. The argument has been made by various sources. For instance, see R. Pool, *Field Evaluation in the Intelligence and Counterintelligence Context: Workshop Summary* (Washington, DC: National Academies Press, 2010); National Research Council, *Intelligence Analysis for Tomorrow: Advances from the Behavioral and Social Sciences* (Washington, DC: National Academies Press, 2011); Mandeep Dhami, David Mandel, Barbara Mellers, and Philip Tetlock, "Improving Intelligence Analysis with Decision Science," *Perspectives on Psychological Science* 106, no. 6 (2015): 753–57.
14. I credit Paul Lehner with this clever framing. See "The Objective Analysis of Analysis," in *Summary Record of the GFF Community of Interest on the Practice and Organization of Intelligence Ottawa Roundtable: What Can the Cognitive and Behavioural Sciences Contribute to Intelligence Analysis? Towards a Collaborative Agenda for the Future*, ed. Anthony Campbell and David Mandel (DRDC Toronto Contractor Report 2010-012, Toronto: DRDC, 2010), 6–7.
15. I put "intuition" in scare quotes since it falsely suggests that analysts are incapable of deliberative reasoning, a proposition that seems highly doubtful to be true.
16. For example, see Coulthart, "Why Do Analysts"; Stephen Artner, Richard Girven, and James Bruce, *Assessing the Value of Structured Analytic Techniques in the U.S. Intelligence Community* (Santa Monica, CA: Rand, 2016).
17. Ziva Kunda, "The Case for Motivated Reasoning," *Psychological Bulletin* 108, no. 3 (1990): 480–98.
18. See Sherman Kent, "Estimates and Influence"; David Mandel and Philip Tetlock, "Debunking the Myth of Value-Neutral Virginity: Toward Truth in Scientific Advertising," *Frontiers in Psychology* 7 (2016): 1–5, doi: 10.3389/fpsyg.2016.00451.
19. For example, see Jack Zlotnick, "Bayes Theorem for Intelligence Analysis," *Studies in Intelligence* 16, no. 2 (Spring 1972): 43–52; David Schum and Jon R. Morris, "Assessing the Competence and Credibility of Human Sources of Intelligence Evidence: Contributions from Law and Probability," *Law, Probability and Risk* 6, no. 1–4 (2007): 247–74; Christopher Karvetski, Kenneth Olson, Donald Gantz, and Glenn Cross, "Structuring and Analyzing Competing Hypotheses with Bayesian Networks for Intelligence Analysis," *EURO Journal on Decision Processes* 1, no. 3–4 (2013): 205–31.
20. David Mandel, "The Psychology of Bayesian Reasoning," *Frontiers in Psychology* 5 (2014): 1–4, doi: 10.3389/fpsyg.2014.01144.
21. Peter Sedlmeier and Gerd Gigerenzer, "Teaching Bayesian Reasoning in Less than Two Hours," *Journal of Experimental Psychology: General* 130, no. 3 (2001): 380–400; Stephanie Kurzenhäuser and Ulrich Hoffrage, "Teaching Bayesian Reasoning: An Evaluation of a Classroom Tutorial for Medical Students," *Medical Teaching* 24,

no. 5 (2002): 516–21; Rachel McCloy, Philip Beaman, Beth Morgan, and Rebecca Speed, "Training Conditional and Cumulative Risk Judgements: The Role of Frequencies, Problem-Structure and Einstellung," *Applied Cognitive Psychology* 21, no. 3 (2007): 325–44.
22. For a detailed report on this research, see David Mandel, "Instruction in Information Structuring Improves Bayesian Judgment in Intelligence Analysts," *Frontiers in Psychology* 6 (2015): 1–12, doi: 10.3389/fpsyg.2015.00387.
23. Instructional materials available at journal.frontiersin.org/article/10.3389/fpsyg.2015.00387/full.
24. For example, Gerd Gigerenzer and Ulrich Hoffrage, "How to Improve Bayesian Reasoning without Instruction: Frequency Formats," *Psychological Review* 102, no. 4 (1995): 684–704; Shahrar Ayal and Ruth Beyth-Marom, "The Effects of Mental Steps and Compatibility on Bayesian Reasoning," *Judgment and Decision Making* 9, no. 3 (2014): 226–42; Mandel, "Psychology of Bayesian Reasoning."
25. See Laura Macchi, Daniel Osherson, and David Krantz, "A Note on Superadditive Probability Judgment," *Psychological Review* 106, no. 1 (1999): 210–14; Gaëlle Villejoubert and David Mandel, "The Inverse Fallacy: An Account of Deviations from Bayes's Theorem and the Additivity Principle," *Memory and Cognition* 30, no. 2 (2002): 171–78; David Mandel, "Violations of Coherence in Subjective Probability: A Representational and Assessment Processes Account," *Cognition* 106, no. 1 (2008): 130–56.
26. David Mandel, "Are Risk Assessments of a Terrorist Attack Coherent?" *Journal of Experimental Psychology: Applied* 11, no. 4 (2005): 277–88.
27. Sedlmeier and Gigerenzer, "Teaching Bayesian Reasoning."
28. Barbara Mellers, Lyle Ungar, Jonathon Baron, Jaime Ramos, Burcu Gurcay, Katrina Fincher, Sydney Scott et al., "Psychological Strategies for Winning a Geopolitical Forecasting Tournament," *Psychological Science* 25, no. (2014): 1106–15.
29. Jack Davis, "Sherman Kent and the Profession of Intelligence Analysis," *The Sherman Kent Center for Intelligence Analysis Occasional Papers* 1, no. 5 (2002): 2–16, http://www.dtic.mil/dtic/tr/fulltext/u2/a526587.pdf.
30. *Canadian Forces Joint Publication (CFJP-2.0): Intelligence* (B-GJ-005-200/FP-001, Ottawa: Department of National Defence, 2011).
31. NATO Standardization Office, *AJP-2.1, Edition B, Version 1: Allied Joint Doctrine for Intelligence Procedures* (Brussels: NATO, 2016), §3.38.
32. Richard Betts, *Enemies of Intelligence: Knowledge and Power in American National Security* (New York: Columbia University Press, 2007); Jeffrey Friedman and Richard Zeckhauser, "Assessing Uncertainty in Intelligence," *Intelligence and National Security* 27, no. 6 (2012): 824–47; Mandel, "Accuracy of Intelligence Forecasts"; Jeffrey Friedman and Richard Zeckhauser, "Why Assessing Estimative Accuracy Is Feasible and Desirable," *Intelligence and National Security* 31, no. 2 (2016): 178–200.
33. Philip Tetlock and Barbara Mellers, "Intelligent Management of Intelligence Agencies: Beyond Accountability Ping-Pong," *American Psychologist* 66, no. 6 (2011):

542–54; also see Loch Johnson, "A Shock Theory of Congressional Accountability for Intelligence," in *Handbook of Intelligence Studies*, ed. Loch Johnson (New York: Routledge, 2007), 343–60.
34. At one time or another, and without effect on the acronym, IAS has also been called the International Assessment Staff.
35. See Barnes, "Making Intelligence."
36. For a detailed report of the results, see David Mandel and Alan Barnes, "Accuracy of Forecasts in Strategic Intelligence," *Proceedings of the National Academy of Sciences* 111, no. 30 (2014): 10984–89.
37. On the "clairvoyance test" in forecasting, see Philip Tetlock, *Expert Political Judgment: How Good Is It? How Can We Know?* (Princeton, NJ: Princeton University Press, 2017), 13.
38. True positives are defined as forecasts greater than 0.5 in which the event occurred, and true negatives are defined as forecasts less than 0.5 in which the event did not occur.
39. Ilan Yaniv, Frank Yates, and Keith Smith, "Measures of Discrimination Skill in Probabilistic Judgment," *Psychological Bulletin* 110, no. 3 (1991): 611–17.
40. David Mandel and Alan Barnes, "Geopolitical Forecasting Skill in Strategic Intelligence," *Journal of Behavioral Decision Making* 31, no. 1 (2018): 127–37.
41. Welton Chang and Philip Tetlock, "Rethinking the Training of Intelligence Analysts," *Intelligence and National Security* 31, no. 6 (2016): 903–20.
42. US Government, *Tradecraft Primer*.
43. Welton Chang, Elissabeth Berdini, David Mandel, and Philip Tetlock, "Restructuring Structured Analytic Techniques in Intelligence Analysis," *Intelligence and National Security* 33, no. 3 (2017): 337–56, doi: 10.1080/02684527.2017.1400230.
44. Steven Rieber, "Intelligence Analysis and Judgmental Calibration," *International Journal of Intelligence and CounterIntelligence* 17, no. 1 (2004): 97–112; see "Recommendation 2," in National Research Council, *Intelligence Analysis for Tomorrow: Advances from the Behavioral and Social Sciences* (Washington, DC: National Academies Press, 2011), 86.
45. Sarah Lichtenstein and Baruch Fischhoff, "Do Those Who Know More Also Know More about How Much They Know?" *Organizational Behavior and Human Performance* 20, no. 2 (1977): 159–83.
46. Mandel and Barnes, "Accuracy of Forecasts."
47. Yaron Shlomi and Thomas Wallsten, "Subjective Recalibration of Advisors' Probability Estimates," *Psychonomic Bulletin and Review* 17, no. 4 (2010): 492–98.
48. Kent, "Words of Estimative Probability."
49. Allan Murphy, Sarah Lichtenstein, Baruch Fischhoff, and Robert Winkler, "Misinterpretation of Precipitation Probability Forecasts," *Bulletin of the American Meteorological Society* 61, no. 7 (1980): 695–701; Wibecke Brun and Karl Teigen, "Verbal Probabilities: Ambiguous, Context-Dependent, or Both?" *Organizational Behavior and Human Decision Processes* 41, no. 3 (1988): 390–404; Thomas Wallsten, David

Budescu, and Rami Zwick, "Preferences and Reasons for Communicating Probabilistic Information in Numeric or Verbal Terms," *Bulletin of the Psychonomic Society* 31, no. 2 (1993): 135–38.

50. Sarah Jenkins, A. J. Harris, and R. M. Lark, "When Unlikely Outcomes Occur: The Role of Communication Format in Maintaining Communicator Credibility," *Journal of Risk Research* (in press) doi:10.1080/13669877.2018.1440415.

51. For a review, see Thomas Wallsten and David Budescu, "A Review of Human Linguistic Probability Processing: General Principles and Empirical Evidence," *Knowledge Engineering Review* 10, no. 1 (1995): 43–62. On effects of demographic heterogeneity, see Valerie Clarke, Coral Ruffin, and David Hill, "Ratings of Orally Presented Verbal Expressions of Probability by a Heterogeneous Sample," *Journal of Applied Social Psychology* 22, no. 8 (1992): 638–56.

52. Granger Morgan, "Commentary: Uncertainty Analysis in Risk Assessment," *Human and Ecological Risk Assessment* 4, no. 1 (1998): 25–39.

53. James Marchio, "'If the Weatherman Can . . . ': The Intelligence Community's Struggle to Express Analytic Uncertainty in the 1970s," *Studies in Intelligence* 58, no. 4 (2014): 31–42; Karl Spielmann, "I Got Algorithm: Can There Be a Nate Silver in Intelligence?" *International Journal of Intelligence and CounterIntelligence* 29, no. 3 (2016): 525–44.

54. As noted earlier, the lexicon developed by Barnes provides an exception. Although I cannot rule out the possibility that some uncertainty lexicons have been developed with a scientific (i.e., evidence-based) approach, in my role as chairman of the NATO Technical Team on Assessment and Communication of Uncertainty in Intelligence to Support Decision-Making (SAS-114), I—along with my team—have spoken to many individuals involved in standards development, but these discussions have not revealed instances that would qualify as evidence-based.

55. Emily Ho, David Budescu, Mandeep Dhami, and David Mandel, "Improving the Communication of Uncertainty in Climate Science and Intelligence Analysis," *Behavioral Science and Policy* 1, no. 2 (2015): 43–55.

56. For example, David Budescu, Tzur Karelitz, and Thomas Wallsten, "Predicting the Directionality of Probability Phrases from Their Membership Functions," *Journal of Behavioral Decision Making* 16, no. 3 (2003): 159–80.

57. Office of the Director of National Intelligence, *Intelligence Community Directive 203: Analytic Standards*, January 2, 2015, https://www.dni.gov/files/documents/ICD/ICD%20203%20Analytic%20Standards.pdf.

58. More specifically, the more favorable evidence-based lexicon used a membership function method; see Thomas Wallsten, David Budescu, Amnon Rapoport, Rami Zwick, and Barbara Forsyth, "Measuring the Vague Meaning of Probability Terms," *Journal of Experimental Psychology: General* 115, no. 4 (1986): 348–65.

59. Kristan Wheaton, "The Revolution Begins on Page Five: The Changing Nature of NIEs," *International Journal of Intelligence and CounterIntelligence* 25, no. 2 (2012): 330–49.

60. For instance, see David Budescu, Han-Hui Por, and Stephen Broomell, "Effective Communication of Uncertainty in the IPCC reports," *Climatic Change* 113, no. 2 (2012): 181–200; David Budescu, Han-Hui Por, Stephen Broomell, and Michael Smithson, "The Interpretation of IPCC Probabilistic Statements around the World," *Nature Climate Change* 4, no. 6 (2014): 508–12.
61. David Piercey, "Motivated Reasoning and Verbal vs. Numerical Probability Assessment: Evidence from an Accounting Context," *Organizational Behavior and Human Decision Processes* 108, no. 2 (2009): 330–41.
62. Thomas Wallsten, Samuel Fillenbaum, and James Cox, "Base Rate Effects on the Interpretations of Probability and Frequency Expressions," *Journal of Memory and Language* 25, no. 5 (1986): 571–87; Elke Weber and Denis Hilton, "Contextual Effects in the Interpretations of Probability Words: Perceived Base Rate and Severity of Events," *Journal of Experimental Psychology: Human Perception and Performance* 16, no. 4 (1990): 781–89; Adam Harris and Adam Corner, "Communicating Environmental Risks: Clarifying the Severity Effect in Interpretations of Verbal Probability Expressions," *Journal of Experimental Psychology: Learning, Memory, and Cognition* 37, no. 6 (2011): 1571–78; Mandel, "Accuracy of Intelligence Forecasts."
63. Adam Harris, Adam Corner, Juemin Xu, and Xiufang Du, "Lost in Translation? Interpretations of the Probability Phrases Used by the Intergovernmental Panel on Climate Change in China and the UK," *Climatic Change* 121, no. 2 (2013): 415–25.
64. Other examples can be found in Baruch Fischhoff and Cherie Chauvin, eds., *Intelligence Analysis: Behavioral and Social Scientific Foundations* (Washington, DC: National Academies Press, 2011); Dhami et al., "Improving Intelligence Analysis."
65. Daniel Kahneman, *Thinking, Fast and Slow* (New York: Farrar, Straus and Giroux, 2011).
66. Campbell and Mandel, *Summary Record*.
67. Davis, "Sherman Kent."
68. For example, see Barbara Mellers, Eric Stone, Pavel Atanasov, Nick Rohrbaugh, S. Emlen Metz, Lyle Ungar, Michael M. Bishop, Michael Horowitz, Ed Merkle, and Philip Tetlock, "The Psychology of Intelligence Analysis: Drivers of Prediction Accuracy in World Politics," *Journal of Experimental Psychology: Applied* 21, no. 1 (2015): 1–14; Tetlock, *Expert Political Judgment*.
69. For an overview, see James Surowiecki, *The Wisdom of Crowds* (New York: W. W. Norton, 2004).
70. For example, Clintin Davis-Stober, David V. Budescu, Jason Dana, and Stephen B. Broomell, "When Is a Crowd Wise?" *Decision* 1, no. 2 (2014): 79–101; Joshua Becker, Devon Brackbill, and Damon Centola, "Network Dynamics of Social Influence in the Wisdom of Crowds," *Proceedings of the National Academy of Sciences of the United States of America* 114, no. 26 (2017): E5070–E5076.
71. For examples of such work funded by IARPA, see Christopher Karvetski, Kenneth C. Olson, David R. Mandel, and Charles R. Twardy, "Probabilistic Coherence

Weighting for Optimizing Expert Forecasts," *Decision Analysis* 10, no. 4 (2013): 305–26; Eva Chen, David V. Budescu, Shrinidhi K. Lakshmikanth, Barbara A. Mellers, and Philip E. Tetlock, "Validating the Contribution-Weighted Model: Robustness and Cost-Benefit Analyses," *Decision Analysis* 13, no. 2 (2016): 128–52.

72. Michael Yi, Mark Steyvers, Michael D. Lee, and Matthew J. Dry, "The Wisdom of the Crowd in Combinatorial Problems," *Cognitive Science* 36, no. 3 (2012): 452–70.

# 8.

# Charting a Research Agenda for Intelligence Studies Using Public Administration and Organization Theory Scholarship

*Rick Caceres-Rodriguez and
Michael Landon-Murray*

Researchers of public sector organizations, broadly speaking, study the multifaceted functioning of executive agencies. This includes examining the many ways agencies execute law and public policy (and the outcomes of those efforts), the specific mechanisms through which they accomplish their diverse missions, and the way they navigate the complex, political environments in which they operate. This entails many areas of research, as public agencies and administrators do many, many things. They turn legislation, at times intentionally vague, into implementable rules, regulations, practices, and public programs. They manage public policy, programs, and organizations, whether concerning environmental protection, transportation infrastructure, or intelligence. Simply said, public administrators are involved in virtually every phase of the policy process, from formulation to implementation to evaluation. These varied roles have critical inputs of their own, including human capital, financial management, and tools for effective policy analysis and program evaluation. And given their varied roles and extensive responsibilities, public administrators have important relationships with a range of stakeholders. Among them are the competing political institutions overseeing bureaucratic action, the private and nonprofit organizations that often implement public programs, and the public and other constituencies encountered in rule-making and program administration.

In an environment of resource constraints, growing intergovernmental and interorganizational complexity, and unruly partisan politics (perhaps better described as tribal politics), the varied tasks of public agencies and bureaucrats are exceedingly challenging and often thankless. The electorate and elected officials ask much of public agencies (in the case of the latter, often to avoid making hard decisions themselves) yet frequently deride the "unelected bureaucrats" who are by and large very specialized and professional. And while at times a source of frustration, bureaucratic "red tape" exists to ensure fair and equitable governmental action, and deviations from such policies can create as many problems as benefits. Balancing values of equity and efficiency is among the many perennial challenges of public administration.

As public sector organizations, intelligence agencies encounter, or are embedded in, many of the same systems, functions, and issues as their overt counterparts: accountability, performance measurement and management, job motivation and satisfaction, contracting and outsourcing, and increasingly, intergovernmental relations, to name a few. Michael Herman has made the simple but profound observation that "intelligence is bound to be influenced by the public administration setting in which it operates."[1] Likewise, Philip H. J. Davies has noted that "how an activity is organized says a great deal about that activity, about how it is conceptualized and how it is undertaken by its participants."[2] Thus, holistically understanding intelligence priorities, processes, and practices cannot be done in a manner disconnected from administrative and organizational settings.

Public administration (PA), and the interrelated field of organization theory, which much PA scholarship is built on, have large, diverse, and rich literatures. Applications of organization theory, like communication science, span several domains, including the private sector and multiple academic disciplines. The field is animated by many topics, among them, the emergence, evolution, and survival of organizations, the impact of organizational design and practice on performance, and the interaction of organizations with their external environment. Intelligence scholars and practitioners can thus learn much from these fields, even when they are not expressly focused on intelligence, and can borrow many questions to more deeply explore the structure, process, and practice of intelligence organizations. On the practitioner side, empirical insights from these fields will help in better understanding not only home organizational contexts but also the organizational contexts of the entities and actors intelligence agencies assess. Likewise, PA scholarship will also benefit from the wider span of organizations closely studied.

This chapter starts with a brief survey of the contemporary place of PA and organization theory in the intelligence studies literature. This section also demonstrates broader connections between intelligence and PA, which will help further elaborate the relationship and application of PA theory to intelligence studies. We then delve more deeply into several specific areas of PA and organization theory—strategic human resources management, performance management and measurement, representative bureaucracy, environmental scanning, and institutional isomorphism—that connect to and build on the existing research on intelligence management, performance, and change. These areas relate not only to intraorganizational dynamics but also to the way organizations relate to their external environments. This section demonstrates how current research topics in intelligence studies can be extended and enhanced by looking more broadly—and deeply—to the study of public sector organizations.

Our chapter by no means offers an exhaustive list or review of applicable PA and organization theory and research, which would be virtually impossible given their inherent connections to intelligence studies. However, it does serve as a bridge from where we are now in intelligence studies to where we might go, concluding with the charting of such a course, theoretically, empirically, and practically.

## An Overview of Contemporary Literature in Intelligence Administration and Organization

Writing in 2010 as guest editor of a special issue of the journal *Public Policy and Administration*, Philip H. J. Davies observed, "Apart from a handful of studies, no systematic effort has yet been made either to incorporate intelligence into the collective knowledge base of public administration as a sub-discipline, or to incorporate the insights of public administration into the study of intelligence either."[3] Earlier Davies had made another central contribution to the field in a book that closely examined the historical and organizational development of the British Secret Intelligence Service (MI6).[4] Davies has thus been at the forefront in this area, and Amy Zegart and Michael Herman are also among those who have provided leadership and attention in stressing the organizational and managerial dimensions of intelligence.

Overall, and to borrow from Sherman Kent's early and seminal framework, intelligence scholars certainly seem to have favored intelligence as "knowledge" and "activity" more than intelligence as "organization."[5] Recent reviews of some of the key journals in intelligence studies support assertions that organizational and management studies are given rather minimal treatment. Looking at the *International Journal of Intelligence and Counterintelligence* (*IJIC*) and *Studies in Intelligence*, one study found that only 6 percent of the intelligence studies literature is chiefly focused on organizational analysis.[6] A similar study, this time of *IJIC* and *Intelligence and National Security*, did not find administrative facets to rate as a primary category.[7]

When compared to that of similar fields, the intelligence studies literature is certainly more practical and practitioner-oriented, generally intended to improve policy and practice.[8] In turn, it has been characterized as "theoretically thin," with intelligence scholars often not looking to their field's own intellectual and research history.[9] This suggests that consistently looking to other fields is even less likely—something this volume will go a long way in addressing. However, the observation has also been made that public administration as an academic discipline can be intellectually detached from the world of practitioners it is meant to serve and has become too focused on quantitative studies at the expense of the rich, contextual understandings afforded by case studies.[10] And to be sure, public administration may not always deeply address key issues for intelligence organizations, including "how to design large-scale organizations whose primary task is to collect and assess information."[11] And given the information-centric nature of intelligence organizations, success and performance are largely functions of how information is organized and managed.[12]

The study of organizational dynamics in contemporary intelligence has often focused on arrangements and cultures that impede effective intelligence sharing, collaboration, and analysis. In addition to the US, many other nations have taken measures in recent years to restructure and better integrate their intelligence agencies and overcome issues relating to collaboration and information sharing.[13] Of course, structural adjustments to intelligence communities are not new (for example, organizing offices along regional or functional lines), though recent changes in the US are perhaps more far-reaching. Such efforts inevitably encounter trade-offs and unintended consequences, for example, as more centrally directed intelligence communities may enhance efficiency but diminish coverage and duplication (potentially increasing the possibility that something is missed).[14] Decentralization may help address such concerns but also complicates coordination and can increase interorganizational rivalries and competition. However, diversity and competition can also compel innovation.[15] A leading challenge for intelligence practitioners and scholars is identifying how the benefits of both centralization and decentralization can be realized, and the benefits of dynamic intelligence organization have been noted.[16] Issues can also emerge when different functions are housed in the same organization (for example, law enforcement and intelligence, as in the Federal Bureau of Investigation [FBI], as well as intelligence and covert action, as in the Central Intelligence Agency [CIA]). As former CIA official James E. Steiner observed, "Organizations tend to excel at only one function."[17]

In the US, the intelligence community (IC) is on the rather large and complex end of the spectrum, and despite the establishment of the director of national intelligence (DNI), interagency cooperation and direction remain tremendous challenges. This is in no small part because a preponderance of US intelligence sits in the Pentagon and the budgetary role of the DNI remains constrained. Further, and like the previous position of director of central intelligence, the DNI does not appoint intelligence leadership in other agencies, is also responsible for overseeing an entire agency, and must balance an IC coordinating role with that of chief intelligence adviser to the president. Thus, the structural and practical impediments are rather daunting, demonstrating perennial and modern challenges to efficient, effective intelligence management.

Thomas H. Hammond concluded, "What allows these debates to continue after so many decades is the fact that most of the key issues remain unresolved, both theoretically and empirically. The problem is that policymakers and legislators simply do not know how to identify the most appropriate structure for the Intelligence Community."[18] Richard Betts reminds us that there will always be limits in looking to structural fixes to intelligence problems and that such changes can be expected to introduce new issues and challenges.[19] This is especially so since predicting future threats and needs is never easy.[20]

Similarly, Hamilton Bean observes that US intelligence reformers have placed great faith in the ability to bolster intelligence performance through efforts to redirect and shape organizational culture, despite scholarly concern that such hopes are largely without empirical merit.[21] The successful imposition of intelligence culture from an outside source is certainly very challenging, and intelligence management cultures can vary drastically from one nation or agency to another.[22] And just as the dispositions of intelligence analysts can vary from policymakers and law enforcement officers, analysts and those in intelligence leadership positions can also exhibit rather different orientations.[23] Speaking to research on intelligence culture, Bean adds that available studies "tend to leave the theoretical and empirical interconnections and interdeterminancies between individuals, systems, and cultures largely unelaborated."[24]

Nonetheless, "although good structure is not a cure-all, bad structure can have devastating effects on organizational performance."[25] In examining the organizational factors contributing to the intelligence failures related to the terrorist attacks of September 11, 2001, with a focus on the FBI and CIA, Zegart highlighted structural fragmentation, including informational and operational silos (both within and between intelligence agencies), poorly devised incentives, antiquated technology (in fact an aversion to technology), and other counterproductive organizational pathologies.[26] Much of this was residual from Cold War and law enforcement orientations and a failure to adapt intelligence organizations, creating organizational gaps that made the collective tracking and prevention of terrorist activity exceedingly challenging. Myriad reforms followed from the events of 9/11, among them a tremendous increase in FBI intelligence analysts, greater closeness between intelligence and criminal investigations in the FBI, and the establishment of the National Counterterrorism Center, among others.

Beyond matters of community and organizational design, the role of leadership and management inside intelligence organizations is central to effective intelligence practice and change, and scholars have noted that much more research and intelligence-specific theory is needed in this area.[27] John A. Gentry has observed that there is a "glaring hole" in the study of intelligence management, a gap that must be addressed because of the roles analytic managers have in decision-making, interagency dynamics, analytic practice and priorities, the building of expert knowledge, resource allocation, and consumer interaction, as well as the organizational problems poor management can result in.[28] Intelligence managers and leaders also face the tension of representing, advocating for, and protecting their agencies and personnel, while also recognizing and balancing the complementary nature of internal and external expertise. Critical information and insight exist outside intelligence agencies, and increasingly, the efficacy of intelligence agencies will be a function of utilizing outside sources. In the US, rapid turnover of high-level intelligence leadership is observed, and this turnover can result in new initiatives displacing just slightly less new initiatives and more generally undermine the sustainable leadership that agencies require.[29]

Dynamic leadership in intelligence organizations can result in envelope-pushing practices, and there are many challenges to be navigated when pursuing organizational change and adaptation. Among them are basic bureaucratic resistance and protective instincts, the need for successfully framing and conveying the purpose of change, budgetary management and authority, and an intimate sense of agency dynamics.[30] The incorporation of new organizational practices, including in the realm of information management, is exceedingly difficult.[31] Of course, different types of intelligence agencies in different places and circumstances (for example, in nations transitioning to democracy) are challenged to adapt not only to changing security conditions but changing legal and societal roles.[32]

To meaningfully study and theorize on intelligence leadership and management, such research "needs to be done in collaboration with intelligence communities, not an isolated activity in the academy."[33] We will return to this topic shortly, and this observation could also be applied to other facets of intelligence. Patrick F. Walsh's model of effective intelligence frameworks, interacting governance with core and enabling intelligence functions (i.e., analysis and IT, respectively), is an example of existing frameworks to be further tested in empirical settings.[34] To be sure, American intelligence organizations at local, state, and federal levels have opened themselves up to outside examination to very good ends.[35] Research from Bridget Nolan's project at the National Counterterrorism Center was presented in an earlier chapter.

One recent example of successful organizational adaptation entailed the adoption of numeric probabilities and systems to measure analytic performance.[36] A deeper investigation into this example can be found in David Mandel's chapter on decision science and intelligence analysis. But such instances remain rare, and in the US, intelligence agencies do little in the way of systematic tracking of how well their analysts, offices, and agencies perform in terms of analytic and forecasting accuracy.[37] The time available for leaders and managers to devote to organizational learning is certainly stretched in intelligence agencies, and learning in networks, such as intelligence communities, is that much more challenging.[38] Of course, it is entirely possible that markedly improved analytic performance will not always mean enhanced foreign and security policymaking. And no doubt additional challenges—including determining what constitutes reasonable standards of accuracy—remain, but scholars and practitioners alike have shown the practicality and benefits of measuring analytic performance.[39] Such measures might help grow the emphasis placed on analytic accuracy as opposed to production (such as the number of current intelligence reports). In the lexicon of public administration, this could be seen as focusing on outcomes rather than outputs, or internals and externals as Michael Herman labeled them, respectively.[40]

Analytic performance also lends itself to the principal-agent theoretical framework, as do consumer-producer relations more generally, whereby principals (policymakers) must overcome information asymmetries in order to truly and meaningfully understand the operations of the agents (intelligence) serving them.[41] Without close and sophisticated knowledge, especially in an esoteric area such as intelligence, principals cannot be sure that agents are acting in a way consistent with their intelligence support needs and preferences. As these information asymmetries are reduced, policymakers can better task and evaluate the work of intelligence agencies. As Martin J. Smith wrote, "Intelligence, because of its particular nature creates a series of power asymmetries that favor those with the most direct access to intelligence."⁴² Of course, the most disadvantaged group in this context is the public, the ultimate political principal.

In his chapter on political science and intelligence studies, Stephen Marrin discusses the role of congressional oversight of the IC, which affords principals (members of Congress) tools to overcome information asymmetries, though such tools are not always used in robust or apolitical fashion. Others have explored market-like contracts (and the associated pitfalls) as a means to compel intelligence consumers to be more purposive and thoughtful about what they need from intelligence.⁴³

The principal-agent framework also has clear implications for intelligence outsourcing, which is a major cost area in much modern intelligence and an area that offers real—and needed—research possibilities in intelligence studies. To be sure, some scholars have begun to examine these issues.⁴⁴ Donald Kettl elaborates, in the process illuminating key theoretical components of principal-agent theory:

> To write a good contract requires good information. But principals can never know enough about their agents to make sure they have selected the best ones, and that lack of insight can produce adverse selection problems, in which ill-chosen agents cannot or choose not to do what their principals want. Moreover, principals can never observe their agents' behavior closely enough to be sure that their performance matches the terms of the contract—this lack of knowledge can produce moral hazard problems, in which agents perform differently than the principals had in mind.⁴⁵

## Extending the Study of Organizations in Intelligence Studies

As we have seen, the intelligence studies literature that expressly and primarily takes on issues of organization, administration, and personnel is advancing but remains less theoretically and empirically developed than it could be. Taking on such questions and issues does not always mean that the depths and dimensions of PA and organization theory are well integrated into the study of intelligence organizations. More generally, intelligence scholarship and instruction, even in the absence of access to intelligence organizations, can benefit from greater theoretical richness, nuance, and even pragmatism when informed by public administration research. And as greater organizational access is granted to intelligence scholars, their research topics and questions will be enriched by a greater command of public administration and organization theory.

Better incorporating the organizational domain into the study of intelligence focuses our attention on the very sites in which the work of intelligence is performed. As socio-organizational processes, intelligence collection, analysis, and dissemination are accomplished through organized action. It is at the organizational level of analysis that one can pose questions about the nature and outcome of such actions and the various factors (e.g., resource allocation, politics, culture, red tape) that influence them. Take, for example, one of the regularly cited intelligence failures in recent history, the 9/11 attacks, to further explore why the organizational sphere matters not only in a practical sense but as scientific pursuit. The 9/11 Commission reported that, among other things, "an overwhelming number of priorities, flat budgets, an outmoded structure, and bureaucratic rivalries" contributed to the IC's inability to predict and respond to the threat posed by transnational terrorism. Each of those factors points to organizational dynamics.[46]

As an interdisciplinary field of inquiry, the study of public sector organizations attempts to tackle a diverse set of questions, many of which span other social sciences, about myriad organizational phenomena. In the next part of the chapter, we review several theoretical and empirical areas being studied in PA and organization theory as a way to specifically illustrate research avenues intelligence studies scholars could pursue. This will also remind intelligence students that intelligence agencies are public sector organizations composed of people and groups that experience and are subject to many of the same forces and factors as their overt counterparts. Ultimately, the focus is on how we can improve our understandings of organizational performance, the management of intelligence professionals, and organizational change and adaptation. Our hope is that each area considered—strategic human resources management, representative bureaucracy, performance management, environmental scanning, and institutional isomorphism—helps do just this.

## Intraorganizational Dynamics

### Strategic Human Resource Management

Similar to the shift in the private sector to people-centric organizations, the public sector has been experiencing its own transition toward strategic human resource management. Under this paradigm, people are the driving force of organizations—making it imperative, therefore, that leaders invest in their development. This line of research attempts to explore and uncover the various factors that influence employee performance and thus organizational effectiveness. While the number of factors this stream of research has studied is too extensive (e.g., job satisfaction, employee morale, organizational attachment, organizational citizenship behavior) for us to discuss all of them, here we just illustrate how they can be incorporated into intelligence studies research.

Take, for one example, job satisfaction. This concept can be defined as "a pleasurable or positive emotional state, resulting from the appraisal of one's job or job experiences."[47] Studies have consistently shown that there is a positive and significant relationship between job satisfaction and performance.[48] That is, on average, effective organizations tend to have a highly satisfied workforce. For instance, in his study of public sector employees, Sangmook Kim found that among four factors (i.e., job satisfaction, organizational commitment, public service motivation, and organizational citizenship behavior), job satisfaction had the greatest impact predicting perceived organizational performance.[49]

Drawing from, and contributing to, this line of research, intelligence scholars could explore the various factors that drive job satisfaction and the way it affects broader organizational phenomena. Given that increased job satisfaction is associated with high performance, it is imperative IC leaders cultivate the work environments and management practices that improve job satisfaction. Similarly, the broader organizational behavior literature would gain empirical results from organizations with working conditions plagued with stress, ambiguity, safety concerns, and (particularly in the foreign field) danger.

## Performance Management and Measurement

Measuring and managing performance have been long-standing research pursuits in, and major sources of debate within, public administration.[50] These tasks have been central to public management scholarship, particularly since the early 1990s with the passage of the Government Performance and Results Act. That law emphasized performance management at the federal level.[51] However, the literature is still attempting to catch up with new modes of governance characterized by intertwined, networked organizational arrangements; multisectoral approaches to public service delivery; and the challenges of globalization, which has eroded national boundaries and brought the world to a new level of interconnectedness and interdependence.[52] Under those realities, how is the performance of government institutions supposed to be measured and managed? What factors influence government's effectiveness? These are, indeed, the central questions of this line of research.

Although the performance management literature is varied, with its own contradictions, here we focus on a couple more recent treatments of this topic. In his study of Danish schools, for example, Nielsen found that managerial authority (especially authority over employees, such as negotiating pay, hiring, and firing) moderates the effects of performance management.[53] In other words, the study suggests that student achievement could be improved by implementing performance management practices (e.g., management by objectives), but these practices are effective when managers have greater authority over employees; in this case, authority over pay negotiations, hiring, and firing. This is an important finding in the public sector context because managers must adhere to strict pay systems and are often required to follow due process procedures for firing. Such lack of authority, then, might diminish any benefit performance management may have in the first place, rendering it fruitless.

In the IC context, performance management often enters the discussion after spectacular organizational failures, that is, when organizations "fail" to perform. The preeminent recent example is the 9/11 attacks on American soil. The events of 9/11 are a formidable reminder of why studying performance management matters when everything is working "fine." At its core 9/11 exemplified the extreme, growing complexities of managing performance in the public sector. As Amy Zegart recounts, citing the 9/11 Commission Report,

On 8 January 2000, the Central Intelligence Agency (CIA) lost track of three suspected al-Qaeda operatives traveling from Kuala Lumpur, Malaysia to Bangkok, Thailand. Several days earlier, intelligence officials had rushed to establish surveillance operations in Malaysia, believing—correctly—that "something nefarious might be afoot." . . . Nobody, however, was prepared for what happened next: When the meeting disbanded, the trail went cold. The three operatives were tracked as far as a Bangkok-bound commercial flight, and although U.S. officials in both Kuala Lumpur and Washington sent urgent request to Bangkok for help, by the time their messages arrived the terrorists had disappeared. Intelligence officials now know that two of the suspects, Khalid al-Mihdhar and Nawaf al-Hazmi, flew to the United States a few days later, where they settled in California and prepared for their 11 September 2001 suicide hijacking mission.[54]

As this and earlier passages demonstrate, intelligence agencies are embedded in an intricate web of organizational relationships, sharing responsibility for mission accomplishment not only with other public but also private entities. Further, owing to their global mission, intelligence agencies rely on foreign partners with their own cultures, ways of performing their roles, and priorities. The proliferation of non-state actors has further challenged intelligence agencies. As Donald Moynihan and colleagues argued, traditional performance regimes assume simple transaction or service-delivery models, which do not reflect today's complex governance, described previously.[55] How then can organizations operating in such a difficult environment design and implement performance management models that are contextual, adaptive to rapidly changing and fluid conditions, and linked to democratic values (e.g., fairness, equity, transparency)? The IC is indeed an ideal site in which to begin to shed light on that important question, and many more, on performance management.

*Representative Bureaucracy*

Another promising theoretical lens intelligence scholars could borrow from PA is representative bureaucracy. This concept generally posits—with some variations—that in performing their roles, bureaucratic actors draw from elements of their social or personal identity (race and ethnicity, gender, social class, age, sexuality, etc.) in ways that may advance the interests of groups sharing those characteristics.[56] That is, during policymaking, program implementation, or perhaps even the most mundane bureaucratic transaction, beliefs, attitudes, and values color the lenses through which these actions are performed. To be sure, representative bureaucracy can take passive and active forms, with certain characteristics of groups being represented in agency settings (passive), on the one hand, and the realization of policy advocacy and benefits for those demographics (active), on the other. More broadly, underlying representative bureaucracy is the notion that public sector organizations will be made more accountable and responsive to the public and key demographics within it by mirroring that public. Such accountability mechanisms may be even more needed in the context of intelligence.

In her widely known study of the Farmers Home Administration Rural Housing Loan Program, Sally Coleman Selden found that representation of racial minority supervisors increased the likelihood of loans being awarded to minorities.[57] These results were consistent across racial groups, namely, blacks, Hispanics, and Asians. In another study of police officers, Vicky Wilkins and Brian Williams found that as the number of black police officers increased in the district, so did cases of racial profiling against blacks in the same area.[58] This is counter to what one would expect. Explaining their findings, the authors put forth the idea that where organizational socialization is robust, as in law enforcement, black officers are trained to conform to organizational expectations. Also, minority officers may hold members of their racial group to harsher standards owing to fear of being perceived as lenient or favoring people of their own racial group. Kenneth Meier and Jill Nicholson-Crotty have also studied representative bureaucracy in law enforcement agencies, finding sexual assault reports and arrests increased with the number of female police officers.[59]

Studies on representative bureaucracy have not yet been extended to intelligence organizations. And while intelligence organizations have important differences from many of their public sector counterparts (e.g., secrecy), representative bureaucracy in those organizations could certainly carry benefits for the American public, its diverse demographics, and the intelligence community. As Brandy Kennedy has noted, there are potentially important benefits for organizational performance and practice to be studied, and if "representation is the key to legitimizing the overall power of bureaucratic agencies, all agency types need to be considered."[60] By examining representative bureaucracy dynamics and outcomes in intelligence organizations, the intelligence studies literature can help contribute to a more complete and comparative view across public bureaucracies.

Direct or tangible intelligence deliverables to the public might be relatively rare, but homeland security and counterterrorism operations—whether the FBI or major city intelligence units—rely critically on public interaction and information. The now defunct demographic mapping unit of the New York City Police Department, which delivered little in the way of actionable intelligence, may have been deemed unnecessary and unwise with more diverse representation, especially at more senior levels (but perhaps not). This would certainly carry benefits to both the NYC public and the targeted demographics, which in turn could even bolster the NYPD's ability to engage needed publics in ways beneficial to counterterrorism activities. With the increased role of state and local governments in national and homeland security intelligence, this is likely of even greater salience than it may have been in the past.

More inclusion of key demographics could also pave the way for greater levels of understanding and acceptance, both in intelligence agencies and among the public.

Hong-Hai Lim has noted the indirect benefits of workplace exposure to minority populations in terms of reducing potentially discriminatory bureaucratic decisions and actions.[61] It is also possible that increasing the minority populations in public sector organizations increases the likelihood of individuals from those populations attaining high-level elected positions in government and affecting public policy.[62]

It may be best to begin research in this area by qualitative means—for example, interviews and observation. As Kennedy has noted, qualitative research on representative bureaucracy will allow for grounded understandings and the identification of important theoretical and empirical questions.[63] These will likely pertain to the unique benefits (and trade-offs) of representative bureaucracy in an intelligence context, as well as the identification of characteristics that can help agencies realize active representation—gender, race, and beyond. Again, identifying potentially unknown or unexpected characteristics and benefits would aid not only intelligence organizations but also the scholarly research on representative bureaucracy. Studying these issues at all levels of intelligence organizations will be helpful for both practical and methodological reasons.

Benefits could be along the lines noted previously but also in the areas of information sharing, collaboration, and analytic performance. These are empirical questions worthy of examination. As the IC is called on to make sense of a complex, diverse world, intelligence scholars should pursue questions about the benefits and challenges of a diverse workforce in the IC. This line of research should explore intraorganizational dynamics and their impact on performance and outcomes. For example, how has increased minority representation changed organizational practices? Other related questions could address the impact certain organizational practices and processes (e.g., security clearance policies and processes) have on the IC's ability to recruit and retain a diverse workforce.

## The Organization-Environment Interface

### Environmental Scanning

The IC is arguably one of the most empirically rich conglomerates in which to test and formulate new theories on environmental scanning in particular and organizational sense making in general. By its very mission, the IC collects, analyzes, and disseminates intelligence to policymakers about myriad global threats and social phenomena. Those threats and social phenomena (e.g., political instability, radicalization, corruption, and drug trafficking) form the dynamic environment that analysts and policymakers must interpret and make sense of. In theory, then, intelligence organizations are environmental scanners and interpretive bodies par excellence—and thus ideal sites for studying such a complex organizational process.

Environmental scanning has been a long-standing focus of organizational theorists and researchers of strategic action concerned with the various mechanisms through which managers perceive, interpret, and collect information about external events and trends.[64] Given the vast, diverse, and often contradictory information emanating from their environment, organizations must be selective—attending to those events or issues that might have an impact on the organization. Such sense-making activities have been directly linked to organizational performance, and that, again, is particularly relevant in the IC context.[65]

One exemplar of this line of research, and from the private sector, is J. B. Thomas, S. M. Clark, and D. A. Gioia's study of the relationship that environmental scanning, interpretation, and action have with organizational performance in the health-care industry.[66] Their results suggest that "information use during scanning was . . . associated with a heightened interpretation of strategic issues as controllable" and led top managers to interpret "strategic issues as positive and as implying potential gains."[67] In other words, the more managers consumed information through various organizational mechanisms, the higher the likelihood they saw issues as potential gains and controllable. This is important because they also found that when CEOs perceived issues as controllable, it had a positive effect on product-service change, which, in turn, had a positive impact on organizational performance (measured as increased profits, admissions, and occupancy).

This private sector study is a formidable example of the kind of research that could influence how the IC designs, builds, and evaluates the sense-making apparatus that attends to both the external and internal environments. Unlike other domains in the public sector—say, for example, land management agencies—the IC operates in a hypercompetitive environment against not only transnational threats but also their foreign counterparts working to mitigate, neutralize, and prevent intelligence collection. In such an environment, strategic action is paramount. This line of research would assist not only top managers in the pursuit of strategic advantage but also intelligence educators who must prepare curricula that cultivate the kind of skills students need to effectively lead in such a complex industry.

This research program, however, does not have to be restricted to the kind of information processing that takes place as part of the development of analytical products for the president or senior policymakers. It should also include studying signals that impact organizational processes, practices, and action. For example, the political environment in which the IC operates is loaded with vast amounts of information about policy preferences that prescribe action. Agencies must weigh information from Congress, the president, and federal courts, to name a few, in order to chart strategic priorities and adapt accordingly. This dynamic, although present across government agencies, is potentially more salient with regard to foreign policy. Therefore, new theories could be developed around how government entities process, analyze, and respond to the flood of information emanating from the environment when the volume is immense, a multiplicity of stakeholders are at play—with their own preferences—and information is conflictive, ambiguous, or contradictory.

## Institutional Isomorphism

Institutional isomorphism has taken on increasing prominence in the study of public sector organizational dynamics. Isomorphism posits that environmental factors and pressures will shape the approaches taken by organizations in a given field of practice. Often, those pressures emanate from public sector organizations, following from laws and regulation. But public sector organizations can also be susceptible to such pressures, even more so than businesses and nonprofits.[68] These pressures can take coercive, mimetic, and normative forms.[69] Coercive isomorphism follows essentially from requirements, whereas normative and mimetic isomorphism results from professional norms and emulation, respectively. Thus, practices and policies can be adopted to improve performance or to gain legitimacy. While the terms may seem a little jargon heavy and complex, the ideas are quite simple and unintimidating.

Exploring the source of and reasons for organizational innovation and practices, and the presence or absence of isomorphic tendencies, is a promising research avenue for those studying intelligence organizations. In the US, for example, such dynamics have likely occurred in phases for state and metro intelligence fusion centers—perhaps first in response to federal guidelines and funding (coercive) and then in response to perceived best practices in other fusion centers, partly as a function of professional conferences, knowledge, and norms (mimetic and normative). Such institutional pressures may also be observed internationally, as younger and smaller agencies seek to gain legitimacy in the eyes of international partners they may be dependent on. While some organizational change will certainly be in response to unique national and domestic circumstances, seeking approval from more mature intelligence organizations could certainly affect practice. This might result in convergence that does not necessarily serve the security interests of a given nation.

Police practice, homeland security, and military agencies have been examined through the lens of isomorphism.[70] Perhaps most salient to intelligence, Jeremy G. Carter has found evidence that intelligence-led policing practices are partly a function of environmental factors, and he stresses the role of making knowledge on best practices available. The frames used in these studies could be further applied to look more closely at various intelligence practices, including analysis, counterterrorism measures, and information sharing. Carter examined isomorphic dynamics chiefly through survey data focused on relations with other law enforcement agencies, the use of professional and academic research, participation in professional opportunities, and indicators of intelligence-led policing practice. Institutional pressures were found to support the diffusion of these practices. Carter urges that the measures used in his study "should be considered a starting position for future scholarly works and not as accepted specification."[71]

Institutional isomorphism provides a highly plausible theoretical framework—one that operates in several diverse organizational contexts—that can advance our understanding of the development and diffusion of intelligence practices. Going forward, such study might take on a more prominent role in the intelligence studies literature.

## Where Do We Go from Here?

### Research Methodologies for Studying Intelligence Organizations

The first step toward further advancing research on intelligence organizations is to identify publicly available sources of data and to compile this data for sharing and analyzing. As information is declassified and archived, researchers can tap into the wealth of materials that shed light on the kinds of questions that could be explored with them in an inductive fashion. For example, the CIA recently published several years of the President's Daily Brief from the Kennedy administration (at that time it was known as the President's Intelligence Checklist). Analyzing a robust sample of such documents could provide insight into the CIA's communication devices and styles.

Assuming the access challenge has been resolved, researchers will be able to use more robust data-collection practices: surveys, interviews, and observations, to name the most commonly used. Organizational research heavily relies on surveys because many researchers are trained psychologists. Thus, using similar survey instruments would be ideal for intelligence studies scholars so that they can contrast their research with that of others. Surveys could help us understand, for example, to what extent the distinctive culture of the IC influences internal employee phenomena (e.g., job satisfaction, organizational attachment, assimilation) and how intelligence agencies differ from other organizational domains (e.g., land management agencies).

Interviews and observations could be—and have been—used as part of a larger effort to engage in theorizing. Interviews and observations provide rich data from which theories can emerge. However, they require researchers to work in sites and to develop a working relationship or rapport with research participants. For these reasons, this kind of data collection takes more resources, especially time. One of the areas in which this approach could advance theorizing is the organization-environment interface, because intelligence agencies are called on to make sense of a complex, ambiguous, and ever-changing environment. Earlier chapters by Damien Van Puyvelde and Bridget Nolan explore these methods in more detail, addressing both the mechanics and outcomes of such research.

### Overcoming Access Challenges for Organizational Research

The secretive nature of intelligence work and the lack of access to the IC make carrying out the research agenda we propose quite arduous. There are many policies and laws in place to ensure that intelligence professionals safeguard classified information. Those policies, coupled with the IC's internal information review infrastructure, often push the IC to err on the side of silence. The security clearance process potentially further reinforces a culture of secrecy and distrust. The 9/11 Commission's report, for instance, documented the overutilization of compartmentalization and overclassification of otherwise nonclassified information. Thus, we not only call on intelligence studies scholars to recalibrate their research agenda. It is similarly paramount for the IC to transform a potentially dangerous culture and legal framework that incentivizes a hermetic paradigm.

One approach to further bridge the academic and applied worlds is for the IC to expand the sponsorship of security clearances for academics who conduct research on the IC (as has been done at the CIA and National Security Agency). Similar to the existing approach with consultants and contractors, the IC could process and grant clearances to academics before they are able to handle and access classified information. Meanwhile, the IC could retain control over what is declassified and publicly disclosed because the same regulations that apply to IC professionals would apply to cleared academics. Once cleared, this cadre of academics could begin to build networks within the IC, pitch research projects to individual agencies, and build partnerships that benefit the IC and the scientific progress of intelligence studies as a field. To be sure, questions of researcher independence and objectivity rightly come to mind, and it would still also be possible to research intelligence agencies as an uncleared academic.[72]

These research partnerships could represent significant savings in public monies if much of what is now done by consultants were performed by academics. Unlike private consultants, academics work for not-for-profit institutions (colleges and universities) and their greatest reward is creating knowledge. Under this approach, agencies in the IC could create grant programs or engage in contractual arrangements directly with cleared academics, in which all the terms (e.g., the nature of the data, potential publications, classified and unclassified versions of products) are discussed and agreed on in advance.

Giving access to classified data and information brings counterintelligence concerns. However, we argue that the same rules and regulations that apply to cleared consultants ought to apply to cleared academics. The same counterintelligence concerns could be mitigated the very same way they are among consultants and contractors. These academics would be trained on how to address the risks associated with having access to classified information.

Of course, we are not arguing for an overnight paradigm shift, but gradual shifts and additions. We contend that once academics and practitioners begin to work closer together and those relationships mature, both sides will develop a deeper understanding of how to nurture win-win partnerships. That is, when intelligence agencies begin to witness the benefits of opening their doors for scientific pursuits, creating and sharing knowledge across the public sector, and advancing intelligence studies as a field—and therefore their own mission—we would have cemented the seeds of a positive and significant institutional shift. After these initial steps have been taken, other approaches could be explored, drawing lessons from successful partnerships and identifying creative ways of building new ones.

## Conclusion

This chapter was borne out of our scholarly interest in the future of intelligence studies. We argue that, as an interdisciplinary field, it should look more deeply to the study of public sector organizations to chart a research program of significantly positive impact on intelligence organizations and practitioners. Doing so would open a range of theoretical frameworks through which the field can be advanced. We gave only a few examples of research avenues based on current developments and debates in the PA scholarship. This review is certainly not comprehensive, as research on public sector organizations is diverse and wide-ranging. We chose to highlight strategic human resources management, performance management and measurement, representative bureaucracy, environmental scanning, and institutional isomorphism from the literatures on public organizations to demonstrate how the existing intelligence literature can further build research insights pertaining to organizational performance and adaptation as well as accountability. And like the other chapters in this section, ours demonstrates for students that varied lenses should be used to inform more holistic and complete thinking about intelligence functions. Some of these lenses are novel and some may seem mundane, but all are ultimately relevant to better serving the critical national security functions of avoiding surprise and supporting sound policy.

## Notes

1. Michael Herman, *Intelligence Power in Peace and War* (Cambridge: Cambridge University Press, 1996).
2. Philip H. J. Davies, *MI6 and the Machinery of Spying: Structure and Process in Britain's Secret Intelligence* (London: Frank Cass, 2004), 2.
3. Philip H. J. Davies, "Intelligence and the Machinery of Government," *Public Policy and Administration* 25, no. 1 (2010): 30.
4. Davies, *MI6 and the Machinery of Spying*.
5. Philip H. J. Davies, "The Missing Dimension's Missing Dimension," *Public Policy and Administration* 25, no. 1 (2010): 5–9.
6. Miron Varouhakis, "What Is Being Published in Intelligence? A Study of Two Scholarly Journals," *International Journal of Intelligence and CounterIntelligence* 26, no. 1 (2013): 176–89.
7. Damien Van Puyvelde and Sean Curtis, "'Standing on the Shoulders of Giants': Diversity and Scholarship in Intelligence Studies," *Intelligence and National Security* 31, no. 7 (2016): 1040–54.
8. Stephen Marrin, "Intelligence Analysis Centers: Making Scholarship on Intelligence Analysis Useful," *Intelligence and National Security* 27, no. 3 (2012): 398–422.
9. Stephen Marrin, "Improving Intelligence Studies as an Academic Discipline," *Intelligence and National Security* 16, no. 2 (2016): 266–79.

10. Phillip Joyce, "How Academia Is Failing Government," *Governing the States and Localities*, August 31, 2016, http://www.governing.com/columns/smart-mgmt/col-how-academia-failing-government.html.
11. Thomas H. Hammond, "Intelligence Organizations and the Organization of Intelligence," *International Journal of Intelligence and CounterIntelligence* 23, no. 4 (2010): 687.
12. Amy Zegart, "Implementing Change: Organizational Challenges," in *Intelligence Analysis: Behavioral and Social Scientific Foundations*, ed. Baruch Fischoff and Cherie Chauvin (Washington, DC: National Academy of Sciences, 2011), 309–25; Kevin C. Desouza, "Information and Knowledge Management in Public Sector Networks: The Case of the US Intelligence Community," *International Journal of Public Administration* 32 (2009): 1219–67.
13. John A. Gentry, "Has the ODNI Improved U.S. Intelligence Analysis?" *International Journal of Intelligence and CounterIntelligence* 28, no. 4 (2015): 637–61; Patrick F. Walsh, "Building Better Intelligence Frameworks through Effective Governance," *International Journal of Intelligence and CounterIntelligence* 28, no. 1 (2015): 123–42; James Whibley, "One Community, Many Agencies: Administrative Developments in New Zealand's Intelligence Services," *Intelligence and National Security* 29, no. 1 (2014): 122–35; David Martin Jones, "Intelligence and the Management of National Security: The Post-9/11 Evolution of an Australian National Security Community," *Intelligence and National Security* 33, no. 1 (2018): 1–20.
14. Richard K. Betts, *Enemies of Intelligence: Knowledge and Power in American National Security* (New York: Columbia University Press, 2009).
15. Herman, *Intelligence Power*.
16. George Christian Maior, "Managing Change: The Romanian Intelligence Service in the 21st Century," *International Journal of Intelligence and CounterIntelligence* 25, no. 2 (2012): 217–39; Christopher Gray and Andrew Sturdy, "A Chaos That Worked: Organizing Bletchley Park," *Public Policy and Administration* 25, no. 1 (2010): 47–66.
17. James E. Steiner, "Restoring the Red Line between Intelligence and Policy on Covert Action," *International Journal of Intelligence and CounterIntelligence* 19, no. 1 (2006): 162.
18. Hammond, "Intelligence Organizations," 687.
19. Betts, *Enemies of Intelligence*.
20. Noel Hendrickson, "Intelligence Analysis as an Academic Discipline: A National Security Education and Recruitment Strategy for a Long-Term Environment of Limited Resources," *American Intelligence Journal* 31, no. 2 (2013): 23–27; Betts, *Enemies of Intelligence*.
21. Hamilton Bean, "Organizational Culture and US Intelligence Affairs," *Intelligence and National Security* 24, no. 4 (2009): 479–98.
22. Davies, "Intelligence and the Machinery"; Nicolas Paul Hare and Paul Collinson, "Organizational Culture and Intelligence Analysis: A Perspective from Senior Managers in the Defense Intelligence Assessment Staffs," *Public Policy and Administration* 28, no. 2 (2012): 214–29.

23. Hare and Collinson, "Organizational Culture."
24. Bean, "Organizational Culture," 491.
25. Amy Zegart, "'CNN with Secrets': 9/11, the CIA, and the Organizational Roots of Failure," *International Journal of Intelligence and CounterIntelligence* 20, no. 1 (2007): 20.
26. Zegart, "CNN with Secrets"; Amy Zegart, "9/11 and the FBI: The Organizational Roots of Failure," *Intelligence and National Security* 22, no. 2 (2007): 165–84; Amy Zegart, *Spying Blind: The CIA, the FBI, and the Origins of 9/11* (Princeton, NJ: Princeton University Press, 2007).
27. Herman, *Intelligence Power*; John A. Gentry, "Managers of Analysts: The Other Half of Intelligence Analysis," *Intelligence and National Security* 31, no. 2 (2016): 154–77; Patrick F. Walsh, "Making Future Leaders in the US Intelligence Community: Challenges and Opportunities," *Intelligence and National Security* 32, no. 4 (2017): 441–59.
28. Gentry, "Managers of Analysts."
29. Zegart, "Implementing Change"; Desouza, "Information and Knowledge"; Walsh, "Building Better Intelligence Frameworks."
30. Michael Fowler, "The Air Force's Predictive Battlespace Awareness: The Siren Song of Ender's Game," *International Journal of Intelligence and CounterIntelligence* 29, no. 1 (2016): 98–109; David Omand, "Creating Intelligence Communities," *Public Policy and Administration* 25, no. 1 (2010): 99–116.
31. Zegart, "Implementing Change"; Desouza, "Information and Knowledge."
32. Maior, "Managing Change."
33. Walsh, "Making Future Leaders in the US Intelligence Community."
34. Patrick F. Walsh, *Intelligence and Intelligence Analysis* (New York: Routledge, 2011).
35. Brian Nussbaum, "Protecting Global Cities: New York, London, and the Internationalization of Urban Counterterrorism" (PhD diss., University at Albany, 2009); Bridget Rose Nolan, "Information Sharing and Collaboration in the United States Intelligence Community: An Ethnographic Study of the National Counterterrorism Center" (PhD diss., University of Pennsylvania, 2013); Carla Lewandowski, "Information Sharing Using a State Fusion Center: A Case Study of the New Jersey Regional Operations Intelligence Center" (PhD diss., University of Pennsylvania, 2012); Rob Johnston, *Analytic Culture in the US Intelligence Community: An Ethnographic Study* (Washington, DC: Studies in Intelligence, 2005).
36. Alan Barnes, "Making Intelligence Analysis More Intelligent: Using Numeric Probabilities," *Intelligence and National Security* 31, no. 3 (2015): 327–44.
37. Gentry, "Managers of Analysts"; Jeffrey A. Friedman and Richard Zeckhauser, "Why Assessing Estimative Accuracy Is Feasible and Desirable," *Intelligence and National Security* 31, no. 2 (2016): 178–200.
38. Desouza, "Information and Knowledge."
39. Mark M. Lowenthal, "Towards a Reasonable Standard for Analysis: How Right, How Often on Which Issues?" *Intelligence and National Security* 23, no. 3 (2008):

303–15; Philip E. Tetlock and Dan Gardner, *Superforecasting: The Art and Science of Prediction* (New York: Crown, 2015); Barnes, "Making Intelligence Analysis."
40. Herman, *Intelligence Power*.
41. Donald F. Kettl, *The Politics of the Administrative Process* (Thousand Oaks, CA: CQ Press, 2017).
42. Martin J. Smith, "Intelligence and the Core Executive," *Public Policy and Administration* 25, no. 1 (2010): 11–28.
43. Herman, *Intelligence Power*.
44. Hamilton Bean, "'Tradecraft versus Science': Intelligence Analysis and Outsourcing" (Research Paper No. 104, Athens: Research Institute for European and American Studies, 2006); Raphael S. Cohen, "Putting a Human and Historical Face on Intelligence Contracting," *Orbis* 54, no. 2 (2010): 232–51; Morton Hansen, "Intelligence Contracting: On the Motivations, Interests, and Capabilities of Core Personnel Contractors in the US Intelligence Community," *Intelligence and National Security* 29, no. 1 (2014): 58–81; Patrick R. Keefe, "'Privatized Spying': The Emerging Intelligence Industry," in *The Oxford Handbook of National Security Intelligence*, ed. Loch Johnson (Oxford: Oxford University Press, 2010); William J. Lahneman, "Outsourcing the IC's Stovepipes?" *International Journal of Intelligence and CounterIntelligence* 16, no. 4 (2003): 573–93; Glenn J. Voelz, "Contractors and Intelligence: The Private Sector in the Intelligence Community," *International Journal of Intelligence and CounterIntelligence* 22, no. 4 (2009): 586–613.
45. Kettl, *Politics*, 104–5.
46. National Commission on Terrorist Attacks, *The 9/11 Commission Report: Final Report of the National Commission on Terrorist Attacks upon the United States* (New York: W. W. Norton, 2004).
47. Edwin Locke, "The Nature and Cause of Job Satisfaction," in *Handbook of Industrial and Organizational Psychology*, ed. Marvin Dunnette (Chicago: Rand McNally, 1976).
48. Lynn McFarlane Shore and Harry Martin, "Job Satisfaction and Organizational Commitment in Relation to Work Performance and Turnover Intentions," *Human Relations* 42, no. 7 (1989): 625–38; Timothy A. Judge, Carj J. Thoresen, Joyce E. Bono, and Gregory K. Patton, "The Job Satisfaction–Job Performance Relationship: A Qualitative and Quantitative Review," *Psychological Bulletin* 127, no. 3 (2001): 376–407.
49. Sangmook Kim, "Individual-Level Factors and Organizational Performance in Government Organizations," *Journal of Public Administration Research and Theory* 15, no. 2 (2005): 245–61.
50. Donald P. Moynihan, Sergio Fernandez, Soonhee Kim, Kelly M. LeRoux, Suzanne J. Piotrowski, Bradley E. Wright, and Kaifen Yang, "Performance Regimes amidst Governance Complexity," *Journal of Public Administration Research and Theory* 21, no. 1 (2011): 141–55.

51. R. S. Kravchuk and R. W. Schack, "Designing Effective Performance-Measurement Systems under the Government Performance and Results Act of 1993," *Public Administration Review* 56, no. 4 (1996): 348–58.
52. Moynihan et al., "Performance Regimes."
53. Poul Aaes Nielsen, "Performance Management, Managerial Authority, and Public Service Performance," *Journal of Public Administration Research and Theory* 24, no. 2 (2013): 431–58.
54. Zegart, "CNN with Secrets," 18–19.
55. Moynihan et al., "Performance Regimes."
56. Mark Bradbury and J. Edward Kellough, "Representative Bureaucracy: Assessing the Evidence on Active Representation," *American Review of Public Administration* 41, no. 2 (2011): 157–67; Brandy Kennedy, "Unraveling Representative Bureaucracy: A Systematic Analysis of the Literature," *Administration and Society* 46, no. 4 (2012): 395–421.
57. Sally Coleman Selden, "Representative Bureaucracy: Examining the Linkage between Passive and Active Representation in the Farmers Home Administration," *American Review of Public Administration* 27, no. 1 (1997): 22–42; Sally Coleman Selden, *The Promise of Representative Bureaucracy: Diversity and Responsiveness in a Government Agency* (Armonk, NY: M. E. Sharpe, 1997).
58. Vicky M. Wilkins and Brian N. Williams, "Black or Blue: Racial Profiling and Representative Bureaucracy," *Public Administration Review* 68, no. 4 (2008): 654–64.
59. Kenneth J. Meier and Jill Nicholson-Crotty, "Gender, Representative Bureaucracy, and Law Enforcement: The Case of Sexual Assault," *Public Administration Review* 66, no. 6 (2006): 850–60.
60. Kennedy, "Unraveling Representative Bureaucracy," 407.
61. Hong-Hai Lim, "Representative Bureaucracy: Rethinking Substantive Effects and Active Representation," *Public Administration Review* 66, no. 2 (2006): 193–204.
62. Kenneth J. Meier and Kevin B. Smith, "Representative Democracy and Representative Bureaucracy: Examining the Top-Down and Bottom-Up Linkages," *Social Science Quarterly* 75, no. 4 (1994): 790–803.
63. Kennedy, "Unraveling Representative Bureaucracy."
64. Raymond E. Miles, Charles C. Snow, and Jeffrey Pfeffer, "Organization-Environment: Concepts and Issues," *Industrial Relations* 13, no. 3 (1974): 244–64; Jeffrey Pfeffer and Gerald Salancik, *The External Control of Organizations: A Resource Dependence Perspective* (New York: Harper & Row, 1978); Donald C. Hambrick, "Environment Scanning and Organizational Strategy," *Strategic Management Journal* 3, no. 2 (1982): 159–74; Richard L. Daft and Karl W. Weick, "Toward a Model of Organizations as Interpretive Systems," *Academy of Management Review* 9, no. 2 (1984): 284–95.
65. J. D. Ford, "The Effects of Casual Attributions on Decision Makers' Responses to Performance Downturns," *Academy of Management Review* 10, no. 4 (1985):

770–86; Paul C. Nystrom and William H. Starbuck, "To Avoid Organizational Crises, Unlearn," *Organizational Dynamics* 12, no. 4 (1984): 53–65.
66. J. B. Thomas, S. M. Clark, and D. A. Gioia, "Strategic Sensemaking and Organizational Performance: Linkages among Scanning, Interpretation, Action, and Outcomes," *Academy of Management Journal* 36, no. 2 (1993): 239–70.
67. Thomas, Clark, and Gioia.
68. Peter Frumkin and Joseph Galaskiewicz, "Institutional Isomorphism and Public Sector Organization," *Journal of Public Administration Research and Theory* 14, no. 3 (2004): 283–307.
69. Paul J. DiMaggio and Walter W. Powell, "The Iron Cage Revisited: Institutional Isomorphism and Collective Rationality in Organizational Fields," *American Sociological Review* 48, no. 2 (1983): 147–60.
70. George W. Burruss and Matthew J. Giblin, "Modeling Isomorphism on Policing Innovation: The Role of Institutional Pressures in Adopting Community-Oriented Policing," *Crime and Delinquency* 60 (2014): 331–55; George W. Burruss, Matthew J. Giblin, and Joseph A. Schafer, "Threatened Globally, Acting Locally: Modeling Law Enforcement Homeland Security Practices," *Justice Quarterly* 27, no. 1 (2010): 77–101; Jeremy G. Carter, "Institutional Pressures and Isomorphism: The Impact on Intelligence-Led Policing Adoption," *Police Quarterly* 19, no. 4 (2016): 435–60; Joelien Pretorius, "The Security Imaginary: Explaining Military Isomorphism," *Security Dialogue* 39, no. 1 (2008): 99–120.
71. Carter, "Institutional Pressures and Isomorphism," 454.
72. Stephen J. Coulthart, "Why Do Analysts Use Structured Analytic Techniques? An In-Depth Study of an American Intelligence Agency," *Intelligence and National Security* 31, no. 7 (2016): 933–48.

# 9.

# How the Field of Communication Can Contribute to the Understanding and Study of National Security Intelligence

*Rubén Arcos*

Communication affects, or has the potential to affect, the decisions of individuals, groups, and organizations of all kinds. In the context of national security intelligence, the dissemination of assessments and analytic products by intelligence agencies is based on the premise that their output can potentially inform decisions affecting national security matters. At the same time, adversaries engaged in disinformation and deception operations can communicate deliberately false and misleading information with the intention of delaying or manipulating decision processes. Less sinister but perhaps no less problematic communication issues—for example, the accumulation of biases at the group level that have "far exceeded initial bias through successive reproductions"—can also be disruptive to intelligence operations and analysis.[1] These communication problems can potentially alter the decisions derived from intelligence inputs.

Effective intelligence support for decision-making in national security is thus largely premised on well-informed communication strategies and practices. To ultimately arrive at finished analytic products, intelligence support is in essence a series of varying communication processes between intelligence agencies, on the one hand, and their targets (e.g., a terrorist organization, an adversary nation), sources, and consumers, on the other. These interactions thus unfold at different organizational levels and different points in the "intelligence cycle," enabled by the use of symbols as well as behaviors.[2] Figure 9.1 identifies communication processes and issues along the intelligence cycle.

The purpose of this chapter is to offer a brief but broad overview of how the field of communication can enhance our understanding of the intelligence enterprise and its various occupational disciplines. The chapter begins with a look at the emergence

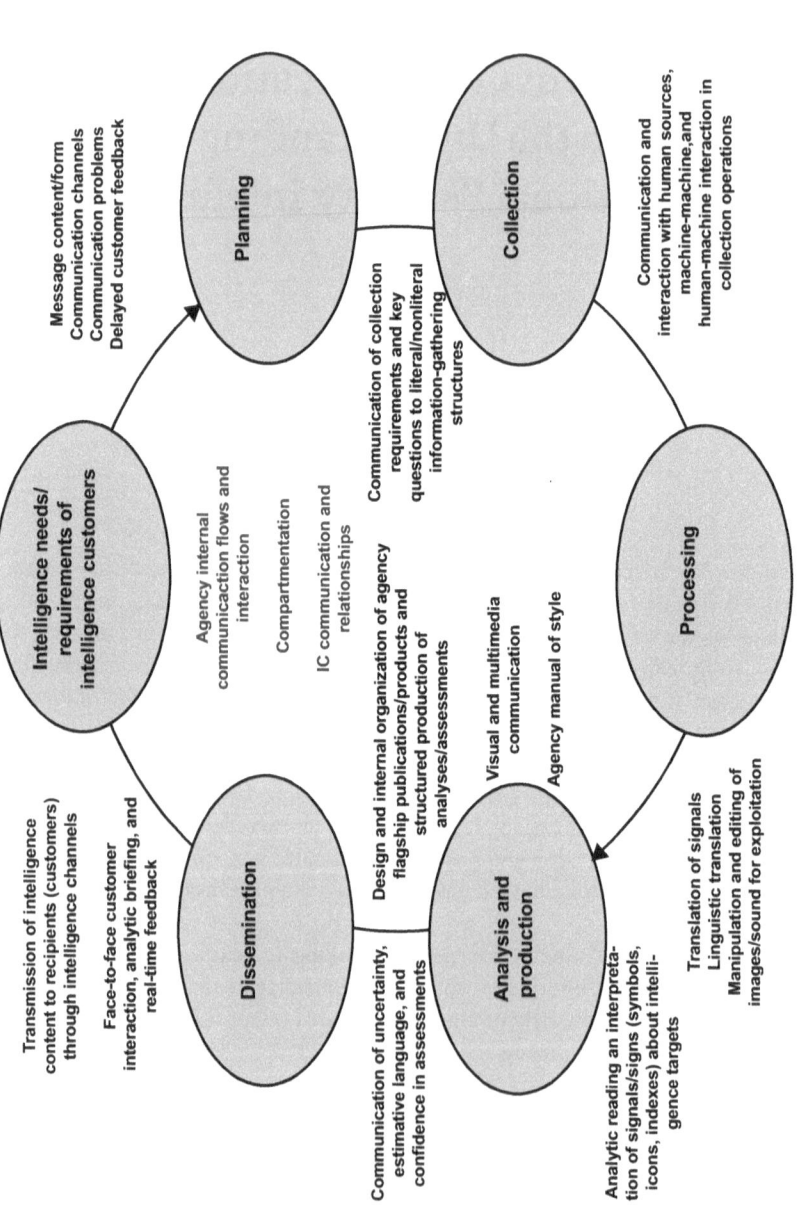

Figure 9.1. Map of communication processes and communication areas along the intelligence cycle

of communication as a field of academic research, its foundations in the service of US national security and intelligence, and its inherent links to intelligence studies and practice. The chapter then moves to an overview of how different research fields and findings in communication can inform a better understanding of intelligence and frame key functions and questions. These functions include collection and analysis, information operations, propaganda and deception, and the transmission of intelligence from producers to consumers. Emerging dynamics such as digital communication are also considered (see fig. 9.2).

## Government, National Security, and Foundations in Communication

Like intelligence studies, communication is a complex field with a varied set of subfields and applications, including journalism, public relations, advertising, and propaganda, among others. Areas as diverse as animal communication and telecommunications technology are captured in the discipline, as well as communication fields specific to political science, social psychology, and sociology. Consequently, there is not a single communication domain. Rather, we find communication phenomena and processes in many scientific fields of knowledge. In fact, some scholars have pointed out the lack of disciplinary status of communication scholarship is rooted in the rise of modern science in the seventeenth century.[3] This argued lack of disciplinary status, according to which communication has evolved more as an interdisciplinary field of study than as a foundational discipline, is something that can also accompany intelligence and intelligence studies.[4]

Wilbur Schramm is considered the founding father of communication study in America.[5] Schramm asserted that communication was the fundamental social process, without which groups and societies would not exist. In his important paper titled "How Communication Works," Schramm presented a model to explain human and mass communication processes. Schramm referred to the Latin origin of the word communication from *communis*, being the act of communication, communicate, to put in common, or "trying to share information, an idea, or an attitude." For Schramm, the process of finding that commonality between a source and an intended receiver consisted of encoding a message in a form adapted so that it can be transmitted (e.g., spoken or written words). The act of communication is not completed until the message has been decoded by the receiver. Sent messages are made up of signs: "signal that stands for something in experience." Humans are thus constantly involved in the process of decoding, interpreting, and encoding messages.[6] Schramm also incorporates the notion of feedback, developed by Norbert Wiener, in the communication process: "An experienced communicator is attentive to feedback, and constantly modifies his messages in light of what he observes in or hears from his audience."[7] This interaction is developed through simultaneous channels. In the case of face-to-face interactions, for example, this includes information conveyed by voice quality, gestures, and facial expressions.

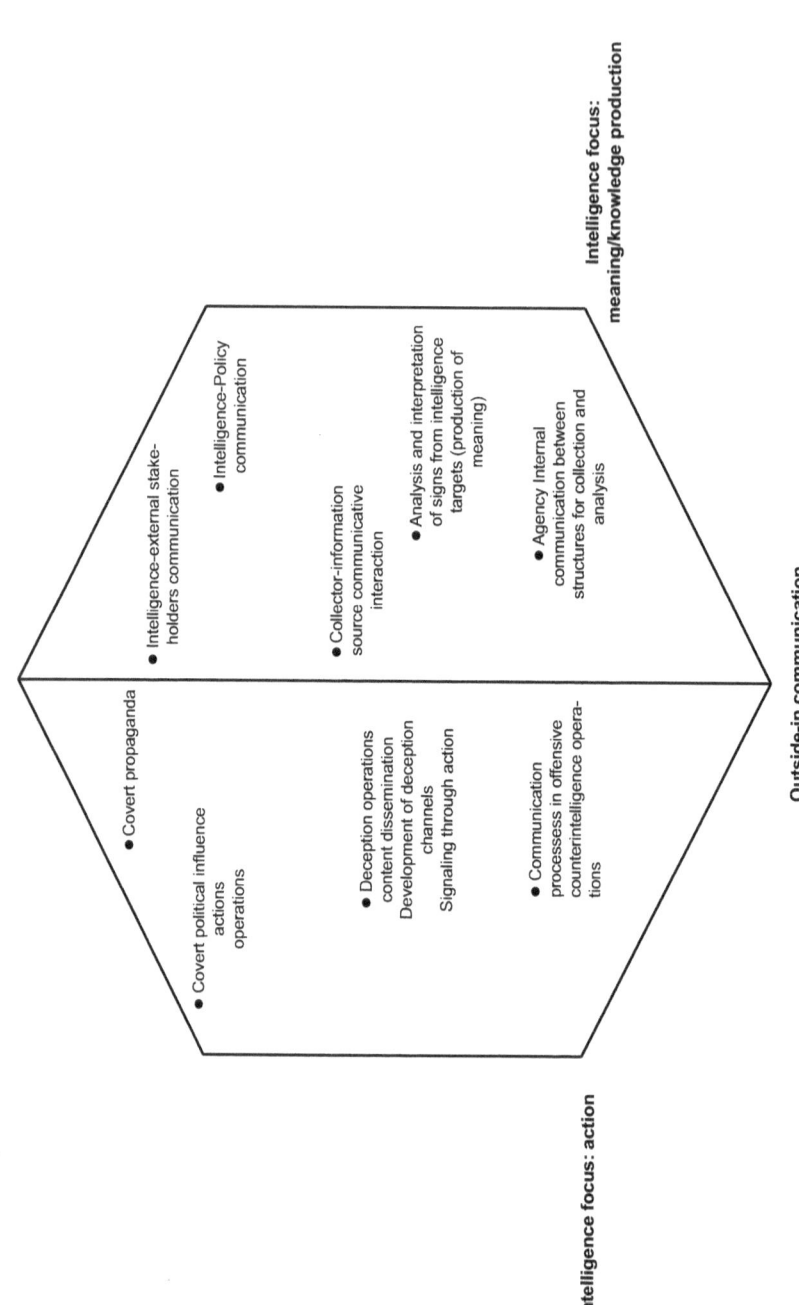

Figure 9.2. Intelligence cube: Topic areas connected with communication

And although not then a formal academic discipline, Schramm described communication as "one of the busiest crossroads in the study of human behavior."[8] He nodded to the interdisciplinary character of communication, highlighting four social scientists, each from a separate discipline, as forerunners of communication research in the United States: Paul Lazarsfeld (a sociologist), Kurt Lewin (a psychologist), Harold Lasswell (a political scientist), and Carl Hovland (a psychologist). According to Schramm, the more productive decades for these forefathers were the 1940s and 1950s. Except Lewin, all are contributing authors in Schramm's influential work *The Process and Effects of Mass Communication*, an edited volume that originated as a book of background materials for the training of personnel at the US Information Agency. During World War II Hovland was appointed chief psychologist and director of experimental studies for the research section of the US War Department. Lasswell directed a research project on "world revolutionary propaganda" for policy guidance during the war years at the US Library of Congress. Lazarsfeld served as a consultant for the Office of Facts and Figures.[9]

This relationship between key academic scholars and US government communication-related research programs has been highlighted by Christopher Simpson in his work *Science of Coercion: Communication Research and Psychological Warfare, 1945–1960*. For Simpson, "taken as whole, it is unlikely that communication research could have emerged in anything like its present form without regular transfusions of money for the leading lights in the field from U.S. military, intelligence, and propaganda agencies."[10]

Other important early communication scholars, such as Claude E. Shannon, drew connections between communication theory and intelligence work and operations, more specifically communications intelligence. Shannon's mathematical theory of communication was closely connected with his mathematical theory of cryptography and secrecy systems.[11] According to Shannon, "I . . . worked at least two or three years on the problems of information and communications . . . then I started thinking about cryptography and secrecy systems. There is this close connection; they are very similar things, in one case trying to conceal information, and in the other case trying to transmit it."[12]

In his declassified paper developing a theory of cryptography, Shannon differentiated between two general types of secrecy systems: "(1) Concealment systems, including such methods as invisible ink, concealing a message in an innocent text, or in a fake covering cryptogram, or other methods in which the existence of the message is concealed from the enemy; (2) 'true' secrecy systems where the meaning of the message is concealed by cipher, code, etc., although its existence is not hidden."[13]

## Intelligence as the Interpretation of Signs and Signals

Human beings are dependent on signs and, being the dominant sign-using species, use very complex systems of signs.[14] Charles Sanders Peirce defined a sign as "an object which stands for another in some mind."[15] Thomas Sebeok has described semiosis as the capacity of human beings (and other organisms) to make and understand signs, from physiological signals to complex symbols.[16] Semiotics is the science that studies these functions.[17]

Likewise, communication signs enable intelligence organizations to fulfill their mission of providing knowledge about national security matters to government decision-makers. Signs mediate the connection between intelligence producers and the intelligence targets, events, and developments (the external-world national security referents) about which policymakers require information and meaning. The reading, verification, and correct interpretation of intentional and unintentional communicative actions from adversaries are essential for intelligence analysis. In fact, James Hoopes has written that "all thinking is inferential interpretation of signs."[18] And it is through the correct reading and interpretation of signs that we can provide early warning, predicting events and behaviors.

Sebeok identified six major types of signs: symptoms, signals, icons, indexes, symbols, and names. One type of sign is of special interest to intelligence practitioners and scholars: signals. Signals are "signs that naturally or conventionally trigger some reaction on the part of a receiver," whether that receiver is an organism or a machine.[19] Sebeok observes that we can deploy either witting or unwitting signals and that we can create systems of signals for social purposes (e.g., Morse code, sirens). Our body can emit unconscious automatic signals in response to a stimulus from the environment, as well as intentional signals, such as winking or nodding, that can act as regulators in an interaction with others in a way that inhibits or provokes subsequent actions.[20] As argued by Robert Jervis, states and international actors can exert influence by affecting the images that others have of them. And this kind of influence is exerted not by military or economic resources but through communication and the use of signals and indexes, issued in the form of statements or actions, with honest or deceitful purposes.[21]

A persistent problem in certain communicative environments, including fields such as national security intelligence, is what Diego Gambetta calls the ubiquitous threat of mimicry. That is to say, signals can be deceptively manipulated: "By lying, imitating, forging, or stealing certain signs, a signaler can mimic the state of affairs one associates with those signs."[22] Signaling theory addresses how deception can be detected and how those who aim to deceive can successfully do so.[23] Understanding the intelligence function, and more precisely, intelligence analysis, as the timely and accurate interpretation of signs related to national security issues can also result in the development of analytic techniques for countering overt and covert influence actions and other national security challenges.

## Persuasion, Deception, and Intelligence

Communication-based human interaction, persuasive communication, and social influence processes are important elements of the disciplines of intelligence collection, counterintelligence, and covert action. Countering disinformation campaigns and influence operations conducted through open communication channels requires an understanding of the communication environment, its processes, and the way communication can affect beliefs, attitudes, and human behaviors.[24] Thus, communication research and a communication-centered approach to the study of intelligence can contribute to intelligence scholarship and to the practice of intelligence. In a globalized world of digital communication, globally interconnected computer networks, massive open-source information, and social media, it is of utmost importance to understand the communication environment, especially in terms of information evaluation and intelligence analysis. Understanding public opinion and its processes, as well as mass media and their influence in the agenda of policymakers, is key for bringing perspective on the social and political dynamics affecting foreign countries and governments and the issues affecting the needs of intelligence customers.

Covert action includes propaganda operations, political action and intervention, paramilitary operations, and the new emergent subset of information warfare operations.[25] Harold Lasswell, one the forefathers of communication study, authored a classic work for understanding propaganda in which he characterizes propaganda as "the control of opinion by significant symbols ... by stories, rumors, reports, pictures and other forms of social communication."[26] Propaganda and the related intelligence functions of denial, deception, and disinformation are thus largely rooted in the art (and science) of communication, and communication science affords us key research tracks and insights, some of which are presented here.

Communication entails the effort to share—via various channels—a message, information, idea, or attitude from a source to a destination, using signs that stand for something in experience.[27] Communication science and research have taught us that messages are much more likely to succeed if they are consistent with the receiver's understandings, attitudes, values, and goals. Further, the effects of communication are influenced by several forces, many of which cannot be controlled by the sender, who controls only the message itself.

The other elements influencing communication effects include the communication situation, the personality of the receiver, and her or his group relationships and standards.[28] Understanding what is likely to increase the persuasiveness of communication and how to effectively structure communication is thus an important endeavor for intelligence practice. Recently, Russian intelligence, in concert with other actors, has shown itself to understand American politics and society well and to be very skilled in using social media in the US, allowing it to conduct disinformation operations and related activities effectively.

Communication research has provided further instruction on how and when efforts at persuasion are likely to be successful. For example, Jane Allyn and Leon Festinger successfully tested the assumption that a persuasive effort to change a person's opinion is more effective when the disagreeing communication is unexpected than when the influence attempt is anticipated.[29] Similarly, experiments by Richard Petty and John Cacioppo found that when the receiver is aware of an incoming strategic communication, the deliberate effort to influence is less likely to affect the receiver.[30]

Highly relevant to human intelligence collection, including interrogation and interviewing, Erving Goffman authored an important work for understanding how the communication field can contribute to the study and practice of intelligence. In his article titled "Expression Games," Goffman explored the human capacity to collect, reveal, and conceal information.[31] He established a distinction between what he called expressions, or expressed information, and communicated information.

Goffman observed that for a party seeking to collect information from an individual, communicated information is not enough for determining the sense of a message. Additionally, observers must pay attention to the expressions from the source. In the case of face-to-face interactions, paralinguistic cues, such as intonation and gestures, provide "framing information" for a message. In a hypothetical interrogation situation involving two players, an interrogator and a subject, Goffman noted key matters to consider: namely, the relation of what is said by the subject to the facts and the relation of what is said by the subject to what is known. When the subject is not willing to provide information to a party seeking to collect and assess the information, he or she may inhibit and fabricate expressions creating gamelike situations in which information becomes strategic. One such example is control moves, intentional efforts by the subject or informant to "produce expressions that he thinks will improve the situation if they are gleaned by the observer."[32]

Goffman's conceptualization of expression games and moves can be useful for explaining deception efforts. Similarly, Donald Daniel and Katherine Herbig developed a deception process model with contributions from communication theory and cybernetics. According to those authors, the channels of communication between deceivers and targets enable the deception by transmitting signals, planted clues, or evidence: "A channel could be a foreign newspaper monitored by the target, his reconnaissance satellites, electronic intercept systems, diplomats, or spies. . . . A signal may be a paragraph in a news article on the activities of a general, a reduction in the level of military radio traffic, or a photo of ships offloading cargo."[33]

## Communicating Analysis and Assessments to Intelligence Consumers

### Communication in Decision-Making

Communication and decision-making are inextricably linked, and it is through communication that nation-states, organizations, and individuals try to affect the decision processes of others. Intelligence dissemination can be understood as a special type of communication process in which the intelligence-producing organization engages in intentional transmission, through language and other signs, of a specific kind of information, produced and protected by using secrecy as a tool and relevant for national security issues. At the same time, intelligence collection and analysis face efforts from adversaries and other actors to conceal or disrupt those activities by engaging in communication and influence processes and, using Goffman's term, in expression games.

This special type of communication is, in turn, a key input in policymaking. When making decisions, policymakers can rely on "simple decision rules" (cognitive decision rules or heuristics) or adopt a different approach: vigilant problem solving. This approach consists of four steps: (1) formulating the problem, (2) using informational resources, (3) analyzing and reformulating, and (4) evaluating and selecting (alternatives). The model "describes what executives can do within the confines of incomplete knowledge, unresolvable uncertainties, limited capacity to process information, and all other usual constraints, which can hamper sound thinking about the generally ill-defined problems that require policy decision."[34]

Intelligence reports and inputs from other experts are resources to be used in step two. Indeed, the quality of the decision-making process, both for policymaking and business management, can be judged by using a list of indicators: the decision-maker surveys a range of objectives; examines alternative courses of action; intensively searches for relevant information; correctly processes information, including unsupportive inputs; reconsiders the originally unaccepted alternatives; examines costs and risks of chosen alternatives; and makes provisions for implementation, monitoring, and contingency plans.[35] The completion of key steps, such as correctly processing information, including inputs that might be counter to policymaker plans and preferences, is in large measure a function of how, and how effectively, intelligence practitioners communicate—through oral or written means—assessments to policymakers. When analysts and agencies convey findings, they must be cognizant of policymakers' information habits, adapting so that their work can be successfully received. But if taken too far, or if assessments are overly padded or softened as to not aggravate the consumer, the charge of "soft politicization" may follow.

In their classic work *Essence of Decision*, Graham Allison and Philip Zelikow describe three models for decision-making: the rational actor model, the organizational behavior model, and the governmental politics model. The rational actor model, as described previously, consists of a rational nation or government, a unitary decision-maker, which in response to a strategic situation, threat, or opportunity, selects from a menu of options the one that will better maximize goals and objectives. The organizational behavior model understands governmental behavior more as "outputs of large organizations functioning according to standard patterns of behavior" than as a deliberate choice of a unitary rational decision-maker. Last, the governmental politics model conceives government behavior as the result of complex bargaining among governmental stakeholders.[36] (See chapter 6 and chapter 8 for further insights into these models.)

## Looking to Journalism: The Production and Communication of Finished Intelligence

In both written and oral forms, including face-to-face interactions, analysts must be effective communicators, including to policymaker audiences that may not always be open and receptive to the assessments they are receiving. Journalism studies and practice, as specific areas of communication inquiry, provide useful principles and best practices for intelligence production and communication as well as for analysis of the communicative quality of intelligence assessments. Some journalistic genres, such as interpretive journalism, can be especially relevant. As explained by Brant Houston, "interpretive journalism goes beyond the basic facts of an event or topic to provide context, analysis, and possible consequences." Reporters "are expected to have expertise about a subject and to look for motives and influences to explain what they are reporting."[37] Descriptive journalism positions the journalist in the role of an observer, while in interpretative journalism the practitioner is also required to be an analyst.[38]

Some professional journalistic concepts, like the inverted pyramid, have in fact been imported to the intelligence community, with clear relevance to the organization and communication of intelligence assessments.[39] Potential applications for college and university intelligence education are also clear. Horst Pöttker has argued that the inverted pyramid became a professional standard in American journalism during the 1880s as a way to improve the communicative quality of news: "The most important information is summarized in the so-called 'lead sentence' that, according to standard practice, has to answer four or five 'w-questions' (who? when? where? what? and perhaps why?). After the lead sentence comes the rest of the story, which may already be redundant for the reader. The information presented after the lead sentence appears in decreasing order of relevance and with an increase in quantity. The details considered least relevant appear at the end."[40]

In an era of digital communication, the study of multimedia journalism practices can also provide insights for evaluating the applicability of digital and interactive news products to the field of intelligence analysis and production.[41] The presentation of relevant information to intelligence consumers in visual and creative ways is, indeed, not new. Dating to the 1940s, the Central Intelligence Agency (CIA) Cartography Center, for example, was making "vital contributions to our Nation's security, providing policymakers with crucial insights that simply cannot be conveyed through words alone."[42] However, new digital communication technologies and tools can make the visual presentation of information and intelligence more powerful and agile in many ways. Such platforms allow for the interaction of the user with multimedia-enhanced maps, bolster the narrative of intelligence products by adding temporal dimensions to static images using video, incorporate real-time data feeds into analytic products, and enable alternative paths for consuming analytic assessments through hypertext and reading the decisions of the intelligence customer through user navigation systems such as tabs. Infographics can help in digesting complex information, presenting data in a narrative way and visualizing alternative courses of action.

Scholarly research and professional practices in information design, interaction design, usability, and user experience are relevant if intelligence products are to be adapted to the digital era.[43] This is consistent with a CIA career opportunity post for its "multimedia production group," advertised through the agency website: "CIA multimedia production units are seeking creative user interface and user experience designers who can convey an analytic story visually through multimedia for the President of the United States, US policymakers, and other officials."[44]

## Conclusion

Intelligence is one of the many contexts to which communication research, concepts, and theories can be applied. To be sure, some communication models, as well as ideas from semiotics, have already been applied in the field of intelligence. In today's world of globalization, digital communication, and fake news, it is more important than ever to provide knowledge on, and develop critical thinking and competences in, communication analysis.

The effective execution of many steps of the intelligence process hinges on communication practices and thus, to be best and most fully understood, requires study from a communication science perspective. This chapter has shown that intelligence collection, analysis, production, and dissemination, as well as covert action, are built on communication, and research insights from that field can help students, scholars, and practitioners conceptualize and improve many intelligence functions.

This chapter, in addition to those on political science, public administration and organization theory, and decision science, also demonstrates that getting toward a fuller view and understanding of the multifaceted field of intelligence requires the application of a range of disciplines. Intelligence research and education, when more fully informed by such a multidisciplinary perspective, will enrich intelligence studies, enhance intelligence practice, and ultimately improve intelligence support to national security policymakers.

## Notes

An earlier version of this chapter was first presented as a paper for the National Security Studies Institute at the University of Texas at El Paso's 2017 colloquium, "Social and Behavioral Science Approaches to the Study of Intelligence," March 23, 2017. The paper was partially based on the draft paper "Communication and Decision-Making: Implications for Intelligence," prepared for presentation at ISA's Fifty-Seventh Annual Convention, March 16, 2016, Atlanta, Georgia. A preliminary work addressing similar questions can be found in Rubén Arcos Martín, "Comunicación, cultura y reservas de inteligencia," in *Inteligencia*, ed. José-Luis González Cussac (Valencia: Tirant lo Blanch, 2010), 411–62.

1. Tiane L. Lee, Michele J. Gelfand, and Yoshihisa Kashima, "The Serial Reproduction of Conflict: Third Parties Escalate Conflict through Communication Biases," *Journal of Experimental Social Psychology* 54 (2014): 71.
2. This applies to the intelligence process, whether it is conceptualized as a cycle that begins and ends with the intelligence customer or by using other alternative models

like Clark's target-centric view. See Robert M. Clark, *Intelligence Analysis: A Target-Centric Approach* (Washington, DC: CQ Press, 2004).
3. Gregory J. Shepherd, "Building a Discipline of Communication," *Journal of Communication* 43, no. 3 (1993): 87.
4. Peter Gill and Mark Phythian, "What Is Intelligence Studies," *International Journal of Intelligence, Security, and Public Affairs* 18, no. 1 (2016): 5–19.
5. Steven H. Chaffee and Everett M. Rogers, "The Establishment of Communication Study in America," in *The Beginnings of Communication Study in America: A Personal Memoir*, ed. Steven H. Chaffee and Everett M. Rogers (Thousand Oaks, CA: Sage, 1997), 127.
6. Wilbur Schramm, "How Communication Works," in *The Process and Effects of Mass Communication*, ed. Wilbur Schramm (Urbana: University of Illinois Press, 1954), 3, 6, 8.
7. Schramm, 9. See also Nobert Wiener, *Cybernetics: Or Control and Communication in the Animal and the Machine* (Cambridge: MIT Press, 1965; first published 1948).
8. Wilbur Schramm, "Communication Research in the United States," in *The Science of Human Communication*, ed. Wilbur Schramm (New York: Basic Books, 1963), 1.
9. Wilbur Schramm, "The Forefathers of Communication Study in America," in Chafee and Rogers, *Beginnings of Communication*, 108.
10. Christopher Simpson, *Science of Coercion: Communication Research and Psychological Warfare, 1945–1960* (Oxford: Oxford University Press, 1994), 4.
11. Claude E. Shannon and Warren Weaver, *The Mathematical Theory of Communication* (Urbana: University of Illinois Press, 1998; first published 1949); Claude E. Shannon, "A Mathematical Theory of Cryptography," declassified paper (1945), https://www.iacr.org/museum/shannon/shannon45.pdf.
12. Robert Price, "A Conversation with Claude Shannon: One Man's Approach to Problem Solving," *Cryptologia* 9, no. 2 (1985): 170.
13. Shannon, "Mathematical Theory of Cryptography," 1.
14. Charles Morris, *Foundations of the Theory of Signs* (Chicago: University of Chicago Press, 1975; first published 1938), 1.
15. James Hoopes, ed., *Peirce on Signs: Writings on Semiotic by Charles Sanders Peirce* (Chapel Hill: University of North Carolina Press, 1991), 141.
16. Thomas A. Sebeok, *Signs: An Introduction to Semiotics* (Toronto: University of Toronto Press, 2001), 8.
17. Sebeok, 8.
18. Hoopes, *Peirce on Signs*.
19. Sebeok, *Signs*, 44.
20. Sebeok, 10.
21. Robert Jervis, *The Logic of Images in International Relations* (New York: Columbia University Press, 1989; first published 1970).

22. Diego Gambetta, *Codes of the Underworld: How Criminals Communicate* (Princeton, NJ: Princeton University Press, 2011).
23. Diego Gambetta "Signaling," in *The Oxford Handbook of Analytical Sociology*, ed. P. Hedström and P. Bearman (Oxford: Oxford University Press, 2009), 168.
24. Rubén Arcos, "Post-Event Analysis of the Hybrid Threat Security Environment: Assessment of Influence Communication Operations," *Hybrid CoE Strategic Analysis*, October 2018, https://www.hybridcoe.fi/wp-content/uploads/2018/11/Strategic-Analysis-2018-10-Arcos.pdf.
25. William J. Daugherty, *Executive Secrets: Covert Action and the Presidency* (Lexington: University Press of Kentucky, 2006), 71–72.
26. Harold D. Lasswell, *Propaganda Technique in World War I* (Cambridge, MA: MIT Press, 1971; first published 1928), 9.
27. Schramm, *How Communication Works*.
28. Schramm, 16–17.
29. Jane Allyn and Leon Festinger, "The Effectiveness of Unanticipated Persuasive Communications," *Journal of Abnormal and Social Psychology* 62, no. 1 (1961): 35–40.
30. Richard E. Petty and John T. Cacioppo, "Forewarning, Cognitive Responding, and Resistance to Persuasion," *Journal of Personality and Social Psychology* 35, no. 9 (1977): 645.
31. Erving Goffman, "Expression Games: An Analysis of Doubts at Play," in *Strategic Interaction* (Philadelphia: University of Pennsylvania Press, 1969), 4.
32. Goffman, 9, 12.
33. Donald C. Daniel and Katherine L. Herbig, "Propositions on Military Deception," *Journal of Strategic Studies* 5, no. 1 (1982): 155–77.
34. Irving L. Janis, *Crucial Decisions: Leadership in Policymaking and Crisis Management* (New York: Free Press, 1989), 90, 91.
35. Janis, 30–31.
36. Graham Allison and Philip Zelikow, *Essence of Decision: Explaining the Cuban Missile Crisis*, 2nd ed. (New York: Addison-Wesley, 1999), 5, 24, 143, 255.
37. Brant Houston, "Interpretive Journalism," in *The Concise Encyclopedia of Communication*, ed. Wolfwang Donsbach (West Sussex, UK: John Wiley and Sons, 2015), 301.
38. Thomas E. Patterson, "The United States: News in a Free-Market Society," in *Democracy and the Media: A Comparative Perspective*, ed. Richard Gunther and Anthony Mughan (New York: Cambridge University Press, 2000), 250.
39. See United Nations Office on Drugs and Crime, *Criminal Intelligence: Manual for Analysts* (New York: United Nations, 2011), 77–78. See also Office of Training and Education, *Analytic Thinking and Presentation for Intelligence Producers* (Washington, DC: Office of Training and Education, n.d.); Brenda Seaver, "From the Ivory Tower to the CIA: Reflections from a Career Intelligence Analyst," *PS: Political Science and Politics* 49, no. 3 (2016): 527–30.

40. Horst Pöttker, "News and Its Communicative Quality: The Inverted Pyramid—When and Why Did It Appear?" *Journalism Studies* 4, no. 4 (2003): 502.
41. Rubén Arcos and Randolph H. Pherson, eds., *Intelligence Communication in the Digital Era: Transforming Security, Defence, and Business* (Basingstoke, UK: Palgrave Macmillan, 2015).
42. "Cartography and Maps 2010s," Central Intelligence Agency, accessed August 12, 2018, https://www.flickr.com/photos/ciagov/sets/72157674854391962.
43. Rubén Arcos, "Communicating Analysis in a Digital Era," in Arcos and Pherson, *Intelligence Communication in the Digital Era*, 10–23.
44. "Interactive Designer," Central Intelligence Agency, accessed August 12, 2018, https://www.cia.gov/careers/opportunities/support-professional/multimedia-specialist-full-performance-cia-university.html.

PART IV

Beyond the Ivory Tower: The Research
and Practice of Intelligence

# 10.

# Bridging the Gap: The Scholar-Practitioner Divide in Intelligence

*Brent Durbin*

In 1993 Alexander George produced a pathbreaking book that set out to "encourage better communication and closer collaboration between academic scholars who study foreign policy and practitioners who conduct it."[1] *Bridging the Gap: Theory and Practice in Foreign Policy* was both a study and a model of the kind of two-way engagement George thought was essential for improving research and practice in international affairs. After a quarter century, George's book continues to serve as a touchstone for those seeking to understand and facilitate the nexus of theory and policymaking.

George saw problems on both sides of the gap between practitioners and scholars. Practitioners had an underdeveloped understanding of concepts and history, leading to poor identification and evaluation of strategic options in policymaking. For their part scholars failed to give enough attention to research questions that would be helpful for improving policies and were ill-equipped to translate their research for policy audiences. George argued that actors in each community had a responsibility to build bridges that could lead to better decision-making, especially in the areas of foreign policy and national security, which were the main focus of his work.

The concept of "bridging the gap" (BTG) has come to guide a range of efforts to improve collaboration and coordination between scholars and policymakers. This chapter considers BTG in the realm of intelligence. First, it explores reasons for the gap, including the different professional norms, practices, and goals found in the two communities. This section shows why bridging efforts are so difficult but also so important. Next, the chapter reviews the long-standing links between scholars and the US intelligence community (IC) and provides recent examples of outreach and collaboration between these groups. The final section discusses the ongoing challenges of the BTG enterprise in intelligence, including the role of secrecy, the limited influence of IC products themselves on policymaking, and the role of intelligence studies in the academy.

## Mapping the Gap

The basic goal of BTG activities is to *facilitate the transfer of knowledge between academic and policy communities to improve the conduct and quality of policymaking*. It is worth noting here that knowledge is only one component of policymaking; there is unlikely to be broad agreement on what constitutes "high-quality" policy because politics and ideology play important roles in policymaking.[2] Even so, BTG advocates such as George believe that the process and content of policy decisions can be improved only with access to more policy-relevant scholarship, which Bruce Jentleson and Ely Ratner define as "research, analysis, writing and related activities that advance knowledge with an explicit priority of addressing policy questions."[3] Such scholarship can enter the policy process through a variety of mechanisms, including scholarly writing, popular or policy writing, cross-fertilization at workshops or conferences, and direct outreach across the gap by individuals on either side.

### *Why Is It So Hard to Bridge the Gap?*

Despite these several ways to share academic knowledge that might be useful to practitioners, problems of timing, translation, and incentives contribute to the uneasy relationship between the academic and policy worlds. These observations are drawn from a growing literature on the scholar-practitioner nexus as well as from my participation in an effort to build institutional and intellectual capacity in support of Alex George's vision. This initiative, now called the Bridging the Gap Project, was founded in 2005 and has hosted hundreds of scholars in workshops aimed at developing policy-relevant research in international relations and finding ways to bring scholarly expertise into the foreign policy process.[4]

First, scholars face an inherent challenge in identifying policy-relevant research questions and completing research in time to make it useful. Policymakers do not need a good idea for research, backed up by an elegant research design, which will eventually fledge into a helpful finding. They need findings quickly, when the policy challenge is current. Moreover, they need research with clear policy implications that can be packaged in a way that is sensitive to existing policies as well as resource constraints and political realities. How can scholars know what kind of research will be useful to policymakers in the future? In some cases they must rely on luck. For almost any given policy area, there is *some* scholar who has been undertaking research on a question that interests policymakers. Like Kingdon's policy entrepreneurs, scholars must be ready when a policy window of opportunity opens for their research.[5] Besides waiting for their research to become relevant, scholars can also draw on their knowledge of politics and history to understand what future policymakers will need and then use this understanding to generate research questions. Some have borrowed forecasting methods from business and other disciplines to this end. For example, at the Bridging the Gap Project, we use scenario analysis to consider multiple possible futures in a five-to-seven-year time frame to try to identify questions that will provide useful findings for policymakers down the road.[6] The National Intelligence Council (NIC), which serves as the IC's "center for long-term strategic analysis," also uses this approach—among others—to develop its products. The NIC's work, such as the *Global Trends* series, informs long-range planning throughout the US government.[7]

The second challenge is that policymakers do not read well and academics do not write well—for each other. This is not due to intellectual deficiencies on either side; the two groups are simply looking for different things. Practitioners have very little time to read and need information that will help them make decisions now. Academics value nuance and methodological rigor, which tends to lead to narrow and contingent findings, often presented in long-form, jargon-riddled prose that is indecipherable to readers outside the discipline. Often, and understandably, scholars do not want to strip away all this nuance and rigor in ways they feel will undermine the integrity of their research. As a result, scholars do not naturally present their work in a form that is accessible to nonacademic readers, and policymakers seldom seek input from academic sources.[8] Beyond this, think tanks and federally funded research and development centers (FFRDCs) have become increasingly adept at packaging research in reports and briefs that are not subject to the long time lines and opaque methods required for peer-reviewed academic publications. These organizations give policymakers in Washington access to a local, attentive community that is trained to understand both research and the policy process. While these relationships provide the policy world with some analysis that includes academic knowledge, this exposure comes through a narrow aperture, as research findings are filtered through the biases and interests—such as fund-raising pressures and ideological or partisan preferences—of the relatively small number of researchers working at these institutions. Much of the research conducted at policy-focused think tanks and consultancies is ideally suited to policymakers' needs, but this "transmission belt" can serve to reduce practitioners' interest in seeking out more diverse scholarship.[9]

Finally, academic incentive structures do not value policy relevance and outreach. This is true at every step of an academic career trajectory. During graduate training students are usually discouraged from pursuing work or internships outside academia and seldom receive instruction on how to write for public and policy audiences. An increasing emphasis on quantitative methods in social science disciplines also pushes against policy relevance. As Anne-Marie Slaughter has observed, "All the disciplines have become more and more specialized and more and more quantitative, making them less and less accessible to the general public"—and to policymakers.[10] While statistics and formal methods have become more prominent in academic coursework and publishing, for example, practitioners report that they are more likely to value deep area studies knowledge, which has become less valued in social science research.[11]

These incentives are also reflected in later stages of a scholar's career. When seeking an academic job, trying to publish in peer-reviewed journals, and pursuing tenure and promotion, academics gain little advantage from policy engagement; such work may even be held against them. *New York Times* columnist Nicholas Kristof has complained that "Ph.D. programs have fostered a culture that glorifies arcane unintelligibility while disdaining impact and audience."[12] While Kristof's claim may seem extreme, it reflects a view held by many in the policy world, where the term "academic" is almost always synonymous with "useless" or "out of touch."[13] One scholar sympathetic to this view has described academic norms as generating a "cult of the irrelevant."[14]

While academic incentives remain centered on scholarly output, there is some anecdotal evidence of movement toward valuing—or at least accepting—policy engagement as part of a scholar's professional role. Publishing rigorous research is still the primary measure of quality in academia, as it should be. Policy outreach should always be in addition to, not instead of, traditional research output. Still, in our work at the Bridging the Gap Project, we have seen several developments that suggest an increasing interest in policy relevance in the academy. For example, since 2005 we have hosted an annual workshop for PhD students aimed at generating research questions that will be of interest to future policymakers.[15] At each of our first few workshops, we were told that several students had not informed their advisers they were coming to a program dedicated to generating policy-relevant research; they knew that any indication of policy interests might suggest that they were not serious scholars. Such concerns have faded since then. We have found a much broader acknowledgment that one can be a strong scholar and still have an interest in and commitment to policy influence. This recognition is found among both students and faculty. Our faculty workshop on policy engagement, the International Policy Summer Institute, has seen ever-increasing numbers of applications in the eight years we have offered it, including among senior faculty.[16] Additionally, in recent years we have convened two meetings of university provosts to discuss the incentive structures embedded in hiring and tenure decisions. We have found an inspiring degree of interest from these provosts in reimagining how nontraditional research and service activities are considered by their administrations. They have reported feeling pressure from funders, state legislatures, alumni, and students to justify their universities' work in light of contributions to the public good. Policy impact can be one way to demonstrate this value.

### Why Should Scholars Try to Influence Policy?

In the face of these challenges, there are at least three reasons scholars should want to engage in BTG activities. Most narrowly, policy engagement can contribute to better academic research. For example, for scholars who study foreign policy, exposure to practitioners can provide valuable access to data—such as documents, potential interview subjects, information on organizational structures and cultures, and information on bureaucratic and partisan political influences—that would difficult, if not impossible, to access without such connections. For those who study the policy process itself, additional benefits derive from watching how events unfold in real time.

The second motivation for engagement with policymakers is to improve the conduct of policy in areas of concern to the scholar. This is the principal focus of George's work on bridging the gap. Many academics enter their studies because they are excited to understand and even improve the world in a particular region or area of policy. They soon find that the norms and practices of academe are rarely focused on changing the world. Research questions are most often driven by the methods and data available to researchers or by marginal gaps in the theoretical literature rather than by problems that would be recognizable as such to members of the policy community. So pursuing policy-relevant research can help scholars remember what motivated them to enter academia in the first place, even if they are uncomfortable adopting the mantle of the scholar-activist.[17] It can also promote accountability in the policy world. Ernest May saw a role for scholars to serve as truth tellers about the possible advantages, drawbacks, and uncertainties of policy choices, including in intelligence.[18] Policy insiders are unlikely to do this in the same way, if at all.

The third benefit is related to the first two but takes an even broader perspective. BTG work provides another avenue through which scholars can contribute to society. In 2002 Robert Putnam used the American Political Science Association presidential address to make the case for the public role of political science, describing "contributions to public understanding and to the vitality of democracy" as core professional responsibilities of the discipline.[19] While these goals may be especially relevant to scholars studying politics and government, I believe the same logic holds across academic fields. If citizenship includes a commitment to promoting the common good, scholars provide a unique contribution through the creation of knowledge, especially when that knowledge helps to improve government decision-making.

## Why Should Practitioners Seek Out Scholarly Knowledge?

Even concentrated efforts by scholars to pursue relevant research and translate it for practitioners will fail if those in policy positions are not paying attention. To overcome practitioners' tendency to ignore or reject academic findings, scholars must be clear about what they can contribute. George identified three types of knowledge that scholars might bring into the policy process: (1) a "conceptualization of strategies," to define the policy options in a given situation; (2) "general, or generic, knowledge of each strategy," to review past experiences with each approach and outline how and when they might succeed; and (3) "actor-specific behavioral models," to understand better the individuals and groups that are party to a strategic interaction and on whom the strategy's success might depend.[20]

George saw these three areas of knowledge as necessary for improving statecraft but found that policy specialists were often resistant to bring "theory" into their thinking. Their mistake, George thought, was believing that they were not already influenced by theories.[21] He argued that the real choice for practitioners was not between theory and no theory but between good theory and bad theory.

## Bridging the Gap in Intelligence

With this framework for understanding general bridging the gap challenges in mind, I now consider the state of affairs in intelligence. The United States' need for academic support of its intelligence mission is more acute now than it has been since the earliest days of the Cold War. Not only is the US role in the world increasingly complex and uncertain, demanding expertise across a wide array of topics and places, but current (short-term) intelligence needs have largely overwhelmed IC resources that were previously devoted to long-term analysis.[22] Knowledge and perspectives from academia can expand the IC's capacity to address these challenges, but only if both scholars and practitioners can overcome professional norms that make collaboration difficult. This is true at all levels of the intelligence enterprise, from senior executives involved in national strategy to frontline analysts seeking expertise to support current intelligence products.

Before considering these connections and the way they can be improved, it is helpful to recall the unique role of scholars in establishing US intelligence during and after the Second World War. This history highlights some of the ways in which the two communities have collaborated to address key national security challenges—and how they might do so again.

### *The Scholarly Origins of US Central Intelligence*

When Franklin Roosevelt first established an independent intelligence office in the summer of 1941, its mission was to "collect . . . pertinent information concerning potential enemies, the character and strength of their troops and their people and their relations with their neighbors or allies."[23] This new organization, the Office of the Coordinator of Information, was quickly subsumed into the wartime Office of Strategic Services (OSS), which itself evolved into the postwar Central Intelligence Group and Central Intelligence Agency (CIA).[24] While OSS took on additional duties, such as espionage, sabotage, and paramilitary activities, during the war—and these later accrued to the CIA as well—its foundational mission was research and analysis, and many of its earliest employees came from the professorial ranks. OSS chief William Donovan even came to refer to his Research and Analysis Branch as his "professors."

It is telling that the early history of US intelligence is written in books with titles such as Robin Wink's *Cloak and Gown* and Ray Cline's *Secrets, Spies, and Scholars*.[25] Former national security adviser McGeorge Bundy later reflected on the "curious fact of academic history that the first great center of area studies in the United States was not located in any university, but in Washington, during the Second World War, in the Office of Strategic Services."[26] This academic orientation continued after the war as OSS transformed first into the Central Intelligence Group and then the CIA. Winks reports that by 1948–49, CIA personnel had come from seventy-seven different colleges and universities.

The persistence of trained academic representation at the CIA was not appreciated by everyone and is partly responsible for the clash of cultures between officers in the agency's Directorate of Intelligence and those in the more action-oriented Directorate of Operations. Over time the scholarly orientation of intelligence analysts led to suspicion on the part of some politicians and members of the military. Richard Nixon famously distrusted the CIA, which he considered populated with "Georgetown liberals." He even ordered H. R. Haldeman and Caspar Weinberger to "quit recruiting from any of the Ivy League schools . . . [or] Stanford or Cal." He wanted to be sure that all new recruits came from those schools that "have presidents or faculty members who have wired us or written us their support."[27] Former director of central intelligence (and retired admiral) Stansfield Turner saw the analytic branch of the CIA as "given to tweedy, pipe-smoking intellectuals who work much as if they were doing research back in the universities whence many of them came."[28]

### Academia and Modern US Intelligence

So an academic orientation is hard-baked into some parts of the IC. Still, much has changed in the time since the CIA's founding in 1947. The IC has grown to include seventeen agencies, including the Office of the Director of National Intelligence, as well as an established network of consultants and contractors.[29] Approximately 1.5 million Americans hold top secret security clearances, and very few of them are employed at universities.[30] How can outside academics contribute?

Bridging the gap efforts in intelligence can help both policy and academic communities in several ways. Scholarship can support the intelligence mission through both empirical and organizational contributions—what George called substantive and process theory. *Substantive theory* describes "standard foreign policy undertakings and strategies such as deterrence, crisis management, coercive diplomacy, détente, war termination, mediation and dispute resolution, and security cooperation." *Process theory* "focuses on how to structure and manage the policymaking process in ways that will improve information processing and foster sound judgments, thus increasing the likelihood of better policy decisions."[31]

In substantive areas scholarship can contribute to the intelligence support mission in the three ways quoted previously: identifying strategic options, evaluating these options on the basis of history and theory, and improving understanding of the actors involved. In addition to helping refine strategic thinking, access to scholarly knowledge can aid the development and understanding of day-to-day intelligence products. A focus on BTG in current intelligence might seem to depart from George's original formulation since he viewed the need for more and better theory in foreign policy as something fundamentally different from a need for "reliable and timely intelligence about situational developments."[32] Presumably he thought that scholars had no comparative advantage in this area, which could be better provided by journalists, diplomats, and especially intelligence analysts. Not only do IC analysts enjoy access to the most up-to-date data gathered from both secret and open sources but many also hold advanced degrees from the same programs that feed scholarly departments across a variety of fields. Yet intelligence professionals suffer from disadvantages in collecting relevant information about the world outside foreign capitals and formal institutions. Most are also beholden to a requirements process that limits the scope of their research attention, keeping their focus on questions that support immediate policy needs rather than scanning for topics that may become important to understand in the future.[33] Scholars are thus able to access data and ask questions that are unavailable to those inside the IC.

The benefits of BTG for intelligence practitioners are even more apparent in organizational and process areas. This is especially true with respect to analysis. Analytical methods in intelligence have been significantly influenced by academic research in psychology, cognitive science, and organizational theory.[34] Of course, these contributions must still grapple with the presence of various forms of bias in the policy process. As Robert Jervis has pointed out, policymakers are subject to significant motivated biases, driven by "powerful political pressures and psychological needs," that would be difficult if not impossible to account for in scholarly studies.[35] Such influences are coupled with a litany of unmotivated biases—those "inappropriate short-cuts to rationality" that Jervis first catalogued fifty years ago[36]—that are especially prevalent in the high-stakes, high-pressure world of national policymaking. It is this latter type of bias that is most susceptible to influence from rigorous scholarship, which can help make policymakers aware when their strategic choices are based on misunderstandings or irrational beliefs.

Academic professionals stand to gain from BTG in intelligence as well. Aside from the inherent benefit of seeing their work have an impact in the world, scholars also can unlock access to communities of knowledge that are typically cut off from public dialogue. Engaging with intelligence insiders can allow academics to test their theoretical and conceptual findings among well-informed colleagues who have deep content knowledge but who bring different questions and perspectives to a research topic. And even in intelligence, scholars may gain access to data that would not have been available outside BTG activities. The expansion of open source intelligence in IC analysis has generated new avenues for collaboration between scholars and practitioners, allowing for the development of dual-use research without the secrecy constraints assigned to most intelligence work.[37]

## IC Efforts to Bridge the Gap

Fortunately, there are signs that the IC is actively seeking to expand its BTG activities. A primary driver of these efforts is IC Directive 205, "Analytic Outreach," which introduces several areas in which the IC seeks assistance from outside experts. Signed by Director of National Intelligence (DNI) Mike McConnell in 2008 and updated under DNI James Clapper in 2013, this document advocates for "outreach to experts beyond the IC to support, improve, and enrich analysis" and directs that "elements of the IC should use outside experts whenever possible to contribute to, critique, and challenge internal products and analysis, and to provide alternative perspectives."38

In recent years the IC has responded to initiatives such as IC Directive 205 by accelerating its efforts to incorporate academic expertise in three ways: scanning, soliciting, and sponsoring. *Scanning* involves actively seeking out scholarly work that might be relevant to intelligence work. Some elements of the IC—especially the State Department's Bureau of Intelligence and Research (INR) and parts of the CIA—have been actively conducting this sort of outreach for years, attending academic talks and conferences, running brown-bag lunch series, and producing in-house research that is then vetted through traditional academic venues. INR's Office of Outreach serves as a hub for this kind of activity, organizing about 170 outreach projects per year as the executive agent for the analytic outreach directive. As another example of scanning, the Intelligence Studies Section (ISS) of the International Studies Association provides an unusual venue for bridging the gap, bringing together a mix of scholars and current and former practitioners that is unique among sections in the major academic associations. Many ISS panels include practitioner members, and each of the dozens of panels I have observed has included current IC professionals in the audience. Additionally, both the current and former ISS section chairs are former practitioners who moved into academia.39

Another approach to BTG in intelligence involves *soliciting* tailored research from scholars to fill gaps in the IC's own production. Both analytical and technical elements of the IC have developed programs for ongoing collaboration with scholars across several disciplines. For example, in 1997 the NIC established the Associates Program as part of the Global Expertise Reserve Program; this was renamed the IC Associates Program in 2008, when INR became executive agent for the analytic outreach directive. The NIC's *Global Trends* initiative has also institutionalized academic input. The Political Instability Task Force—formerly, the State Failure Task Force—has been working for more than twenty years to build and maintain a database of conflicts that might lead to state failure. This work began as an unclassified effort housed at US universities and sponsored by the CIA's Directorate of Intelligence. In addition to these ongoing efforts, the IC regularly solicits white papers and other products through the National Academies and other venues and provides grant support through the Intelligence Advanced Research Projects Activity and other vehicles for targeted research from university-based academics.

Finally, the IC *sponsors* connections with the academic world by shaping the ways that universities train future intelligence officers and develop understandings of the intelligence mission. These efforts include twenty universities that have participated in the IC Centers for Academic Excellence program, which is administered by the Defense Intelligence Agency.40 Smaller but related efforts have been undertaken by the National Security Agency (NSA)—the National Centers of Academic Excellence in Cyber Operations—and the CIA, which launched its Signature School Program in 2016.

These examples of outreach suggest that the IC understands the benefits of seeking academic resources and people to support its mission. While this recognition indicates progress toward narrowing the academic-practitioner gap in intelligence, it is unlikely to eliminate the gap owing to persistent and unresolvable challenges in this relationship.

## Ongoing Challenges to Bridging the Gap in Intelligence

The efforts described in the previous section are necessary because there remains an inherent divide between academia and government intelligence. To understand why this is true, first recall the general challenges to BTG described previously, such as the different goals and norms of academic and policy professionals. These also hold for intelligence work, despite historical connections between the two communities. In addition, the intelligence enterprise presents several significant barriers to effective bridging. These include secrecy, the role of intelligence in policy, and perceptions of intelligence in academic culture.

Not surprisingly, secrecy remains a barrier to the effective integration of scholars into the intelligence process. Recent IC initiatives have helped by allowing for a more flexible range of secrecy conditions in outreach efforts, including unclassified conferences and short-term clearances for targeted conversations with academic experts. Still, the need to uphold internal security protocols presents a high hurdle for practitioners seeking scholarly input on intelligence products. The problem of secrecy is exacerbated by the devolved nature of the IC; it is hard for scholars to know who might be interested in their expertise and how to package research findings for use by intelligence officials. As Ernest May notes, "Scholars dealing with modern international relations need to try to understand tribes in governments much as anthropologists try to understand tribal communities elsewhere."[41] For a scholar hoping to connect with intelligence practitioners, the complex networks that make up the modern US IC can be difficult to map out, let alone understand sufficiently to find useful access points.

Scholars must also be cognizant of how the IC fits within the broader policy process. While George's "reliable and timely intelligence about situational developments" is important for decision-making, the IC is not the only—or even the main—source of such intelligence. In fact, it is not only scholars who believe their work should be more influential among policymakers; intelligence analysts often have the same complaint.[42] Scholars seeking to bridge the gap should also seek other avenues for drawing the attention of policymakers, such as through op-eds and other media strategies and affiliations with think tanks and advocacy organizations.

A final challenge relates to the status of intelligence within the broader landscape of academic research. This manifests in two ways. First, the field of intelligence studies is relatively new and somewhat isolated from mainstream work in international relations. For scholars to contribute to the intelligence mission through their research and writing, they need more than just data for developing theories; they also need to be part of an active research community that can assess, test, and extend their findings. The intelligence studies community is robust and growing, but it remains somewhat sequestered from the mainstream of academic discourse. Much political science and international relations scholarship is not particularly attentive to intelligence, even when it should be.

Second, not all academics would agree that scholars should be supporting the work of agencies such as the CIA and NSA. For some this is part of the general academic discomfort with policy relevance that I described earlier in this chapter. For others the history of US intelligence—which includes assassination plots, spying on Americans, torture of detainees, and other illegal and unethical activities—makes collaboration with these agencies anathema to many academics.[43]

## Conclusion

None of these barriers to bridging the gap are likely to disappear soon. Despite these challenges, scholars should seek pathways to influence policy in whatever areas they feel their expertise might be helpful. The IC provides a range of opportunities for BTG efforts, not least because of its own efforts to incorporate scholarly knowledge into its work. Even so, scholars should understand the different goals, norms, and practices that govern the policy process, including the specific context of intelligence work. Practitioners should recognize how academic research can help improve strategies and processes of foreign policymaking. There are many reasons for the divide between the academic and policy communities; some of these reflect necessary and appropriate differences, while others undermine potentially fruitful collaboration that could improve the quality of work on both sides of the gap. Recent outreach efforts within the IC show a commitment to expanding opportunities for BTG. We should hope that these attempts continue, even if the gap can never—and should never—disappear completely.

## Notes

1. Alexander George, *Bridging the Gap: Theory and Practice in Foreign Policy* (Washington, DC: US Institute of Peace Press, 1993), xvii.
2. See Henry Nau, "Scholarship and Policy-Making: Who Speaks Truth to Whom?" in *The Oxford Handbook of International Relations*, ed. Christian Reus-Smit and Duncan Snidal (Oxford: Oxford University Press, 2008), 635–48; and James M. Goldgeier, "The Academic and Policy Worlds," in *Security Studies: An Introduction*, ed. Paul D. Williams (New York: Routledge, 2012), 567.
3. Bruce W. Jentleson and Ely Ratner, "Bridging the Beltway-Ivory Tower Gap," *International Studies Review* 13, no. 1 (2011): 6–11.
4. The Bridging the Gap Project is housed at American University's School of International Service and receives principal funding from the Carnegie Corporation of New York, which has played a major role in advancing such efforts over the past ten years. For more information, see www.bridgingthegapproject.org.
5. John Kingdon, *Agendas, Alternatives, and Public Policies* (New York: Longman, 1984).

6. For an explanation of scenario analysis and its use in generating research questions, see Naazneen Barma, Brent Durbin, Eric Lorber, and Rachel Whitlark, "'Imagine a World in Which': Using Scenarios in Political Science," *International Studies Perspectives* 17, no. 2 (May 2016): 117–35.
7. The NIC has produced a *Global Trends* report every four years since 1997. See https://www.dni.gov/index.php/global-trends-home.
8. Avey and Desch report that policymakers "are skeptical of much of academic social science which they see as jargon-ridden and overly focused on technique, at the expense of substantive findings." Paul C. Avey and Michael C. Desch, "What Do Policymakers Want from Us? Results of a Survey of Current and Former Senior National Security Decision Makers," *International Studies Quarterly* 58, no. 2 (June 2014): 227–46.
9. See Jentleson and Ratner, "Bridging the Beltway," 7–8.
10. Quoted in Nicholas Kristof, "Professors, We Need You!" *New York Times*, February 14, 2014, https://www.nytimes.com/2014/02/16/opinion/sunday/kristof-professors-we-need-you.html. For a more thorough discussion of the rise of specialization and quantitative and formal methods in political science, see Lawrence M. Mead, "Scholasticism in Political Science," *Perspectives on Politics* 8, no. 2 (June 2010): 453–64.
11. Daniel Malinak, Amy Oakes, Susan Peterson, and Michael Tierney, "International Relations in the US Academy," *International Studies Quarterly* 55, no. 2 (2011): 437–64. See also Avey and Desch, "What Do Policymakers Want?"
12. Kristof, "Professors, We Need You!"
13. For a summary of academic responses to Kristof, see Tadween Editors, "The (Ir)relevance of Academia? Academics Lash Back at Kristof for NYT Column," *Al-Diwan* (blog), February 28, 2014, https://tadweenpublishing.com/blogs/news/12565169-the-irrelevance-of-academia-academics-lash-back-at-kristof-for-nyt-column.
14. Michael C. Desch, *Cult of the Irrelevant: The Waning Influence of Social Science on National Security* (Princeton, NJ: Princeton University Press, 2019).
15. More information about the New Era Workshop can be found at http://bridgingthegapproject.org/programs/new-era/.
16. For more on the International Policy Summer Institute, see http://bridgingthegapproject.org/programs/ipsi/.
17. Scholar-activists take an explicitly normative approach to their research, focusing on questions and methods that can help effect specific changes in policies and practices of interest. While this tradition is strongest in fields such as anthropology (where it is often called "participatory action research") and geography, it has gained traction among other social scientists in recent years. See Jessica F. Green, "Why We Need a More Activist Academy," *Chronicle of Higher Education*, July 15, 2018, https://www.chronicle.com/article/Why-We-Need-a-More-Activist/243924; Cathy MacDonald, "Understanding Participatory Action Research: A Qualitative Research Methodology Option," *Canadian Journal of Action Research* 13, no. 2 (2012): 34–50.

18. Ernest May, "Studying and Teaching Intelligence," Central Intelligence Agency, 1993, https://www.cia.gov/library/center-for-the-study-of-intelligence/kent-csi/vol38no5/html/v38i5a01p.htm.
19. Robert D. Putnam, "APSA Presidential Address: The Public Role of Political Science," *Perspectives on Politics* 1, no. 2 (June 2003): 249.
20. George, *Bridging the Gap*, xvii.
21. George, 6–7.
22. See John G. Heidenrich, "The Intelligence Community's Neglect of Strategic Intelligence," *Studies in Intelligence* 51, no. 2 (2007).
23. Memorandum from William Donovan to Franklin Roosevelt, reprinted in Thomas F. Troy, *Donovan and the CIA: A History of the Establishment of the Central Intelligence Agency* (Washington, DC: CIA Center for the Study of Intelligence, 1981), 419–20.
24. For more on this transition, see Brent Durbin, *The CIA and the Politics of U.S. Intelligence Reform* (Cambridge: Cambridge University Press, 2017).
25. Robin Wink, *Cloak and Gown: Scholars in the Secret War, 1939–1961* (New Haven, CT: Yale University Press, 1996); Ray Cline, *Secrets, Spies, and Scholars: The Essential CIA* (Washington, DC: Acropolis, 1976).
26. Quoted in Cline, *Secrets, Spies*.
27. Cline.
28. Stansfield Turner, *Secrecy and Democracy: The CIA in Transition* (New York: HarperCollins, 1986).
29. In 2007 the United States spent approximately 70 percent of its classified intelligence budget on private contractors. Tim Shorrock, "The Corporate Takeover of U.S. Intelligence," *Salon*, June 1, 2007, https://www.salon.com/2007/06/01/intel_contractors/.
30. Bart Jansen, "Who Has a Security Clearance? More than 4.3 Million People," *USA Today*, June 6, 2017, https://www.usatoday.com/story/news/2017/06/06/who-has-security-clearance/102549298/.
31. George, *Bridging the Gap*, xxi–xxiii.
32. George.
33. For a discussion of the changing nature of requirements, see Thomas Fingar, *Reducing Uncertainty: Intelligence Analysis and National Security* (Stanford, CA: Stanford University Press, 2011), 28–30.
34. For a thorough review of scholarly contributions to intelligence analysis, see Stephen Marrin, *Improving Intelligence Analysis: Bridging the Gap between Scholarship and Practice* (New York: Routledge, 2011).
35. Robert Jervis, "Bridges, Barriers, and Gaps: Research and Policy," *Political Psychology* 29, no. 4 (2008): 571–72.
36. See Robert Jervis, "Hypotheses on Misperception," *World Politics* 20, no. 3 (April 1968): 454–79.
37. For more on recent developments in open-source intelligence, see Heather J. Williams and Iliana Blum, *Defining Second Generation Open Source Intelligence (OSINT)*

*for the Defense Enterprise* (Santa Monica, CA: Rand, 2018), https://www.rand.org/pubs/research_reports/RR1964.html.

38. "Intelligence Community Directive 205," Office of the Director of National Intelligence, August 28, 2013, https://www.dni.gov/files/documents/ICD/ICD%20205%20-%20Analytic%20Outreach.pdf.
39. Current chair Erik Dahl, associate professor of national security affairs at the Naval Postgraduate School, served twenty-one years in naval intelligence. His predecessor, Stephen Marrin, worked as a CIA analyst before entering academia. Marrin founded the section and now serves as associate professor in the Intelligence Analysis Program at James Madison University.
40. For more on the IC Centers for Academic Excellence program, see http://www.dia.mil/Training/ICCAE/.
41. May, "Studying and Teaching."
42. See James A. Barry, Jack Davis, David Gries, and Joseph Sullivan, "Bridging the Intelligence-Policy Divide," *Studies in Intelligence* 37, no. 3 (1993), https://www.cia.gov/library/center-for-the-study-of-intelligence/kent-csi/vol37no3/html/v37i3a02p_0001.htm.
43. CIA recruitment efforts at colleges and universities have sometimes been met with protests or even efforts to ban the agency from conducting business on campus. For a critical history of these relations, see Daniel Golden, *Spy Schools: How the CIA, FBI, and Foreign Intelligence Secretly Exploit America's Universities* (New York: Holt, 2017). For an insider's effort to address these and related concerns, see Robert M. Gates, "CIA and the University," *Studies in Intelligence* (Summer 1986), https://catalog.archives.gov/id/7283209.

# 11.

# The Ivory Tower and the Fourth Estate

*Paul Lashmar*

In early 2013 the disaffected National Security Agency (NSA) contractor Edward Snowden sought out two campaigning journalists, filmmaker Laura Poitras and *Guardian* columnist Glenn Greenwald. Snowden then provided Poitras and Greenwald with access to the tranche of up to 1.7 million classified NSA documents that, among other significant issues, revealed the massive growth in surveillance capability of the "Five Eyes" network of signals intelligence agencies of the US, UK, Canada, Australia, and New Zealand. Using the pseudonym "Verax," Snowden was also in contact with Barton Gellman, an investigative journalist with national security expertise working for the *Washington Post*. Another investigative journalist with national security reporting experience, Ewen MacAskill from the *Guardian*, joined the Poitras-Greenwald team in Hong Kong to structure and coordinate the release of their stories beginning in June 2013. Over the next months, investigative journalists from major news organizations across many countries cooperated with the core team to release documents into their regional media.

The Snowden documents caused a worldwide sensation and a polarizing debate in the Five Eyes countries about the merits of publication. Gen. Keith B. Alexander, then director of the NSA, said in June 2013, "These leaks have caused significant and irreversible damage to our nation's security." He added, "The irresponsible release of classified information about these programs will have a long-term detrimental impact on the intelligence community's ability to detect future attacks."[1] Sir Iain Lobban, the director of Britain's Government Communication Headquarters (GCHQ), said his spies had picked up "near-daily discussion" of the unauthorized disclosures among his agency's targets. His colleague Sir John Sawers, the head of the Secret Intelligence Service (MI6), was even more critical. "It's clear that our adversaries are rubbing their hands in glee," he told a British parliamentary committee. "Al Qaeda is lapping it up."[2] Heads of other Five Eyes eavesdropping agencies responded with similar criticisms. Others saw it as a fine example of the fourth estate at work, and the *Guardian* and *Washington Post* shared a Pulitzer Prize for their work on the Snowden story.

An anthropological method is to look for the silences in any situation, and when it came to the Snowden leaks, one group had surprisingly little impact on this splenetic public debate. A group of specialists, drawn from universities across the world, spend their time monitoring, researching, advising, and critiquing intelligence. For all their research activity, these academics did not alert the public to a massive growth in the Five Eyes signals intelligence (SIGINT) capabilities, with its concomitant potential not only for global mass surveillance but also Orwellian nation-state control. Furthermore, it took years for these academics to produce substantive responses to the Snowden documents in academic journals. The question this chapter addresses is, If academic responses are so delayed, what impact do they really have on policy about a controversial issue like global surveillance? Is scholarship there for the sake of scholarship? Or as intelligence studies academic Peter Gill asks, "If journalists produce the first draft of history, do academics produce the second?"[3]

This chapter was commissioned to explore what academics might learn from investigative journalists and whether cooperation between the two groups is possible in a more formal setting. First, I describe the two cohorts and some of the conditions they work under. Then I explore the commonalities and the differences between the two groups before considering the lessons academics can learn. At various points I compare the two groups to a third group—the intelligence community—as this community is the common point of research for both journalists and academics in what is an overlapping Venn diagram of three professional fields. To help conceptualize how the groups function, I find Pierre Bourdieu's field theory useful. In his lifetime he applied it to the "field" of journalism, among other groups, and it was further elucidated by Rodney Benson and Erik Neveu. I suggest that this theory describes better than other theories the relational self-reinforcing environment of journalism I know and that it could equally well be applied to the academy or the intelligence community. Within field theory Bourdieu proposed the concepts of *habitus*, which can be summarized as "socialized subjectivity," and *doxa*, or the "universe of tactic presuppositions." Both concepts are apposite, but in this chapter his concept of *illusio* has the most relevance. It describes "an agent's emotional and cognitive 'investment' in the stakes involved in any field," or more simply, the belief that the game is worth playing.[4]

A note of caution is that the cohorts of journalists and academics relevant to this discussion are relatively small, and this chapter tries to steer a path, making some general observations and suggestions, while recognizing that some dominant figures within the considered cohorts challenge those generalizations. Another point of fact is that the author is British and a journalism practitioner academic, so while the chapter refers to the landscape in the Five Eyes countries, it does tend to call on UK examples to make illustrations.

## Describing the Cohorts

### Who Are the Journalists Covering Intelligence?

Kenneth Payne notes that covering national security for the mainstream media draws in what he defines as the "access," the "clippings," and the "investigative" journalists.[5] The access journalists are those for whom national security is their specialism, or beat. They tend to be experienced staff journalists as the beat is recognized as a difficult, if not the most difficult, one. One distinct feature of national security reporting is how challenging it is to cultivate meaningful contacts. In any beat the reporter needs not only the official media contacts for the organization but knowledgeable individuals formerly of or within the organization who are prepared to talk on a confidential basis and may challenge the official line.[6] These reporters are, in effect, access or lobby journalists, and the danger for us and them is if they are not skeptical of any official line. In the UK most major news organizations have one or two reporters who are "accredited" and have mutually authorized contact with intelligence organizations. In the UK the agencies, with the exception of GCHQ, do not have press offices, and even GCHQ's is mainly for community liaison. In the US, access seems more liberal but varies across the seventeen or so intelligence agencies. Experienced journalists from Canada, Australia, and New Zealand have told me that media access is restricted, difficult, and sometimes tense, unless you are deemed "a safe pair of hands," for which you can read "lacking criticality."

When a major story involving national security occurs, an influx of general reporters may cover it, making the best contacts they can in the moment and using the news organization's "cuttings" or "clippings" library. This is routine and ephemeral and does not deploy any specialist knowledge of the sector.

Within investigative journalism in developed democratic countries, a subset of reporters tends to cover national security. Investigative journalists are largely driven by the search for exclusive revelatory stories and not by a particular beat. But by dint of stories covered and contacts developed, they usually have areas of special interest that they return to. National security is seen to be an important and newsworthy area, and for instance, in each of the Five Eyes countries, there are investigative journalists who cover national security time and time again. This is the group this chapter's discussion centers on (see fig. 11.1). The US academic Loch Johnson has noted the role of rigorous journalism in bringing accountability to the intelligence world: "I think that (in the United States at least) the media has done much more than any other organization or group to advance intelligence accountability. Especially investigative journalists, in their drive for a good story that might lead to their professional advancement and honors (Pulitzers and Polks, for example), have been successful in sniffing out stories and alerting elected overseers in Congress to carry out investigations."[7]

I conform to this characterization as a journalist who, for a large part of my career, was an investigative journalist in the UK national media with specialist knowledge of

| Name | Nationality | Affiliation/Notes |
|---|---|---|
| Heidi Blake | United Kingdom | *Buzzfeed* |
| Jim Bronskill | Canada | *Canada Press* |
| Dr. Duncan Campbell | United Kingdom | Intelligence expert and freelance journalist |
| David Fisher | New Zealand | *New Zealand Herald* |
| Andrew Fowler | Australia | Formerly, Australia Broadcasting Corporation's *Four Corners* program |
| Colin Freeze | Canada | *Globe and Mail* |
| Barton Gellman | United States | Formerly of the *Washington Post*, a Pulitzer Prize–winning reporter and now a lecturer and author in residence at Princeton University |
| Stephen Grey | United Kingdom | Thomson Reuters |
| Nicky Hager | New Zealand | Freelance journalist and NZ's leading investigative reporter |
| Ewen MacAskill | United Kingdom | *Guardian* |
| Mark Mazzetti | United States | *New York Times* |
| Jenna McLaughlin | United States | *The Intercept* |
| Greg Miller | United States | Covers intelligence and national security for the *Washington Post* and was awarded the Pulitzer working with Barton Gellman |
| Andrew Mitrovica | Canada | Freelance journalist |
| Ellen Nakashima | United States | *Washington Post* |
| Dana Priest | United States | *Washington Post* |
| James Risen | United States | *The Intercept* |
| David Seglins | Canada | *CBC* |
| Scott Shane | United States | *New York Times* |
| Jeff Stein | United States | Covers the spy agencies and foreign policy for *Newsweek* |
| Peter Taylor | United Kingdom | BBC TV's *Panorama* |
| Ali Watkins | United States | *New York Times* |
| Dylan Welch | Australia | ABC's *7.30* |

Figure 11.1. Examples of investigative journalists who have national security reporting experience

intelligence. While working for the UK's Independent Newspapers, I was an accredited reporter with the security services, and up to 2008 I dealt with intelligence agencies, including during the controversial weapons of mass destruction; July 7, 2005, London bombings; and extraordinary rendition briefings.[8] More recently, I became a journalism academic practitioner whose research interests include the study of intelligence and media relations.

## Who Are the Intelligence Academics?

A key group of academics this book addresses are those whose discipline is intelligence studies. As a branch of the international relations discipline, intelligence studies has as its core academic body the US-centered International Studies Association (ISA). I have engaged with the intelligence studies discipline with varying degrees of success over the years, noting reticence to engage from some members of that group. Some investigative journalists and some intelligence-focused academics contact each other, but to make a generalization based on experience, cooperation remains occasional and unsystematic. Richard Norton-Taylor was the *Guardian*'s security correspondent until his recent retirement. He has a reputation for critical investigative journalism and observed that both journalists and academics can get too close to the intelligence people they are researching: "The security and intelligence agencies need [us journalists and academics], even more than 'we' need them especially now with pressure on MI5 (because of terrorist attacks) and on MI6 (on the back foot because of lack of protection of their Russian agents and over rendition), and GCHQ (desperately in need of recruits and good PR because of its increasing role re: cyber, etc.)."[9] Why is this important? The intelligence agencies have the potential to exercise power through secrecy that, in certain circumstances, has been and again could be undemocratic. John le Carré, with his usual erudition, encapsulated the key question for intelligence in "Fifty Years Later," a foreword to a new edition of his novel *The Spy Who Came in from the Cold*: "How far can we go in the rightful defence of our Western values without abandoning them along the way?"

As Tina Basi and Mona Sloane have written about the UK higher education institutions, academics are driven by targets for affecting public and government policy, attracting research funds, and producing high-ranking scholarship.[10] "While many higher education institutions (HEI) have come up with innovative ways to build impact case studies, the focus of impact practices has been increasingly narrowed down to tech transfer or policy impact." Basi and Sloane critically worry, "The 'impact agenda' is fueled, in part, by a cost-benefit framework." They place this in a wider context: "The discussion of impact is bound by both a poorly articulated purpose of higher education within social policy at large and a shift towards the marketisation of universities."[11]

Gill pointed out that academics manifest different approaches to producing output from their intelligence-focused work: "For example, I would distinguish those academics who conduct research from those who focus on scholarship. The former seeks to mine primary sources for material hitherto unpublished while the latter relies primarily on secondary sources and seeks to develop new perspectives, models or theories."[12] As Robert Dover, Michael Goodman, and Martha White note of the UK intelligence-academic environment, "There has historically been a measure of ad-hoc interaction between the UK's intelligence community with individual academics and, of course, with those in privileged or knowledgeable positions outside of the community." They go on to write that although universities are "public institutions, albeit funded in an increasingly private way," they "are a key source of knowledge and innovation for the country."[13] The number of former intelligence practitioners turned academics is increasing. There are many in United States, fewer in the UK; Michael Herman and David Omand (both ex-GCHQ) are obvious examples. Over many years I have engaged with intelligence-focused academics both as a journalist and as an academic and have observed the following distinct groupings.

The first group, acolytes, see themselves as an academic adjunct of the professional intelligence community and seek to analyze and improve intelligence methodology. Their closeness to the intelligence community positions them better to achieve the career-enhancing grants that will meet impact criteria. This group engages in both research and scholarship, and they often share, as Bourdieu might have described it, the *illusio* of the intelligence community.[14] These academics are often seen by intelligence leaders as useful aides-de-camp but best kept in the *vicus* and not the *castrum*. (One of the interviewees for this chapter pointed out that the idea that intelligence officials may welcome contact with useful outsiders in informal environments while not welcoming them into their inner sanctum could equally apply to journalists.)[15]

The second group, historians, seeks to portray the history of intelligence, and there tends to be a substantial time lag as official data and interviews with operatives may become available only many years after the events described. Some historians are sufficiently trusted to write the official histories with access to still classified archives. Interestingly, and somewhat counterintuitively, it is this group that is most called on by the media to commentate on intelligence-related stories, perhaps as they are seen to provide the long view and to have greater "respectability."

The third group, critical friends, see themselves as rigorous academic analysts of the intelligence community and its wider political and social context. They seek an overview, even a sense making and search for truth, of the larger ontological question of intelligence and, while engaging with the intelligence community, seem to exercise resistance to the pull of the intelligence field's *doxa*.

The fourth group, critical theorists, see themselves as very much a counter to the intelligence studies grouping and are outsiders, often Marxists, to the intelligence community. This group bases its analyses on the negative historical record of the intelligence community and can veer into conspiracy theory. They do provide a useful counter to the acolytes in any debate.

## The Commonalities

The first commonality between academics and journalists is that both face the shared obstacle intrinsic to obtaining data on intelligence: secrecy. Abram Shulsky and Gary Schmitt have observed, "The connection between intelligence and secrecy is central to most of what distinguishes intelligence from other intellectual activities."[16] As Dover, Goodman, and White noted, "The practical business of government intelligence and security communities exist, for the most part, in necessary secrecy."[17] While secrecy may be an essential of intelligence activity, it can mask groupthink, incompetence, illegality, domain expansion, and political meddling. Thus intelligence organizations need to be accountable, although the more usual open government oversight is not a comfortable fit. As Gill noted in his work on the democratization of intelligence, the media must be much more than a mouthpiece for governments. They are the fourth estate and provide a crucial, if informal, accountability mechanism. He recommends they act as a watchdog against corruption and other abuses of power, including providing an outlet for whistle-blowers, and argues that since "formal intelligence oversight mechanisms are often relatively weak [it] is often some combination of civil society organisations and the media that brings abuses to public attention."[18]

Gill also noted that the problem for media in covering security and intelligence issues is often presented as one of penetrating the "veil of secrecy," but that is just one dimension of the problem. The job of journalists (and academic researchers) is similar in many respects to that of intelligence officers: both are seeking information, often from or about people who guard their privacy closely. Even if information can be obtained, the problem is making sense of it and drawing some reasonable conclusion.[19] The most productive method for journalists to obtain intelligence insights is through sources. Access to those working in intelligence is difficult, and if access is to be achieved, the question has to be asked, At what cost?[20]

Given the protective secrecy and the strength of their *habitus* and *illusio*, those within intelligence rarely feel compelled to explain themselves or discuss the ethical and conceptual basis on which they operate. They tend to talk to journalists or academics only if they feel they will gain something—the rare exception to this is the whistle-blower. While journalists have a good deal of freedom within legal and ethical constraints, academics find constraints embedded in the research infrastructure. It is clear that to remain relevant to public policy and opinion, academics need to become more agile and timely.

The second commonality is the research cycle, the process of identifying knowledge gaps, collecting information, analyzing it, and reporting it (fig. 11.2).[21] Dover, Goodman, and White undertook an exercise to see what the intelligence community could learn from academics and compared the intelligence cycle with the academic research process using the eight-step hourglass model, which they summarize as using eight key steps in the research process. "Whilst academic research 'models' are neither uniform nor universally adhered to, the Hourglass Model represents the ideal

| Intelligence cycle | Academic research model (hourglass) | Investigative journalism model |
|---|---|---|
| Identifying requirements | Identification of the research problem | Initial facts or clues |
| Consulting organizational memory—the files and open sources | Literature review | Cuttings review |
| Specific targeting | Specification of the purpose of research | |
| | Determination of specific research questions | Determination of specific research questions |
| Possible source identification and management | | Possible source identification and management |
| Collection of information | Data collection | Data collection |
| Processing of information | | Verification |
| Analysis of information | Analysis and interpretation of data | Analysis and interpretation of information |
| Evaluation by managers | Reporting and evaluation of research | Evaluation of story with editors and lawyers |
| Dissemination of analytic product, that is, "intelligence" | Communication of research findings and recommendations | Dissemination |
| Feedback from customer and policymakers | Citations | Feedback from targets and audience |

Figure 11.2. Intelligence cycle, academic research model (hourglass), and investigative journalism model

process of academic research."[22] As a complementary exercise, I extend the comparison to include a third element, investigative journalism, using Mark L. Hunter's "story-based inquiry model," which is widely considered the best practice research method for in-depth journalism. Hunter writes that unlike most routine journalism, the story-based inquiry model takes "the hypothesis-based inquiry approach, which takes the basic assumption that a story is only a hypothesis until verified."[23]

The processes of research and analysis in all three cohorts closely correspond. The notion of hypothesis works across all cohorts as they use methods (not philosophical truth determinations) that provide the best available means of approaching "truth." While the journalist does not explicitly state a hypothesis, it is usually paraphrased in the introductory sentence or paragraph of the story. As Gill noted, he had much sympathy with the idea that what analysts, academics, and journalists are trying to do is "make sense" of the world. "The idea of 'sensemaking' seems highly appropriate to issues of such complexity. As someone once said, 'truth is a difficult concept.'"[24]

## Core Differences

The three cohorts are in other regards quite different. Funding is different for each of the three groups, and Gill observed that, for academics, funding is more crucial for research than scholarship: "The former seeks to mine primary sources for material hitherto unpublished while the latter relies primarily on secondary sources and seeks to develop new perspectives, models or theories." But, he adds, perhaps it is less so now that so much material is available online:

> There has never been much funding available for academic research into intelligence but I believe much can be done without it. Now I think there will be more funding available for historical research than social science research into current organisational/governance issues because they raise trickier questions of getting access and may frighten donors. The lack of availability of big grants for research into intelligence (compared with elections, parties etc.) is one of a number of reasons why the number of intelligence studies academics is so small. Academics don't really face the risk of capture by funders but may risk capture by agencies if they seek to bargain access for control over output.[25]

Gill warned that even though there are differences in funding, journalists are also not free agents and will be subject to whatever editorial constraints are put on them. In many cases these restraints will reflect the preferences of owners and, in turn, may be shaped by informal or formal pressures from the state.[26]

A second difference is dissemination. Dr. Duncan Campbell observed, "In journalism, we publish, and meet legal, professional, and/or situational restrictions and responses. We are de facto subject to 'review' (taking a very broad meaning) by anyone without restriction including targets of enquiries." By comparison, he noted, "intelligence reports are 'disseminated' only to selected recipients, who are likely to be de facto paying or payment enabling customers, with strict and severe controls. The broad 'reviews' consequent on genuine publication are wholly and inevitably absent."[27] The main academic dissemination is in peer-reviewed journals for which the audience is usually in three figures if the metrics are to be believed.

A third difference is in the collection of information. Sources are used across all groups, but academics do not tend to use sources in the same way as either journalists or intelligence officers. Gill noted, "Covert methods are standard and essential for intelligence, OK sometimes for journalists subject to editors and codes and regulators; but rarely OK in academic studies." He expanded the point, saying it is easier and cheaper to gather information from open sources, but intelligence agencies are specifically empowered to infringe on privacy and deploy many methods to gather information covertly: "Journalists do not possess such legal powers but may well deploy various forms of subterfuge up to and including illegal behaviour in order to gather what is not publicly available. How else could investigative journalism proceed? Once gathered, much effort is made to protect not just what has been learnt but also the sources."[28]

When it comes to technologically assisted intelligence, neither journalists nor academics can rival GCHQ for technological SIGINT data capture and imagery intelligence. That said, the availability of commercial imagery and the broader availability of open source information has empowered journalists and academics. For example, the crowd-sourced investigative group Bellingcat has done quite remarkable work with commercially available satellite imagery, notably in the case of the Malaysian airliner shot down over Ukraine in 2014. In this example, Bellingcat made a strong case for a mobile Russian missile launcher unit to have been the culprit.[29]

A fourth difference is confidentiality. Information barriers are common to all three cohorts. They are especially prevalent in intelligence but are very small in academia. While predisposed to publication, journalists have an ontological duty of confidentiality to some sources. Academics, in contrast, do not usually operate with live issues, so confidentially is not such a concern, except that university ethics committees push academics toward confidentiality even when it is not necessary.[30]

A fifth difference is time. Urgency is a factor for both intelligence and journalist groups, whereas academics prioritize perceived authority of reporting. Intelligence collection and analysis can be a race against time to prevent catastrophic events. Journalism has a publication imperative, but investigative journalists are not so subject to the 24-7 news regime. Gill noted academic research is mainly historical and therefore urgency does not arise, except if there is a race to publish some new findings from recently opened archives. He wrote, "I'd draw a distinction between urgency of analysis in a developing counterterrorism investigation compared with anything journalists may face, e.g., fear of being beaten to publication by rivals."[31]

As Gill observed, all three cohorts are subject to review by peers: "For intelligence analysts, the first people they have to convince with their product are managers who intervene between them and the policy people; for academics the equivalent is the external reviewer and for journalists, the editor."[32] Dover, Goodman, and White observed that intelligence analysis may utilize a range of structured analytical techniques or may be performed without any methodological approach: "Structured analytical techniques range from simple brainstorming instructions to the application of Subjective Bayesian Analysis."[33] Within intelligence, analysis is a crucial element in producing a "product" ready for dissemination and involves assessing the credibility of both the information's source and the information itself. This assessment may involve using sophisticated models but at the very minimum will involve seeking independent verification or cross-checking different sources.[34] The argument goes that despite the similarity of interests, journalists, unlike academics, operate with an imperative to inquire and publish, and their outlets are conceptually framed around speedy delivery to the wider public sphere. Academics are under lesser temporal or dissemination imperatives. Gill wrote, "I think academics can learn much from investigative journalism, but taking the longer view, I don't think there is any point in academics trying necessarily to produce quicker—it's more important that one's work passes the test of 'intersubjectivity.'" However, like journalists, academics are facing more and more fiscal and productivity pressures in their institutions. Some of these are common across international borders, some are national in character, and others institutional. There are the systemic pressures of an increasingly consumer-driven higher education sector. Contemporary research academics express incredulity at the suggestion that they still have time to read and think within their contracted work hours.

The sixth difference lies in the ethics mechanisms. Professional journalists operate with an ethical framework, and ethics is integral to most journalism university training syllabi. In the UK most belong to the National Union of Journalists, which has an ethical structure and code, and they are also subject to self-regulation (print), an official regulatory body (broadcast), and the law. Nevertheless, they are generally free to contact potential interviewees without much ado, unless the interviewees are vulnerable or under the age of eighteen. Only when it comes to undercover work for interviews do matters become more complicated, especially for public service broadcasters, for whom the regulatory bodies now stringently require compelling evidence that subterfuge is justified.

In contrast, even if it is possible for academics to interview former and current intelligence officers, they almost certainly could not interview people on the periphery, like agents and contractors. In some cases these peripheral characters have engaged in criminal activity, and ethics committees are reticent to let academics interview criminals (unless they are in prison and supervised) or to enter environments where criminal activity may take place. From my experience, academic ethics committees tend to be one-size-fits-all enterprises and prefer risk-averse proposals. An academic's prior experience of these situations often holds no sway, and researchers who have previously done ethnographic work in environments frequented by criminals are just as likely to have their projects rejected as inexperienced doctoral researchers. These ethics committees and processes also push academics toward confidentiality for interviewees, which reduces their ability to fully authenticate their sources as valuable. (In fairness, insider sources will normally insist of anonymity anyway.) This is because these committees, in seeking to protect the vulnerable, treat all groups as though they are unable to see the bigger picture. It is as if highly experienced people from law enforcement and intelligence cannot manage their own risks, even though in most cases the potential interviewees have been doing just that for their entire careers. The danger of ethics committees is that they can infantilize both the academic and the sources. Ethics committees need to consider ethics from a real world rather hypothetical perspective. If journalists were subject to such committees, little quality reporting would ever be undertaken. Some of the most important research is to be found in areas that ethics committees will veto.

## How Can Journalists and Intelligence-Focused Academics Cooperate?

For academic engagement with the public debate to be made timelier, all academics will have to challenge systemic barriers like overly rigorous ethics approval and the slow peer review publication process. Academics in the intelligence-related disciplines could, if so minded, take their cue from the journalists and improve certain areas. As noted, one measure academics have to consider now is impact. When an intelligence story breaks, journalists turn to existing or former intelligence insiders or oversight entities or even politicians. Stuart Hall and colleagues noted decades ago the role of elite interviewers, who they characterized as "primary definers. . . . Such spokesmen are understood to have access to more accurate or specialized information on particular topics than the majority of the population."[35] I argue that the debate around Snowden was framed within the first weeks, if not days, of the story. Here the notion of an elite discourse fits well with Hall and colleagues' way of thinking about where the debate was framed.[36] After the Snowden leaks, in most of the Five Eyes countries, the debate was polarized: government and the intelligence community, supported by parts of the press, stood on one side against the Snowden release, and journalists, some politicians, and considerable elements of civil society stood on the other, defending Snowden's release.

Some academics do seek to get op-ed pieces in the media and are available to comment on major events in intelligence. In recent years academics, with encouragement from their universities, have been seeking to influence policy by writing for commentary websites, like The Conversation in Australia and Open Democracy in the UK. Although the actual impact is not yet clear, these websites do get accessible academic analysis into the public sphere quickly. Being concise and engaging is not a skill known to all academics. Richard Norton-Taylor noted, "Whenever there is an incident, I get a stream of comments or offers of comments from academics and universities and the vast majority of the comments are extremely banal."[37] Countering, Gill noted that in the post-Snowden debate, academics have started to make contributions in other ways that are quicker than waiting for journal or book publication: "There were several post-Snowden inquiries: by the Intelligence and Security Committee (ISC), the Royal United Services Institute (RUSI), and that conducted by the UK Independent Reviewer of Terrorism legislation, David Anderson, to which academics contributed and in some cases were invited to public hearings. For example, I appeared with John Naughton, Julian Richards before ISC. Whether any of us had any impact on their conclusions, let alone policy, is another matter!"[38]

### *Interdisciplinarity*

For investigative journalists to work with academics would require a level of interdisciplinarity. Journalists are without a discipline and are by their nature interdisciplinary.

Their stories come from diverse sources, and journalists tend not to be constrained by boundaries. How about academics? Most universities say they encourage multi- or interdisciplinarity, and grant-awarding councils and bodies see it as advantage. This seems to work best in the sciences. As a research academic, I am surprised, despite the rhetoric, how reluctant academics, especially social scientists, are to engage with other related disciplines. When it enables understanding, I use an interdisciplinary approach, incorporating useful concepts from outside journalism studies. I have engaged with the intelligence studies discipline, in which there are discourse and methodologies for testing theory. My experience in the UK is that the silos are still concrete and not yet porous. Intelligence studies academics seem reluctant to integrate with security studies, surveillance studies, or terrorism studies and vice versa. Perhaps my view is harsh, as Gill argues that intelligence studies is itself at least multidisciplinary, if not interdisciplinary.

There is a small but growing discourse around intelligence and the media that a cross-discipline engagement adds value. However, as a journalism academic, I have felt deliberately discouraged by colleagues in UK intelligence studies at times. Some positively arbitrate against journalists (including journalism academics) attending their events or engaging in discourse. This is especially true when current or even former intelligence operatives are present. Essentially they think the presence of someone who has journalistic credentials will deter contributions from "the industry." It is worth noting that journalism practitioners do understand Chatham House Rules, which state that "participants are free to use the information received, but neither the identity nor the affiliation of the speaker(s), nor that of any other participant, may be revealed."[39] There have been some moves to persuade intelligence-focused academics to be more multidisciplinary, notably by Mark Phythian (see chapter 1 in this book).

*Matters to Consider*

Journalists are often quite willing to share their research material with academics once their story has been disseminated, as they frequently obtain far more data than they are able to use. I have noticed, however, that academics seem reluctant to use documents unless they are released by official sources or archives. For example, surprisingly little use has been made of the WikiLeaks Cablegate documents, a treasure trove of US State Department analysis of a wide range of countries, though some have suggested to me that could be because US academics who might want to obtain a security clearance in the future are reluctant to use Wikileaks documents. Such sensitivities do not cross the minds of journalists, who believe that "information is information" and the source of information is less important than its verification.

In addition to access to research material, academics might see other benefits of engaging with investigative journalists. A journalist who has been considering intelligence for many decades, for example, can bring mature subjectivity to the topic, especially given the data drought in intelligence.

## International Cooperation

In the last decade or so, journalists have turned from being solo, retentive story hunters to far more collaborative operators. There have now been many stories in which journalists have collaborated across borders to exploit data leaks. The series of data leaks regarding offshore banking secrecy have been exemplary and have taught many lessons. The International Consortium of Investigative Journalists worked with the German newspaper *Suddeutsche Zeitung* and more than a hundred other media partners over the course of a year to sift "through 11.5 million leaked files to expose the offshore holdings of world political leaders, links to global scandals, and details of the hidden financial dealings of fraudsters, drug traffickers, billionaires, celebrities, sports stars and more."[40] Academics of course often have international connections, and intelligence studies academics have the annual ISA conference. But it is worth considering whether these kinds of groupings could become more proactive in analyzing the contemporary landscape. Intelligence has international real-time links, and that raises serious oversight issues to consider and monitor.

## Forums

In the UK, journalists and academics from a range of security and international relations disciplines meet in certain venues, like the Royal United Services Institute and Chatham House. In the US, they meet in venues such as the Brookings Institution in Washington. Some UK intelligence and security research groups invite investigative journalists to attend meetings and conferences. Duncan Campbell, for example, was invited to a Ditchley Foundation conference to discuss the impact of Snowden.[41] Norton-Taylor, the most respected UK security correspondent, was invited regularly to such events but said he had attended only twice.[42] The picture across the Five Eyes countries is varied, with the US being rather more open than others, especially with the intelligence-focused departments in its higher education institutions, like Georgetown University and University of Texas–Austin. Most specialist centers in UK universities do not engage with journalists. Academics could seek to organize forums in which intelligence matters are addressed by investigative journalists with experience in the field. The UK has a need for a new intelligence forum and research hub (similar in principle to the security hub created by a consortium of universities led by Lancaster University) that would engage more systematically with investigative journalists with national security interests.[43]

## Conclusion

The academic, often sitting in a single-occupancy office, is still often a lone operator and may benefit from a more collaborative and timely approach. This chapter argues for greater engagement and interdisciplinarity. Dover, Goodman, and White noted the key benefit of academic and intelligence interaction "is the enrichment of knowledge and intelligence picture."[44] This can be extended to include journalists, especially those with a national security specialization. While intelligence-focused academic research and scholarship have integrated well-tested methodologies, academics might benefit from studying the ways and ethos of investigative journalism. Engagement might also reduce the polarization that featured so destructively in the Snowden debate. Taking their cue from investigative journalists, academics might consider a more proactive approach, perhaps taking on more contemporary research instead of historical scholarship and forgoing the consequential delay and lack of impact of the peer-reviewed publication process. However, the journalist-academic relationship is not a one-way street. Academics can also bring insight to journalists in understanding the processes of intelligence.

Given the too frequent failure of official oversight and accountability mechanisms for intelligence entities, there is a clear need for rigorous external monitoring from journalists and academics alike. In the UK I was involved with the interdisciplinary project DataPSST!, which successfully trialed this approach.[45] Despite the revelations from and the debate over the Snowden case, it caused only a delay, rather than a rethink, of the expansion of Five Eyes' capability and mass surveillance. Bulk collection (as the intelligence community likes to frame it) continues its dangerous expansion; a US intelligence agency report stated the NSA had collected more than 500 million phone call records from Americans in 2017, more than triple the number gathered in 2016.[46] And there are new problems to confront. As this chapter was being written, Privacy International released a report titled *Secret Global Surveillance Networks: Intelligence Sharing between Governments and the Need for Safeguards*, which warned of "alarming weaknesses" in the oversight arrangements governing intelligence sharing between state agencies.[47] Engagement between journalists and academics would see enhanced cooperation and agility from the journalism side but also more measure and proportionality from the academic side.[48]

There is work to be done. As Phythian points out, ethical issues are inseparable from intelligence activities and, like the question of failure, can take in the entire intelligence cycle:

> Targeting of "friendly" states, the very notion of covert surveillance, and the more intrusive forms of collection, together with the question of covert action and other intelligence-led policy responses, all raise fundamental ethical questions. There is a growing body of work on this subject most recently clearly informed by developments in the "war on terror," specifically the torture debate in the US and the associated question of extraordinary rendition, in effect the outsourcing of torture by the US. Hence, more than ever before there is a need to adapt the just war paradigm to construct a concept of *jus in intelligentia*.[49]

An ethical failure that brings a short-term gain (of information) but a long-term loss (of moral high ground) is illustrated in the case of Libyan dissident Abdel Hakim Belhaj and his wife, Fatima Boudchar. In 2004 MI6 (and the CIA) aided Belhaj's rendition to Muammar al-Qaddafi's Libya, where the dissident was imprisoned and tortured. In 2018 British prime minister Theresa May had to make a full public apology for the rendition in front of the world.[50] Compelling evidence of British collusion in rendition had exposed a government cover-up. On matters of such importance, a mature dialogue across disciplines with experienced practitioners and academics may prevent repeating the mistakes of history.

## Notes

I would to thank the following for their advice and insight: Dr. Duncan Campbell, investigative journalist specializing in intelligence; Dr. Richard Danbury, ex-BBC investigative journalist and now associate professor at de Monfort University; Peter Gill, honorary visiting fellow at Leicester University; Richard Norton-Taylor, security correspondent at the *Guardian*, retired; Dr. Eamonn O'Neill, investigative journalist and now associate professor at Edinburgh Napier University; and Dr. Kenneth Payne, ex-BBC journalist and now senior lecturer at King's College, University of London.

1. Claudette Roulo, "Leaks Damage National Security, NSA Director Says," American Forces Press Service, June 28, 2013.
2. "Spy Chief: Adversaries 'Rubbing Hands Together with Glee' after Snowden Revelations," *Daily Telegraph*, November 7, 2013, https://www.telegraph.co.uk/news/uknews/terrorism-in-the-uk/10431349/Spy-chief-adversaries-rubbing-hands-together-with-glee-after-Snowden-revelations.html.
3. Peter Gill, email correspondence with the author, 2018.
4. Rodney Benson and Erik Neveu, *Bourdieu and the Journalistic Field* (Malden, MA: Polity, 2005), 3.
5. Kenneth Payne, email correspondence with the author, 2018.
6. This is difficult in national security reporting, especially in light of Snowden revelations, as journalists now know the full invasive capabilities of electronic surveillance methods that can be used to track sources. See Paul Lashmar, "'No More Sources?' The Impact of Snowden's Revelations on Journalists and Their Confidential Sources," *Journalism Practice* 11, no. 6 (2017): 665–88.
7. Loch Johnson, email correspondence with the author, 2015.
8. Paul Lashmar, "Urinal or Conduit? Institutional Information Flow between the UK Intelligence Services and News Media," *Journalism: Theory, Practice and Criticism* 14, no. 8 (2013): 1024–40.
9. Richard Norton-Taylor, email correspondence with the author, 2018.
10. In the UK, academics are under increasing pressure to engage with what is known as the "publish or die" culture of the government-inspired Research Excellence Framework (REF), a periodic review of academic research that will next be conducted in 2021. In the UK, papers are ranked by a four-star system, and for the REF, academics are under intense pressure to achieve three-star (nationally significant) or preferably four-star (internationally significant) ratings.

11. Tina Basi and Mona Sloane, "Impact Is Crippling Higher Education: But It Is Still Part of the Solution," *LSE Impact Blog* (blog), April 23, 2018, http://blogs.lse.ac.uk/impactofsocialsciences/2018/04/23/impact-is-crippling-higher-education-but-it-is-still-part-of-the-solution/.
12. Gill, email correspondence.
13. Robert Dover, Michael Goodman, and Martha White, "Two Worlds, One Common Pursuit: Why Greater Engagement with the Academic Community Could Benefit the UK's National Security," in *The Palgrave Handbook of Security, Risk and Intelligence*, ed. Robert Dover, Huw Dylan, and Michael Goodman (London: Palgrave, 2017), 461.
14. Related to Bourdieu's concept of the field with the *habitus*. *Illusio* is described most simply as the phenomenon whereby individuals are "taken in and by the game."
15. Gill, email correspondence.
16. Abram N. Shulsky and Gary J. Schmitt, *Silent Warfare: Understanding the World of Intelligence* (Washington, DC: Brassey's Inc., 2002), 171.
17. Dover, Goodman, and White, "Two Worlds," 461.
18. Peter Gill, *Intelligence Governance and Democratisation: A Comparative Analysis of the Limits of Reform* (Abingdon, UK: Routledge, 2016).
19. Gill.
20. Although sometimes it is easier for academics (especially if they have a reputation for discretion) since interviewees know that they are not seeking immediate publication.
21. I have made minor amendments to these models and included in the intelligence cycle the evaluation of open-source material, which is now commonplace at an early stage, and the identification of source intelligence and sources (important in both journalism and intelligence).
22. Dover, Goodman, and White, "Two Worlds," 465–66.
23. Mark Hunter, Nils Hanson, Rana Sabbagh, Luuk Sengers, Drew Sullivan, Flemming Tait Svith, and Piva Thordse, *Story-Based Inquiry: A Manual for Investigative Journalists* (Paris: United Nations Educational, Scientific, and Cultural Organization, 2011), http://www.unesco.org/new/en/communication-and-information/resources/publications-and-communication-materials/publications/full-list/story-based-inquiry-a-manual-for-investigative-journalists/.
24. Gill, email correspondence.
25. Gill, email correspondence.
26. Gill, email correspondence.
27. Duncan Campbell, email correspondence with the author, February 23, 2018.
28. Gill, email correspondence.
29. For details of the full Bellingcat investigation, see https://www.bellingcat.com/tag/mh17/page/9/.
30. Campbell, email correspondence.
31. Gill, email correspondence.
32. Gill, email correspondence.
33. Dover, Goodman, and White, "Two Worlds," 470.

34. Gill, *Intelligence Governance*.
35. Stuart Hall, Charles Critcher, Tony Jefferson, John Clarke, and Brian Robert, *Policing the Crisis, Mugging, the State and Law and Order* (London: Palgrave Macmillan 1978), 61.
36. Entman said of framing, "To frame is to select some aspects of a perceived reality and make them more salient in a communicating text, in such a way as to promote a particular problem definition, causal interpretation, moral evaluation, and/or treatment recommendation for the item described." R. M. Entman, "Framing: Towards a Clarification of a Fractured Paradigm," *Journal of Communication* 43, no. 4 (1993): 51–58.
37. Norton-Taylor, email correspondence.
38. John Naughton is professor of the public understanding of technology at the Open University. Dr. Julian Richard of the University of Buckingham spent nearly twenty years working in intelligence and security for the British government. Gill, email correspondence.
39. "Chatham House Rule," Chatham House, accessed May 31, 2018, https://www.chathamhouse.org/chatham-house-rule.
40. "About the Investigation," International Consortium of Investigative Journalists, accessed August 11, 2018, https://www.icij.org/investigations/panama-papers/pages/panama-papers-about-the-investigation/.
41. Ryan Gallagher, "Apple and Google Attended a Confidential Spy Summit in a Remote English Mansion," *The Intercept*, May 22, 2015, https://theintercept.com/2015/05/22/apple-google-spy-summit-cia-gchq-ditchley-surveillance/.
42. Norton-Taylor, email correspondence.
43. Dover, Goodman, and White, "Two Worlds," 471.
44. Dover, Goodman, and White, 472.
45. "Welcome to Debating and Assessing Transparency Arrangements," Prifysgol Bangor University, accessed August 11, 2018, http://data-psst.bangor.ac.uk/.
46. Charlie Savage, "N.S.A. Triples Collection of Data from US Phone Companies," *New York Times*, May 4, 2018.
47. Privacy International, *Secret Global Surveillance Networks: Intelligence Sharing between Governments and the Need for Safeguards*, April 2018, https://privacyinternational.org/sites/default/files/2018-04/Secret%20Global%20Surveillance%20Networks%20report%20web%20%28200%29.pdf.
48. Paul Lashmar, "Spies and Journalists: Towards an Ethical Framework," *Ethical Space: International Journal of Communication Ethics* 12, no. 3/4 (2015): 4–14.
49. Peter Gill, Stephen Marrin, and Mark Phythian, eds., *Intelligence Studies: Key Questions and Debates* (Abingdon, UK: Routledge, 2009), 63–64.
50. Declan Walsh, "Britain Apologizes for Role in Libyan Dissident's C.I.A. Nightmare," *New York Times*, May 10, 2018.

# 12.

# The Ethics of Intelligence Research

*Ross Bellaby*

There are some key challenges for intelligence studies that other research fields are not likely to face. First among them is that intelligence is inherently secretive. What intelligence operatives do, how they do it, against whom, and whether they are successful are all closely guarded secrets. And to some extent, this is justified. Intelligence plays an important ethical role in society when it aims to detect, locate, and prevent threats others wish to keep hidden before they have a chance to materialize, and being able to act in secret represents a key means to achieving this. A second challenge for intelligence researchers is the topic focus on national security, which raises concerns over how much information should be released and the extent to which it might actually undermine future intelligence operations. On the one hand, therefore, there can be serious implications when too much or sensitive information is revealed, putting operatives and operations in jeopardy. On the other hand, the researcher—whether in academia or journalism—faces an ethical obligation to inform the wider population by providing not only raw information but also critical analysis and evaluation to inform and educate so that people can judge the intelligence agencies' actions. There are therefore various, and invariably conflicting, duties put on the intelligence researcher: the duty one has to the political community, to keep them informed and to speak truth unto power; the duty one has to the security of the nation, to limit the harm one's revelations can cause; the duty to the intelligence agencies themselves, to keep them educated and self-reflective; and the duty to academic integrity and practice, to ensure the methods used are in line with what the profession as a whole requires.

## Duty to the People

Transparency and the duty to have an informed public are well established as ethical goods, to fulfill both the general need for information so individuals can make autonomous decisions in relation to their government and the specific needs of democratic systems to have an informed sovereign population. Being able to act autonomously means having enough information to critically examine one's choices.[1] Without information people's ability to reflect on how they should engage with their government (whether to cooperate or resist, to reside or move, to contribute or undermine) is severely limited. Add to this the special powers and allowances made for the intelligence actors—in terms of their ability to monitor, detain, and coerce people in ways deemed unacceptable for the general public—and it is clear that intelligence activity has the potential to cause individuals and society a significant degree of harm. There is a clear ethical demand, therefore, that regardless of political structure people know how intelligence activities are likely to affect them so they can decide how they wish to act.

Moreover, in democratic societies there is a specialized pressure to have an informed sovereign public. For instance, classical liberals such as John Stuart Mill and John Locke argued for an informed populous to keep check on state powers and its representatives, while John Rawls considered transparency as a key means of ensuring a just society.[2] Secrecy limits access to information and in doing so undermines the people's role as the sovereign power. This is the Madisonian argument that "meaningful participation in democratic processes requires informed participants. Secrecy reduces the information available to the citizenry, hobbling their ability to participate *meaningfully.*"[3] Furthermore, this recognizes that decision-makers, like all humans, are fallible, and public scrutiny is the most effective check on individual shortcomings. As Mill argued, "The only stimulus which can keep the ability of the body itself up to a high standard is liability to the watchful criticism of equal ability outside the body."[4] Secrecy is therefore considered wrong inasmuch as it challenges democracy by delaying its processes, limiting engagement, or weakening an individual's role. Having public involvement ensures not only that government policies and practices are a reflection of the public will but also that the intelligence agencies do not unduly undermine democratic necessities, including the right to privacy, liberty, autonomy, equality, and the freedoms of speech, assembly, and press.[5]

Where transparency cannot be guaranteed, then decision-makers should act as if it could be. This promotes the publicity principle, Kant's argument that the first test for a political maxim is to ask oneself, "Could I still get away with this if my action and reason for doing it were publically known?"[6] Indeed, Simone Chambers argues, "All theories of deliberative democracy contain something that could be called a publicity principle," whereby determining what secrets should be kept involves "having to defend one's policy preferences in public" so that the decision "leans one towards using public reason" or "reasons that this public at large could accept."[7] Such a principle "encourages participants to examine their own beliefs and arguments," promoting critical self-reflection by decision-makers, and confers legitimacy as the policy "ought to be in the general interest."[8]

What this means for the intelligence researcher is that as special actors in the community—born from their knowledge, training, position, and area of concern—they have a duty to inform the public. Social science research needs a strong strain of activism that places an ethical drive to be proactive and promote an informed population and that holds intelligence actors to account through the dissemination of scholarship. This means piercing the protective intelligence shield in order to put the publicity principle into practice and to ensure that there is no disjuncture between what people think is occurring and what is actually occurring. For intelligence the existing government oversight mechanisms are arguably too passive and have failed in revealing some serious unethical behavior, placing an even greater pressure on academics and journalists to act as this penetrating oversight presence.[9] Journalists in practice have an immediate obligation to actively penetrate secretive protections around intelligence and provide timely updates for the population. Academics, on the other hand, have a duty to investigate, analyze, critique, and provide an informed reflection of intelligence activity.

## Duty to the Nation's Security

This argument does not mean that all intelligence activity should be made publicly available. Indeed, there are general arguments for the benefits of secrecy in a democracy; secret keeping can aid processes and further democratic ends, including juries, peace negotiations, trade agreements, hiring and admission committees, and constitution writing.[10] The general argument put forward by many in the intelligence profession and by politicians is that any release of information or greater awareness of intelligence practice will put their activity, and their operatives, in jeopardy and will threaten the security of the nation. Intelligence secrecy is, therefore, often framed in terms of the "reasons of state"; that is, "certain actions that would be deemed immoral if performed by individuals are justified when performed by the state"—keeping secrets included.[11] As political theorist Micheal Walzer argues, "The survival and freedom of political communities . . . are the highest values of international society."[12] So regardless of whether you place a separate moral value on the state or whether the state is just a means of protecting the moral value found in the individual, secret national security is, to some extent, justified. As a result, there is "near universal consensus that some measure of secrecy is justified and necessary to protect authorized national security activities, such as intelligence gathering and military operations."[13]

In addition, some warn that too much openness and availability to external critique can have direct detrimental effects on the culture of the intelligence agencies. Njord Wegge argues that in addition to problems faced when intelligence partners have their own secrets revealed, including loss of cooperation, an excessive public gaze could create "oversensitivity, even passivity, among service employees, where the fear of doing something wrong and of public criticism could overshadow the responsibility to avert threats."[14] So while the intelligence professional should show concern about committing ethical wrongs, not all operations will be successful, and the fear of failure itself should not prevent action. That is, there is a difference between causing unnecessary harm to someone through excessive or unjustified surveillance and failing to produce results despite a justified level of surveillance on a legitimate target.

Moreover, the public can respond inappropriately when it does not have all the information, is constrained by time, or is being manipulated by powerful actors. The resultant mob mentality can be a detrimental influencer on the intelligence operative's decision to act.

However, national security should not be viewed strictly as protecting the state, as this perspective often offers little limit other than what the state deems as being expedient. Rather, as philosopher Adam Moore argues, "We value national security, not because some specific political union is valuable in itself, but because it is a necessary part of protecting individual rights."[15] The value of the state, and the need for national security, is drawn from the value of those individuals it is charged with protecting; "Whatever rights and privileges states have, they have them only in so far as they thereby serve individuals' fundamental interests."[16] Indeed, I have argued elsewhere that the ethical value found in intelligence activity comes from its role in protecting the individual and the political community, and this end shapes what activities intelligence agencies can justly carry out.[17] Therefore, the state and its institutions are currently the most appropriate means by which an individual's vital interests are protected and allowed to flourish, and they also include the most usable means of representing the people. When the state fails in its role or becomes an unjustified threat to someone's vital interests, then it loses its moral authority.

This means that narratives that portray security and liberties as opposing qualities that must be traded or balanced, while pervasive, are dangerous.[18] Framing the debate as a binary trade-off between liberties and security, in which security is a trump card, it is not surprising that "after 9/11 countries around the globe unhesitatingly adopted policies to enhance their government's capacity to prevent terrorism ... at the expense of individual civil liberties."[19] Jeremy Waldron warns that even these framings are problematic in terms of unequal distribution of the trade-off, unclear returns for any given exchange, and the problem of trading liberties at will. It is more accurate to see security as a means of offering the necessary protections that secure all an individual's vital interests, including physical and mental integrity, liberty, autonomy, privacy, and self-worth.[20] These interests exist as a matrix, viewed holistically so the individual can carry out his goals and therefore be deemed secure. Security is therefore not separate from people's interests, but an overarching formula by which they are ensured. This includes, first, recognizing that these vital interests do not exist in binary form—whole one minute and destroyed the next—but that they can be affected to various degrees. Second, they need to be present to a minimum level, but interests in physical and psychological integrity will often precede interests in autonomy, liberty, privacy, and self-worth when the severity is equal. Third, an excess of one cannot make up for the absence of another, so you cannot have no privacy in exchange for great physical security.[21]

For the intelligence researcher, a negotiation is therefore required between the understanding that the revealed information is likely to cause harm by undermining intelligence goals or by threatening an operative's safety and the important role information plays in maintaining autonomy in the people and preventing intelligence abuse. Negotiating these points can be aided by answering some key questions. First, what is the justifying argument for retention or release, or what specific individual or public interest is likely to be served by revealing or retaining secretive information? That is, of the different threats to people's vital interests, which of them is under threat and by whom if the information were to be released, and realistically how real is that threat? For example, will the revelations prevent the en masse violation of people's privacy, or will they reveal an intelligence operative's location in a dangerous terrorist organization? This negotiation also involves balancing the amount of good produced or harm avoided by revealing or retaining information. So avoiding embarrassment of state institutions or leaders would fare poorly as a justifying argument for information retention as compared to poor conduct, misuse of funds, or harmful behavior as arguments for release.

Second, who is likely to be affected, and what is the driving force for wider public engagement? Whereas revealing tactical information is likely to cause more harm because it involves specifics on operations and people that would put lives in jeopardy, revealing policy information can affect society as a whole and lead to public engagement that may ensure practices are a reflection of the population's will. Third, can the message be delivered while minimizing the potentially detrimental fallout? For example, a general program of activity could be revealed without too many specifics or details. That is, the devil often exists in the details, but a clear picture can still be revealed without giving away too many specifics that could render current or future operations redundant or dangerous for those involved—unless, that is, those specifics play an important role in ending unethical behavior or bringing those responsible to justice.

The story of the Central Intelligence Agency (CIA) "black sites" in foreign countries, which were established through bribes and the reported use of torture, is an interesting case. Dana Priest broke the story in the *Washington Post* in 2005 but withheld the names of the countries involved "at the request of senior US officials" after they argued that it would "disrupt counterterrorism efforts." Priest contacted the White House before the story was released, and Vice President Dick Cheney and President George W. Bush both personally asked her not to run the story. Priest responded that the *Post* would run the story but would redact parts if necessary. This selective release and redaction, however, was criticized by groups such as Fairness and Accuracy in Reporting and the *Guardian*'s Glen Greenwald, who accused Priest of "purposely concealing the identity of the countries . . . in order to enable the plainly illegal program to continue." On the other side, the House Speaker and Senate majority leader criticized the story for revealing too much, calling it an "egregious disclosure" with "long-term and far-reaching damaging and dangerous consequences."[22]

In contrast, in 2010 Chelsea Manning indiscriminately gave thousands of classified documents to Wikileaks, which published them in unredacted form in 2011. Critics argued that if this kind of uncontrolled information release became the norm, it could undermine both military and diplomatic capabilities. Others were concerned that information that was embarrassing yet not necessarily revealing of unethical behavior—for example, disrespectful diplomatic discussions regarding world leaders, such as former French president Nicolas Sarkozy and Afghan president Hamid Karzai—could lessen local sources' or diplomats' willingness to share sensitive information or engage in dialogue with American officials.[23] Referring to the leaks of Palestinian negotiations with Al Jazeera in 2011, *The Economist* said, "Diplomacy necessarily involves tentatively exploring, in private, ideas that at first seem radical: talks would never get anywhere if the parties involved offered only what was conceded."[24] Deliberation in private must be allowed, in the short term at least, for any effective negotiating to occur. Furthermore, in their private exchanges, diplomats can speak freely, give their unmediated assessments of global political situations, and offer a glimpse at what they really think. For example, Russia's diplomatic cables "painted a bleak and despairing picture of a kleptocracy centered on Putin's leadership, in which officials, oligarchs and organized crime are bound together in a virtual mafia state," and revealing these cables "offered a rare moment of truth-telling about a regime normally accorded international respectability."[25]

Wikileaks also included revealing instances of unethical behavior by US officials, and the *New York Times* defended its decision to publish American diplomatic cables, arguing that they "tell the unvarnished story of how the government makes its biggest decisions, the decisions that cost the country most heavily in lives and money. . . . It would be presumptuous to conclude that Americans have no right to know what is being done in their name." Also among the material the *Times* published was "Collateral Murder," a video of an Apache helicopter killing unarmed civilians in Iraq in July 2007, and the "Afghan War Logs" and "Iraq War Logs," which detailed significant abusive behavior and cover-ups by both military and political actors. The "Afghan War Logs" revealed military accounts of civilian killings that contradicted official public reports given at the time, including a report that a new US weapon fired five rockets on a religious school, failing to kill a senior al-Qaeda fighter and resulting in the deaths of seven children. The "Iraq War Logs" revealed extensive secrecy and distortion by the UK and US governments regarding statistics on the number of civilians who died in the Iraq War. In addition, there were examples of US government engagement in unlawful or undiplomatic activity. Cable 219058, published by Germany's *Der Spiegel*, revealed that "the United States State Department (on behalf of the CIA) had ordered its diplomats to spy on senior United Nations (UN) officials and collect their 'detailed biometric information'" and that the United States had been spying on the UN and its secretary general, Ban Ki-moon.[26]

From these two quite different examples, it can be argued that Priest could have released more information to promote a quicker resolution to the unethical activity. She could have brought those involved into the light, forcing them under greater general scrutiny. Indeed, revealing that level of detail would not have created an immediate threat to operative life, and the counterterrorism methods used were in themselves unjustified, so the claim that the release of this information would undermine counterterrorism efforts is redundant. Wikileaks, in contrast, could have taken greater care to limit the details released and to filter out activity that did not reveal unethical (but merely embarrassing) behavior, but given the importance of revealing the abusive behavior detailed in the war logs and US spying on UN officials, a general release is better than no release.

## Duty to Intelligence and Its Practitioners

The intelligence agencies represent a community of individuals and institutions with their own culture and mentality, one that often makes critical decisions separate from those public politicians who are meant to have ultimate oversight. Researchers, therefore, face a separate set of obligations toward this group of actors. First among them is the duty to educate. Universities, research institutions, and think tanks all produce knowledge in order to better understand the world, and as an important part of this mission, many of these institutions take on educational roles, some specially targeted to prospective or current intelligence practitioners. Researchers, therefore, are obligated to provide the necessary tools for practitioners to be better educated—that is, to be informed on how the world works; to possess the necessary skills for processing, analyzing, and understanding the information presented to them; and to understand the ethical limits and implications of one's actions. This duty is broad, but one that intelligence researchers must give specific attention to in order to best pass on good practice to those who will become or are intelligence practitioners. One key aspect of the researcher's education role is improving the effectiveness and efficiency of intelligence activity, helping to increase the likelihood of threat prevention and examining and advancing both the knowledge and skills of intelligence practitioners. This aspect includes examining intelligence practices, policies, and tools with the aim of increasing their success and aiding professionals by, for example, providing new tools, contexts, or training on analyzing raw intelligence data.[27]

A key part of this duty is for academics to act as an outside point of reference, both as a moral compass and as a means of encouraging reflection on practices, behaviors, and internal cultures. When secretive environments establish clear demarcations between those in the know on the inside and everyone else on the outside, they create and promote a closed-off mentality. Those on the outside are unaware and unable to engage, while for those on the inside, this process of in-group and out-group differentiation dehumanizes others and, when coupled with a lack of outside input, means there is no differential method for measuring one's moral compass.[28] As a result intelligence officers learn to exclude those considered outsiders from their universe of obligation.[29] Cognitive restructuring redefines violence or harm as honorable, for a greater abstract good, and increasingly socially and morally acceptable to those inside.[30] A secretive environment normalizes this process, feeding on itself to reinforce both the need for greater secrecy and a lack of regard for the negative consequences for those on the outside. In such an environment, internal criticism is limited as it is considered a betrayal to the group, and so alternative analysis is restricted and group mentality smothers dissenting points of view.[31] In the field of intelligence, the absence of dissension could result in tactics far harsher than those originally planned, including escalating interrogation techniques, increasingly intrusive collection methods, or unequal treatment based on race or ethnicity.

Intelligence researchers thus have an expressed ethical duty to act as an engaging force, one that actively critiques and seeks to gain ever greater insight in order to show intelligence actors when they have gone too far. This duty involves understanding what intelligence agencies have done previously, highlighting where they have caused unjustified harm, and thinking about how they might act to prevent future harm.

## Duty to Academia and Academic Practice

Finally, researchers have a duty to academia that comes with its own particular challenges, including reflecting on how one's own positioning and biases can unduly shape the research, who is funding the research, how one's research might be used, and whether one can be held accountable for intentional or accidental misunderstandings of the research.[32] One of the most important questions for intelligence researchers is confidentiality and determining when to give it, to whom, and what (if any) limits should be placed on it.

As a general concept, confidentiality is extensively discussed in the professional fields of medicine, law, and journalism, with each body of literature debating the particular pressures placed on researchers and practitioners. However, although it is given general importance and ethical priority in many instances, confidentiality is not absolute, and intelligence researchers have the added pressure of dealing with whistle-blowers who reveal state secrets and with individuals who detail their own illegal activity. For researchers, three key interests inform their decisions to maintain confidentiality or not. First is the interest of the individuals being researched. Offering subjects confidentiality and anonymity can play an important role not only in gaining their trust and encouraging them to provide information but can be vital in protecting them from severe repercussions. For example, in medical ethics, aside from individuals' right to control their own information, confidentiality is considered important given that released information could result in direct harm to those connected to it in the form of embarrassment, loss of social and financial standing, disgrace, anxiety, and general distress, especially if the individuals are judged or perceive themselves to be judged poorly by others.[33] For those who conduct research on vulnerable groups, protecting identities can become vital given the potential for backlash and harm when vulnerable individuals express their views or reveal their identities.[34] Indeed, retaliation against whistle-blowers has been reported in the literature across a range of instances and societies. Philip Jos, Mark Tomkinson, and Steven Hays reported that 60 percent of the whistle-blowers they surveyed answered that they had been fired or forced to retire.[35] Joyce Rothschild and Terance Miethe reported that this was the case for 69 percent of their survey participants, with 84 percent of participants reporting suffering from anxiety or depression as a result.[36] Joseph McGlynn and Brian Richardson detailed how the possibility of slander, physical intimidation, and death threats is very real for those who blow the whistle.[37] In intelligence agencies this possibility is further heightened given the sense of betrayal expressed both within and outside the agencies, the severe legal repercussions faced by and limited protections offered to the whistle-blower, and the high-tension nature of national security.

Second are the interests of the profession. Offering and then maintaining confidentiality is one of the most important means of establishing trustworthiness and maintaining the integrity within a profession.[38] All professions that rely on trust—doctors, lawyers, journalists, and academics—should maintain trust not only for the particular benefits it can bring or harms it can avoid but for the sake of future engagements for the profession generally. People will not tell the truth if they fear that information might harm them later on, and any broken trust can have wide, harmful repercussions for others in the profession. In addition, journalists argue that as professionals they should not be compelled to reveal their sources as this would represent a threat to their freedom of speech and expression. Any overly draconian state interference could reduce sources' willingness to cooperate with journalists and could even undermine the journalist's drive and willingness to take risks and investigate more sensitive topics from fear of ending up in a professionally difficult or even personally dangerous position.

Third are the interests of those who would benefit from confidentiality being broken. For example, as Matthew Wynia points out, medical ethics has "typically allowed for breaches of confidentiality when there is a credible threat of significant harm to an identifiable third party."[39] Indeed, the American Public Health Association's code of conduct suggests that an exception to confidentiality "must be justified on the basis of the high likelihood of significant harm to the individual or others."[40] It can be argued that this threshold could be pushed further if the information could be used to broadly protect "public health" by preventing disease, prolonging life, and promoting general human health by allowing greater access to and pooling of medical data.[41] In this case the benefit to the wider population would outweigh the harm caused by breaking confidentiality.

The importance of confidentiality came to the forefront in the legal fight over the Belfast Project at Boston College. The Belfast Project was "an oral history with former republican and loyalist paramilitaries who had first-hand knowledge about bombings, kidnapping and murders committed during The Troubles in Northern Ireland."[42] When the US attorney sought the identities of contributors to the project, pursuant to a request by the UK government under the Mutual Legal Assistance Treaty, a conflict arose between the researchers, who argued for maintaining the confidentiality of their contributors, and college administrators, who argued that they must obey the court's subsequent subpoenas. For Ted Palys and John Lowman, the conflict served to highlight that researchers should be "suspicious of universities." In this case, despite originally offering confidentiality and recognizing the benefit the archive would potentially bring the university, Boston College opted not to fight the law of the land. Further, the Belfast Project conflict underlined how important it is for researchers to "walk their talk" and live up to their "unlimited promise of confidentiality."[43] The practical lesson here is that attention should be given to who has access to what information regarding a source's identity, as research institutions will not necessarily support the wishes of the researcher.

So where does this leave the debate, especially for intelligence studies? First, researchers in intelligence studies could face a much greater potential backlash if they reveal sensitive information. Indeed, whistle-blower legislation explicitly does not protect those in the security apparatus, and the cases of Edward Snowden and Wikileaks highlight not only the severe legal repercussions but also the potential social backlash that can come with revealing sensitive information.[44] For researchers, a particularly extreme emphasis on the importance of intelligence specifically and national security generally creates a lot of pressure to either refuse the offer of confidentiality or reveal sources. But arguably, given the inherent and obsessive secrecy surrounding intelligence activity, getting the most useful information can involve going against this pressure. Excessive secrecy, reports of intelligence abuse, and weak oversight mechanisms increase the burden on the intelligence researcher to penetrate the protective bubble and reveal unethical behavior—even if this includes retaining protective confidentiality against the wishes of the state. However, while retaining confidentiality might represent the researcher's ethical duty, in practice the answer is actually less bold: do not promise that which you cannot guarantee. The repercussions of refusing to reveal a source can be severe for the researcher—ranging from loss of reputation and career to financial costs to emotional and psychological stress and aggravation to even incarceration—and withstanding pressure from the state in order to maintain one's promise to a source can be difficult. While the right thing to do is to maintain one's promise, this is understandably an exceptional thing to do.

Before researchers grant confidentiality to their sources, they must decide whether they would be happy to face the consequences of maintaining that confidentiality. Failing to uphold the promise of confidentiality is wrong not only in the general ethical terms of breaking a promise but in terms of the repercussions the informant will now face, repercussions that would not have arisen without the researcher's original promise. Without the promise of confidentiality, the informant might have found another (more secure or reliable) route for information release; by making the offer of confidentiality, the researcher shut down those avenues and made him or herself the only viable option. Therefore, to avoid repercussions for oneself and the informant, it is better to avoid offers of confidentiality and hope a better, more secure option will come along.

## Notes

1. Martha Nussbaum, *Women and Human Development: The Capabilities Approach* (Cambridge: Cambridge University Press, 2000), 79.
2. John Stuart Mill, *Considerations on Representative Government* (London: Parker, Son, and Bourn, 1861), 104. On Locke's work, see Ajume H. Wingo, *Veil Politics in Liberal Democratic States* (Cambridge: Cambridge University Press, 2003), 16–18; John

Rawls, *A Theory of Justice* (Cambridge, MA: Harvard University Press, 1971), 454; and John Rawls, *Political Liberalism* (New York: Columbia University Press, 1993), 35, 68.
3. Joseph Stiglitz, "On Liberty, the Right to Know, and Public Discourse: The Role of Transparency in Public Life," in *Globalising Rights: Oxford Amnesty Lecture 1999* (Oxford: Oxford University Press, 1999), 125. Emphasis in original.
4. John Stuart Mill, *On Liberty* (New York: Cosimo, 2005), 138.
5. Thomas Emerson, "The First Amendment and the Right to Know: Legal Foundations of the Right to Know," *Washington University Law Quarterly* 976, no. 1 (1976): 14; Robert Dahl, *Polyarchy: Participation and Opposition* (New Haven, CT: Yale University Press, 1971).
6. David Luban, "The Publicity Principle," in *The Theory of Institutional Design*, ed. Robert E. Goodin (Cambridge: Cambridge University Press, 1998), 156.
7. Simone Chambers, "Behind Closed Doors: Publicity, Secrecy, and the Quality of Deliberation," *Journal of Political Philosophy* 12, no. 4 (2004): 390.
8. Chambers, 390.
9. Ross Bellaby, "The Ethics of Whistleblowing: Creating a New Limit on Intelligence Activity," *Journal of International Politics Theory* 14, no. 1 (2018): 60–84.
10. Chambers, "Behind Closed Doors," 392. Also see Mark Chinen, "Secrecy and Democratic Decisions," *Quinnipiac Law Review* 27, no. 1 (2009): 9.
11. Edward H. Spense, "Government Secrecy, the Ethics of Wikileaks, and the Fifth Estate," *International Review of Information Ethics* 17, no. 7 (2012): 40.
12. Michael Walzer, *Just and Unjust Wars: A Moral Argument with Historical Illustrations* (New York: Basic Books, 2000), 254.
13. Steven Aftergood, "National Security Secrecy: How Limits Change," *Social Research* 77, no. 3 (2010): 839.
14. Njord Wegge, "Intelligence Oversight and Security of the State," *International Journal of Intelligence and CounterIntelligence* 30, no. 4 (2017): 691.
15. Adam Moore, "Privacy, Security, and Government Surveillance: Wikileaks and the New Accountability," *Public Affairs Quarterly* 25, no. 2 (2011): 142.
16. Cecile Fabre, "Cosmopolitanism, Just War Theory and Legitimate Authority," *International Affairs* 84, no. 5 (2008): 964.
17. Ross Bellaby, *The Ethics of Intelligence: A New Framework* (London: Routledge, 2014).
18. Jeremy Waldron, "Security and Liberty: The Image of Balance," *Journal of Political Philosophy* 11, no. 2 (2003): 191–210; David Pozen, "Privacy-Privacy Tradeoffs," *University of Chicago Law Review* 83, no. 1 (2016): 221–47; Robert McArthur, "Reasonable Expectations of Privacy," *Ethics and Information Technology* 3, no. 2 (2001): 123–28.
19. Tiberiu Dragu, "Is There a Trade-off between Security and Liberty? Executive Bias, Privacy Protections, and Terrorism Prevention," *American Political Science Review* 105, no. 1 (2011): 64–78. For more on this debate, see Derek E. Bambauer, "Privacy versus Security," *Journal of Criminal Law and Criminology* 103, no. 3 (2013):

667–83; Moore, "Privacy, Security." For arguments for security trumping privacy, see Ken Himma, "Privacy vs. Security: Why Privacy Is Not an Absolute Value or Right," *San Diego Law Review* 44 (2007): 857.
20. Jeremy Waldron, "Security and Liberty: The Image of Balance," *Journal of Political Philosophy* 11, no. 2 (2003): 191–210.
21. Severity refers to the degree to which the vital interest is violated, because a prick on the finger would not be considered worse than incarceration just because it is a physical as compared to a liberty violation.
22. William H. Harwood, "Secrecy, Transparency and Government Whistleblowing," *Philosophy and Social Criticism* 43, no. 2 (2017): 167, 168.
23. "WikiLeaks Embassy Cables: The Key Points at a Glance," *Guardian*, December 7, 2010, http://www.theguardian.com/world/2010/nov/29/wikileaks-embassy-cables-key-points; Rahul Sagar, *Secrets and Leaks: The Dilemma of State Secrecy* (Princeton, NJ: Princeton University Press, 2016), 1; L. N. Rangarajan, "Diplomacy, States and Secrecy in Communications," *Diplomacy and Statecraft* 9, no. 3 (1998): 18–24.
24. "Leaks Must Not Poison Diplomacy," *The Economist*, January 27, 2011, http://www.economist.com/node/18010593.
25. David Leigh and Luke Harding, *WikiLeaks: Inside Julian Assange's War on Secrecy* (London: Guardian Books, 2011), 216.
26. Leigh and Harding, 117, 129, 178, 200. The UN has asserted that bugging the secretary general is illegal, citing the 1946 Convention on Privileges and Immunities of the United Nations, Section 3, Section 30, and the 1961 Vienna Convention on Diplomatic Relations, Article 22.2, Article 27.2, Article 29, Article 30.2.
27. For such efforts, see Joseph Caddell Jr. and Joseph Caddell Sr., "Historical Case Studies in Intelligence Education: Best Practices, Avoidable Pitfalls," *Intelligence and National Security* 32, no. 7 (2017): 889–904; Stephen Marrin, "Improving Intelligence Studies as an Academic Discipline," *Intelligence and National Security* 32, no. 1 (2016): 266–79; Nicholas Dujmovic, "Less Is More, and More Professional: Reflections on Building an 'Ideal' Intelligence Program," *Intelligence and National Security* 32, no. 7 (2017): 935–43; Mark M. Lowenthal, "My Take on Teaching Intelligence: Why, What, and How," *Intelligence and National Security* 32, no. 7 (2017): 986–94; Welton Chang and Philip E. Tetlock, "Rethinking the Training of Intelligence Analysts," *Intelligence and National Security* 31, no. 6 (2016): 903–20.
28. Albert Bandura, "Moral Disengagement in the Perpetration of Inhumanities," *Personality and Social Psychology Review* 3, no. 3 (1999): 194.
29. Helen Fein, *Human Rights and Wrongs: Slavery, Terror and Genocide* (Boulder, CO: Paradigm, 2007), 11.
30. Albert Bandura, *Social Foundations of Thought and Action: A Social Cognitive Theory* (Englewood Cliffs, NJ: Prentice Hall, 1986), 376; Jacques-Philippe Leynes, Brezo Cortes, Stéphanie Demoulin, John F. Dovidio, Susan T. Fiske, Ruth Gaunt, Maria-Paola Paladino, Armando Rodriguez-Perez, Ramon Rodriguez-Torres, and Jeroen Vaes, "Emotional Prejudice, Essentialism, and Nationalism," *European Journal of Social Psychology* 33, no. 6 (2003): 703–17; Brian Mullen, Rupert Brown, and

Colleen Smith, "In-Group Bias as a Function of Salience, Relevance, and Status: An Integration," *European Journal of Social Psychology* 22, no. 2 (1992): 103–22; R. Johnson, "Institutions and the Promotion of Violence," in *Violent Transactions: The Limits of Personality*, ed. Anne Campell and John Gibbs (Oxford: Oxford University Press, 1986); James Waller, *Becoming Evil: How Ordinary People Commit Genocide and Mass Killing* (Oxford: Oxford University Press, 2002).

31. US Senate Select Committee on Intelligence, "Committee Study of the Central Intelligence Agency's Detention and Interrogation Program," December 3, 2014, http://fas.org/irp/congress/2014_rpt/ssci-rdi.pdf.

32. See Betsy W. Bach, "The Organizational Tension of Othering," *Journal of Applied Communication Research* 33, no. 3 (2005): 258–68; Mark Israel and Deborah Hersh, "Research Ethics," in *From Postgraduate to Social Scientist: A Guide to Key Skills*, ed. Nigel Gilbert (London: Sage, 2006), 43–58; and J. Michael Oakes, "Risks and Wrongs in Social Science Research: An Evaluator's Guide to the IRB," *Evaluation Review* 26, no. 5 (2002): 443–79.

33. For privacy as the right of control, see G. Stoney Alder, Marshall Schminke, and Terry W. Noel, "The Impact of Individual Ethics on Reactions to Potentially Invasive HR Practices," *Journal of Business Ethics* 75, no. 2 (2007): 201–14; James Boyle, *Shamans, Software and Spleens: Law and the Construction of the Information Society* (Cambridge, MA: Harvard University Press, 1997), 54; Jerry Kang, "Information Privacy in Cyberspace Transactions," *Stanford Law Review* 50, no. 4 (1998): 1207; Edward Shils, "Privacy: Its Constitution and Vicissitudes," *Law and Contemporary Problems* 31, no. 2 (1966): 290; Alan Westin, *Privacy and Freedom* (New York: Atheneum, 1967).

34. David Kennamer, "What Journalists and Researchers Have in Common about Ethics," *Journal of Mass Media Ethics* 20, no. 1 (2005): 85.

35. Philip H. Jos, Mark E. Tompkins, and Steven W. Hays, "In Praise of Difficult People: A Portrait of the Committed Whistleblower," *Public Administration Review* 49, no. 6 (1989): 552–61.

36. Joyce Rothschild and Terance Miethe, "Whistle-Blower Disclosures and Management Retaliation," *Work and Occupations* 26, no. 1 (1999): 107–28.

37. Joseph McGlynn III and Brian K. Richardson, "Private Support, Public Alienation: Whistle-Blowers and the Paradox of Social Support," *Western Journal of Communication* 78, no. 2 (2014): 213–37.

38. Wendy Rogers, "Pressures on Confidentiality," *The Lancet* 367, no. 9510 (2006): 553–54; Robert Bogdan and Sari Knopp Biklen, *Qualitative Research in Education: An Introduction to Theory and Methods*, 3rd ed. (Boston: Allyn and Bacon, 1998); J. L. Fitzgerald and M. Hamilton, "Confidentiality, Disseminated Regulations and Ethico-legal Liabilities in Research with Hidden Populations of Illicit Drug-Users," *Addiction* 92, no. 9 (1997): 1099–1108; John M. McGuire, Sanford Graves, and Burton Blau, "Depth of Self-Disclosure as a Function of Assured Confidentiality and Videotape Recording," *Journal of Counseling and Development* 64, no. 4 (1985): 259–63.

39. Matthew K. Wynia, "Breaching Confidentiality to Protect the Public: Evolving Standards of Medical Confidentiality for Military Detainees," *American Journal of Bioethics* 7, no. 8 (2007): 1–2.
40. American Public Health Association, *Principles of the Ethical Practice of Public Health* (n.p.: Public Health Leadership Society, 2002), 7, https://www.apha.org/-/media/files/pdf/membergroups/ethics/ethics_brochure.ashx. Also see "Code of Medical Ethics Opinion 3.2.1," American Medical Association, accessed August 12, 2018, https://www.ama-assn.org/delivering-care/confidentiality.
41. Wynia, "Breaching Confidentiality," 3.
42. Ted Palys and John Lowman, "Defending Research Confidentiality 'to the Extent the Law Allows': Lessons from the Boston College Subpoenas," *Journal of Academic Ethics* 10, no. 4 (2012): 271–72.
43. Palys and Lowman, 294–95.
44. G. Robert Vaughn, *Successes and Failures of Whistleblower Laws* (Cheltenham, UK: Edward Elgar, 2012), 314.

# Conclusion: The Past, Present, and Future of Intelligence Research

*Stephen Coulthart, Michael Landon-Murray, and Damien Van Puyvelde*

In October 2000 an email with the subject line "Please Spread This Letter as Widely as Possible—Let Them Know We Exist" was distributed to members of the American Political Science Association (APSA).[1] The email was signed by a figure known only as "Mr. Perestroika," a reference to the 1980s Communist Party movement to restructure Soviet politics and economics. The email included aims such as making political science accessible to the public, diversifying the association's leadership, and challenging the dominance of quantitative methodologies and rational actor theory in the field. The manifesto sparked controversy among political scientists and led to a flurry of journal articles and an edited book.[2] Almost twenty years later, political scientists still debate the impact and legacy of the movement. Some claim it was ineffectual, while others point to modest changes to the discipline, such as the decision by APSA's flagship journal to print more nonquantitative articles and the creation of training programs for qualitative research.[3]

Contemporary intelligence research and American political science of the 2000s are quite different. Whereas political science is a well-established disciplinary field, intelligence research is a newer, multidisciplinary field, drawing from disparate areas of knowledge (including political science). There are other differences as well: intelligence research is not dominated by quantitative approaches. Quite the opposite, it seems most intelligence research is qualitative. These differences aside, the "perestroika movement" and its overarching emphasis on openness and diversity of perspectives make a useful rhetorical framing for our own pluralist call to develop intelligence research that is more rigorous, better integrated, and more relevant for policy and practice. We share this vision with several colleagues who have written thoughtfully about the importance of charting the future of intelligence scholarship by developing theory and engaging practitioners.[4] This chapter weaves these ideas into an overarching pluralist framework and places an aspirational stake in the ground, signaling where we think the field should go over the next decade and beyond. Our message, in short, is that intelligence research is ready to be opened up further in a variety of exciting ways this volume started to explore, including examining new sources of evidence, bringing in more diverse disciplinary perspectives, and actively and ethically engaging the world of policy and practice.

### Questions to Ponder Over

Mr. Perestroika's manifesto contains eleven "questions to ponder over," covering concerns such as the gender and racial representation of APSA's leadership and critiques of the perceived focus on formal modeling and quantitative research methodologies, among many others.[5] In the following we list our own "questions to ponder" along with some ideas to address them. The content, focus, and tone of our questions depart from Mr. Perestroika's—our goal is not to dismantle an "Orwellian system" as he had in mind for political science.[6] Instead, we believe intelligence research is heading in a positive direction, evidenced by its growth and increased interest from scholars in many fields. In calling for our own perestroika movement in intelligence research, we draw on themes and observations made in this volume about the characteristics of intelligence scholarship that ought to be addressed for the field to reach its full potential in the coming years. Related to these themes and observations, we conclude the volume by asking and answering the following fundamental questions.

### How Can Intelligence Scholars Gather More Diverse Sources of Evidence?

Part 2, "Data Sources and the Study of National Security Intelligence," explores how the secrecy surrounding intelligence agencies imposes high costs on researchers seeking to collect evidence. Misty Duke explains how behavioral observation can help researchers understand intelligence functions, but there are still limitations. For example, using an experimental research design provides more control of the research variables but may limit the ability to generalize the findings to other contexts. Damien Van Puyvelde cautions that interviews can be time-consuming and require close scrutiny of biases among interviewees. The high costs of collecting evidence in intelligence research increase the likelihood of the streetlight effect, the tendency to analyze subjects, cases, and theories that are easier to study and, therefore, skew research findings. This type of bias gets its name from an old social science parable:

> Late at night, a police officer finds a drunk man crawling around on his hands and knees under a streetlight. The drunk man tells the officer he's looking for his wallet. When the officer asks if he's sure this is where he

dropped the wallet, the man replies that he thinks he more likely dropped it across the street. Then why are you looking over here? the befuddled officer asks. Because the light's better here, explains the drunk man.[7]

As the parable explains, researchers can end up selecting cases and theories that are easier to collect evidence on and, therefore, test. For example, intelligence practitioners and researchers alike frequently complain that we know more about intelligence failures, which tend to be very apparent, than intelligence successes, which are often jealously (and reasonably) guarded by agencies keen to maintain their most effective modus operandi.

In intelligence research the conditions that create the streetlight effect are not worse than most other fields, but they are different. This difference stems from the fact that unlike in many other fields, the subjects of study in intelligence—intelligence organizations—often seek to hide their sources and methods. Intelligence scholar Michael Warner points out intelligence "resists scholarship."[8] Scholars who study other difficult-to-access research problems, such as terrorism, transnational crime, and corruption, face a similar issue.[9] In intelligence research the streetlight effect emphasizes the experiences of English-speaking intelligence services over non-English-speaking ones. A recent study finds that more than 70 percent of articles from the leading intelligence journals focused on intelligence communities in the United States and United Kingdom.[10] While there is also a small but promising strand of scholarship in comparative intelligence systems from non-English-speaking countries, much work remains to fill a number of geographical gaps.[11] Even within well-studied intelligence communities, such as those of the United States and United Kingdom, there are new areas for inquiry waiting to be explored. As Bridget Rose Nolan points out, much of what we know about the culture of the US intelligence community (IC) is based on studies of a small number of agencies. We simply do not know much about intelligence at the Department of Energy, the Department of Treasury, or the Drug Enforcement Administration. The combined effect of this bias is that intelligence theories and findings could be omitting key variables as well as mischaracterizing intelligence functions and processes.

A pluralist approach assumes that an emphasis on increasing the diversity of evidence sources is a helpful way to mitigate the streetlight effect. The availability of research material to study diverse intelligence practices partly depends on government declassification decisions. Yet recent research suggests that we might have entered a new era of transparency in which unauthorized disclosures will force intelligence organizations to assume their activities will become public sooner or later.[12] Beyond examining intelligence agencies outside the Anglosphere, researchers can increase their coverage of law enforcement and business uses of intelligence. There is a growing body of literature in these areas, and students of national security intelligence could examine these cases for theory generation and testing purposes.[13] In addition, advances in technology have led to new opportunities to learn about intelligence agencies in unconventional ways. In 2017 an Australian undergraduate student realized that since US and allied armed forces personnel were uploading their daily jogging routes to a fitness application called Strava, he could produce high-resolution maps of bases from around the world.[14] This case and others, like the leaks orchestrated by Wikileaks, illustrate how new digital open sources are leveling the playing field for data collection and in the process raise new ethical conundrums for researchers. As Ross Bellaby notes in his contribution, scholars have an ethical duty to avoid doing harm when the release of information could risk the lives of government personnel or innocent bystanders. Among other opportunities, intelligence fiction provides another set of underutilized sources to explore public perceptions on intelligence, explain the dilemmas practitioners confront, and imagine the possible futures of intelligence.[15]

## How Can Disciplinary Perspectives Be Better Integrated in Intelligence Scholarship?

Intelligence research evolves between and within multiple disciplines. Mark Phythian argues intelligence scholarship focuses on four projects: the research/historical, the definitional/methodological, the organizational/functional, and the governance/societal/policy projects. Many possible perspectives can be applied to each type of project. The governance/societal/policy project is largely undertaken by policy analysts, public administration specialists, and political scientists, as the contributions by Michael Landon-Murray, Rick Caceres-Rodriguez, and Stephen Marrin demonstrate. However, this project can also be analyzed fruitfully by other specialists, like anthropologists and sociologists working on organizational culture. Nolan's discussion of sociological data collection in the US is a good example of the potential of this perspective.[16] Despite the diversity of perspectives in intelligence research, the field is still not well integrated. Intelligence scholars have insufficiently engaged with the growing body of research and methods developed by behavioral scientists to study interviewing, secrecy, and security behaviors, for instance.[17] As John Ferris points out, historians and policy scholars have traditionally dominated intelligence research. The evolution of intelligence practices, most notably since the information technology revolution of the 1990s, opens new windows of opportunities to reassess core intelligence processes and theories.[18]

What explains the lack of integration between disciplinary perspectives? Influential social scientist Donald Campbell argues that the division of the modern university into disciplinary departments has led scholars to focus on their own specializations, leading to "a redundant piling up of highly similar specialties leaving interdisciplinary gaps." Even within these clusters of specialization, Campbell speculates that scholars can cover only about one-tenth of their own disciplinary literature because they must become highly specialized in one subject area to become experts in their fields. The interdisciplinary gaps Campbell describes constrain intelligence scholarship, creating productive but disconnected islands of intelligence scholarship in political science, history, and policy studies, to name a few disciplines, surrounded by vast seas of untapped interdisciplinary potential. This disconnect is solidified by the norms of publishing, tenure, and promotion in the ivory tower. When scholars write research articles and books on intelligence, they naturally focus on their own discipline's theoretical frameworks rather than on intelligence theory from other disciplines. Disciplinary boundaries reinforce what Campbell describes as "disciplinary ethnocentrism," the tendency to view a research problem through a rigid disciplinary framework.[19] This type of bias can prevent intelligence scholarship from being cumulative and constrain research to omit key findings as well as theories in other relevant disciplines.[20]

The lack of disciplinary integration and resulting disciplinary ethnocentrism leads to an important question: How can intelligence researchers bridge the gaps between them? An option is to develop a "fish-scale approach" to interdisciplinary collaboration, built on the overlapping expertise of researchers.[21] This approach requires scholars to accept the limits of their own mastery of research problems and to seek out collaborators in adjacent specialties to supplement their expertise. For example, intelligence researchers in political and policy fields can partner with those from science, technology, engineering, and mathematics (STEM) fields to investigate research topics requiring technical expertise, such as cybersecurity and bulk data collection and analysis programs. Beyond engagement with STEM researchers, there are countless other possible collaborations for intelligence scholars in fields ranging from area studies to museum studies.[22] Recent volumes, like ours, have sought to give a voice to a more diverse pool of researchers based in different countries and working in a variety of fields.[23]

There is also a need for research projects on the body of intelligence scholarship itself. Research projects in this area could implement research designs similar to those in terrorism studies and build on the small but promising scholarship that examines publishing trends in the field.[24] Damien Van Puyvelde and Sean Curtis analyzed articles in *Intelligence and National Security* and the *International Journal of Intelligence and CounterIntelligence* to determine authors' country of origin and research methods, among other variables.[25] Future analyses could answer research questions, such as, Are there "hub" institutions where most research is occurring? What are the main funding sources of intelligence research? Are there identifiable clusters of authors who are working together? We also know little about the backgrounds, opinions, and attitudes of intelligence scholars—all factors that matter for shaping these individuals' worldviews and, therefore, their research. To tap researchers' perspectives, an option is to conduct a survey similar to the Teaching, Research, and International Policy survey of international relations scholars.[26] This survey is updated regularly and sheds light on, for example, the main theoretical debates, most important journals, and leading research areas. Introspective studies, along with increasing interdisciplinary collaboration, would go a long way to understanding and improving disciplinary integration and the structure of the field.

### Does Intelligence Scholarship Influence Policy and Practice—and Should It?

Intelligence scholars often seem to be working on the periphery of public discussions of intelligence matters. Paul Lashmar points out that in the immediate aftermath of the Snowden disclosures, academics were largely unengaged with the ensuing public debate, leading him to ask, "What impact do [intelligence scholars] really have on policy about a controversial issue like global surveillance? Is scholarship there for the sake of scholarship?" The current answer to both questions is wholly unsatisfying: we just do not know. While intelligence scholarship has some influence, we lack systematically collected evidence on how much it is involved in the public debate and whether it is having a tangible effect on decision-makers and public perceptions.

Some important first steps for understanding the influence of intelligence scholarship include surveying relevant literatures and conducting careful studies of how agencies use research findings. Intelligence scholars could examine the well-established knowledge utilization literature, a field that investigates the factors that affect how and why practitioners use academic knowledge.[27] Additionally, as Brent Durbin pointed out in his contribution, there is a robust strand of literature on bridging the gap in international relations.[28] For example, Paul Avey and Michael Desch conducted a survey of hundreds of US national security policymakers to understand how they use international relations research.[29] Their findings support the belief that there is "trickle-down" influence of scholarship on policymakers; the impact of scholarship is not immediate and can take years, if not decades.[30] Avey and Desch also find that among policymakers substantive expertise of academics is more helpful than the results of sophisticated quantitative analysis. A similar study to Avey and Desch's could explore the types of academic research made available to and used by different types of intelligence professionals. These research findings could then be used to inform policy-oriented academics on practitioners' perceived need for scholarship and the best methods for disseminating their research findings.

In the absence of research evidence on the most effective strategies to disseminate research, there are several well-established best practices for bridging the gap between scholarship and policy and practice. On the government side, the US IC, among others, has developed collaborative agreements to bring in academics to consult and assist in the development of some analytical projects, both classified and open source.[31] On the academic side, there are several initiatives under way to prepare scholars for engagement outside the ivory tower, with the most notable being the Bridging the Gap (BTG) Project at American University. Durbin explains how BTG helps scholars hone skills to design and disseminate their research outside academia, such as learning how to write jargon-free and concisely for practitioners.

Beyond the question of how well scholars are bridging the gap between scholarship and practice, another is whether they should even try to bridge it in the first place. The answer to this question depends on the perspective of the individual scholar.[32] To one group, whom Lashmar calls "acolytes," an important duty of intelligence research is to assist practitioners. Bellaby describes this point of view well: the intelligence scholar's role is to improve "effectiveness and efficiency of intelligence activity, helping to increase the likelihood of threat prevention and examining and advancing both the knowledge and skills of intelligence practitioners." In short, acolytes see their role as influencing practitioners and policymakers. The second type, "critical friends," falls somewhere in the middle of the spectrum. These researchers seek answers to the "big questions" about the role of intelligence in society, relating to topics such as privacy, reform, and surveillance. They are willing to engage with practitioners but keep more distance from government than the acolytes. Critical friends may also have concerns that making the field an applied inquiry—as the acolytes would have it—could weaken its academic credibility. On the opposite end of the spectrum from the acolytes are outsiders to the intelligence world we might call purists. Lashmar points out how some of these researchers critically analyze intelligence, often based on "the negative historical record of the intelligence community." These scholars do not see intelligence as an applied field to assist practitioners. A pluralist approach to intelligence studies recognizes the different incentives and approaches that motivate all these researchers and seeks to keep a dialogue open between all of them to move the field forward.

## *What Are the Trade-Offs between Academic Expertise and Practical Experience?*

Current and former practitioners bring a wealth of experience to intelligence scholarship. Their backgrounds help them to illustrate the complexities of life in secretive institutions—the mundane and the extraordinary—with nuance that is difficult or even impossible for outsiders to convey in detail. Nolan's discussion of culture and socialization in the National Counterterrorism Center is a good example of how insider accounts can shed light on the dynamics of culture on intelligence practices. Beyond these important observations, practitioners have developed some of the most influential concepts in the field. These range from Richards Heuer Jr.'s importation of cognitive biases research findings into intelligence analysis to Gregory Treverton's "puzzles, mysteries, and complexities" and countless other practitioner-made contributions that are simply too numerous to list here.[33]

Practical experience also comes with trade-offs. Even with careful management, the strong government-academic nexus of intelligence research creates a significant risk of observer bias. This bias is commonly discussed in a variety of disciplines from psychology to anthropology and occurs when researchers' experiences and worldviews affect their ability to objectively view the phenomenon they are investigating. If anything, a form of observer bias is most visible in the memoirs of former senior officials whose interpretation of their own history is questionable and questioned.[34] Addressing observer bias is a difficult task for researchers. Even if it is noticed, there is a strong possibility it cannot be fully resolved.

Scholars, of course, bring their own unique biases, blind spots, and contributions. Biases and blind spots can include unwavering hostility toward intelligence agencies among some and, as noted, a lack of detailed inside organizational knowledge that can diminish research quality. However, more complete understandings of intelligence functions and processes require examinations from a variety of disciplinary perspectives and with a variety of tools. More detached scholars can also be more dispassionate and critical in their examination of intelligence agencies, contributing to their role in helping hold intelligence agencies accountable.

Scholars and practitioners should continue to discuss the trade-offs between practical and academic expertise because of the contributions both perspectives bring to intelligence studies. Such a conversation could take place in a special edition of a journal or edited volume and address questions like, What are the pros and cons of academic and practitioner approaches to research? How can we mitigate the negatives and increase the positives? How can organizational arrangements between governments and universities improve collaboration while maintaining analytic rigor? Such an effort would represent another critical facet in advancing the field of intelligence studies, hopefully encouraging an intellectually honest conversation on the strengths and limits of both approaches so that the quality of intelligence research can be maximized.

## Pondering the Future

The preceding chapters have included a wide range of scholars representing different disciplinary and methodological approaches to the study of intelligence. This volume is a reflection of the growing diversity of the field, and it is critical that that diversity continues to evolve, incorporating a greater variety of voices, not only along multidisciplinary lines but also along gender and geographic lines. This edited volume will help equip and encourage more scholars, both early and veteran, and from a range of disciplines, to pursue and advance intelligence studies as a field of inquiry. Just as important, this text offers students of intelligence an exploration of the many disciplines and tools that need to be engaged to most fully understand—and thus improve—contemporary intelligence scholarship. This volume will also further engender an appreciation and culture among intelligence practitioners of engaging external stakeholders, including academics from a range of disciplines. Bridging the gaps that remain between scholars and practitioners, while not surrendering the oversight role of intelligence academics, will help in the design, conduct, and application of intelligence research. This is not an easy balance, as those in academia seek to both enhance and check intelligence functions, and an increased diversity of scholars and approaches helps ensure that both approaches are utilized. Nonetheless, the purposive combination of scholars and practitioners, as well as scholars from various disciplines, will contribute to innovative research agendas. Diverse teams of researchers can ask and answer more ambitious and challenging questions informed by the many fields that bear on the practice and process of intelligence. The use of publicly available evidence, and robust efforts to make more data available to intelligence researchers, can mitigate the "streetlight effect," providing complete insights into intelligence practices. Such efforts will require changes in policy and classification but also the promotion of activities and approaches that allow practitioners and academics to engage with each other. In these ways intelligence researchers can build on the strong foundations in place, further expanding and advancing intelligence studies as the practice of intelligence itself undergoes rapid and profound changes in the twenty-first century.

## Notes

1. Mr. Perestroika, "Please Spread This Letter as Widely as Possible—Let Them Know We Exist," October 15, 2000, https://ia800208.us.archive.org/0/items/OnThe IrrelevanceOfApsaAndApsrToTheStudyOfPoliticalScience/mrperestroika.pdf.
2. For example, see Kristen Monroe, *Perestroika: The Raucous Rebellion in Political Science* (New Haven, CT: Yale University Press, 2005).
3. Michael Lerner and Ethan Hill, "The New Nostradamus," *Good*, October 4, 2007, https://www.good.is/articles/the-new-nostradamus; Stephen E. Bennett, "'Perestroika' Lost: Why the Latest 'Reform' Movement in Political Science Should Fail," *PS: Political Science and Politics* 35, no. 2 (2002): 177–79.
4. For several examples, see Peter Gill and Mark Phythian, eds., "Developing Intelligence Theory," special issue, *Intelligence and National Security* 33, no. 4 (2018).
5. Perestroika, "Please Spread This."
6. Perestroika.
7. David Freedman, "Why Scientific Studies Are So Often Wrong: The Streetlight Effect," *Discover Magazine*, December 10, 2010, http://discovermagazine.com/2010/jul-aug/29-why-scientific-studies-often-wrong-streetlight-effect.
8. Michael Warner, "Sources and Methods for the Study of Intelligence," in *Handbook of Intelligence Studies*, ed. Loch Johnson (New York: Routledge, 2007), 35–45.
9. For a conceptual discussion of difficult-to-access research problems, see Patrick von Maravic, "Limits of Knowing or the Consequences of Difficult-Access Problems for Multi-method Research and Public Policy," *Policy Sciences* 45, no. 2 (2012): 153–68.
10. Damien Van Puyvelde and Sean Curtis, "'Standing on the Shoulders of Giants': Diversity and Scholarship in Intelligence Studies," *Intelligence and National Security* 31, no. 7 (2016): 1040–54.
11. For an example from Latin America, see Eduardo Estévez, "Comparing Intelligence Democratization in Latin America: Argentina, Peru and Ecuador Cases," *Intelligence and National Security* 29, no. 4 (2014): 552–80. For other examples, see Phillip Davies and Kristian Gustafson, eds., *Intelligence Elsewhere: Spies and Espionage Outside the Anglosphere* (Washington, DC: Georgetown University Press, 2013).
12. Richard Aldrich and Christopher Moran, "Delayed Disclosure: National Security, Whistle-Blowers and the Nature of Secrecy," *Political Studies* (in press): 1–16, https://journals.sagepub.com/doi/abs/10.1177/0032321718764990.
13. For example, see Jerry H. Ratcliffe, *Intelligence-Led Policing* (New York: Routledge, 2016); and Eamon Javers, *Broker, Trader, Lawyer, Spy: The Secret World of Corporate Espionage* (New York: HarperCollins, 2010).
14. Liz Sly, "Australian Learns How Strava Heat Map Reveals Dangerous Information from Jogging US Soldiers," *Sydney Morning Herald*, January 29, 2018, https://www

.smh.com.au/technology/australian-learns-how-strava-heat-map-reveals-dangerous-information-from-jogging-us-soldiers-20180129-h0pq5i.html.
15. See, for example, Wesley Wark, *Spy Fiction, Spy Films and Real Intelligence* (London: Frank Cass, 1991); and Yves Trotignon, *Politiques du Secret* (Paris: Presse Universitaires de France, 2018).
16. Rob Johnston, *Analytic Culture in the U.S. Intelligence Community: An Ethnographic Study* (Washington, DC: Central Intelligence Agency Center for the Study of Intelligence, 2005).
17. For example, see Misty Duke and Damien Van Puyvelde, "What Science Can Teach Us about 'Enhanced Interrogation,'" *International Journal of Intelligence and CounterIntelligence* 30, no. 2 (2017): 310–39.
18. Aaron Brantly, "When Everything Becomes Intelligence: Machine Learning and the Connected World," *Intelligence and National Security* 33, no. 4 (2018): 562–73.
19. Donald Campbell, "Ethnocentrism of Disciplines and the Fish-Scale Model of Omniscience," in *Interdisciplinary Relationships in the Social Sciences*, ed. Muzafer Sherif and Carolyn W. Sherif (New Brunswick, NJ: Aldine Transaction, 1969), 3, 4, 7.
20. For a critique of intelligence research as not cumulative, see Stephen Marrin, "Improving Intelligence Studies as an Academic Discipline," *Intelligence and National Security* 31, no. 2 (2016): 266–79.
21. Campbell, "Ethnocentrism of Disciplines," 3.
22. See, for example, Dustin Dehéz, "Security Sector Reform and Intelligence Services in Sub-Saharan Africa: Capturing the Whole Picture," *African Security Review* 19, no. 2 (2010): 3846; and Andrew Hammond, "Deciphering Museums, Politics and Impact," *British Politics* 13, no. 3 (2018): 409–31, https://link.springer.com/article/10.1057/s41293-018-0086-8.
23. See, for example, Philip H. J. Davies and Kristian C. Gustafson, eds., *Intelligence Elsewhere* (Washington, DC: Georgetown University Press, 2013); and Bob de Graaf and James M. Nyce, *The Handbook of European Intelligence Cultures* (New York: Rowman and Littlefield, 2016).
24. For example, see Edna Reid and Hsinchun Chen, "Mapping the Contemporary Terrorism Research Domain," *International Journal of Human-Computer Studies* 65, no. 1 (2007): 42–56.
25. Van Puyvelde and Curtis, "Standing on the Shoulders."
26. "About Us," Teaching, Research, and International Policy, accessed August 13, 2018, https://trip.wm.edu/about-us.
27. For example, see Carol H. Weiss, "The Many Meanings of Research Utilization," *Public Administration Review* 39, no. 5 (1979): 426–31; and Réjean Landry, Nabil Amara, and Moktar Lamari, "Climbing the Ladder of Research Utilization: Evidence from Social Science Research," *Science Communication* 22, no. 4 (2001): 396–422.
28. For a foundational text in this research strand, see Alexander George, *Bridging the Gap: Theory and Practice in Foreign Policy* (Washington, DC: US Institute of Peace Press, 1993), xvii.

29. Paul C. Avey and Michael C. Desch, "What Do Policymakers Want from Us? Results of a Survey of Current and Former Senior National Security Decision Makers," *International Studies Quarterly* 58, no. 2 (June 2014): 227–46.
30. Weiss, "Many Meanings," 429–30.
31. In addition to classified research initiatives like the IC associates program, US academics interested in unclassified research have options like the Department of Homeland Security's Analytic Exchange Program: "Analytic Exchange Program (AEP) Deliverables," Department of Homeland Security, August 13, 2018, https://www.dhs.gov/aep-deliverables. For an example from Canada, see "Academic Outreach," Government of Canada, accessed August 14, 2018, https://www.canada.ca/en/security-intelligence-service/corporate/academic-outreach.html.
32. Lashmar mentions another group, historians. We omit this group because historians can fall into any of these categories.
33. Richards J. Heuer, *Psychology of Intelligence Analysis* (Washington, DC: Central Intelligence Agency Center for the Study of Intelligence, 1999); Gregory F. Treverton, *"Addressing Complexities" in Homeland Security* (Stockholm: Swedish National Defence College, 2008).
34. See, for example, Michael V. Hayden, *Playing to the Edge: American Intelligence in the Age of Terror* (New York: Penguin Books, 2017). And for a list of errors, see Dianne Feinstein, "Factual Errors and Other Problems in 'Playing to the Edge: American Intelligence in the Age of Terror,' by Michael V. Hayden," staff summary, March 2016, https://www.feinstein.senate.gov/public/_cache/files/e/7/e7fde6e8-4053-454a-a15c-47234daf175e/1FB727F237C5E0C97F075462081B6DAC.hayden-book-response-march-2016.pdf.

# Contributors

**Rubén Arcos**, PhD, is lecturer of communication sciences at Rey Juan Carlos University (Madrid). He is the founder and chapter chair of Strategic and Competitive Intelligence Professionals for Spain and founding codirector of IntelHub. He is a freelance contributor to *Jane's Intelligence Review* and deputy editor of the *International Journal of Intelligence, Security, and Public Affairs*. He has served for almost ten years as coordinating director of the first ever master's degree in intelligence analysis in Spain. Arcos has published extensively in intelligence studies, strategic communications, and experiential learning in intelligence through simulations and games.

**Ross Bellaby**, PhD, is a senior lecturer at the University of Sheffield's Politics Department. His main research examines the application of ethics to violence and war, with specific attention to developing an ethical framework for intelligence activity. This involves developing ethical frameworks for intelligence, terrorism, counterterrorism, and cybersecurity. His ethical framework is set out in his book *The Ethics of Intelligence: A New Framework*. Recent works also examine the dark web and hacker groups as ethical vigilantes and the moral obligation that intelligence professionals have to blow the whistle when they witness wrongdoing.

**Rick Caceres-Rodriguez** completed his PhD in public administration and policy at the University at Albany's Rockefeller College and is an adjunct professor at American University. His research focuses on representative bureaucracy, diversity and inclusion programs, social equity, and human resource (HR) management. He has published in *Administration and Society*, presented at academic conferences, and served as a reviewer for the *Public Administration Review* and the *Review of Public Personnel Administration*. Caceres-Rodriguez is currently an HR professional in the intelligence community, and before that he worked at the Department of the Interior.

**Stephen Coulthart** is an assistant professor of security studies in the National Security Studies Institute at the University of Texas at El Paso. He earned a PhD in public and international affairs from the University of Pittsburgh. His research focuses on intelligence analysis and emerging national security technologies, and he has been published in *Intelligence and National Security*, *International Affairs*, and *Journal of Conflict Resolution*, among others. He has provided training and analytical support to numerous governmental and nongovernmental entities in the United States and Europe.

**Misty Duke** is a lecturer in the National Security Studies Institute at the University of Texas at El Paso, where she teaches courses on intelligence interviewing and interrogation, cognitive bias in intelligence analysis, and applied research methods and statistics in intelligence analysis. She has published research on intelligence interviewing and interrogation methods, juror decision-making, and child suggestibility. Duke's research has been funded by the High-Value Detainee Interrogation Group (HIG). Duke has frequently presented research on interrogation interviewing methods to both academics and practitioners.

**Brent Durbin** is associate professor of government at Smith College. His research centers on the political dynamics of US national security, with a particular focus on the Central Intelligence Agency (CIA). His book *The CIA and the Politics of U.S. Intelligence Reform* was published by Cambridge University Press in 2017. With support from a Mellon Foundation New Directions Fellowship, Durbin is currently studying the social and political effects of data analytics in government and business. Durbin is codirector of the Bridging the Gap Project, which promotes connections between scholars and the broader foreign policy community.

**John Ferris** is a fellow of the Royal Society of Canada. He is professor of history at the University of Calgary. He is honorary professor at the School of Law and Politics, Brunel University, and in the Department of International Politics, the University of Aberystwyth, and he is an associate member of Nuffield College, Oxford. He has published widely in air, diplomatic, imperial, intelligence, international, and diplomatic history and in intelligence studies and strategic studies. He is completing the authorized history of the British code-breaking agency, Government Communications Headquarters, which will be published in October 2019.

**Michael Landon-Murray** is an assistant professor at the University of Colorado–Colorado Springs, where he teaches courses in intelligence analysis and public administration and policy. He is a graduate of Rockefeller College at the University at Albany and was formerly a visiting assistant professor at the University of Texas at El Paso's National Security Studies Institute. His research focuses on intelligence analysis, education, and oversight and has been published in the *International Journal of Intelligence and CounterIntelligence*, the *International Journal of Intelligence, Security, and Public Affairs*, and the *Washington Post*.

**Paul Lashmar**, PhD, is deputy head of journalism at City, University of London. His research interests include investigative journalism, intelligence-media relations, organized crime reporting, digital journalism, and media bias. Lashmar has been an investigative journalist in television and print and on the staff of *The Observer*, Granada Television's World in Action current affairs series, and *The Independent*. Paul is an adviser to the Centre for Investigative Journalism. He was previously head of journalism at University of Sussex (2015–17) and Brunel University (2014–15). His latest book is *Spin, Spies and the Fourth Estate: British Intelligence and the Media* (Edinburgh University Press, 2019).

**David R. Mandel** is a senior defense scientist with Defence Research and Development Canada and adjunct professor of psychology at York University. He has published widely on the topics of reasoning, judgment, and decision-making and has coedited *The Psychology of Counterfactual Thinking*, *Neuroscience of Decision Making*, and *Improving Bayesian Reasoning: What Works and Why?* Mandel is chairman of the NATO System Analysis and Studies Panel Research Technical Group on Assessment and Communication of Uncertainty in Intelligence to Support Decision Making (SAS-114) and principal investigator of multiple Canadian government projects aimed at improving intelligence production.

**Stephen Marrin,** PhD, is an associate professor and director of the Intelligence Analysis Program at James Madison University. He has also previously held positions with Brunel University's Centre for Intelligence and Security Studies and Mercyhurst University's Intelligence Studies Department, and he spent five years as an analyst with the Central Intelligence Agency and the Government Accountability Office. Holder of a BA from Colgate University and MA and PhD degrees from the University of Virginia, he has until recently been the chair of the International Studies Associations' Intelligence Studies Section and was previously on the board of the International Association for Intelligence Education.

**Bridget Rose Nolan** is a postdoctoral research fellow at the National Security Studies Institute at the University of Texas at El Paso. She has an undergraduate degree in psychology from Princeton University and a PhD in sociology from the University of Pennsylvania. Nolan's research interests include organizations, culture, gender, terrorism (particularly in sub-Saharan Africa and Northern Ireland), counterterrorism, and national security. From 2007 to 2011, she worked as a counterterrorism analyst for the Central Intelligence Agency.

**Mark Phythian** is professor of politics in the School of History, Politics, and International Relations at the University of Leicester. He is the author or editor of several books on aspects of intelligence, most recently *Principled Spying: The Ethics of Secret Intelligence*, coauthored with David Omand (Oxford University Press / Georgetown University Press, 2018), and a third edition of *Intelligence in an Insecure World*, coauthored with Peter Gill (Polity Press, 2018). He is the coeditor of *Intelligence and National Security* and a fellow of the UK Academy of Social Sciences.

**Damien Van Puyvelde** is lecturer in intelligence and international security at the University of Glasgow. His research focuses on the governance of intelligence and security practices in contemporary democracies. He is the author of *Outsourcing U.S. Intelligence: Contractors and Government Accountability* (Edinburgh University Press, 2019) and coauthor of *Cybersecurity: Politics, Governance and Conflict in Cyberspace*, with Aaron Brantly (Polity, 2019). Van Puyvelde serves as program cochair for the Intelligence Studies Section of the International Studies Association, and coconvenes the Intelligence Studies Group of the Association pour les Études sur la Guerre et la Stratégie.

# Index

*Figures and notes are indicated by f and t following the page number.*

Abawajy, Jemal, 72
Aberbach, Joel D., 54
academic research model (hourglass), 199–200, 200f
academics. *See* scholars
accountability: intelligence failures and, 124–25; journalism and, 195, 199; representative bureaucracy and, 151; of scholars and researchers, 1–2, 17–18, 213, 218; secrecy and, 199
ACH (Analysis of Competing Hypotheses), 118–21
acolytes, 198, 230
activism, 183, 190n17, 213
Afghanistan War, 216–17
agent recruitment, 83–85, 87–88, 192n43
Aldrich, Richard, 14, 15, 101
Alexander, Keith B., 193
Allison, Graham, 4, 108, 171
Allyn, Jane, 169
American Political Science Association (APSA), 97, 225–26
Analysis of Competing Hypotheses (ACH), 118–21

*Analytic Culture in the U.S. Intelligence Community* (Johnston), 54
Anderson, David, 204
Andrew, Christopher, 13–14, 30, 31
anonymity. *See* confidentiality
APSA (American Political Science Association), 97, 225–26
archival release policies: barriers to intelligence research and, 12; biographical projects and, 15, 24n24; declassified information, delaying release of, 49–50; democracy and, 47; in former Communist bloc states, 15; intelligence history and, 14, 15, 24n24, 32–33, 198; ongoing classification and, 15–16; public record sanitation and, 15, 49; research on intelligence organizations and, 155; in Soviet Union, 15
Arcos, Rubén, 5, 163
*Army Field Manual,* 70
Association of Former Intelligence Officers, 11
*Asylums* (Goffman), 84
Avey, Paul C., 190n8, 230

Ban Ki-moon, 216
Bar-Joseph, Uri, 105
Barnes, Alan, 119–20, 125, 127, 137n54
Basi, Tina, 197
Bauman, Zygmunt, 17
Bayesian reasoning, 122–24, 202
Bean, Hamilton, 102, 144–45
Beesly, Patrick, 32
behavior: coding of, 66, 67–73; deceptive, 40, 70–71, 163, 168–70; manipulation through technology, 19; nonverbal language and, 55, 65, 71, 168, 170; self-reports of, 63, 72, 74; surveillance and skewed interpretation of, 15; verbal, 65–66, 71. *See also* communication; structured behavioral observation systems
Belfast Project, 219–20
Belhaj, Abdel Hakim, 207–8
Bellaby, Ross, 1–2, 6, 211, 228, 230
Bellingcat, 202
Belton, Ian, 120
Benson, Robert, 194
Betts, Richard, 31, 144
bias: communication and, 163; disciplinary specialties and, 229; in forecasting, 127–28; in intelligence history, 34, 227; of interviewees, 57, 80, 226; misperceptions resulting from, 104; policymaking and, 186; in research, 218; in sampling, 52–53; of scholars, 231–32. *See also specific types of bias*
Bigo, Didier, 17
biographical projects: archival release policies and, 15, 24n24; credibility of, 50; information security and, 56; national contexts, understanding through, 20; observer bias and, 231; researcher use of, 49, 53
biographical questions, 55
block quotations, 57–58

*Blowing My Cover: My Life as a CIA Spy* (Moran), 87–88
body language. *See* nonverbal language and behavior
Bourdieu, Pierre, 194, 198, 209n14
bridging the gap. *See* scholar–practitioner divide in intelligence
*Bridging the Gap* (George), 179
Bridging the Gap (BTG) Project, 180, 182, 189n4, 230
Budescu, David, 129, 130
Bundy, McGeorge, 184
Bureau of Intelligence and Research (INR), 187
Bush, George W., 215

Caceres-Rodriguez, Rick, 5, 141, 228
Cacioppo, John, 169
calibration feedback, 127
Cambridge Intelligence Seminar, 52
Campbell, Donald, 228–29
Campbell, Duncan, 201, 206
Carter, Jeremy G., 154
case studies, 19–20, 197
CBCA (Criteria-Based Content Analysis), 71–72
Center for the Study of Intelligence (CSI), 81–82, 92
Centers for Academic Excellence, 187
Central Intelligence Agency (CIA): academic outreach of, 187; "black sites" of, 215; culture of, 85–86; data leaks from, 47; declassified data from, 155; emotion management of agents in, 87; Freedom of Information Act requests and, 2; as greedy institution, 84–85; Iran, coup involvement in (1953), 15–16; multimedia communications of, 172–73; online records search tools of, 2; public opinion on, 92; recruitment of agents for, 87–88, 192n43; rendition of Libyan dissident, 207–8; researching, 81–82, 92,

155; scholarly origins of, 184–85; September 11, 2001, terrorist attacks and, 88, 145, 150
Chamberlain, Neville, 36
Chambers, Simone, 212
Cheney, Dick, 215
civil liberties, 103, 214. *See also* surveillance
Clapper, James, 51, 186
Clark, S. M., 153
coding of behaviors, 66, 67–73
coercive isomorphism, 154
cognitive bias, 4, 118, 231
Cold War, 15, 38–40, 44n28
collaboration. *See* cooperation and collaboration
communication, 5, 163–76; in decision-making, 170–71; of finished intelligence, 171–73; government, national security, and foundations in, 165–67, 166f; intelligence as interpretation of signs and signals, 167–68; with interview subjects, 54–55; nonverbal language and behavior, 55, 65, 71, 168, 170; persuasion and deception in, 168–70; political science theory and, 99; processes and areas of, 163, 164f; technology for, 99, 172; of uncertainty in intelligence, 128–31, 130f
communism, 15, 103
comparative analysis, 19–20, 229
confidence levels, 127–28
confidentiality: ethical duty of researchers and, 218–20; journalism and, 202, 203; qualitative interviews and, 54, 56, 58
confirmation bias, 118
congressional oversight of intelligence, 106–7, 147
conspiracy theories, 34, 42, 198
constructivism, 101–2
consultants, 156

continuous narrative of intelligence history, 33–42
cooperation and collaboration: among intelligence agencies, 79, 80, 85–86, 91–92, 144–45, 207, 227; interdisciplinary, 4, 41–42, 204–5, 207–8, 228–29; between journalists and scholars, 197, 204–6. *See also* scholar–practitioner divide in intelligence
Cormac, Rory, 14
Coser, Lewis, 79, 84–85
Coulthart, Stephen, 1, 51, 225
counterintelligence, 41, 44n28, 64, 156
counterterrorism. *See* terrorism and counterterrorism
count system for behavior observation, 66
covert action, 109, 169. *See also* deceptive behavior
Criteria-Based Content Analysis (CBCA), 71–72
critical friends, 198, 230–31
critical intelligence studies, 18
critical theorists, 198
cryptography, 30, 33, 38, 167
CSI (Center for the Study of Intelligence), 81–82, 92
Cunningham-Sabot, Emanuelle, 56
Curtis, Sean, 20, 229
cybersecurity, 19, 58, 72–73

Dahl, Erik, 192n39
Daniel, Donald, 170
data leaks: consequences of, 47; ethical issues and, 2–3, 228; international cooperation on, 206; journal articles on, 21; transparency and, 49, 227; whistle-blowers and, 199, 218–20; WikiLeaks, 2, 205, 215–17, 220, 228. *See also* Snowden data leaks
DataPSST! project, 207

data sources: barriers to intelligence research and, 2–3; confidentiality and, 54, 56, 58, 202, 203, 218–20; declassified information, 2, 49–50, 105, 155–56, 227, 235n31; diversity of, 226–28; interrogations and, 65, 66–72, 170, 207–8, 218; intrusive methods of collection, 218; political science theory and, 99; protecting, 2, 55–58, 202, 208n6, 218, 219–20; public as, 151–52; for research on intelligence organizations, 2, 53, 155–56, 227, 235n31; scholarly vs. journalistic uses of, 199, 201–2; whistle-blowers, 199, 218–20. *See also* archival release policies; interviews; structured behavioral observation systems; surveillance

data triangulation, 15, 49, 59

David, Stephen, 103

Davies, Philip H. J., 51, 142, 143

deceptive behavior, 40, 70–72, 163, 168–70

decision-making processes, 35–38, 104–5, 108, 170–71

decision science, 5, 117–39; application to intelligence analysis, 121–30; communication of uncertainty in intelligence, 128–31, 130*f*; exploitation in intelligence, 118–21; forecasting skill and, 124–28, 126*f*; probabilistic reasoning and, 121–24, 123*f*

declassified information: delaying release of, 49–50; individual-level data analysis and, 105; for research on intelligence organizations, 2, 155–56, 227, 235n31. *See also* archival release policies

Defense Intelligence Agency, 187

Delcassé, Théophile, 13–14

democracy: archive availability and, 47; ethical duty to public and, 211–13;

intelligence services, purpose of, 106; international relations theory and, 103; secrecy vs., 17, 197, 212

democratic peace theory, 103

Department of Homeland Security Analytic Exchange Program, 235n31

Desch, Michael C., 190n8, 230

descriptive journalism, 172

Dhami, Mandeep, 120, 129

Dilks, David, 13–14

diplomacy, 216

direct-questioning technique, 69

disciplinary integration, 3–4, 41–42, 204–5, 207–8, 228–29

discrimination accuracy, 71

disinformation campaigns, 39, 168–69

documentary research, 49, 57, 59

Donovan, William, 184

Dover, Robert, 198, 199, 202, 206–7

Doyle, Michael, 103

drones, 19

Duke, Misty, 5, 63, 226

Durbin, Brent, 6, 179, 230

dynamic behavior observations, 66

education and training: in cybersecurity, 72–73; decision science and, 132; degrees and faculty positions in intelligence studies, 1, 11, 33, 97, 109–10, 181–82; disciplinary integration, 3–4, 41–42, 205, 207–8, 228–29; evidence-based, 124; intelligence studies as field of study, 30–32, 38, 42; in mindsets and biases, 127; preprofessional training for intelligence agents, 12; in probabilistic reasoning, 122–24, 123*f*

electroencephalographs, 63

elicitation methods, 73–74

emotion work, 86–90

encryption, 58

Entman, R. M., 210n36

environmental scanning, 152–53
espionage, 83–84, 99, 216–17
*Essence of Decision* (Allison & Zelikow), 171
ethical duties, 6, 211–24; to academia and academic practice, 218–20; data leaks and, 2–3, 228; to intelligence practitioners, 217–18; of interviewers, 56–57; of journalists, 203; to national security, 213–17; to public, 1–2, 211–13; short-term gains vs., 207–8; surveillance and, 17, 207
ethnicity, 150–52, 218
ethnography, 80
evidence-based lexicons, 119, 128–30, 130*f*, 137n54
evidence-based practice, 1, 3, 67–72
evidence-based training, 124
expression games, 170
extremism, 64, 74

Fairness and Accuracy in Reporting, 215
false statements. *See* deceptive behavior
Federal Bureau of Investigation (FBI), 73, 145
federally funded research and development centers (FFRDCs), 181
feedback, 165
Feinstein, Dianne, 50
Ferris, John, 4, 29, 228
Festinger, Leon, 169
field theory (Bourdieu), 194
Five Eyes countries, 193–95, 206
forecasting, 124–28, 126*f*, 132, 180–81
foreign policy, 108–9, 180, 185
Foucault, Michel, 19
fourth estate. *See* journalists
framing, 210n36
Freedom of Information Act (FOIA, 1967), 2
French, David, 31

functional magnetic resonance imaging, 63

Gambetta, Diego, 168
Gellman, Barton, 193
Gentry, John A., 145
George, Alexander, 179, 180, 183, 185, 188
Germany, 15, 35–38
Gill, Peter, 16, 194, 197–205
Gioia, D. A., 153
*Global Trends* (NIC), 181, 187
Goffman, Erving, 80, 82–84, 92, 170
Goodman, Michael, 198, 199, 202, 206–7
goodness heuristic, 131
governmental politics model of decision-making, 108, 171
Government Communications Headquarters (GCHQ), 195, 202
Government Performance and Results Act (1993), 149
Granhag, Par Anders, 69, 70
greedy institutions, 84–86
Greenwald, Glenn, 193, 215

Haldeman, H. R., 185
Hall, Stuart, 204
Hammond, Thomas H., 144
Handel, Michael, 31–32, 40
Happ, Christian, 73
hard-easy effect, 127
Hasler, Susan, 89
Hastedt, Glenn, 106
Hatch Act (1939), 90
Hayden, Michael, 50
Hays, Steven, 218
Herbig, Katherine, 170
Herman, Michael, 32, 142, 143, 146, 198
Hesketh, Roger, 40
Heuer, Richards, Jr., 118–20, 231
Hilsman, Roger, 106

Hitler, Adolf, 36–37
Ho, Emily, 129
Hochschild, Arlie, 80, 86–87
Hoopes, James, 168
Hourglass Model of academic research, 199–200, 200*f*
House Permanent Select Committee on Intelligence (HPSCI), 106–7
Houston, Brant, 172
Hovland, Carl, 167
human resource management, 148–49
Hunter, Mark L., 200

IC Directive 205 "Analytic Outreach" (2008), 186–87
imagery intelligence, 202
impression management, 82–84
individual-level IR theories, 104–5
information asymmetries, 146–47
information security, 55–58
information sharing. *See* cooperation and collaboration
innovation, 144, 154
INR (Bureau of Intelligence and Research), 187
institutional isomorphism, 154–55
institutional review boards, 56
intelligence, defined, 16, 98–99, 132
Intelligence Advanced Research Projects Activity, 187
intelligence agencies: agent recruitment for, 83–85, 87–88, 192n43; cooperation and collaboration among, 79, 80, 85–86, 91–92, 144–45, 207, 227; culture of, 85–86, 144–45, 155–56, 213, 231; emotion management of agents in, 86–90; as greedy institutions, 84–86; history and historians of, 32–33, 39; individual-level data analysis of, 105; intelligence education as preprofessional training for, 12; intelligence failures and, 145, 147–48; intelligence

theory and, 16–17; leadership and management of, 145–46; prepublication boards of, 2; public opinion on, 42, 92, 213–15, 228; researching, 2–3, 80–82, 92, 155–56; restricted access to headquarters of, 55; secrecy vs. democracy and, 17; surveillance and, 17. *See also* public administration; scholar–practitioner divide in intelligence; *specific agencies*
intelligence analysis: accuracy of, 146; analyst selection and, 132; cognitive bias and, 4; education for, 12, 33, 110; emotion work and, 86–90; forecasting and, 124–28, 126*f*, 132, 180–81; influence of scholarly research in, 186; policymaking and, 99; publication of reports and, 91–92; research limitations and, 185–86; structured techniques for, 202. *See also* decision science; intelligence failures
*Intelligence and National Security:* founding and purpose of, 16, 31; interview use in, 48, 48*f*, 59–60n6; on organizational analysis, 143; on principal debate in intelligence studies, 13; survey of countries covered in, 20, 229
intelligence cycle: communication and, 163, 164*f*, 173–74n2; ethics and, 207; journalism and academic research models compared to, 199–200, 200*f*, 209n21
intelligence failures: accountability and, 124–25; decision making and, 104; fear of, 213; flipside errors and, 124–25; foreign policy analysis and, 108; intelligence studies focus on, 18, 227; organizational factors contributing to, 90, 145, 147–50; sociological research in, 90–91; transparency following, 49

intelligence fiction, 228
intelligence history and historians, 4, 29–44; archival release policies and, 14, 15, 24n24, 32–33, 198; bias and, 34, 227; Cold War and, 38–40, 44n28; continuous narrative of, 33–42; as field of study, 30–32, 38; intelligence agencies and, 32–33; as journalists' sources, 198; as project of intelligence studies research, 14–16; role in intelligence studies, 228; WWII and, 35–38
intelligence management, 33, 145–46, 149
intelligence outsourcing, 147, 156
intelligence studies research, 4, 11–27; behavior studies and, 63–77; central debate in, 13, 16; challenges of, 2–4, 6, 12, 47, 91–92; communications and, 163–76; decision science and, 117–39; degrees and faculty positions in, 1, 11, 33, 97, 109–10, 181–82; disciplinary integration for, 3–4, 41–42, 204–5, 207–8, 228–29; ethical duties in, 211–24; evidence-based practice and, 1, 3; explanation of, 11–14; four projects of, 14–18, 228; funding for, 1, 3, 201, 218; future of, 232–33; history and historians of, 29–44, 198, 228; incentives for, 181–82, 197–98, 231; issues cutting across projects of, 18–20; journalism and, 193–210; opportunities of, 20–22; pluralistic approach to, 4–6; policymaking influence and, 180–83, 190n8, 204, 229–31; political science and, 97–115, 225; public administration and organizational theory, 141–62; qualitative interviews for, 47–62; scholar–practitioner divide and, 179–92; secrecy as barrier to, 2, 12, 31–32, 47, 91, 155, 188, 211; security clearances for scholars and, 156, 185, 188; sociological approach to, 79–94; streetlight effect in, 226–27
intelligence theory, 98–105; critical theorist and, 198; disciplinary framework and, 228–29; history of intelligence and, 31, 33–34, 40; individual-level IR theories, 103–5; intelligence agencies and, 16–17; international relations and, 100–105; political theory and, 98–100; state-level IR theories, 103–4; systemic-level IR theories, 101–3
interdisciplinary collaborations, 4, 41–42, 204–5, 207–8, 228–29
International Association for Intelligence Education, 52
International Consortium of Investigative Journalists, 206
International Intelligence History Association, 15
*International Journal of Intelligence and Counterintelligence*, 20, 59–60n6, 143, 229
International Policy Summer Institute, 182
international relations, 21–22, 100–105, 182–83, 230
International Studies Association (ISA), 52, 187, 197, 206
*The International Who's Who*, 52
interpretive journalism, 172
inter-rater reliability, 65
interrogations, 65, 66–72, 170, 207–8, 218
interval coding, 66, 68, 70
interviews: behavior observation systems for, 66–72; bias and, 57, 80, 226; disadvantages of, 79–80; ethical issues and, 203; interviewees, choosing, 51–53; organizational research and, 155; preparation of, 53–57;

interviews (*continued*)
  protecting sources, 55–58, 202, 208n6, 218–20; recording, 56, 57, 65–66, 68–71; semistructured, 54; skills of interviewers, 67–68; structured, 53, 55; unstructured, 53–54; using material from, 57–58. *See also* interrogations; qualitative interviews
intuition, 121
investigative journalism. *See* journalists
Iran-US relations, 15–16
Iraq War, 216–17
Ireland, 219–20
ISA (International Studies Association), 52, 187, 197, 206
isomorphism, 154–55

Jeffery, Keith, 14
Jeffreys-Jones, Rhodri, 50
Jenkins, Sarah, 128
Jentleson, Bruce, 180
Jervis, Robert, 31, 104, 168, 186
job satisfaction, 148–49
Johnson, Loch, 13, 17, 31, 106, 107, 195
Johnston, Rob, 54, 64, 80
Jos, Philip, 218
journalists, 6, 193–210; accountability of, 195, 199; commonalities between scholars and, 199–201, 200*f*; cooperation with scholars, 197, 204–6; differences between scholars and, 201–3; finished intelligence, communication of, 171–73; intelligence scholars and, 197–98; interdisciplinarity of, 204–5; investigative journalism model, 200, 200*f*; national security reporting, 195, 208n6; oversight role of, 213; overview of, 195–97, 196*f*; protecting sources, 202, 219–20; Snowden data leaks and, 193–94, 204

journals of intelligence studies: disciplinary integration and, 4, 21; English-speaking intelligence services, 227; journalism vs., 201; overview, 20–21; qualitative interviews used in articles of, 48, 48*f*, 59–60n6; research needs for, 229; response to Snowden data leaks in, 194. *See also specific journals*

Kahn, David, 31
Kahneman, Daniel, 131
Kant, Immanuel, 103, 212
Kelly, Christopher, 68
Kennedy, Brandy, 151, 152
Kennedy, John F., 155
Kent, Sherman, 117, 124, 128, 132, 143
Kettl, Donald, 147
Kim, Sangmook, 148
Kingdon, John, 180
Kiriakou, John, 47
Klepak, Hal, 20
Kristof, Nicholas, 182

Landon-Murray, Michael, 1, 5, 12, 141, 225, 228
Lashmar, Paul, 6, 193, 229–31
Lasswell, Harold, 167, 169
Lazarsfeld, Paul, 167
leaked information. *See* data leaks
Le Carré, John, 197
Lehner, Paul, 120
Lewin, Kurt, 167
liberty. *See* civil liberties
Libya, 207–8
lies. *See* deceptive behavior
Lilleker, Darren G., 54
Lim, Hong-Hai, 152
LinkedIn, 52
Lobban, Iain, 193
Locke, John, 212
Lowman, John, 219
Lyon, David, 17

MacAskill, Ewen, 193
Maddrell, Paul, 20
Madigan, Michael, 107
*Man, the State, and War* (Waltz), 100
*The Managed Heart* (Hochschild), 86
Mandel, David R., 5, 117, 146
Manning, Chelsea, 215
Marrin, Stephen, 5, 97; background of, 192n39; on congressional oversight, 147; disciplinary integration and, 228; on intelligence failure, 18; on intelligence studies, 12
May, Ernest, 188
May, Theresa, 208
McConnell, Mike, 186
McDermott, Rose, 63, 105
McGlynn, Joseph, 218
Mearsheimer, John, 21–22
media. *See* journalists
Meier, Kenneth, 151
memoirs. *See* biographical projects
METIS research group, 52
MI5 (British Security Service), 14–15
MI6 (British Secret Intelligence Service), 14, 206–7
Miethe, Terance, 218
Mill, John Stuart, 212
mimetic isomorphism, 154
mimicry, 168
minorities, 150–52, 218
misperceptions, decision-making and, 104–5
*The Missing Dimension* (Andrew & Dilks), 13–14
Mitrokhin, Vasili, 14
Mitrokhin archive, Churchill College, Cambridge, 15
Moore, Adam, 214
morality, 147, 213, 217
Moran, Christopher, 20
Moran, Lindsay, 87–88
Moynihan, Donald, 150
Murphy, David, 50

Mussolini, Benito, 36
Mutual Legal Assistance Treaty, 219

National Intelligence Estimates (US), 130
national security reporting, 195, 208n6
NATO (North Atlantic Treaty Organization), 124
natural sampling trees, 122
Naughton, John, 204, 210n38
NCTC (National Counterterrorism Center), 80, 86, 87, 88, 231
Neilson, Keith, 31
networking, 52–53
Neveu, Erik, 194
NIC (National Intelligence Council), 181, 187
Nicholson-Crotty, Jill, 151
Nielsen, Poul Aaes, 149
9/11 Commission Report, 80, 86, 148–50, 155–56
Nixon, Richard, 185
Nolan, Bridget Rose, 5, 79, 146, 227, 228, 231
nonverbal language and behavior, 55, 65, 71, 168, 170
normative isomorphism, 154
North Atlantic Treaty Organization (NATO), 124
Norton-Taylor, Richard, 197, 204, 206
NSA (National Security Agency), 33, 187, 193, 207. *See also* Snowden data leaks
nuclear weapons, 39–40

observation of behavior. *See* structured behavioral observation systems
observer bias, 231
offshore banking secrecy, 206
off-the-record interview questions, 55
Omand, David, 198
open-minded thinking, 132

250  Index

open source intelligence, 186, 201–2, 209n21, 228
operationalization, 63. *See also* structured behavioral observation systems
organizational behavior model of decision-making, 108, 171
organizational bias, 127–28
organizational failure, 90, 145, 147–50
organization theory. *See* public administration
overconfidence, 127–28
Owen, John, 99

PA. *See* public administration
Palys, Ted, 219
Payne, Kenneth, 195
PEACE interviews, 67
Peirce, Charles Sanders, 167
perfect information, 104, 108
performance management and measurement, 149–50
Perrow, Charles, 90
persuasion, 168–70
Petraeus, David, 56
Petty, Richard, 169
physiology, behavior study and, 63
Phythian, Mark, 4, 11, 102, 205, 207, 228
Poitras, Laura, 193
policy and policymaking: bias in, 186; environmental scanning and, 153; individual influences on, 104; intelligence analysis and, 18, 99; interpreting to discern states' intentions, 21; policy-relevant scholarship, 180–82, 190n8; realism and, 102; scholar-activists and, 183, 190n17; scholars' influence in, 180–83, 190n8, 204, 229–31
Political Instability Task Force, 187
political policing, 41
political psychology, 105

political science, 5, 97–115; American politics and, 105–9; intelligence studies compared, 225; international relations and, 100–105; political theory and, 98–100; power and, 98–99, 101; role in intelligence studies, 109–10, 228
polygraph tests, 87–88
Popper, Karl, 119–20
Porter, Stephen, 71
Poznansky, Michael, 103
prepublication boards, 2
*The Presentation of Self in Everyday Life* (Goffman), 82
President's Daily Brief, 91, 155
Priest, Dana, 215–16
primary source data. *See* qualitative interviews
principal-agent theory, 146–47
privacy, 103, 215. *See also* confidentiality; data leaks; surveillance
Privacy International, 207
private contractors, 191n29
probabilistic reasoning, 121–24, 123f
problem solving, 171
*The Process and Effects of Mass Communication* (Schramm), 167
process theory, 185
propaganda, 169
pro-social behaviors, 65, 73
provocative statements, 73–74
psychological testing, 88
public: civil liberties and, 103, 214; as data source, 151–52; ethical duty to, 1–2, 211–13; opinion on intelligence community, 42, 92, 213–15, 228; sanitation of records for, 15, 49
public administration (PA), 5, 141–62; access challenges for researching, 155–56; environmental scanning and, 152–53; institutional

isomorphism and, 154–55; literature overview on, 143–47; performance management and measurement, 149–50; representative bureaucracy and, 150–52; research methodologies for studying, 155; role in intelligence studies, 228; strategic human resource management and, 148–49; study of, 147–48

publications: analysts and, 91–92; intelligence fiction, 228; periodic review and ranking of, 208n10; policy-relevant scholarship, 180–82, 190n8; restrictions on, 2, 12. *See also* archival release policies; biographical projects; journalists; journals of intelligence studies

publicity principle, 212–13

Putnam, Robert, 103

Qazi, Aimal, 89

qualitative interviews, 5, 47–62; bias and, 57, 226; choosing interviewees, 51–53; importance of, 49–50; percentage used in journal articles, 48, 48f, 59–60n6; preparation of, 53–57; protecting sources, 55–58; using material from, 57–58

question design, 54, 55

questionnaire surveys, 53, 155

quotations, interview material and, 57–58

race and ethnicity, 150–52, 218

radicalization, 64, 74

random sampling, 51

Ransom, Harry Howe, 16, 17, 106

rapport, 55, 56, 65, 155

rating scales for behavior observation, 66, 67–69

rational actor model of decision-making, 104, 108, 171

Ratner, Ely, 180

Rawls, John, 212

realism, 101–2

Reality Monitoring (RM), 71–72

recordings of interviews, 56, 57, 65–66, 68–71

reliability in structured observation, 65

reporters. *See* journalists

representative bureaucracy, 150–52

research. *See* intelligence studies research

Research Excellence Framework (REF), 208n10

response bias, 71

Richards, Julian, 204, 210n38

Richardson, Brian, 218

Rockman, Bert A., 54

Romanian Orthodox Church, 24n21

Rothschild, Joyce, 218

Russia/Soviet Union: Cold War and, 15, 38–40, 44n28; disinformation operations of, 39, 169; World War II and, 36–37

sampling, 51–53, 122

satellite imagery, 202

Sawers, John, 193

scenario analysis, 180–81

Scharff technique, 69

Schmitt, Gary, 199

scholar-activists, 183, 190n17, 213

scholar–practitioner divide in intelligence, 6, 179–92; bridging the gap, 4, 155–56, 184–88; challenges in bridging the gap, 188–89, 228–29; CIA origins and, 184–85; intelligence community efforts to bridge the gap, 186–88, 230, 235n31; mapping the gap, 180–83; modern intelligence and, 185–86; policy-making influence and, 182–83, 190n8, 230; policy-relevant scholarship and, 180–82

scholars: academic vs. practical experience of, 231–32; accountability of, 1–2, 17–18, 213, 218; biases of, 231–32; commonalities between journalists and, 199–200, 200*f*; cooperation with journalists, 197, 204–6; degrees and faculty positions in intelligence studies, 1, 11, 33, 97, 109–10, 181–82; differences between journalists and, 201–3; disciplinary specialization of, 3–4, 41–42, 205, 228–29; incentives for research and scholarship, 181–82, 197–98, 231; policymaking influence of, 182–83, 190n8, 204, 229–31; security clearances for, 2, 81, 156, 185, 188, 205; Snowden data leaks, response to, 12, 21, 193–94, 229–30; streetlight effect and, 226–27; writing style of, 181, 190n8, 230. *See also* ethical duties; intelligence studies research; publications; scholar–practitioner divide in intelligence
Schramm, Wilbur, 165, 167
*Science of Coercion* (Simpson), 167
Sebeok, Thomas, 167–68
secrecy: accountability of intelligence organizations and, 199; agent recruitment and, 83–84; as barrier to intelligence research, 2, 12, 31–32, 47, 91, 155, 188, 211; cryptography and, 30, 33, 38, 167; democracy vs., 17, 197, 212; ethics of research and, 220; in-group mentality and, 217; interview techniques and, 53–54; national security and, 213; of offshore banking, 206; scholar-practitioner divide in intelligence and, 188. *See also* data leaks

*Secret Global Surveillance Networks* (Privacy International), 207
Securitate, 24n21
security awareness, 73
security clearances: limitations created by, 81, 155–56; requirements of, 85; for scholars, 2, 81, 156, 185, 188, 205; short-term, 188
Selden, Sally Coleman, 151
self-reports of behavior, 63, 72, 74
semiotics, 168
semistructured interviews, 54
Senate Select Committee on Intelligence (SSCI), 106–7
senior officials, interviewing, 51–52, 56, 58
September 11, 2001, terrorist attacks, 49, 88, 145, 147–50. *See also* 9/11 Commission Report
SERUM (Social Engineering Resistant User Model), 72–73
Shannon, Claude E., 167
Shelton, Allison, 50
Shulsky, Abram, 199
signals intelligence (SIGINT): Cold War and, 39–40; signal detection theory, 71, 168; study of, 30, 33, 167–68, 170, 193–94; technologically assisted, 202; WWII and, 38
Simpson, Christopher, 167
Sims, Jennifer, 101
Singer, David, 100
Slaughter, Anne-Marie, 181
Sloane, Mona, 197
Smist, Frank, 107
Smith, Brad, 31–32
Smith, Martin J., 146–47
snowballing for interview subjects, 52–53
Snowden data leaks: academic response to, 12, 21, 193–94, 229–30; as forced transparency, 49; social

backlash and legal repercussions of, 220; surveillance studies and, 12, 17, 193–94, 204
social control, 19
social engineering. *See* structured behavioral observation systems
Social Engineering Resistant User Model (SERUM), 72–73
social media, 74
sociology, 5, 79–94; emotion work and, 86–90; future considerations for, 90–92; greedy institutions and, 84–86; opportunities and challenges in, 80–82; role in intelligence studies, 228; streetlight effect in research and, 226–27; surveillance and, 19; symbolic interactionism and, 82–84; theoretical considerations for, 82–90
sources. *See* data sources
sovereignty norm, 102
Soviet Union. *See* Russia/Soviet Union
spies, 83–84, 99, 216–17
*The Spy Who Came in from the Cold* (Le Carré), 197
SSCI (Senate Select Committee on Intelligence), 106–7
Stalin, Joseph, 36
Stampnitzky, Lisa, 12
Stasi archives, 15, 24n20
state-level IR theories, 103–4
state of nature, 98–100
static behavior observations, 66
Steiner, James E., 144
story-based inquiry model (Hunter), 200, 200*f*
Strategic and Competitive Intelligence Professionals Association, 52
strategic human resource management, 148–49
streetlight effect, 226–27
structural realism, 102

structured analytic techniques (SATs), 118–21
structured behavioral observation systems, 5, 63–77; intelligence interviewing and interrogation, 66–72; limitations of, 226; overview, 64–66; political and religious radicalization, 74; in secure environments, 72–74
structured interviews, 53, 55
*Studies in Intelligence,* 143
substantive theory, 185
surveillance: ethics and, 17, 207; increase in, 207; intelligence defined, 16; political policing and, 41; protecting interview sources from, 208n6; suspicion and skewed interpretation of behavior, 15; technology for, 18, 19, 202. *See also* Snowden data leaks
surveys, 53, 155
symbolic interactionism, 82–84
systemic-level IR theories, 101–3

technology: for communication, 99, 172; cybersecurity and, 19, 58, 72–73; for imagery intelligence, 202; intelligence studies research and, 19, 227–28; multimedia journalism and, 172; social control through, 19; for surveillance, 18, 19, 202
telephone interviews, 55
terrorism and counterterrorism: ethics of data leaks and, 215–17; intelligence agencies' response to, 88–90; intelligence collection methods and, 66–67, 151; liberty vs. security and, 214; radicalization and, 64, 74; terrorism studies programs, 11–12, 18–19. *See also specific terrorist attacks*

Thayer, Carl, 20
Thomas, J. B., 153
Tomkinson, Mark, 218
torture, 207–8, 215
*The Tragedy of Great Power Politics* (Mearsheimer), 21–22
training. *See* education and training
transparency, 33, 49, 211–12, 227
Treverton, Greg, 17–18, 231
triangulation of data, 15, 49, 59
true positives and negatives, 136n38
trustworthiness of researcher, 219
Turner, Stansfield, 185

Ulam, Adam, 30
Ultra, 37
uncertainties in intelligence, 128–31, 130*f*, 137n54
underconfidence, 127–28
United Kingdom: consistency rates of evidence-based lexicons in, 129–30; declassified information, delaying release of, 50; democracy vs. secrecy in, 197; Government Code and Cypher School (GC and CS), 30; intelligence studies in, 14; interviewing model used in, 67–69; journalists' access to intelligence community in, 195; National Union of Journalists, 203; rendition of Libyan dissident, 207–8; World War II, 35–38. *See also specific intelligence agencies*
United Nations, 216, 222n26
United States: congressional oversight of intelligence in, 106–7, 147; consistency rates of evidence-based lexicons in, 129–30, 130*f*; democracy vs. secrecy in, 17; foreign and national security policy, 108–9; history of intelligence community in, 184–85; intelligence agency organization in, 144–46; journalists' access to intelligence community in, 195; as political science subfield focus, 105–9. *See also specific intelligence agencies*
unstructured interviews, 53–54

Valero, Larry, 33
validity in structured observation, 65
Van Puyvelde, Damien, 1, 5, 20, 47, 225, 226, 229
Vaughan, Diane, 90
verbal behavior, 65–66, 71
verbal probabilities. *See* words of estimative probability
Verona, 41, 44n28
video recordings of interviews, 65–66, 68, 71
Vrij, Aldert, 71

Waldron, Jeremy, 214
Walsh, Patrick F., 146
Walton, Calder, 15
Waltz, Kenneth, 100–101, 102
Wark, Wesley, 14, 16, 31
Warner, Michael, 32, 47, 59, 227
Weber, Max, 79
Wegge, Njord, 213
Weinberger, Caspar, 185
We Know All interrogation approach, 70
Wendt, Alexander, 102
WEPs (words of estimative probability), 119, 126, 128–31, 130*f*, 137n54
whistle-blowers, 199, 218–20. *See also* data leaks
White, Martha, 198, 199, 202, 206–7
Wiener, Norbert, 165
WikiLeaks, 2, 205, 215–17, 220, 228
Wilkins, Vicky, 151
Williams, Bill, 33

Williams, Brian, 151
Wohlstetter, Roberta, 31
words of estimative probability
 (WEPs), 119, 126, 128–31, 130f,
 137n54
World War II, 35–38
writing style, 181, 190n8, 230
Wynia, Matthew, 219

WYSIATI (what you see is all there is)
 principle, 131

Yarhi-Milo, Keren, 104

Zegart, Amy, 90, 97, 106, 143, 145,
 149–50
Zelikow, Philip, 171

www.ingramcontent.com/pod-product-compliance
Lightning Source LLC
Chambersburg PA
CBHW050901300426
44111CB00010B/1333